A TREASURY OF KNITTING PATTERNS

A Treasury of
Knitting Patterns

BARBARA G. WALKER

Photography by William J. Williams

CHARLES SCRIBNER'S SONS · NEW YORK

DEDICATED TO THE CREATIVE KNITTERS OF THE PAST
AND THE CREATIVE KNITTERS OF THE FUTURE

She seekath wool, and flax,
and worketh willingly with her hands.
—PROVERBS 31:13

Charles Scribner's Sons
Macmillan Publishing Company
866 Third Avenue, New York, NY 10022
Collier Macmillan Canada, Inc.

Library of Congress Catalog Card Number 67-24064

ISBN 0-684-17314-X

Macmillan books are available at special discounts for bulk purchases
for sales promotions, premiums, fund-raising, or educational use.
For details, contact:

Special Sales Director
Macmillan Publishing Company
866 Third Avenue, New York, NY 10022

17 16 15 14 13 12 11 10

Printed in the United States of America

ACKNOWLEDGMENTS

I wish to express my gratitude to my husband, Gordon N. Walker, for his help and encouragement; to my photographer, William J. Williams, for his patient and painstaking work, to my editor, Elinor Parker, for her gracious and wise handling of the innumerable details of putting a book into print; and to my book designer, Barbara Rasmussen. I am grateful, also, for the efforts of an army of pattern designers whose names are unknown to me, but whose ingenuity enriches every modern needlework publication and contributes to the continuing growth of the ancient and living art of knitting.

B. G. W.

CONTENTS

Chapter Three

RIBBINGS 38

Chapter Four

COLOR-CHANGE PATTERNS 50

CONTENTS

Chapter Five

SLIP-STITCH PATTERNS   92

CONTENTS

Chapter Six

TWIST STITCH PATTERNS 114

Chapter Seven

FANCY TEXTURE PATTERNS 128

CONTENTS

Chapter Eight

PATTERNS MADE WITH YARN-OVER STITCHES 148

Chapter Nine

EYELET PATTERNS 168

CONTENTS

Chapter Ten

LACE   183

CONTENTS

Chapter Eleven

CABLES 238

Chapter Twelve

CABLE-STITCH PATTERNS 272

CONTENTS

A TREASURY OF KNITTING PATTERNS

CHAPTER ONE

Introduction

There are three things about knitting of which many a knitter is—but should not be—ignorant. The first is that knitting is one of the oldest of crafts, its history extending back almost to the origins of human culture. The second is that knitting was developed largely by men, not by women. And the third is that the variety, flexibility, and adaptability of patterns in knitting are practically infinite. This book, being a book on patterns, is mostly concerned with the third point. But to introduce the subject, a few words should be said about the first two.

There is something in every human soul which seeks to create a thing of beauty, given any sort of opportunity and materials to do so. Throughout all the ages people have pursued their own ideas of beauty, building, shaping, weaving, painting, decorating. They have carried on that pursuit through every medium that ever came to hand: wood, stone, feathers, bone, ivory, cloth, jewels, metals, glass, clay, shell, leather, pigment . . . and yarn. Knitting is very much a part of that age-old pursuit of the beautiful. Many patterns known today were first formed by hands that have become dust hundreds or even thousands of years ago; but the same patterns may still be formed by other hands. Thus knitting is a true folk art, in that it has been developed over the course of centuries by millions of ordinary people, whose delight it was to create beauty with their hands.

The origin of knitting is lost in antiquity, but it is known to have come from the near East, probably Arabia. Scraps of knitted fabric have been found in Egyptian tombs. Possibly Cleopatra herself wore knitted garments. Certainly by Cleopatra's day the art of knitting was well established, and at a fairly early date it was carried from its Eastern home into Europe.

During the Middle Ages the famous "knitters' guilds"—which were, of course, composed entirely of men—brought the art of knitting to a very high degree of refinement. A young man who wished to become a member of such a guild had to serve as an apprentice to a Master Knitter for a minimum of three years, and spend another three years in travel, learning foreign techniques and patterns. After this he had to pass a grueling examination, knitting a number of original "masterpieces" of his own in a very short time, and then was admitted to the guild as a Master in his own right. The men of these guilds made exquisite garments that were worn by kings and princes, and every member of the nobility had his or her favorite Master Knitter, as well as a favorite tailor or dressmaker.

The time-honored tradition that knitting is a manly art, rather than, or as well as, a womanly one, still persists in areas of northern Europe and the British Isles. Quick-fingered males such as sailors and fishermen, who were adept with sails, ropes, and nets, also originated several types of fancy knitted garments. The men of the Aran Isles in Ireland, who made their own "ganseys" or jerseys (which are known today under the generic term of fisherman sweaters) believed that it was the duty of women to spin the wool, but the privilege of men to knit it. It is possible that at various times knitting has been considered an unwomanly activity, just as more recently such things as smoking or wearing pants were considered unwomanly.

Eventually women got into the picture, as they usually do, and today all the great and ancient traditions of knitting are literally at their fingertips. Our legacy from the ages is a truly marvelous variety of patterns, which every knitter should learn and apply to her own work. In this way, and only in this way, a true folk art grows and reproduces its beauty.

To learn the techniques of pattern stitches is not only exciting, but it is to learn also that knitting can be almost anything, from the most cobwebby lace to the sturdiest blankets. All sorts of fabrics are possible. Some patterns are sporty and "tweedy", some are quaint, some are dainty and fine, some are sophisticated, some are simple and childlike. But all are charming. Each one has its own special quality that can turn your garment into a real creation—your own creation. In learning various pattern stitches, you can raise what is otherwise a mere craft to the height of a real art. You can "mix-and-match" from literally hundreds of sources, and choose patterns to express your own personality and taste as never before. In the wonderful world of pattern stitches knitting is never a bore. There are endless possibilities which will fascinate and delight every true knitter. Some patterns almost seem to cry out to be used. They say, "Don't just knit something—knit something beautiful!"

Now let us begin at the beginning, and suppose that you are a novice knitter or one who has done only "plain knitting" for years and imagines that "all that fancy work is too complicated." It is important, then, for you to realize that many of the most attractive patterns are astonishingly simple to do. All of the pattern stitches in this book can be done by anyone who knows just four basic knitting operations: how to knit, how to purl, how to make a yarn-over stitch and how to use a cable needle. Few handicraft skills can do so much with so little. But of course you must also know (and this applies to the learning of any skill, from cooking to cabinetmaking) how to read and follow directions carefully.

Here is a hint to help you follow directions. When you begin to knit, *always* have a pencil and paper at hand. Jot down the number of each row completed as you finish it. Then you will never have to wonder, "Now where was I? Was it Row 18 or Row 20?" Another bugaboo which often leads to mistakes is the "visual jump" from one line of print to another, which mixes up directions for separate rows, and can easily happen when you are glancing back and forth from page to work. To prevent this, it is a good idea to take a piece of paper or a card, and lay it on the page in such a way that it covers the rows you have finished and shows you only the one you are working on. This is particularly important in patterns which have more than four or six rows to a repeat. Nothing is more frustrating than to be feeling your way carefully through a complicated pattern and then to forget where you were.

Of course if you are inexperienced, you should not begin with a complicated pattern, such as a fancy lace which may have 30 or 40 rows to the repeat. There are hundreds of simple patterns which are wonderfully effective and rewarding to work. You should begin with these and move on to fancier ones as you gain confidence and skill.

But how to apply all these wonderful patterns to your own garments? This brings us to one of the most important subjects in knitting: the test swatch. In the first place, it cannot be too strongly emphasized that the only way to master a new pattern stitch is to pick up needles and yarn and *try it out*. You cannot learn it just by looking at an illustration or by reading the directions. Even the best of illustrations are often deceptive, and no one can visualize the total effect of a pattern by reading it, any more than the reading of a recipe can give you the exact taste of the finished dish. It is essential to *see* and *feel* a knitted pattern before you really know how, or whether, to use it. And in making a test swatch, make it big enough to give you a good look. A little shred eight or ten stitches wide can't show you much. If the pattern is a multiple of eight or less stitches, cast on enough to repeat the pattern at least four or five times. If the pattern is more than eight stitches wide, repeat it at least three times. Then repeat the pattern rows enough times to make the swatch roughly square, or until you have become thoroughly familiar with the way the pattern is worked.

Never sit down and begin a garment, then, in a new and unfamiliar pattern without first making a test swatch. Most really experienced knitters do this as a matter of course. Having made the test swatch and blocked it, you must take its gauge. Let's say you are working on a sweater which calls for stockinette stitch, but you would like to vary it with a fancier pattern. You make your pattern swatch and ascertain the gauge. If it is roughly the same as your stockinette gauge, then you can go ahead and make the garment according to the directions given. If the pattern tends to compress or pull together laterally, as most cables do, then you will have to cast on more stitches. If the pattern is compressed vertically, as most slip-stitch patterns are, then you will have to work more rows. If the pattern opens up somewhat, as do most laces, eyelets, and other patterns composed of open spaces, then you will need fewer stitches. All this is what the test swatch tells you.

In working without a garment pattern, the test swatch is even more important. Though you may not believe it in the beginning, it is surprisingly easy to design your own garments to your own measurements. The test swatch is what does it. Having made the swatch and checked the gauge, you have only to multiply the pattern enough times to achieve the desired number of inches in each section of the garment, increasing or decreasing as required. After you have made several garments you begin to acquire a "feel" for the number of stitches and rows required for any given measurement. The more different patterns you work with, the more you develop and broaden this sense of proportion.

Every knitter should keep a "sample box" of patterns that have been learned, to serve for future reference. Test swatches can be saved, so that they can be reconsulted and re-checked for gauge when you are deciding on a pattern for a new garment. A very pleasant way to learn many patterns, and still make good use of the yarn, is to knit some article as a sampler. Delightful afghans can be made in sampler style out of squares, each knitted in a different pattern. If you are careful to block all the squares to the same size and shape, they can be sewn or crocheted together into a real treasure of an afghan that will be your "reference" as well as a thing of beauty and utility. Lace samplers, incorporating as many different lace patterns as you like, can make lovely stoles or scarves, fancy shawls or table runners—even curtains!

It is the purpose of this book to help you learn many new and exciting patterns, thereby extending your knitting skill. It is not a book to be *read*; it is a book to be *worked with*, needles and yarn in hand. Whether you are a novice or an expert, you will find plenty of novelty, challenge, and inspiration in working with this book. After you have mastered a number of new patterns, you will never want to return to the drab tedium of "plain knitting." You will develop ideas for combining two, three, four or more different patterns in your own way, to produce effects that no one has ever produced before; and herein lies the thrill of making a garment that is uniquely your own. Here, also, is the ultimate achievement of real knitting. *Combinations* are the key to true artistry in knitting. Combinations are what gives hand knitting its incomparable look of originality, which no machine knitting can ever copy. Thus the more patterns you learn, the more you enlarge the repertoire from which you draw your combinations, and the closer you come to the creation of beauty. And—as people through the ages have known instinctively—there are few joys in life like the deep joy of knowing that your own mind and your own hands have created a beautiful thing.

So—don't just knit something. Knit something beautiful.

Glossary of Terms and Abbreviations

K—Knit.

P—Purl.

St—Stitch. Sts—stitches.

K2 tog—Knit two stitches together as one stitch.

P2 tog—Purl two stitches together as one stitch.

B—Work through the back loop of the stitch. "K1-b" means: knit one stitch through its back loop, inserting the needle into the stitch from the right-hand side. "P1-b" means: purl one stitch through its back loop, turning the work over slightly toward the knitter, inserting the needle into the back of the stitch from the left-hand side, and wrapping the yarn around the needle in front to complete a purl stitch in the usual way.

K2 tog-b—Insert the needle into the back loops of two stitches and knit them together as one stitch; the same action as "k1-b" performed on two stitches at once.

P2 tog-b—Turn the work over slightly and insert the needle from the left-hand side into the back loops of the second and the first stitches, in that order, then wrap the yarn around the needle in front to complete the purl stitch. Same action as "p1-b" performed on two stitches at once.

Sl—Slip. To pass a stitch or stitches from the left-hand needle to the right-hand needle without working them. The right-hand needle is always inserted into a stitch that is to be slipped *as if to purl* (i.e., from the right-hand side) unless directions specify "as if to knit" or "knitwise" (i.e., from the left-hand side).

Sl-st—Slip-stitch. A stitch that has been slipped.

Psso—Pass slipped stitch over. Insert the tip of left-hand needle into a stitch that has been slipped, and draw the slipped stitch to the left over the stitch just knitted, over the tip of right-hand needle, and off needle.

Ssk—Slip, slip, knit. In this book the abbreviation "ssk" is used instead of the usual decrease "sl 1, k1, psso", because it is shorter, less easily confused with "sl 1, k2 tog, psso", and when done as directed makes a neater-looking decrease then the usual one. Instead of "sl 1, k1, psso", work "ssk" as follows: slip the first and second stitches *knitwise,* one at a time, then insert the tip of left-hand needle into the *fronts* of these two stitches from the left, and knit them together from this position.

Sl 2 knitwise—k1—p2sso—A double decrease sometimes used instead of the usual "sl 1—k2 tog—psso", when it is more desirable to have the central stitch of the three more prominent. It is done as follows: inserting the needle into the fronts of the second and first stitches, in that order, slip them both together as if to knit; then knit the next stitch, then insert the left-hand needle into the two slipped stitches at once and draw them together over the knitted stitch and off needle, as in "psso".

Wyib—With yarn in back. Used with slip-stitches, it means that the yarn is carried across behind the stitch, i.e., on the side of the needles away from the knitter, as the stitch is slipped. When working on a right-side row, a slip-stitch is always slipped with yarn in back unless otherwise specified.

Wyif—With yarn in front. When a stitch is slipped, the yarn is carried across in front of the stitch, i.e., on the side of the needles toward the knitter.

Rep—Repeat.

Rep from *—Repeat all that comes after the *, in the same order.

( ) Parentheses—Indicates a repeat of material written inside the parentheses as many times as specified; i.e., "(k2 tog, k1) twice" means: knit two stitches together, knit one stitch, then knit two stitches together and knit one stitch again.

Yo—Yarn over. Take the yarn over the top of the needle once before making the next stitch. If the next stitch is to be knitted, then the yarn is simply taken over the top of the right-hand needle to the back, where it is in position to knit the next stitch; if the next stitch is to be purled, then the yarn is taken over the top of the right-hand needle and then under the needle to the front, where it is in position to purl the next stitch. On the return row, a yo is usually worked as a separate stitch.

(Yo) twice—A double yarn-over. The yarn passes twice over the top of the right-hand needle before making the next stitch; i.e., over the needle to the back, under the needle to the front, over to the back again to position to knit the next stitch. If the next stitch is to be purled, the yarn is brought under the needle to the front once more to purl position.

Running thread—The horizontal strand lying between two stitches from the base of one to the base of the other.

M1—Make One. A method of adding a new stitch without leaving a hole. It is usually done by lifting the running thread onto the tip of the left-hand needle so that it lies over the needle from the left, behind, to the right, in front; then the right-hand needle is inserted into the back or left-hand portion of this thread to knit a new stitch as in "k1-b".

Dpn—Double-pointed needle or cable needle.

FC—Front Cross. In cabling, this means that the double-pointed needle carrying a stitch or stitches is left in front of the work while other stitches are being worked behind it.

BC—Back Cross. In cabling, the double-pointed needle carrying a stitch or stitches is left in back of the work while other stitches are being worked in front.

Panel—A portion of the knitting that develops a narrow vertical pattern, such as a cable, or a vertical insertion in lace. In panel patterns, the directions are given for the entire panel a specified number of stitches in width.

Band—A horizontal panel.

Motif—The dominant figure or shape of a pattern.

Spot-pattern—An arrangement of motifs scattered over the entire fabric at regular intervals both vertically and horizontally.

Half-drop—A method of converting a panel pattern into a spot-pattern, by working the second half of the pattern rows in one panel along with the first half of the pattern rows in the adjoining panel, and so on alternately across the fabric.

A NOTE ABOUT NOMENCLATURE

Most of the patterns in this book have their own names which, for better or worse, have been honored by time. In some cases, either the pattern has no name or the author has been unable to discover it; therefore the author has taken the liberty of naming it herself. In other cases, the pattern is one invented by the author, who consequently claims the right to name it.

CHAPTER TWO

Simple Knit-Purl Combinations

A large number of very attractive designs can be worked with no more knowledge of knitting than how to form knit stitches and purl stitches. In such designs one type of stitch is played against the other to make embossed patterns on the surface of the fabric.

It is a basic principle of such combinations that knit stitches, worked vertically, will tend to stand up away from purl stitches (forming ribs) and that purl stitches, worked horizontally, will tend to stand up away from knit stitches (forming ridges or welts). Thus one type of stitch is often used as a background for the other. Cables, being worked usually with knit stitches against a purled background, constitute another illustration of this principle.

In the purely embossed type of knit-purl pattern, the two types of stitches are scattered or grouped more or less evenly over the surface of the fabric, so that a subtle design is formed which neither "takes in" like ribbing nor "takes up" like welting. This kind of pattern is usually interchangeable with stockinette stitch as far as gauge is concerned, and may be used in any garment calling for "plain knitting" with delightful effect.

Knit-purl combinations should be worked with solid colors. They are not suitable for yarns dyed in variegated color, as the alteration in color detracts from the pattern. Nor are they usually suitable for stripes of contrasting colors, since the color-change rows give a "wrong side" appearance to those stitches which are purled on the right side.

Many of the patterns in this section do not have specified right and wrong sides. This means either that they look the same on both sides, or that it does not matter which side is shown as the right side and this is left to the option of the knitter.

Two Basic Stitches: Stockinette Stitch and Garter Stitch

1. STOCKINETTE STITCH

This is the "plain sweater" stitch. All stitches on the right side are knitted, all stitches on the wrong side purled. When Stockinette Stitch is worked on a circular needle or a set of double-pointed needles in rounds, all stitches are knitted.

When worked in flat, rather than circular, knitting, Stockinette Stitch has a tendency to curl. Thus it usually requires blocking to make the fabric lie flat.

Two interesting variations on Stockinette Stitch are Crossed Stockinette and Twisted Stockinette. In the Crossed version, all the stitches on the right side of the fabric are knitted through the back loops, which causes the strands to cross at the base of each stitch. On the wrong side, all stitches are purled in the usual way. In the Twisted version, the right-side stitches are knitted through the back loops, *and* the wrong-side stitches are purled through the back loops. This twists each little column of stitches and gives a firm texture to the fabric. Both Crossed and Twisted Stockinette derive from ancient Arabic methods of knitting, and either one may be used in place of plain Stockinette for a somewhat more decorative effect.

2. GARTER STITCH

Garter Stitch is "plain knitting"—every stitch on every row, both right and wrong sides, being knitted when the piece is being worked from both sides. In circular knitting, however, Garter Stitch is made by alternating one round of knit stitches and one round of purl stitches.

Garter Stitch looks the same on both sides: a series of purl-stitch ridges and knit-stitch troughs. It is a flat, firm fabric, having no tendency to curl, and thus is often used for borders, buttonhole bands, and edgings for articles made in lace or some other delicate pattern. It has more lateral spread than Stockinette Stitch, and less vertical spread. Indeed it was used to make garters, or the tops of stockings where the most horizontal elasticity was required, whereas Stockinette Stitch was used for the stockings themselves; in England the latter is still called Stocking Stitch.

UPPER BAND: *Stockinette Stitch, plain*
SECOND BAND: *Stockinette Stitch, Crossed*
THIRD BAND: *Stockinette Stitch, Twisted*
LOWER BAND: *Garter Stitch*

Seed Stitch

This stitch is very frequently used for borders and for a texture effect, as it lies flat, looks the same on both sides, and tends to make a slightly tighter fabric than stockinette stitch. It is sometimes called Rice Stitch or Moss Stitch, although it is different from true Moss Stitch. Seed Stitch is really a k1, p1 ribbing broken on every row, so that every knit stitch is placed above a purl stitch and every purl stitch is placed above a knit stitch.

Even number of sts.

Row 1—* K1, p1; rep from *.
Row 2—* P1, k1; rep from *.

Repeat Rows 1 and 2.

UPPER BAND: *Seed Stitch*
CENTER BAND: *Moss Stitch*
LOWER BAND: *Double Seed Stitch*

Moss Stitch

Moss stitch is probably the most popular of the broken-rib-texture patterns, being used very often to point up cable patterns, and giving a pleasing nubby effect when used in large areas. It should not be confused with Seed Stitch, as the latter changes from knit to purl stitches on every row whereas Moss Stitch changes every other row.

Even number of sts.

Rows 1 and 2—* K1, p1; rep from *.
Rows 3 and 4—* P1, k1; rep from *.

Repeat Rows 1–4.

Double Seed Stitch

Double Seed Stitch probably should be called "double moss stitch", since like Moss Stitch it requires four rows to complete the pattern. It consists of a k2, p2 ribbing broken every other row. For all its simplicity it gives a very beautiful texture, and may be used in place of plain stockinette for almost any type of garment. It resists curling out of shape, looks the same on both sides, and seldom requires any extensive blocking.

Multiple of 4 sts.

Rows 1 and 2—* K2, p2; rep from *.
Rows 3 and 4—* P2, k2; rep from *.

Repeat Rows 1–4.

SIMPLE KNIT-PURL COMBINATIONS   11

Sand Stitch

ABOVE: *Sand Stitch*
BELOW: *Dot Stitch or Spot Stitch*

Sand Stitch is a handsome, nubby purl fabric that is very good for sport wear and sweaters for men and boys. The reverse side, which shows isolated bumps of purl stitches, is called Dot Stitch or Spot Stitch.

Even number of sts.

Rows 1 and 3 (Wrong side)—Knit.
Row 2—* K1, p1; rep from *.
Row 4—* P1, k1; rep from *.

Repeat Rows 1–4.

Broken Rib Pattern

ABOVE: *Broken Rib*
BELOW: *Double Broken Rib*

This is a very popular pattern for sport sweaters and jackets. It resembles ribbing but does not have the elasticity of a true ribbing. When a Broken Rib forms the fabric of a sweater, it should be used as a continuation of Knit-One Purl-One Ribbing—the knit stitches of the pattern falling directly above the knit stitches of the ribbing. Double Broken Rib is used in the same manner as a continuation of Knit-Two Purl-Two Ribbing. Both of these patterns show an interesting texture on the wrong side, for anyone in search of a rough, nubby fabric that is easy to work.

Odd number of sts.

Row 1 (Right side)—K1, * p1, k1; rep from *.
Row 2—Purl.

Repeat Rows 1 and 2.

VARIATION: *DOUBLE BROKEN RIB*

Multiple of 4 sts plus 2.

Row 1 (Wrong side)—Purl.
Row 2—Knit.
Row 3—K2, * p2, k2; rep from *.
Row 4—P2, * k2, p2; rep from *.

Repeat Rows 1–4.

Roman Stitch

This is a very simple pattern consisting of seed-stitch stripes across a stockinette fabric.

Even number of sts.

Rows 1 and 3 (Right side)—Knit.
Rows 2 and 4—Purl.
Row 5—* K1, pl; rep from *.
Row 6—* P1, k1; rep from *.

Repeat Rows 1–6.

VARIATION: *ROMAN RIB STITCH*

In this variation the knits and purls are still alternated as in Roman Stitch, but in different stripes. The result is a pleasing texture of horizontal corrugations.

Even number of sts.

Row 1 (Right side)—Knit.
Row 2—Purl.
Rows 3 and 4—* K1, p1; rep from *.
Row 5—Knit.
Row 6—Purl.
Rows 7 and 8—* P1, k1; rep from *.

Repeat Rows 1–8.

ABOVE: *Roman Stitch*
BELOW: *Roman Rib Stitch*

Ripple Stitch

Multiple of 8 sts plus 6.

Row 1 (Right side)—K6, * p2, k6; rep from *.
Row 2—K1, * p4, k4; rep from *, end p4, k1.
Row 3—P2, * k2, p2; rep from *.
Row 4—P1, * k4, p4; rep from *, end k4, p1.
Row 5—K2, * p2, k6; rep from *, end p2, k2.
Row 6—P6, * k2, p6; rep from *.
Row 7—P1, * k4, p4; rep from *, end k4, p1.
Row 8—K2, * p2, k2; rep from *.
Row 9—K1, * p4, k4; rep from *, end p4, k1.
Row 10—P2, * k2, p6; rep from *, end k2, p2.

Repeat Rows 1–10.

Ripple Stitch

Ripple Rib Stitch

Ripple Rib Stitch

This pattern consists of Knit-Two Purl-Two ribs, broken, one stitch at a time, to form alternating diagonals.

Multiple of 4 sts.

Rows 1 and 2—* P2, k2; rep from *.
Row 3—P1, * k2, p2; rep from *, end k2, p1.
Row 4—K1, * p2, k2; rep from *, end p2, k1.
Rows 5 and 6—* K2, p2; rep from *.
Row 7—Repeat Row 4.
Row 8—Repeat Row 3.
Rows 9 and 10—Repeat Row 1.
Row 11—Repeat Row 4.
Row 12—Repeat Row 3.
Rows 13 and 14—Repeat Row 5.
Row 15—Repeat Row 3.
Row 16—Repeat Row 4.

Repeat Rows 1–16.

Escalator Pattern

Escalator Pattern

This pattern shows an interesting use of purl-stitch welts.

Multiple of 32 sts.

Rows 1 and 3 (Right side)—* K5, p11; rep from *.
Row 2—* K11, p5; rep from *.
Rows 4 and 6—Purl.
Row 5—Knit.
Rows 7 and 9—P4, * k5, p11; rep from *, end k5, p7.
Row 8—K7, * p5, k11; rep from *, end p5, k4.
Rows 10 and 12—Purl.
Row 11—Knit.
Rows 13 and 15—P8, * k5, p11; rep from *, end k5, p3.
Row 14—K3, * p5, k11; rep from *, end p5, k8.
Rows 16 and 18—Purl.
Row 17—Knit.
Rows 19 and 21—K1, p11, * k5, p11; rep from *, end k4.
Row 20—P4, * k11, p5; rep from *, end k11, p1.
Row 22—Purl.
Row 23—Knit.
Row 24—Purl.

Repeat Rows 1–24.

Waving Rib Pattern

Though the ribs are knitted straight, a hint of a wave is imparted to them by the purl stitches, which draw them slightly left and right. The reverse side of this pattern is a most attractive little block stitch arranged in basketweave fashion.

Waving Rib Pattern

Multiple of 6 sts plus 2.

Rows 1 and 3 (Right side)—P2, * k4, p2; rep from *.
Rows 2 and 4—K2, * p4, k2; rep from *.
Rows 5 and 7—K3, p2, * k4, p2; rep from *, end k3.
Rows 6 and 8—P3, k2, * p4, k2; rep from *, end p3.

Repeat Rows 1-8.

Quaker Ridging

Quaker Ridging is only one example of an almost limitless number of possible combinations in knit-purl stripes. Any knitter, even the least experienced, can vary this pattern at will, simply by establishing purled stripes of any desired width across a stockinette fabric at any desired intervals. If the purled ridges are to be more than five rows in width it is a good idea to work them in Garter Stitch so that the fabric does not draw up too much. For instance: if the broader stripe, in the pattern as given, were to be worked in Garter Stitch, then Row 13 would be knitted instead of purled.

For a simple single-row stripe, repeat Rows 1-6 only.

Quaker Ridging

Any number of sts.

Rows 1, 3, and 5—(Right side)—Knit.
Rows 2 and 4—Purl.
Row 6—Knit.
Rows 7, 9, and 11—Knit.
Rows 8 and 10—Purl.
Row 12—Knit.
Row 13—Purl.
Row 14—Knit.

Repeat Rows 1-14.

Wager Welt or All Fools' Welt

Wager Welt or All Fools' Welt

This type of ridging owes its fame to an amusing little side-light in the history of knitting. The "wager" was concerned with the question, out of eight pattern rows, how many rows are purled? From the appearance of the pattern it is very hard to guess, and so the French called it Puzzle Stitch and the Germans called it Dispute Stitch; but the English, who seemed to believe that only a fool could be stumped by the problem, called it All Fools' Welt. The answer, of course, is "one."

Any number of sts.

Row 1 (Right side)—Knit.
Row 2—Purl.
Rows 3 through 8—Knit.

Repeat Rows 1–8.

Banded Insertion Pattern

Banded Insertion Pattern

When worked in fine yarn, this pattern has a soft, lacy effect which is probably the easiest approach to lace in all knitting.

Any number of sts.

NOTE: Two pairs of needles are used, one pair 4 to 5 sizes larger than the other. Odd-numbered rows are right-side rows.

Rows 1–4—Using small needles, knit.
Row 5—Using large needle, knit.
Row 6—Using large needles, purl.

Repeat Rows 1–6.

Basketweave

This famous pattern is notable for its ease of working and handsome appearance. It is often done with 7 purl sts across the horizontal bars, instead of 5 as given here; but the shorter 5-stitch span is preferable. Basketweave is not to be confused with Basket Stitch.

Multiple of 8 sts plus 5.

Row 1 (Right side)—Knit.
Row 2—K5, * p3, k5; rep from *.
Row 3—P5, * k3, p5; rep from *.
Row 4—Repeat Row 2.
Row 5—Knit.
Row 6—K1, * p3, k5; rep from *, end last rep k1 instead of k5.
Row 7—P1, * k3, p5; rep from *, end last rep p1 instead of p5.
Row 8—Repeat Row 6.

Repeat Rows 1-8.

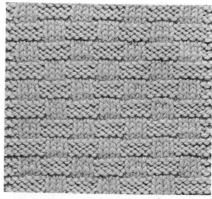

Basketweave

Basket Rib and Basket Welt Patterns

Here are two variations on Basketweave, which together illustrate very plainly how knit and purl stitches are played each against a background of the other. Though Basket Rib consists mostly of purl, or horizontal, stitches, its effect is vertical, like a ribbing. And though Basket Welt consists mostly of knit, or vertical stitches, its quality is definitely horizontal.

BASKET RIB

Multiple of 4 sts plus 1.

Row 1 (Right side)—K1, * p1, k1; rep from *.
Row 2—K2, * p1, k3; rep from *, end p1, k2.
Row 3—P2, * k1, p3; rep from *, end k1, p2.
Row 4—P1, * k1, p1; rep from *.
Row 5—K1, * p3, k1; rep from *.
Row 6—P1, * k3, p1; rep from *.

Repeat Rows 1-6.

BASKET WELT

Multiple of 10 sts. Odd-numbered rows are right-side rows.

Rows 1 and 2—* K5, p5; rep from *.
Row 3—Knit.
Rows 4 and 5—* P5, k5; rep from *.
Row 6—Purl.

Repeat Rows 1-6.

ABOVE: *Basket Rib Pattern*
BELOW: *Basket Welt Pattern*

SIMPLE KNIT-PURL COMBINATIONS   17

Double Basket Pattern

Double Basket Pattern

This pattern has nearly as much lateral stretch as a ribbing. It is quite fascinating when left entirely unblocked, so that the vertical ribs can close up together except where they are pushed apart by the purled welts. This produces a series of highly embossed waves that look almost as if they were done with the aid of a cable needle.

Multiple of 18 sts plus 10.

Row 1 (Right side)—* K11, p2, k2, p2, k1; rep from *, end k10.
Row 2—P1, k8, p1, * p1, (k2, p2) twice, k8, p1; rep from *.
Row 3—* K1, p8, (k2, p2) twice, k1; rep from *, end k1, p8, k1.
Row 4—P10, * p1, k2, p2, k2, p11; rep from *.
Rows 5, 6, 7, and 8—Repeat Rows 1, 2, 3, and 4.
Row 9—Knit.
Row 10—(P2, k2) twice, p2, * p 10, (k2, p2) twice; rep from *.
Row 11—* (K2, p2) twice, k2, p8; rep from *, end (k2, p2) twice, k2.
Row 12—(P2, k2) twice, p2, * k8, (p2, k2) twice, p2; rep from *.
Row 13—* (K2, p2) twice, k10; rep from *, end (k2, p2) twice, k2.
Rows 14, 15, 16, and 17—Repeat Rows 10, 11, 12, and 13.
Row 18—Purl.

Repeat Rows 1–18.

ABOVE: *Elongated Rib Check*
BELOW: *Variation*

Elongated Rib Check

This is a variant of Double Seed Stitch which also looks the same on right and wrong sides. It gives a pretty texture of knit-stitch checks, each 2 sts wide and 6 rows high.

Multiple of 4 sts plus 2.

Rows 1, 3, and 5—K2, * p2, k2; rep from *.
Rows 2, 4, and 6—P2, * k2, p2; rep from *.
Rows 7, 9, and 11—P2, * k2, p2; rep from *.
Rows 8, 10, and 12—K2, * p2, k2; rep from *.

Repeat Rows 1–12.

VARIATION

Establishing odd-numbered rows as wrong-side rows, work as above except: *Knit* every stitch across Rows 5, 6, 11, and 12.

Swedish Block Pattern

This Scandinavian version of Block Stitch enlarges some of the squares and reduces others, to produce a sort of cross-rib which is very attractive for sports wear—and *so* easy to knit!

Multiple of 6 sts plus 2.

Row 1 (Right side)—K2, * p4, k2; rep from *.
Row 2—P2, * k4, p2; rep from *.
Rows 3, 5, and 7—P2, * k4, p2; rep from *.
Rows 4, 6, and 8—K2, * p4, k2; rep from *.

Repeat Rows 1–8.

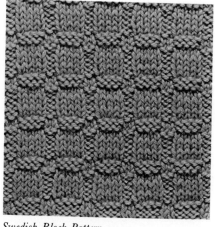

Swedish Block Pattern

Squared Check Pattern

Multiple of 10 sts plus 2.

Row 1 (Right side)—Knit.
Row 2—Purl.
Row 3—K2, * p8, k2; rep from *.
Row 4—P2, * k8, p2; rep from *.
Rows 5, 7, and 9—K2, * p2, k4, p2, k2; rep from *.
Rows 6, 8, and 10—P2, * k2, p4, k2, p2; rep from *.
Row 11—Repeat Row 3.
Row 12—Repeat Row 4.

Repeat Rows 1–12.

Squared Check Pattern

Block Stitch or Dice Pattern

This is the simplest form of knit-purl check, and like most very simple knitting patterns it has been much varied. Three variations at once are given here. In all three the basic checks are made of knit stitches, and the contrasting checks of (1) purl stitches, (2) Garter Stitch, and (3) Seed Stitch. Only (1), the Knit-Purl Block Stitch, looks the same on both sides.

For all three variations: Multiple of 10 sts plus 5.

(1) KNIT-PURL BLOCK STITCH

Rows 1, 3, 5, 6, and 8—K5, * p5, k5; rep from *.
Rows 2, 4, 7, and 9—P5, * k5, p5; rep from *.
Row 10—K5, * p5, k5; rep from *.

Repeat Rows 1–10.

ABOVE: *Knit-Purl Block Stitch*
CENTER: *Garter Block Stitch*
BELOW: *Seed Block Stitch*

SIMPLE KNIT-PURL COMBINATIONS   19

(2) GARTER BLOCK STITCH

Rows 1, 3, 5, 7, 9, and 11 (Right side)—Knit.
Rows 2, 4, and 6—K5, * p5, k5; rep from *.
Rows 8, 10, and 12—P5, * k5, p5; rep from *.

Repeat Rows 1–12.

(3) SEED BLOCK STITCH

Rows 1, 3, and 5—(Wrong side)—P5, * (k1, p1) twice, k1, p5; rep from *.
Rows 2 and 4—K5, * (k1, p1) twice, k6; rep from *.
Rows 6, 8, and 10—(P1, k1) twice, p1, * k5, (p1, k1) twice, p1; rep from *.
Rows 7 and 9—(P1, k1) twice, p1, * p5, (p1, k1) twice, p1; rep from *.

Repeat Rows 1–10.

Swedish Check and Twisted Check Patterns

Here are two very nice allover textured fabrics for "tweedy" sports wear, coats, and sweaters. Twisted Check has a little more depth to it than Swedish Check, but Swedish Check is somewhat faster to work.

SWEDISH CHECK

Multiple of 4 sts plus 2.

Row 1 (Right side)—Knit all sts through back loops.
Row 2—Purl.
Row 3—K2-b, * p2, k2-b; rep from *.
Row 4—P2, * k2, p2; rep from *.
Rows 5 and 6—Repeat Rows 1 and 2.
Row 7—P2, * k2-b, p2; rep from *.
Row 8—K2, * p2, k2; rep from *.

Repeat Rows 1–8.

TWISTED CHECK

Odd number of sts.

Row 1 (Right side)—Knit all sts through back loops.
Rows 2 and 4—* K1, p1-b; rep from *, end k1.
Row 3—* P1, k1-b; rep from *, end p1.

ABOVE: *Swedish Check Pattern*
BELOW: *Twisted Check*

Row 5—Knit all sts through back loops.
Row 6—* P1-b, k1; rep from *, end p1-b.
Row 7—* K1-b, p1; rep from *, end k1-b.
Row 8—Repeat Row 6.

Repeat Rows 1–8.

Little Check

This is a very old pattern, possibly dating back to the earliest Arabic knitting. It is formed of small squares of stockinette stitch (knit stitches) on a ground of reverse stockinette (purl stitches).

Multiple of 10 sts plus 1.

Row 1 (Right side)—Purl.
Row 2—K4, * p3, k7; rep from *, end last rep k4.
Row 3—P4, * k3, p7; rep from *, end last rep p4.
Row 4—Repeat Row 2.
Row 5—Purl.
Row 6—Knit.
Row 7—K2, * p7, k3; rep from *, end last rep k2.
Row 8—P2, * k7, p3; rep from *, end last rep p2.
Row 9—Repeat Row 7.
Row 10—Knit.

Repeat Rows 1–10.

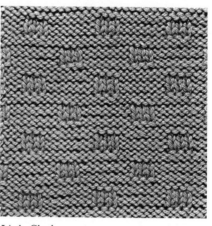

Little Check

Garter and Rib Check

The name of this pattern explains it—checks of garter stitch alternating with ribbing.

Multiple of 10 sts.

Row 1—* (K1, p1) twice, k6; rep from *.
Row 2—* K5, (p1, k1) twice, p1; rep from *.
Rows 3 and 5—Repeat Row 1.
Rows 4 and 6—Repeat Row 2.
Row 7—* K6, (p1, k1) twice; rep from *.
Row 8—* (P1, k1) twice, p1, k5; rep from *.
Rows 9 and 11—Repeat Row 7.
Rows 10 and 12—Repeat Row 8.

Repeat Rows 1–12.

Garter and Rib Check

Vandyke Check Pattern

Vandyke Check Pattern

Multiple of 8 sts.

Row 1—(Right side)—Knit.
Row 2—* K4, p4; rep from *.
Row 3—P1, * k4, p4; rep from *, end last rep p3 instead of p4.
Row 4—K2, * p4, k4; rep from *, end last rep k2 instead of k4.
Row 5—P3, * k4, p4; rep from *, end last rep p1 instead of p4.
Row 6—* P4, k4; rep from *.
Row 7—Knit.
Rows 8, 9, 10 and 11—* K4, p4, rep from *.
Row 12—Purl.
Row 13—* P4, k4; rep from *.
Row 14—K1, * p4, k4; rep from *, end last rep k3 instead of k4.
Row 15—P2, * k4, p4; rep from *, end last rep p2 instead of p4.
Row 16—K3, * p4, k4; rep from *, end last rep k1 instead of k4.
Row 17—* K4, p4; rep from *.
Row 18—Purl.
Rows 19, 20, 21 and 22—* P4, k4; rep from *.

Repeat Rows 1–22.

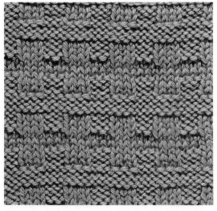

Harris Tweed Pattern

Harris Tweed Pattern

Multiple of 6 sts.

Rows 1–3—* K3, p3; rep from *.
Row 4—Knit.
Row 5—Purl.
Row 6—Knit.
Rows 7–9—* K3, p3; rep from *.
Row 10—Purl.
Row 11—Knit.
Row 12—Purl.

Repeat Rows 1–12.

Arabic Cross

This is an ancient pattern using the crossed stockinette stitch, which is formed into short-armed crosses on a purl-stitch ground.

Multiple of 12 sts plus 1.

Row 1 (Right side)—Purl.
Row 2—Knit.
Rows 3 and 5—P5, * k3-b, p9; rep from *, end last rep p5 instead of p9.

Rows 4 and 6—K5, * p3, k9; rep from *, end last rep k5 instead of k9.

Rows 7 and 9—P2, * k9-b, p3; rep from *, end last rep p2 instead of p3.

Rows 8 and 10—K2, * p9, k3; rep from *, end last rep k2 instead of k3.

Rows 11 and 13—Repeat Rows 3 and 5.

Rows 12 and 14—Repeat Rows 4 and 6.

Row 15—Purl.

Row 16—Knit.

Repeat Rows 1–16.

UPPER AND LOWER BANDS: *Arabic Cross*
CENTER BAND: *Arabic Diamonds*

Arabic Diamonds

If desired, the diamonds in this pattern may be knitted in Crossed or Twisted knit stitches for a more authentic Eastern look.

Multiple of 8 sts plus 1.

Row 1 (Right side)—Purl.

Row 2—Knit.

Row 3—P4, * k1, p7; rep from *, end last rep p4.

Row 4—K4, * p1, k7; rep from *, end last rep k4.

Row 5—P3, * k3, p5; rep from *, end last rep p3.

Row 6—K3, * p3, k5; rep from *, end last rep k3.

Row 7—P2, * k5, p3; rep from *, end last rep p2.

Row 8—K2, * p5, k3; rep from *, end last rep k2.

Row 9—Repeat Row 5.

Row 10—Repeat Row 6.

Row 11—Repeat Row 3.

Row 12—Repeat Row 4.

Repeat Rows 1–12.

Organ-Pipes Pattern

Multiple of 6 sts plus 4.

Rows 1 and 3 (Right side)—K4, * p2, k4; rep from *.

Rows 2 and 4—P4, * k2, p4; rep from *.

Rows 5 and 7—P1, k2, * p4, k2; rep from *, end p1.

Rows 6 and 8—K1, p2, * k4, p2; rep from *, end k1.

Row 9—Purl.

Row 10—Knit.

Repeat Rows 1–10.

Organ-Pipes Pattern

SIMPLE KNIT-PURL COMBINATIONS 23

Diagonal Rib

This pattern may be varied by increasing or decreasing the number of purl stitches on the right side (i.e., p2, k4 etc.) or by knitting and purling into the back loops of those stitches which form a knit stripe on the right side. In any case, the pattern is developed by moving the stripes one stitch over to the left or right on every row.

Multiple of 8 sts plus 6.

Row 1—K1, * p4, k4; rep from *, end p4, k1.
Row 2—K4, * p4, k4; rep from *, end p2.
Row 3—K3, * p4, k4; rep from *, end p3.
Row 4—K2, * p4, k4; rep from *, end p4.
Row 5—P1, * k4, p4; rep from *, end k4, p1.
Row 6—P4, * k4, p4; rep from *, end k2.
Row 7—P3, * k4, p4; rep from *, end k3.
Row 8—P2, * k4, p4; rep from *, end k4.

Repeat Rows 1–8.

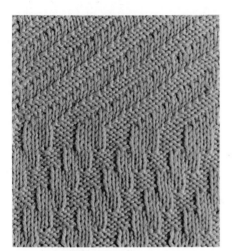

ABOVE: *Diagonal Rib*
BELOW: *Broken Diagonal Rib*

Broken Diagonal Rib

This is similar to Diagonal Rib but progresses in a zigzag design.

Multiple of 8 sts.

Rows 1, 2, 3, and 4—* P4, k4; rep from *.
Rows 5 and 7—K2, * p4, k4; rep from *, end last rep k2 instead of k4.
Rows 6 and 8—P2, * k4, p4; rep from *, end last rep p2 instead of p4.
Rows 9, 10, 11, and 12—* K4, p4; rep from *.
Rows 13 and 15—P2, * k4, p4; rep from *, end last rep p2 instead of p4.
Rows 14 and 16—K2, * p4, k4; rep from *, end last rep k2 instead of k4.

Repeat Rows 1–16.

Parallelogram Check

There are two ways of making this pattern. In the first version (Vertical), the parallelogram checks are slanted at the top and bottom, and straight at the sides. In the second version (Horizontal), the checks are slanted at the sides, and straight at the top and bottom. In both versions, if odd-numbered rows are used on the right side, the checks will slant to the left as shown; whereas if the even-numbered rows are used on the right side, the checks will slant to the right instead. The pattern should be thus reversed if there are to be two panels of it on either side of a common center.

I. VERTICAL PARALLELOGRAM CHECK

Multiple of 5 sts.

Row 1—* P1, k4; rep from *.
Rows 2 and 3—* P3, k2; rep from *.
Row 4—Repeat Row 1.
Row 5—* K1, p4; rep from *.
Rows 6 and 7—* K3, p2; rep from *.
Row 8—Repeat Row 5.

Repeat Rows 1–8.

II. HORIZONTAL PARALLELOGRAM CHECK

Multiple of 10 sts.

Row 1—* K5, p5; rep from *.
Row 2—K4, * p5, k5; rep from *, end p5, k1.
Row 3—P2, * k5, p5; rep from *, end k5, p3.
Row 4—K2, * p5, k5; rep from *, end p5, k3.
Row 5—P4, * k5, p5; rep from *, end k5, p1.
Row 6—* P5, k5; rep from *.

Repeat Rows 1–6.

ABOVE: *Vertical Parallelogram Check*
BELOW: *Horizontal Parallelogram Check*

Tulip Pattern

Multiple of 3 sts.

Rows 1 and 3 (Right side)—Knit.
Rows 2 and 4—Purl.
Rows 5 and 7—K1, * p1, k2; rep from *, end p1, k1.
Rows 6 and 8—P1, * k1, p2; rep from *, end k1, p1.
Rows 9 and 11—* P2, k1; rep from *.
Rows 10 and 12—* P1, k2; rep from *.

Repeat Rows 1–12.

Tulip Pattern

SIMPLE KNIT-PURL COMBINATIONS   25

Chevron

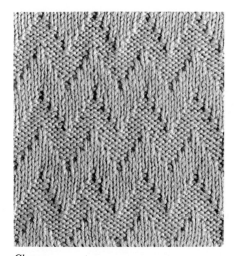

Chevron

This is an interesting pattern of transverse zigzags, of the "Vandyke" type. It looks the same on both sides although the pattern is reversed. Note that in the second half of the pattern the odd-numbered rows are switched to the even-numbered side.

Multiple of 8 sts plus 1.

Row 1—K1, * p7, k1; rep from *.
Row 2—P1, * k7, p1; rep from *.
Row 3—K2, * p5, k3; rep from *, end p5, k2.
Row 4—P2, * k5, p3; rep from *, end k5, p2.
Row 5—K3, * p3, k5; rep from *, end p3, k3.
Row 6—P3, * k3, p5; rep from *, end k3, p3.
Row 7—K4, * p1, k7; rep from *, end p1, k4.
Row 8—P4, * k1, p7; rep from *, end k1, p4.
Row 9—Repeat Row 2.
Row 10—Repeat Row 1.
Row 11—Repeat Row 4.
Row 12—Repeat Row 3.
Row 13—Repeat Row 6.
Row 14—Repeat Row 5.
Row 15—Repeat Row 8.
Row 16—Repeat Row 7.

Repeat Rows 1–16.

Pinnacle Chevron

Pinnacle Chevron

This pattern is remarkable for beauty of texture. It is formed of a broken Knit-Two Purl-Two ribbing arranged in chevrons, and is almost as simple to work as the ribbing itself. If it is pressed only lightly, or left altogether unblocked, the knit stitches will close up and twist around each other so that they resemble little Mock Cables.

Multiple of 18 sts plus 1.

Rows 1 and 3—P1, * (k2, p2) twice, k1, (p2, k2) twice, p1; rep from *.
Rows 2 and 4—K1, * (p2, k2) twice, p1, (k2, p2) twice, k1; rep from *.
Rows 5 and 7—P1, * p1, k2, p2, k2, p3, (k2, p2) twice; rep from *.
Rows 6 and 8—K1, * k1, p2, k2, p2, k3, (p2, k2) twice; rep from *.

Rows 9 and 11—Repeat Rows 2 and 4.
Rows 10 and 12—Repeat Rows 1 and 3.
Rows 13 and 15—Repeat Rows 6 and 8.
Rows 14 and 16—Repeat Rows 5 and 7.

Repeat Rows 1–16.

Seeded Chevron

If the odd-numbered rows are used on the right side, then the chevrons are in Seed Stitch outlined in purl, as shown. If the even-numbered rows are used on the right side, then the chevron is double: one of Seed Stitch, and one of purl, alternated upon a knit-stitch ground. Both sides are very pretty, and it is up to the knitter which one is to be preferred.

Seeded Chevron

Multiple of 22 sts plus 1.

Row 1—K1, * p3, (k1, p1) twice, k1, p5, k1, (p1, k1) twice, p3, k1; rep from *.

Row 2—P1, * p1, k3, (p1, k1) twice, p1, k3, p1, (k1, p1) twice, k3, p2; rep from *.

Row 3—K1, * k2, p3, (k1, p1) 5 times, k1, p3, k3; rep from *.

Row 4—K1, * p3, k3, (p1, k1) 4 times, p1, k3, p3, k1; rep from *.

Row 5—P1, * p1, k3, p3, (k1, p1) 3 times, k1, p3, k3, p2; rep from *.

Row 6—K1, * k2, p3, k3, (p1, k1) twice, p1, k3, p3, k3; rep from *.

Row 7—K1, * p3, k3, p3, k1, p1, k1, p3, k3, p3, k1; rep from *.

Row 8—K1, * (p1, k3, p3, k3) twice, p1, k1; rep from *.

Row 9—K1, * p1, k1, p3, k3, p5, k3, p3, k1, p1, k1; rep from *.

Row 10—K1, * p1, k1, p1, (k3, p3) twice, k3, (p1, k1) twice; rep from *.

Row 11—K1, * (p1, k1) twice, p3, k3, p1, k3, p3, (k1, p1) twice, k1; rep from *.

Row 12—K1, * (p1, k1) twice, p1, k3, p5, k3, (p1, k1) 3 times; rep from *.

Row 13—P1, * (p1, k1) 3 times, p3, k3, p3, (k1, p1) twice, k1, p2; rep from *.

Row 14—K1, * k2, (p1, k1) twice, (p1, k3) twice, (p1, k1) 3 times, k2; rep from *.

Repeat Rows 1–14.

Dotted Chevron

Dotted Chevron

Multiple of 18 sts.

Row 1 (Right side)—* K8, p2, k8; rep from *.
Row 2—* P7, k4, p7; rep from *.
Row 3—* P1, k5, p2, k2, p2, k5, p1; rep from *.
Row 4—* K2, p3, k2, p4, k2, p3, k2; rep from *.
Row 5—* P1, k3, p2, k6, p2, k3, p1; rep from *.
Row 6—* P3, (k2, p3) 3 times; rep from *.
Row 7—* K2, p2, k3, p4, k3, p2, k2; rep from *.
Row 8—* P1, k2, (p5, k2) twice, p1; rep from *.
Row 9—* P2, k14, p2; rep from *.
Row 10—* K1, p16, k1; rep from *.

Repeat Rows 1–10.

Garter Stitch Zigzag

Garter Stitch Zigzag

Multiple of 6 sts.

Row 1 (Wrong side) and all other wrong-side rows—Purl.
Row 2—* K3, p3; rep from *.
Row 4—P1, * k3, p3; rep from *, end last rep p2 instead of p3.
Row 6—P2, * k3, p3; rep from *, end last rep p1 instead of p3.
Row 8—* P3, k3; rep from *.
Row 10—P2, * k3, p3; rep from *, end last rep p1 instead of p3.
Row 12—P1, * k3, p3; rep from *, end last rep p2 instead of p3.

Repeat Rows 1–12.

Triangular Stitch

This is a Scottish pattern, sometimes known as Mock Kilting, for the reason that if left unpressed it will tend to roll up into soft pleats.

Multiple of 7 sts.

Row 1—* P6, k1; rep from *.
Row 2—* P2, k5; rep from *.
Row 3—* P4, k3; rep from *.
Row 4—* P4, k3; rep from *.
Row 5—* P2, k5; rep from *.
Row 6—* P6, k1; rep from *.

Repeat Rows 1–6.

ABOVE: *Triangular Stitch*
BELOW: *Pennant Stitch*

Pennant Stitch

Pennant Stitch, a close relative of Triangular Stitch, has an even stronger tendency to form pleats. Thus it is sometimes called Pennant Pleating. Thanks to this natural pleating ability it is particularly useful for skirts.

Multiple of 6 sts.

Row 1—* K1, p5; rep from *.
Row 2—* K4, p2; rep from *.
Row 3—* K3, p3; rep from *.
Row 4—* K2, p4; rep from *.
Row 5—* K5, p1; rep from *.
Row 6—Repeat Row 4.
Row 7—Repeat Row 3.
Row 8—Repeat Row 2.

Repeat Rows 1-8.

Lozenge Pattern

This is a traditional Italian knitting pattern of some antiquity.

Multiple of 5 sts.

Row 1—* P1, k4; rep from *.
Rows 2 and 3—* P3, k2; rep from *.
Row 4—* P1, k4; rep from *
Row 5—* K4, p1; rep from *
Rows 6 and 7—* K2, p3; rep from *.
Row 8—* K4, p1; rep from *.

Repeat Rows 1-8.

Lozenge Pattern

Pyramid Pattern

This is an Italian pattern, but the pyramid design, with minor variations, is common to many European countries.

Multiple of 8 sts plus 1.

Rows 1 and 3 (Right side)—* P1, k1; rep from *, end p1.
Rows 2 and 4—* K1, p1; rep from *, end k1.
Rows 5 and 7—* P2, (k1, p1) 3 times; rep from *, end p1.
Rows 6 and 8—* K2, (p1, k1) 3 times; rep from *, end k1.
Rows 9 and 11—* P3, k1, p1, k1, p2; rep from *, end p1.
Rows 10 and 12—* K3, p1, k1, p1, k2; rep from *, end k1.
Rows 13 and 15—* P4, k1, p3; rep from *, end p1.
Rows 14 and 16—* K4, p1, k3; rep from *, end k1.

Repeat Rows 1-16.

Pyramid Pattern

Dutch Pyramids

Dutch Pyramids

This pattern combines two different pyramid formations in the same design.

Multiple of 15 sts plus 7.

Row 1 (Right side)—* P1, k5-b, p1, k8; rep from *, end p1, k5-b, p1.
Row 2—* K1, p5-b, k1, p8; rep from *, end k1, p5-b, k1.
Row 3—* P1, k5-b, p9; rep from *, end p1, k5-b, p1.
Row 4—* K1, p5-b, k9; rep from *, end k1, p5-b, k1.
Row 5—* P2, k3-b, p3, k6, p1; rep from *, end p2, k3-b, p2.
Row 6—* K2, p3-b, k3, p6, k1; rep from *, end k2, p3–b, k2.
Row 7—* P2, k3-b, p10; rep from *, end p2, k3-b, p2.
Row 8—* K2, p3-b, k10; rep from *, end k2, p3-b, k2.
Row 9—* P3, k1-b, p5, k4, p2; rep from *, end p3, k1-b, p3.
Row 10—* K3, p1-b, k5, p4, k2; rep from *, end k3, p1-b, k3.
Row 11—* P3, k1-b, p11; rep from *, end p3, k1-b, p3.
Row 12—* K3, p1-b, k11; rep from *, end k3, p1-b, k3.

Repeat Rows 1–12.

Diamond Brocade

ABOVE: *Diamond Brocade*
BELOW: *Double Diamond Brocade*

This is a very famous pattern. For centuries it has recommended itself to knitters by virtue of its simplicity of working and its handsome appearance. Thus, as is inevitable when a pattern passes through many hands, many different versions of it exist.

Multiple of 8 sts plus 1.

Row 1 (Right side)—K4, * p1, k7; rep from *, end p1, k4.
Row 2—P3, * k1, p1, k1, p5; rep from *, end last repeat p3.
Row 3—K2, * p1, k3; rep from *, end last repeat k2.
Row 4—P1, * k1, p5, k1, p1; rep from *.
Row 5—* P1, k7; rep from *, end p1.
Row 6—Repeat Row 4.
Row 7—Repeat Row 3.
Row 8—Repeat Row 2.

Repeat Rows 1–8.

VARIATION: *DOUBLE DIAMOND BROCADE*

Multiple of 12 sts.

Row 1 (Right side)—K5, * p2, k10; rep from *, end p2, k5.
Row 2 and all other wrong-side rows: Knit all knit sts and purl all purl sts.
Row 3—K3, * p2, k2, p2, k6; rep from *, end last repeat k3.

Row 5—K1, * p2, k6, p2, k2; rep from *, end last repeat k1.
Row 7—P1, * k10, p2; rep from *, end k10, p1.
Row 9—Repeat Row 5.
Row 11—Repeat Row 3.
Row 12—Knit all knit sts and purl all purl sts.

Repeat Rows 1–12.

King Charles Brocade

This elegant version of Diamond Brocade carries a historical footnote of a rather gruesome nature. It is one of the patterns in a vest worn by King Charles I of England on the day of his execution in 1649. This vest, a marvelous piece of master knitting of the period, was worked in blue silk. It was preserved in the London Museum.

Multiple of 12 sts plus 1.

Row 1 (Right side)—K1, * p1, k9, p1, k1; rep from *.
Row 2—K1, * p1, k1, p7, k1, p1, k1; rep from *.
Row 3—K1, * p1, k1, p1, k5, (p1, k1) twice; rep from *.
Row 4—P1, * (p1, k1) twice, p3, k1, p1, k1, p2; rep from *.
Row 5—K1, * k2, (p1, k1) 3 times, p1, k3; rep from *.
Row 6—P1, * p3, (k1, p1) twice, k1, p4; rep from *.
Row 7—K1, * k4, p1, k1, p1, k5; rep from *.
Row 8—Repeat Row 6.
Row 9—Repeat Row 5.
Row 10—Repeat Row 4.
Row 11—Repeat Row 3.
Row 12—Repeat Row 2.

King Charles Brocade

Repeat Rows 1–12.

English Diamond Block Pattern

Multiple of 14 sts plus 5.

Row 1 (Right side)—P5, * k4, p1, k4, p5; rep from *.
Row 2—K5, * p3, k3, p3, k5; rep from *.
Row 3—K7, * p5, k9; rep from *, end last repeat k7.
Row 4—P6, * k7, p7; rep from *, end last repeat p6.
Row 5—K5, * p9, k5; rep from *.
Row 6—Repeat Row 4.
Row 7—Repeat Row 3.
Row 8—Repeat Row 2.

Repeat Rows 1–8.

English Diamond Block Pattern

Inverness Diamonds

Derived from fishermen's sweaters of the port of Inverness.

Inverness Diamonds

Panel of 17 sts.

Row 1 (Right side)—K1, p3, k9, p3, k1.
Row 2—P2, k3, p7, k3, p2.
Row 3—K3, p3, k5, p3, k3.
Row 4—P4, k3, p3, k3, p4.
Row 5—K5, p3, k1, p3, k5.
Row 6—P6, k5, p6.
Row 7—K7, p3, k7.
Row 8—Repeat Row 6.
Row 9—Repeat Row 5.
Row 10—Repeat Row 4.
Row 11—Repeat Row 3.
Row 12—Repeat Row 2.

Repeat Rows 1–12.

Giant Diamond Pattern

The wrong side of this pattern may be presented as the right side if desired. It shows the same design, in reverse.

Giant Diamond Pattern

Multiple of 15 sts.

Row 1 (Right side)—* K1, p13, k1; rep from *.
Row 2—* P2, k11, p2; rep from *.
Row 3—* K3, p9, k3; rep from *.
Row 4—* P4, k7, p4; rep from *.
Row 5—* K5, p5, k5; rep from *.
Row 6—* K1, p5, k3, p5, k1; rep from *.
Row 7—* P2, k5, p1, k5, p2; rep from *.
Row 8—* K3, p9, k3; rep from *.
Row 9—Repeat Row 7.
Row 10—Repeat Row 6.
Row 11—Repeat Row 5.
Row 12—Repeat Row 4.
Row 13—Repeat Row 3.
Row 14—Repeat Row 2.

Repeat Rows 1–14.

Diamond Stripe

This pattern gives a vertical stripe with diamonds formed of Moss Stitch indented into a knit-stitch ground. The panel may be combined with ribbings or cables or other texture patterns, or simply repeated across.

Panel of 13 sts.

Row 1 (Right side)—K6, p1, k6.
Row 2—P6, k1, p6.
Row 3—K5, p1, k1, p1, k5.
Row 4—P5, k1, p1, k1, p5.
Row 5—K4, (p1, k1) twice, p1, k4.
Row 6—P4, (k1, p1) twice, k1, p4.
Row 7—K3, (p1, k1) three times, p1, k3.
Row 8—P3, (k1, p1) three times, k1, p3.
Row 9—K2, p1, k1, p1, k3, p1, k1, p1, k2.
Row 10—P2, k1, p1, k1, p3, k1, p1, k1, p2.
Row 11—(K1, p1) twice, k5, (p1, k1) twice.
Row 12—(P1, k1) twice, p5, (k1, p1) twice.
Row 13—Repeat Row 9.
Row 14—Repeat Row 10.
Row 15—Repeat Row 7.
Row 16—Repeat Row 8.
Row 17—Repeat Row 5.
Row 18—Repeat Row 6.
Row 19—Repeat Row 3.
Row 20—Repeat Row 4.

Repeat Rows 1–20.

CENTER PANEL: *Diamond Stripe*
SIDE PANELS: *Jacob's Ladder, or Ladder of Life*

Jacob's Ladder or Ladder of Life

This pattern is also known as Cross-Rib. It is often seen in fisherman sweaters, where its comparative simplicity sets off more complicated cables in a pleasing fashion.

Panel of 7 sts.

Rows 1, 3, and 5 (Wrong side)—K1, p5, k1.
Rows 2 and 4—P1, k5, p1.
Row 6—Purl 7.

Repeat Rows 1–6.

SIMPLE KNIT-PURL COMBINATIONS   33

Halved Diamond Pattern

Multiple of 12 sts plus 1.

Row 1 (Wrong side)—P6, * k1, p11; rep from *, end k1, p6.
Row 2—K6, * p1, k11; rep from *, end p1, k6.
Row 3—P5, * k3, p9; rep from *, end k3, p5.
Row 4—K5, * p3, k9; rep from *, end p3, k5.
Row 5—P4, * k5, p7; rep from *, end k5, p4.
Row 6—K4, * p5, k7; rep from*, end p5, k4.
Row 7—P3, * k7, p5; rep from *, end k7, p3.
Row 8—K3, * p7, k5; rep from *, end p7, k3.
Row 9—P2, * k9, p3; rep from *, end k9, p2.
Row 10—K2, * p9, k3; rep from *, end p9, k2.
Row 11—P1, * k11, p1; rep from *.
Row 12—K1, * p11, k1; rep from *.
Rows 13, 14, 15, 16, 17, 18, 19, 20, 21, 22, 23, and 24—Repeat
    Rows 12, 11, 10, 9, 8, 7, 6, 5, 4, 3, 2, and 1.

Repeat Rows 1–24.

ABOVE: *Halved Diamond Pattern*
BELOW: *Garter Stitch Version*

GARTER STITCH VERSION

Repeat all odd-numbered or wrong-side rows exactly as given
above. All even-numbered or right-side rows: Knit. On this version
the even-numbered rows must be kept to the right side; on the
basic Halved Diamond Pattern above, either side can be shown.

Imitation Lattice

This pattern bears some resemblance to the regular cabled
Lattice, but is constructed entirely of simple knit and purl
stitches. The "lattice" is seen when odd-numbered rows are used
as the *wrong* side. If even-numbered rows are placed on the wrong
side instead, then the result is a pretty pattern of embossed knit-
stitch diamonds on a purled ground.

Multiple of 12 sts plus 1.

Row 1—K4, * p5, k7; rep from *, end p5, k4.
Row 2 and all other even-numbered rows—Knit all knit sts and
    purl all purl sts.
Row 3—K3, * p3, k1, p3, k5; rep from *, end last repeat k3.
Row 5—K2, * p3, k3; rep from *, end last repeat k2.
Row 7—K1, * p3, k5, p3, k1; rep from *.
Row 9—P3, * k7, p5; rep from *, end k7, p3.

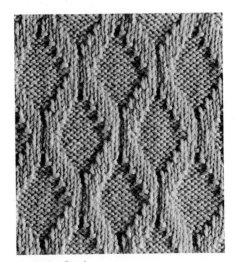

Imitation Lattice

Row 11—P2, * k9, p3; rep from *, end k9, p2.
Row 13—Repeat Row 9.
Row 15—Repeat Row 7.
Row 17—Repeat Row 5.
Row 19—Repeat Row 3.
Row 21—Repeat Row 1.
Row 23—K5, * p3, k9; rep from *, end p3, k5.
Row 24—See Row 2.

Repeat Rows 1–24.

Elongated Diamond Pattern

The wrong side of this pattern is very attractive, and might be preferred by some knitters for use on the right side of the fabric.

Elongated Diamond Pattern

Multiple of 22 sts plus 1.

Rows 1 and 3 (Right side)—K1, * k1, p2, k2, p1, k3, p1, k1, p1, k3, p1, k2, p2, k2; rep from *.

Rows 2 and 4—P1, * p1, k2, p2, k5, p1, k5, p2, k2, p2; rep from *.

Rows 5 and 7—K1, * p2, k2, (p1, k3) 3 times, p1, k2, p2, k1; rep from *.

Rows 6 and 8—Pl, * k2, p2, k5, p3, k5, p2, k2, p1; rep from *.

Rows 9 and 11—P1, * p1, k2, p1, k3, (p1, k2) twice, p1, k3, p1, k2, p2; rep from *.

Rows 10 and 12—K1, * k1, p2, k5, p2, k1, p2, k5, p2, k2; rep from *.

Rows 13 and 15—P1, * k2, p1, k3, p1, k2, p3, k2, p1, k3, p1, k2, p1; rep from *.

Rows 14 and 16—K1, * p2, k5, p2, k3, p2, k5, p2, k1; rep from *.

Rows 17 and 19—K1, * k1, p1, k3, p1, k2, p2, k1, p2, k2, p1, k3, p1, k2; rep from *.

Rows 18 and 20—P1, * p1, k5, p2, k2, p1, k2, p2, k5, p2; rep from *.

Rows 21 and 23—K1, * p1, k3, p1, k2, p2, k3, p2, k2, p1, k3, p1, k1; rep from *.

Rows 22 and 24—P1, * k5, p2, k2, p3, k2, p2, k5, p1; rep from *.

Rows 25 through 28—Repeat Rows 17 through 20.
Rows 29 through 32—Repeat Rows 13 through 16.
Rows 33 through 36—Repeat Rows 9 through 12.
Rows 37 through 40—Repeat Rows 5 through 8.

Repeat Rows 1–40.

UPPER AND LOWER BANDS: *X-and-Diamond Border*

CENTER BANDS: *Welted Leaf Pattern*

Welted Leaf Pattern

Multiple of 8 sts.

Row 1 (Right side)—Knit.
Row 2—Purl.
Row 3—* K4, p4; rep from *.
Row 4—K3, * p4, k4; rep from *, end p4, k1.
Row 5—P2, * k4, p4; rep from *, end k4, p2.
Row 6—K1, * p4, k4; rep from *, end p4, k3.
Rows 7, 8, and 9—Repeat Rows 4, 5, and 6.
Row 10—* P4, k4; rep from *.
Row 11—Knit.
Rows 12 and 13—Purl.
Row 14—Knit.

Repeat Rows 1–14.

X-and-Diamond Border

Multiple of 16 sts plus 1.

Row 1 (Right side)—Knit.
Row 2—Knit.
Row 3—K1, * k4, (p1, k5) twice; rep from *.
Row 4—P1, * (p3, k1) 3 times, p4; rep from *.
Row 5—K1, * k2, p1, k3, p1, k1, (p1, k3) twice; rep from *.
Row 6—P1, * p1, k1, (p3, k1) 3 times, p2; rep from *.
Row 7—K1, * p1, k3, p1, k5, p1, k3, p1, k1; rep from *.
Row 8—K1, * p3, k1, p7, k1, p3, k1; rep from *.
Row 9—Repeat Row 7.
Row 10—Repeat Row 6.
Row 11—Repeat Row 5.
Row 12—Repeat Row 4.
Row 13—Repeat Row 3.
Row 14—Knit.

NOTE: The pattern rows as given make a horizontal border 14 rows high. To continue the pattern in horizontal bands, omit Rows 1 and 2 from subsequent repeats, and repeat only Rows 3–14.

Moss-Bordered Diamonds

Although there are many similar patterns, this one is surely one of the prettiest possible arrangements of knit and purl stitches in the diamond form. If the odd-numbered rows are used as right-side rows, the diamonds will be formed of knit and moss stitches on a purled ground as shown. If the even-numbered rows are used as right-side rows, then the diamonds will be formed of purl and moss indented in a knit-stitched ground.

Moss-Bordered Diamonds

Multiple of 22 sts plus 1.

Row 1—P1, * p4, (k1, p1) twice, k5, (p1, k1) twice, p5; rep from *.

Row 2 and all other even-numbered rows—Knit all knit sts and purl all purl sts.

Row 3—K1, * p5, (k1, p1) twice, k3, (p1, k1) twice, p5, k1; rep from *.

Row 5—P1, * k1, p5, (k1, p1) 5 times, p4, k1, p1; rep from *.

Row 7—K1, * p1, k1, p5, (k1, p1) 4 times, p4, k1, p1, k1; rep from *.

Row 9—P1, * (k1, p1) twice, p4, (k1, p1) 3 times, p4, (k1, p1) twice; rep from *.

Row 11—K1, * (p1, k1) twice, p5, (k1, p1) twice, p4, (k1, p1) twice, k1; rep from *.

Row 13—K1, * (k1, p1) 3 times, p4, k1, p5, (k1, p1) twice, k2; rep from *.

Row 15—K1, * k2, (p1, k1) twice, p9, (k1, p1) twice, k3; rep from *.

Row 17—K1, * k3, (p1, k1) twice, p7, (k1, p1) twice, k4; rep from *.

Rows 19, 21, 23, 25, 27, 29, 31, and 33—Repeat Rows 15, 13, 11, 9, 7, 5, 3, and 1.

Row 35—P1, * p3, (k1, p1) twice, k7, (p1, k1) twice, p4; rep from *.

Row 36—See Row 2.

Repeat Rows 1–36.

CHAPTER THREE

Ribbings

Everyone who has ever made a sweater knows what ribbing is. But not many people know how many variations there are, aside from the usual "k2, p2," or "k1, p1." A novelty ribbing can make a big difference in giving a garment the "original" look. But remember that when trying out new ribbings it is very important to make a test swatch. Some ribbings are looser than others, which means that they vary in elasticity. You would not want a very loose ribbing in some circumstances, such as at the bottom of a sweater, where the purpose of the ribbing is to hold the fabric close to the figure. On the other hand, some of the looser ribbings are very effective when used over the entire body of the garment, or as cuffs for jackets and coats, or as borders at the bottom of a jacket which is to fall straight rather than hug like a sweater. After you have tried out a few different ones in test swatches, their appearance will suggest innumerable possibilities for their use.

Some of the ribbings included here are rather fancy, employing twist stitches, yarn-over stitches and the like. If you are unfamiliar with any of these specialized stitches it is suggested that you read the Introduction to their particular section, before proceeding with the ribbing pattern.

A number of fancy ribbings are very successful when used in combination with each other. The usual method is to alternate ribs: that is, to work one rib in one pattern and the second in the other, and so on. Some combinations are suggested in this section. Many other combinations of two—or even three or four—different ribbing patterns are possible. You should try out combinations for yourself, alternating whatever patterns you please to see which ones look well together. As well as the ribbing patterns in this section, there are many other patterns included in other sections which are highly suitable for use as fancy ribbings. See Little Mock Cables, Yarn-Over Cable, Fuchsia Pattern, Simple Cable, Little Plait Cable, etc.

Knit-One Purl-One Ribbing

This is the simplest form of ribbing, most often used on sweaters at lower edges, neckbands and cuffs. It can be pleasantly varied and made to look a little fancier by crossing the stitches on the right side; that is, by knitting each right-side knit stitch through the back loop.

Even number of sts.

* K1, p1. Repeat from * across.

Repeat this same row.

VARIATION

Twisted ribbing, in which the stitches are twisted on both right and wrong sides, gives a corded effect. It is worked as follows:

Even number of sts.

Row 1—* K1-b, p1; rep from *. (This is right side.)
Row 2—* K1, p1-b; rep from *.

Repeat Rows 1 and 2.

LEFT: *Knit-One Purl-One Ribbing*
RIGHT: *Knit-Two Purl-Two Ribbing*
BOTH PATTERNS: (ABOVE) *Plain* (CENTER)
Crossed (BELOW) *Twisted*

Knit-Two Purl-Two Ribbing

This ribbing is just as popular as Knit-One Purl-One, but a trifle looser. Knit-Two Purl-Two may also be crossed by knitting through the back loops of knit stitches on the right side.

Multiple of 4 sts.

* K2, p2. Repeat from * across.

Repeat this row.

When Knit-Two Purl-Two Ribbing is twisted on both sides of the fabric, it is sometimes known as Cross Cord Ribbing. This variation is worked as follows:

Multiple of 4 sts.

Row 1 (Right side)—* K2-b, p2; rep from *.
Row 2—* K2, p2-b; rep from *.

Repeat Rows 1 and 2.

Mistake-Stitch Ribbing

Mistake-Stitch Ribbing

This handsome ribbing may very well have been discovered by an accident. The "mistake" consists of working Knit-Two Purl-Two ribbing on one less stitch than required—though anyone who first made this mistake would have perceived it very soon, as the two ribbings appear quite different.

Multiple of 4 sts plus 3.

* K2, p2; rep from *, end k2, p1.

Repeat this row.

Embossed Moss Stitch Ribbing

Embossed Moss Stitch Ribbing

This ribbing is formed by two stitches of Moss enclosed by vertical ribs of knit stitches. It may also be used as an allover fabric.

Multiple of 7 sts plus 3.

Row 1 (Right side)—P3, * k1, p1, k2, p3; rep from *.
Row 2—K3, * p2, k1, p1, k3; rep from *.
Row 3—P3, * k2, p1, k1, p3; rep from *.
Row 4—K3, * p1, k1, p2, k3; rep from *.

Repeat Rows 1–4.

Baby Cable Ribbing

This method of twisting two stitches to make a miniature cable is superior to the method used in the classic Mock Cable; the result is smoother and more symmetrical. Baby Cable Ribbing is a delightful pattern for an allover sweater fabric. It may be used to replace almost any Knit-Two Purl-Two Ribbing with great success.

Multiple of 4 sts plus 2.

Rows 1 and 3 (Wrong side)—K2, * p2, k2; rep from *.
Row 2—P2, * k2, p2; rep from *.
Row 4—P2, * k2 tog, but leave on needle; then insert right-hand needle between the 2 sts just knitted together, and knit the 1st st again; then sl both sts from needle together; p2; rep from *.

Repeat Rows 1–4.

Baby Cable Ribbing

Cross-Stitch Ribbing and Little Hourglass Ribbing

Here are two fancy ribbings that combine prettily. Both are highly embossed. Either may be used alone, of course, or in combination with some other pattern, and thus they are given separately.

CROSS-STITCH RIBBING

This ribbing is a straight two-stitch twist, worked like a Classic Mock Cable except that the twist is performed on every right-side row.

Multiple of 4 sts plus 2.

Row 1 (Right side)—P2, * skip 1 st and knit into 2nd st, then knit into skipped st, then sl both sts from needle together; p2; rep from *.
Row 2—K2, * p2, k2; rep from *.

Repeat Rows 1 and 2.

LITTLE HOURGLASS RIBBING

See also Yarn-Over Cable for a somewhat similar technique.

Multiple of 4 sts plus 2.

Row 1 (Wrong side)—K2, * p2, k2; rep from *.
Row 2—P2, * k2 tog-b, then knit same 2 sts tog again through *front* loops; p2; rep from *.
Row 3—K2, * p1, yo, p1, k2; rep from *.
Row 4—P2, * ssk, k1, p2; rep from *.

Repeat Rows 1-4.

ABOVE, LEFT: *Cross-Stitch Ribbing*
ABOVE, RIGHT: *Little Hourglass Ribbing*
BELOW: *In combination*

Braided Ribbing

Multiple of 5 sts plus 2.

Row 1 (Right side)—P2, * insert needle from back to front between 1st and 2nd sts on left-hand needle and knit the 2nd st, then knit the 1st st and sl both sts from needle together; k1, p2; rep from *.
Row 2—K2, * skip 1 st and purl the 2nd st, then purl the skipped st, sl both sts from needle together; p1, k2; rep from *.

Repeat Rows 1 and 2.

ABOVE: *Braided Ribbing*
BELOW: *Variation*

VARIATION   *(See illustration, page 41)*

When the plain knitted and purled stitches are placed before the twisted stitches instead of after them, the result is a rounder, tighter, and more highly embossed braided ribbing.

Multiple of 5 sts plus 2.

Row 1 (Right side)—P2, * k1, insert needle from back to front between 1st and 2nd sts on left-hand needle and knit the 2nd st, then knit the 1st st and sl both sts from needle together; p2; rep from *.

Row 2—K2, * p1, skip 1 st and purl the 2nd st, then purl the skipped st, sl both sts from needle together; k2; rep from *.

Repeat Rows 1 and 2.

Reverse Cross-Stitch Ribbing and Mock Cable Rib

These two ribbings combine well, because the Mock Cable Rib tends to be a little flat and the Reverse Cross-Stitch, in high relief, compensates for this and gives the combination more elasticity.

REVERSE CROSS-STITCH RIBBING

Multiple of 4 sts plus 2.

Row 1 (Right side)—P2, * k2, p2; rep from *.

Row 2—K2, * skip 1 st and purl the 2nd st, then purl the skipped st, then sl both sts from needle together; k2; rep from *.

Repeat Rows 1 and 2.

MOCK CABLE RIB

Multiple of 5 sts plus 2.

Rows 1 and 3 (Wrong side)—K2, * p3, k2; rep from *.

Row 2—P2, * k3, p2; rep from *.

Row 4—P2, * skip 2 sts and insert needle knitwise into front of 3rd st, then taking point of needle in *front* of the 2 skipped sts, past these sts and around to the right, catch yarn and knit; then sl the 3rd st off left-hand needle over the 2 skipped sts, taking care not to let the skipped sts come off with it; k2, p2; rep from *.

Repeat Rows 1–4.

ABOVE, LEFT: *Reverse Cross-Stitch Ribbing*
ABOVE, RIGHT: *Mock Cable Rib*
BELOW: *In combination*

Wheat Ear Rib

Multiple of 5 sts plus 2.

Row 1 (Right side)—* P3, insert needle from back to front between 1st and 2nd sts on left-hand needle and knit the 2nd st, then knit the 1st st and sl both sts from needle together; rep from *, end p2.

Row 2—* K3, skip 1 st and purl the 2nd st, then purl the skipped st, then sl both sts from needle together; rep from *, end k2.

Repeat Rows 1 and 2.

VARIATION: *ZIGZAG KNOTTED RIB*

Although the change in knitting technique is very minor, this variation is remarkably different in appearance from Wheat Ear Rib.

Multiple of 5 sts plus 2.

Row 1 (Right side)—P2, * insert needle from back to front between 1st and 2nd sts on left-hand needle and knit the 2nd st, then knit the 1st st, then sl both sts from needle together; p3; rep from *.

Row 2—K2, * skip 1 st and purl the 2nd st, then purl the skipped st, then sl both sts from needle together; k3; rep from *.

Repeat Rows 1 and 2.

ABOVE: *Wheat Ear Rib*
BELOW: *Zigzag Knotted Rib*

Figure-Eight Twisted Ribbing

Multiple of 10 sts plus 7.

Row 1 (Wrong side) and all other wrong-side rows—K2, * p3, k2; rep from *.

Row 2—P2, * skip 2 sts and knit into 3rd stitch, then knit into 2nd stitch, then knit into 1st stitch, then sl all 3 sts from needle together (Twist Three, Tw 3); p2; rep from *.

Row 4—P2, * k3, p2, Tw 3, p2; rep from *, end k3, p2.

Row 6—Repeat Row 2.

Row 8—Repeat Row 4.

Row 10—Repeat Row 2.

Row 12—P2, * Tw 3, p2, k3, p2; rep from *, end Tw 3, p2.

Row 14—Repeat Row 2.

Row 16—Repeat Row 12.

Repeat Rows 1–16.

Figure-Eight Twisted Ribbing

Rickrack Ribbing

Rickrack Ribbing

Multiple of 3 sts plus 1.

Row 1 (Right side)—P1, * take right-hand needle behind left-hand needle, skip 1 st and knit in *back* loop of 2nd st; then knit skipped st through front loop, then sl both sts from needle together; p1; rep from *.

Row 2—K1, * with yarn in front skip 1 st and purl the 2nd st, then purl the skipped st, then sl both sts from needle together; k1; rep from *.

Repeat Rows 1 and 2.

Fisherman's Rib

Fisherman's Rib

This pattern, a member of the Waffle Stitch family, makes a deep fluffy ribbing and is also very handsome as an allover fabric for sports sweaters.

Even number of sts.

Cast on and purl one row.

Row 1—* P1, knit next st in the row below; rep from *, end p2.

Repeat this same row.

ABOVE: *Slip-Stitch Ribbing*
BELOW: *Variation*

Slip-Stitch Ribbing

This pattern makes a full, rounded rib with plenty of spring to it. Left unpressed, the ribbing will close tightly together in a firm hold such as is desired at the lower edge or cuff of a sweater, or a turtleneck collar, or a ribbed hat. The Variation, p. 45, is also a good firm ribbing but a little flatter, with the ribs somewhat broadened by placing the slip-stitches at the sides instead of in the center.

Multiple of 5 sts plus 2.

Row 1 (Wrong side)—K2, * p3, k2; rep from *.
Row 2—P2, * k1, sl 1 wyib, k1, p2; rep from *.

Repeat Rows 1 and 2.

Multiple of 5 sts plus 2.

Row 1 (Wrong side)—K2, * p3, k2; rep from *.
Row 2—P2, * sl 1 wyib, k1, sl 1 wyib, p2; rep from *.

Repeat Rows 1 and 2.

Diagonal Ribbing

This ribbing is thick and dense, and "takes in" very effectively. It does well as an allover fabric, i.e., for a coat or jacket. The wrong side is attractive also.

Multiple of 3 sts.

Row 1 (Wrong side)—K2, * sl 1 wyif, k2; rep from *, end k1.
Row 2—K1, p2, * skip 1 st and knit into the *back* loop of 2nd st, then knit the skipped st through front loop, then sl both sts from needle together (Twist Two, Tw 2); p1; rep from * to last 3 sts, end Tw 2, k1.
Row 3—K1, * sl 1 wyif, k2; rep from *, end sl 1, k1.
Row 4—K1, * Tw 2, p1; rep from *, end k2.
Row 5—K1, * k2, sl 1 wyif; rep from *, end k2.
Row 6—K1, *p1, Tw 2; rep from *, end p1, k1.

Repeat Rows 1–6.

Diagonal Ribbing

Brioche Stitch

Brioche Stitch is the basic member of a large family of patterns of Eastern origin (see Double Brioche, Waffle Brioche, Syncopated Brioche, Tunisian Knitting, etc.). The elements of all such patterns are (1) a slipped stitch, and (2) a yarn-over; these are knitted together on the return row.

Brioche Stitch, worked in medium-weight yarn on average needles, forms a deep, soft, tidy-looking ribbing that is useful in many ways. It has a lot of "give", and thus is good for knitted articles that are likely to be subjected to pulling and twisting, such as scarves, baby blankets, and shawls. Worked in fine yarn, it makes a mesh-like lace that is ideal for fancy stockings.

Brioche Stitch

If Brioche Stitch is used as a straight ribbing on the lower edge or cuff of a garment, the last row at the end of the ribbing should be worked as follows: omit the yo, (p1, k2 tog) across. The same applies to binding off. It is important to bind off *very* loosely. All slip-stitches are slipped with yarn in back.

Even number of sts.

Row 1 (preparation row)—* Yo, sl 1, k1; rep from *.
Row 2—* Yo, sl 1, k2 tog (slip-stitch and yo of previous row); rep from *.

Omit first row, repeat Row 2 only.

Single Eyelet Rib and Double Eyelet Rib

These two patterns look very nice in combination. Either or both will make a pretty border for any garment worked in fine yarn, particularly if the body of the garment is done in some openwork pattern. The Double Eyelet is a broad rib, and so has not very much elasticity; but its springiness can be increased by inserting Single Eyelet or some other ribbing pattern between Double Eyelet ribs.

ABOVE, LEFT: *Single Eyelet Rib*
ABOVE, RIGHT: *Double Eyelet Rib*
BELOW: *In combination*

SINGLE EYELET RIB

Multiple of 5 sts plus 2.

Row 1 (Wrong side) and all other wrong-side rows—K2, * p3, k2; rep from *.
Row 2—P2, * k3, p2; rep from *.
Row 4—P2, * k2 tog, yo, k1, p2; rep from *.
Row 6—Repeat Row 2.
Row 8—P2, * k1, yo, ssk, p2; rep from *.

Repeat Rows 1–8.

DOUBLE EYELET RIB

Multiple of 7 sts plus 2.

Rows 1 and 3 (Wrong side)—K2, * p5, k2; rep from *.
Row 2—P2, * k5, p2; rep from *.
Row 4—P2, * k2 tog, yo, k1, yo, ssk, p2; rep from *.

Repeat Rows 1–4.

Italian Chain Ribbing

Like most openwork ribbings, this quite fancy pattern tends to be loose. Thus when used as a ribbing it should be worked on small needles. In a larger gauge it makes a pleasing allover pattern for the body of a garment. Both sides are attractive, though different; therefore the pattern could also be used for such articles as scarves and baby blankets.

Italian Chain Ribbing

Multiple of 6 sts plus 2.

Row 1 (Wrong side)—K2, * p4, k2; rep from *.
Row 2—P2, * k2 tog, (yo) twice, ssk, p2; rep from *.
Row 3—K2, * p1, purl into front of 1st yo, purl into back of 2nd yo, p1, k2; rep from *.
Row 4—P2, * yo, ssk, k2 tog, yo, p2; rep from *.

Repeat Rows 1-4.

Two Novelty Textures: Little Shell Rib and Puff Rib

These novelty patterns do very well as an allover fabric, and equally well in isolated vertical panels to add texture interest. Puff Rib in particular has a very deep texture and a good deal of lateral stretch.

LITTLE SHELL RIB

Multiple of 5 sts plus 2.

Row 1 (Right side)—P2, * k3, p2; rep from *.
Row 2—K2, * p3, k2; rep from *.
Row 3—P2, * sl 1—k2 tog—psso, p2; rep from *.
Row 4—K2, * (p1, k1, p1) all in the same stitch, k2; rep from *.

Repeat Rows 1-4.

PUFF RIB

Multiple of 3 sts plus 2.

Row 1 (Right side)—P2, * yo, k1, yo, p2; rep from *.
Row 2—K2, * p3, k2; rep from *.
Row 3—P2, * k3, p2; rep from *.
Row 4—K2, * p3 tog, k2; rep from *.

Repeat Rows 1-4.

ABOVE: *Little Shell Rib*
BELOW: *Puff Rib*

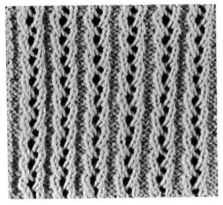

Lace Rib

Lace Rib

Either side of this delicate ribbing may be used as the right side, though they are different in appearance. This pattern makes a lovely finish on lace-stitch blouses or dresses.

Multiple of 5 sts plus 2.

Rows 1 and 3—K2, * p3, k2; rep from *.
Row 2—P2, * k1, yo, ssk, p2; rep from *.
Row 4—P2, * k2 tog, yo, k1, p2; rep from *.

Repeat Rows 1–4.

Knotted Rib and Broad Spiral Rib

These two ribbing patterns combine handsomely. The Knotted Rib is tight, whereas the Broad Spiral Rib projects from the fabric in a series of rounded columns with the stitches spiraling around them to the right. Either pattern, or a combination of them, is very good for heavy, fancy cable sweaters full of texture interest.

KNOTTED RIB

Multiple of 3 sts plus 2.

Row 1 (Right side)—P2, * knit into front and back of next st, p2; rep from *.
Row 2—K2, * p2 tog, k2; rep from *.

Repeat Rows 1 and 2.

BROAD SPIRAL RIB

Multiple of 6 sts plus 2.

Rows 1 and 3 (Wrong side)—K2, * p4, k2; rep from *.
Row 2—P2, * (k2 tog but do not sl from needle; insert right-hand needle between the sts just knitted together, and knit the first st again; then sl both sts from needle together) twice; p2; rep from *.
Row 4—P2, * k1, k2 tog and knit 1st st again as before; k1, p2; rep from *.

Repeat Rows 1–4.

ABOVE, LEFT: *Knotted Rib*
ABOVE, RIGHT: *Broad Spiral Rib*
BELOW: *In combination*

Corded Ribbing

This is a traditional Italian pattern that makes quite a handsome fabric.

Multiple of 4 sts plus 2.

Row 1—K1, * ssk, lift running thread between st just worked and the next st, and knit into back of this thread (M1), p2; rep from *, end k1.

Repeat this same row.

Corded Ribbing

Cable Ribbing

While not particularly elastic, these rows of fancy little cables will make an appropriate border for garments containing cables or cable-stitch patterns.

Multiple of 5 sts plus 2.

Rows 1 and 3 (Wrong side)—K2, * p1-b, k1, p1-b, k2; rep from *.
Row 2—P2, * k1-b, p1, k1-b, p2; rep from *.
Row 4—P2, * sl next 2 sts to dpn and hold in front, k1-b, then sl the purl st back to left-hand needle and purl it; then k1-b from dpn; p2; rep from *.

Repeat Rows 1–4.

Cable Ribbing

CHAPTER FOUR

Color-Change Patterns

There are few things that give so much novelty and originality to a hand-knitted garment as the interplay of contrasting colors. Yet the patterns in this section are easy to work—almost effortless, compared with some other knitting techniques. The reason for this is simple: all of them, excepting only the last two, employ the delightful and infinitely adaptable slip-stitch method of color knitting.

The last two patterns, "Fair Isle" Pattern and Houndstooth Check, are done in quite a different way. Instead of using the same strand of color all the way along any given row, these patterns change color from stitch to stitch. This type of knitting is generically termed Fair Isle knitting, although such a general application of the term is decidedly inaccurate. True Fair Isle knitting has its roots in the Spanish tradition, and uses only certain definite patterns which are based on the Armada Cross. Therefore "Fair Isle" is put in quotes to indicate that it really is a misnomer.

Actually, "Fair Isle" knitting does not belong in this book, because it is not a stitch pattern at all. It is all done in plain stockinette stitch, the right-side rows being knitted and the wrong-side rows purled. But these two patterns are included just to give you an idea of it. The knitter can invent any sort of pattern for this kind of knitting, simply by marking the colors on graph paper, each square representing a stitch, and then knitting plain with her own "art work" as a guide. There are only two rules to follow: first, the unused strand is carried lightly across the back of the fabric; second, the new color is always picked up from *under* the one that is being dropped, in order to avoid leaving holes in the work.

Slip-stitch color knitting is easier to do than the "Fair Isle" type, and its patterns are true stitch patterns. The colors are changed only at the end of a row. Unused strands are carried up the side of the piece from row to row, where they will be concealed in a garment seam. To make the neatest possible edge, remember to drop the strand just used on the *right* side of the fabric, and pick up the new strand behind it, on the wrong side. In this way the strands will be woven tidily around each other up the edge, all being drawn from the front to the back of the fabric. In circular knitting, it makes little difference whether the new strand is picked up to the left or to the right of the old strand at the end of a round, as long as all are done the same way. This will make a continuous spiral of strands running up the inside of the garment from round to round. Care must be taken not to pull the strands too tight, as this might cause a vertical pucker.

Directions for slipping stitches specify "with yarn in front" (wyif) or "with yarn in back" (wyib). These are directions for straight, not circular, knitting, and do *not* refer to the right or wrong side of the fabric, but rather to the fabric in relation to the knitter. "Front" is the side of the fabric that is toward the knitter, and "back" is the side that is away from the knitter. Whether the knitter is looking at the right or wrong side of the fabric does not matter. After the stitch has been slipped, the yarn is returned to position for knitting or purling, whichever the following stitch calls for. Thus if a stitch is slipped with yarn in front, and the next stitch is to be knitted, then the yarn is put to the back again to be in position for knitting. If, on the other hand, a stitch is slipped with yarn in back, and the next stitch is to be purled, then the yarn is brought forward again for purling. Remember that in slipping stitches the needle is always inserted into the stitch *as if to purl,* i.e., from the right-hand side, unless otherwise specified.

Not all of these patterns need be done in contrasting colors. Some give very interesting texture effects even when the yarn is all the same color; which clearly shows that they are stitch patterns and not just color patterns. Experiment with them. In knitting, experimentation is usually rewarded with novelty.

Simple Vertical Stripes

Multiple of 4 sts. Colors A and B.

Cast on with Color B and purl one row.

Row 1 (Right side)—With A, k1, * sl 2 wyib, k2; rep from *, end sl 2, k1.
Row 2—With A, k1, * sl 2 wyif, p2; rep from *, end sl 2, k1.
Row 3—With B, k1, * k2, sl 2 wyib; rep from *, end k3.
Row 4—With B, k1, * p2, sl 2 wyif; rep from *, end p2, k1.

Repeat Rows 1–4.

Simple Vertical Stripes

Simple Check Pattern

There are so many ways of varying this pattern that it is hardly possible to list them all. But here are a few ideas: (1) For a three-color check, a Color C can be introduced in Rows 7 and 8 of either version. (2) A little added texture can be had by *knitting* instead of purling the wrong-side rows of contrasting color (Rows 4 and 8). (3) Two more knit and purl rows can be inserted between the rows of Color B, thus spacing the checks farther apart. (4) The pattern can be widened even more than Version II, working a six- or eight-stitch check.

VERSION I: TWO-STITCH CHECK

Multiple of 4 sts. Colors A and B.

Row 1 (Right side)—With A, knit.
Row 2—With A, purl.
Row 3—With B, k3, * sl 2 wyib, k2; rep from *, end k1.
Row 4—With B, p3, * sl 2 wyif, p2; rep from *, end p1.
Rows 5 and 6—With A, repeat Rows 1 and 2.
Row 7—With B, k1, * sl 2 wyib, k2; rep from *, end sl 2, k1.
Row 8—With B, p1, * sl 2 wyif, p2; rep from *, end sl 2, p1.

Repeat Rows 1–8.

VERSION II: FOUR-STITCH CHECK

Multiple of 6 sts plus 4. Colors A and B.

Row 1 (Right side)—With A, knit.
Row 2—With A, purl.
Row 3—With B, k4, * sl 2 wyib, k4; rep from *.
Row 4—With B, p4, * sl 2 wyif, p4; rep from *.
Rows 5 and 6—With A, Repeat Rows 1 and 2.
Row 7—With B, k1, * sl 2 wyib, k4; rep from *, end sl 2, k1.
Row 8—With B, p1, * sl 2 wyif, p4; rep from *, end sl 2, p1.

Repeat Rows 1–8.

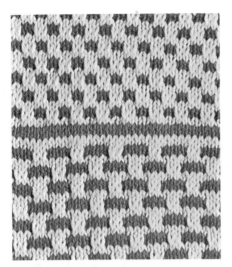

Simple Check Pattern
ABOVE: *Two-Stitch Check*
BELOW: *Four-Stitch Check*

Elongated Check Pattern

This pattern is an elaboration of Simple Vertical Stripes; a good example of how basic patterns may be built into many different designs.

NOTE: On right-side rows (odd numbers) sl all sl-sts with yarn in back; on wrong-side rows (even numbers) sl all sl-sts with yarn in front.

Multiple of 22 sts plus 1. Colors A and B.

Row 1 (Right side)—With A, knit.
Row 2—With A, purl.
Row 3—With B, k1, * sl 3, k2, sl 2, k3, sl 1, k3, sl 2, k2, sl 3, k1; rep from *.

Elongated Check Pattern

Row 4—With B, p1, * sl 3, p2, sl 2, p3, sl 1, p3, sl 2, p2, sl 3, p1; rep from *.
Row 5—With A, k1, * k3, sl 2, k2, sl 3, k1, sl 3, k2, sl 2, k3, sl 1; rep from *, end last repeat k1 instead of sl 1.
Row 6—With A, p1, * p3, sl 2, p2, sl 3, p1, sl 3, p2, sl 2, p3, sl 1; rep from *, end last repeat p1 instead of sl 1.
Rows 7–14—Repeat Rows 3–6 twice more.
Row 15—With A, knit.
Row 16—With A, purl.
Rows 17 and 18—With B, repeat Rows 5 and 6.
Rows 19 and 20—With A, repeat Rows 3 and 4.
Rows 21–28—Repeat Rows 17–20 twice more.

Repeat Rows 1–28.

Three-and-One Tweed

This is the classic Three-and-One slip-stitch pattern worked in two colors.

Multiple of 4 sts plus 3. Colors A and B.

Cast on with Color B and knit one row.

Row 1 (Right side)—With A, k3, * sl 1 wyib, k3; rep from *.
Row 2—With A, k3, * sl 1 wyif, k3; rep from *.
Row 3—With B, k1, * sl 1 wyib, k3; rep from *, end sl 1, k1.
Row 4—With B, k1, * sl 1 wyif, k3; rep from *, end sl 1, k1.

Repeat Rows 1–4.

Three-and-One Tweed

Maltese Cross

In this pattern a slight variation on Three-and-One Tweed makes a surprisingly large difference.

Multiple of 4 sts plus 3. Colors A and B.

Row 1 (Wrong side)—With A, purl.
Row 2—With B, k3, * sl 1 wyib, k3; rep from *.
Row 3—With B, k3, * sl 1 wyif, k3; rep from *.
Row 4—With A, k1, * sl 1 wyib, k3; rep from *, end sl 1, k1.
Row 5—With A, k1, * sl 1 wyif, k3; rep from *, end sl 1, k1.
Row 6—With B, repeat Row 2.
Row 7—With B, purl.
Row 8—With A, repeat Row 4.

Repeat Rows 1–8.

Maltese Cross

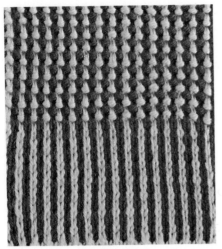

ABOVE: *Corn on the Cob Stitch*
BELOW: *Pin Stripe Pattern*

Corn on the Cob Stitch

This fabric, knitted in narrow vertical stripes, is nubby and very dense. It is well suited to heavy knitted coats and jackets calculated to keep the wind out; and it can be done also in fine yarn for such articles as gloves.

Even number of sts. Colors A and B.

Cast on with Color A and knit one row.

Row 1 (Right side)—With B, k1, * k1, sl 1 wyib; rep from *, end k1.
Row 2—With B, k1, * sl 1 wyif, k1; rep from *, end k1.
Row 3—With A, k1, * sl 1 wyib, k1-b; rep from *, end k1.
Row 4—With A, k1, * k1, sl 1 wyif; rep from *, end k1.

Repeat Rows 1–4.

VARIATION: *PIN STRIPE PATTERN*

Work Pin Stripe Pattern the same as Corn on the Cob Stitch, except in Rows 2 and 4 *purl* instead of knit.

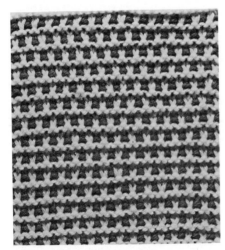

ABOVE: *Waffle Check*
BELOW: *Variation*

Waffle Check

This pattern is the same as Pin Check, except that it has a garter-stitch basis which lends it a nubby texture.

Odd number of sts. Colors A and B.

Row 1 (Wrong side)—With A, knit.
Row 2—With B, k1, * sl 1 wyib, k1; rep from *.
Row 3—With B, k1, * sl 1 wyif, k1; rep from *.
Rows 4 and 5—With A, knit.
Row 6—With B, k2, * sl 1 wyib, k1; rep from *, end k1.
Row 7—With B, k2, * sl 1 wyif, k1; rep from *, end k1.
Row 8—With A, knit.

Repeat Rows 1–8.

WAFFLE CHECK VARIATION

To align the checks vertically instead of alternating them, repeat Rows 1–4 only.

Pin Check

This pattern is identical with Waffle Check except for Rows 1 and 5. Yet this small difference gives quite a different texture.

Odd number of sts. Colors A and B.

Row 1 (Wrong side)—With A, purl.
Row 2—With B, k1, * sl 1 wyib, k1; rep from *.
Row 3—With B, k1, * sl 1 wyif, k1; rep from *.
Row 4—With A, knit.
Row 5—With A, purl.
Row 6—With B, k2, * sl 1 wyib, k1; rep from *, end k1.
Row 7—With B, k2, * sl 1 wyif, k1; rep from *, end k1.
Row 8—With A, knit.

Repeat Rows 1–8.

PIN CHECK VARIATION

Repeat Rows 1–4 only. In this way the checks are aligned vertically above one another instead of being alternated.

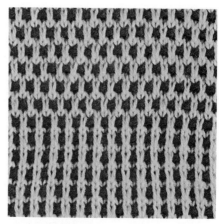

ABOVE: *Pin Check*
BELOW: *Variation*

Tricolor Wave Stripes

Multiple of 4 sts plus 1. Colors A, B, and C.

Cast on with Color A and purl one row.

Row 1 (Right side)—With B, k1, * sl 3 wyib, k1; rep from *.
Row 2—With B, p2, * sl 1 wyif, p3; rep from *, end sl 1, p2.
Row 3—With B, knit.
Row 4—With B, purl.
Rows 5–8—With C, repeat Rows 1–4.
Rows 9–12—With A, repeat Rows 1–4.

Repeat Rows 1–12.

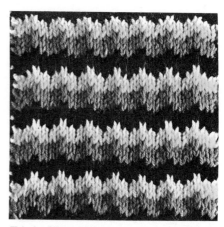

Tricolor Wave Stripes

Ripple Stripes

This is a smaller version of Tricolor Wave Stripes.

Multiple of 4 sts plus 2. Colors A and B.

Rows 1 and 3 (Right side)—With A, knit.
Rows 2 and 4—With A, purl.
Row 5—With B, k2, * sl 2 wyib, k2; rep from *.
Row 6—With B, purl.
Row 7—With A, repeat Row 5.
Row 8—With A, purl.

Repeat Rows 1–8.

Ripple Stripes

Dotted Ladder Pattern

In this pretty vertical-stripe variation, each stripe contains accents of its opposite color, which makes the overall effect more interesting than plain vertical stripes.

Dotted Ladder Pattern

Multiple of 6 sts plus 5. Colors A and B.

Cast on with Color A and purl one row.

Row 1 (Right side)—With B, k1, * sl 1 wyib, k1, sl 1 wyib, k3; rep from *, end last repeat k1.
Row 2—With B, k1, * sl 1 wyif, k1, sl 1 wyif, p3; rep from * to last 4 sts, end (sl 1 wyif, k1) twice.
Row 3—With A, k1, * k3, sl 1 wyib, k1, sl 1 wyib; rep from * to last 4 sts, end k4.
Row 4—With A, k1, * p3, sl 1 wyif, k1, sl 1 wyif; rep from *, end p3, k1.

Repeat Rows 1–4.

Stripe and Spot Pattern

This is another traditional French pattern which has innumerable variations. Colors A and B may be carried up the side of the piece, but it is better to break off Color C at the end of Row 8 and re-join it at the next repeat.

Stripe and Spot Pattern

Odd number of sts. Colors A, B, and C.

Rows 1 and 3 (Right side)—With A, knit.
Rows 2 and 4—With A, purl.
Rows 5 and 6—With B, knit.
Row 7—With C, k1, * sl 1 wyib, k1; rep from *.
Row 8—With C, k1, * sl 1 wyif, k1; rep from *.
Rows 9 and 10—With B, knit.
Row 11—With A, k2, * sl 1 wyib, k1; rep from *, end k1.
Row 12—With A, p2, * sl 1 wyif, p1; rep from *, end p1.

Repeat Rows 1–12.

Tricolor Fabric Stitch

This is one of the most fascinating of three-color patterns, adaptable to dozens of useful and decorative knitted articles. It must be worked on fairly large needles. For further discussion and suggestions for using this pattern, see Fabric Stitch.

Odd number of sts. Colors A, B, and C.

Cast on with Color A and purl one row.

Row 1 (Right side)—With B, k1, * sl 1 wyif, k1; rep from *.
Row 2—With C, k1, p1, * sl 1 wyib, p1; rep from *, end k1.
Row 3—With A, repeat Row 1.
Row 4—With B, repeat Row 2.
Row 5—With C, repeat Row 1.
Row 6—With A, repeat Row 2.

Repeat Rows 1–6.

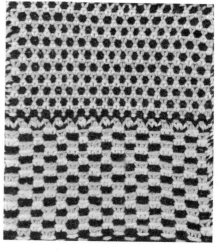

ABOVE: *Tricolor Fabric Stitch*
BELOW: *Double Tricolor Fabric Stitch*

Double Tricolor Fabric Stitch

Multiple of 4 sts. Colors A, B, and C.

Cast on with Color A and purl one row.

Row 1 (Right side)—With B, k1, * sl 2 wyif, k2; rep from *, end sl 2 wyif, k1.
Row 2—With C, k1, p2, * sl 2 wyib, p2; rep from *, end k1.
Row 3—With A, repeat Row 1.
Row 4—With B, repeat Row 2.
Row 5—With C, repeat Row 1.
Row 6—With A, repeat Row 2.

Repeat Rows 1–6.

Honeycomb Tweed

There seems little reason to give this pattern the name of "Honeycomb"—there are far too many different Honeycombs in knitted patterns already—but nevertheless, this tweed pattern makes one more. It is a most adaptable pattern, of French origin.

Odd number of sts. Colors A and B.

Cast on with Color A.

Row 1 (Right side)—With B, k1, * sl 1 wyib, k1; rep from *.
Row 2—With B, purl.
Row 3—With A, k2, * sl 1 wyib, k1; rep from *, end k1.
Row 4—With A, purl.

Repeat Rows 1–4.

Honeycomb Tweed

Windowpane Stripes

Windowpane Stripes

A two-color version of the Stripe and Spot Pattern.

Odd number of sts. Colors A and B.

Cast on with Color B.

Row 1 (Right side)—With A, k1, * sl 1 wyib, k1; rep from *.
Row 2—With A, p1, * sl 1 wyif, p1; rep from *.
Rows 3 and 4—With B, knit.
Rows 5 and 6—With A, knit.
Rows 7 and 8—With B, knit.

Repeat Rows 1–8.

Tricolor Stripe Pattern

The advantage in using three different colors of yarn in a color-contrast pattern is that the color may be changed on every row without cutting or breaking any of the strands. Color A takes you across to Color B, which brings you back to Color C, which takes you across again to Color A, and so on. There are two methods of doing this stripe pattern, either of which may be used alone, or they may be combined—12 rows of Woven Method, then 12 rows of Stranded Method, etc.—for an even fancier effect.

I. WOVEN METHOD

Odd number of sts. Colors A, B, and C.

Cast on with Color A and purl one row.

Row 1 (Right side)—With B, k1, * sl 1 wyif, k1; rep from *.
Row 2—With C, purl.
Row 3—With A, k2, * sl 1 wyif, k1; rep from *, end k1.
Row 4—With B, purl.
Row 5—With C, repeat Row 1.
Row 6—With A, purl.
Row 7—With B, repeat Row 3.
Row 8—With C, purl.
Row 9—With A, repeat Row 1.
Row 10—With B, purl.
Row 11—With C, repeat Row 3.
Row 12—With A, purl.

Repeat Rows 1–12.

II. STRANDED METHOD

Work exactly the same as Woven Method except: sl all sl-sts with yarn in back instead of with yarn in front.

Tricolor Stripe Pattern
ABOVE: *Woven Method*
BELOW: *Stranded Method*

Striped Check Pattern

Four-Color Fancy Pattern

Striped Check Pattern

This French pattern makes a beautiful and simple-to-work four-color tweed.

Multiple of 4 sts plus 3. Colors A, B, C, and D.

Cast on with Color D.

Row 1 (Right side)—With A, k1, * sl 1 wyib, k3; rep from *, end sl 1, k1.
Row 2—With A, p1, * sl 1 wyif, p3; rep from *, end sl 1, p1.
Row 3—With B, * k3, sl 1 wyib; rep from *, end k3.
Row 4—With B, * p3, sl 1 wyif; rep from *, end p3.
Rows 5 and 6—With C, repeat Rows 1 and 2.
Rows 7 and 8—With D, repeat Rows 3 and 4.

Repeat Rows 1–8.

Four-Color Fancy Pattern

This is a very pleasing pattern for ski sweaters, mittens, and hats. It is gay, colorful, and a lot simpler than it looks.

Multiple of 4 sts plus 3. Colors A, B, C, and D.

Cast on with Color A.

NOTE: On all even-numbered rows, all slip-stitches are slipped with yarn in back. On all odd-numbered rows, all slip-stitches are slipped with yarn in front.

Row 1 (Wrong side)—With A, k1, purl to last st, k1.
Row 2—With B, k2, * sl 1, k1; rep from *, end k1.
Row 3—With B, k1, p1, * sl 1, p1; rep from *, end k1.
Row 4—With C, k1, * sl 1, k1; rep from *.
Row 5—With C, k1, purl to last st, k1.
Row 6—With D, k1, * sl 1, k3; rep from *, end sl 1, k1.
Row 7—With D, k1, * sl 1, p3; rep from *, end sl 1, k1.
Row 8—With B, k2, * sl 3, k1; rep from *, end k1.
Row 9—With B, k1, p2, * sl 1, p3; rep from *, end sl 1, p2, k1.
Row 10—With A, repeat Row 6.

Repeat Rows 1–10.

Triangle Check

Triangle Check

NOTE: On all right-side rows (odd numbers) sl all sl-sts with yarn in back; on all wrong-side rows (even numbers) sl all sl-sts with yarn in front.

Multiple of 6 sts plus 3. Colors A and B.

Cast on with Color B and purl one row.

Row 1 (Right side)—With A, k1, * sl 1, k5; rep from *, end sl 1, k1.
Row 2—With A, k1, * sl 1, p5; rep from *, end sl 1, k1.
Row 3—With B, k3, * sl 3, k3; rep from *.
Row 4—With B, k1, p2, * sl 3, p3; rep from *, end sl 3, p2, k1.
Row 5—With A, k1, sl 2, * k3, sl 3; rep from *, end k3, sl 2, k1.
Row 6—With A, k1, sl 2, * p3, sl 3; rep from *, end p3, sl 2, k1.
Row 7—With B, k4, * sl 1, k5; rep from *, end sl 1, k4.
Row 8—With B, k1, p3, * sl 1, p5; rep from *, end sl 1, p3, k1.

Repeat Rows 1–8.

Semi-Woven Tweed

Semi-Woven Tweed

Odd number of sts. Colors A and B.

Cast on with Color A and purl one row.

Row 1 (Right side)—With B, k1, * sl 1 wyib, k1; rep from *.
Row 2—With B, purl.
Row 3—With A, k1, * sl 1 wyif, k1; rep from *.
Row 4—With A, purl.
Row 5—With B, k2, * sl 1 wyib, k1; rep from *, end k1.
Row 6—With B, purl.
Row 7—With A, k2, * sl 1 wyif, k1; rep from *, end k1.
Row 8—With A, purl.

Repeat Rows 1–8.

Woven Stripe Pattern

Here is a gay and easy-to-work pattern adapted from Woven Stitch in two colors. It is delightful for children's garments or for ski sweaters where a colorful and informal look is desired. For a four-color version, simply work the pattern once through in colors A and B, then the second time through in colors C and D.

Odd number of sts. Colors A and B.

Row 1 (Right side)—With A, knit.
Row 2—With A, purl.
Row 3—With B, k1, * sl 1 wyif, k1; rep from *.
Row 4—With B, purl.
Row 5—With A, k2, * sl 1 wyif, k1; rep from *, end k1.
Row 6—With A, purl.
Row 7—With A, knit.
Row 8—With A, purl.
Row 9—With B, k1, * sl 1 wyif, k1; rep from *.
Row 10—With B, purl.
Rows 11 and 12—With B, repeat Rows 1 and 2.
Rows 13 and 14—With A, repeat Rows 3 and 4.
Rows 15 and 16—With B, repeat Rows 5 and 6.
Rows 17 and 18—With B, repeat Rows 7 and 8.
Rows 19 and 20—With A, repeat Rows 9 and 10.

Repeat Rows 1–20.

Woven Stripe Pattern

Three-Color Tweed

This is a lovely version of the infinitely versatile Woven Stitch.

Odd number of sts. Colors A, B, and C.

Cast on with Color C.

Row 1 (Right side)—With B, k1, * sl 1 wyif, k1; rep from *.
Row 2—With B, purl.
Row 3—With A, k1, * sl 1 wyib, k1; rep from *.
Row 4—With A, purl.
Row 5—With C, k1, * sl 1 wyif, k1; rep from *.
Row 6—With C, purl.
Rows 7 and 8—With B, repeat Rows 3 and 4.
Rows 9 and 10—With A, repeat Rows 1 and 2.
Rows 11 and 12—With C, repeat Rows 3 and 4.

Repeat Rows 1–12.

Three-Color Tweed

Bricks

This version of the checkered pattern is fun to use. It consists of knit-stitch "bricks" in one color set off by garter-stitch "mortar" in the second color.

Multiple of 4 sts plus 3. Colors A and B.

Rows 1 and 2—With A, knit. (This is the "mortar" color).
Row 3—With B, k1, * sl 1 wyib, k3; rep from * to last 2 sts, sl 1, k1. (Right side).
Row 4—With B, p1, * sl 1 wyif, p3; rep from * to last 2 sts, sl 1, p1.
Rows 5 and 6—With A, knit.
Row 7—With B, k3, * sl 1 wyib, k3; rep from *.
Row 8—With B, p3, * sl 1 wyif, p3; rep from *.

Repeat Rows 1–8.

Bricks

Broken Plaid Pattern

Multiple of 8 sts plus 7.

Colors A, B, and C. Color B is the background color.

Row 1 (Right side)—With A, knit.
Row 2—With A, k3, insert needle knitwise into next st and wrap yarn 3 times around point of needle, then knit the st (k1-3 wraps); * k7, k1-3 wraps; rep from *, end k3.
Row 3—With B, k3, * sl 1 wyib, k3; rep from *. (Throughout pattern, the extra wraps are dropped from the elongated stitches when these stitches are slipped.)
Row 4—With B, p3, * sl 1 wyif, p3; rep from *.
Row 5—With C, k3, * sl 1 wyib, k7; rep from *, end sl 1, k3.
Row 6—With C, k3, * sl 1 wyif, k7; rep from *, end sl 1, k3.
Rows 7 and 8—With B, repeat Rows 3 and 4.
Row 9—With C, knit.
Row 10—With C, k7, * k1-3 wraps, k7; rep from *.
Rows 11 and 12—With B, repeat Rows 3 and 4.
Row 13—With A, k7, * sl 1 wyib, k7; rep from *.
Row 14—With A, k7, * sl 1 wyif, k7; rep from *.
Rows 15 and 16—With B, repeat Rows 3 and 4.

Repeat Rows 1–16.

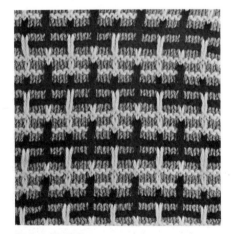

Broken Plaid Pattern

Basket Stitch

Not to be confused with Basketweave or Basket Cable, the Basket Stitch works equally well in a single-color version but is most adaptable to color contrast. It is a variation of Slipped-Stitch Ridges, with horizontal stripes of Garter Stitch worked in behind the ridges. It may also be worked in the same manner as the Bricks pattern, i.e., with two rows of stockinette in place of four rows of garter stitch for Color B, and two rows of garter stitch for Color A in place of stockinette.

Basket Stitch

Multiple of 4 sts plus 3. Colors A and B.

Cast on with Color A and purl one row (This is the wrong side).

Rows 1 and 3—With B, k3, * sl 1 wyib, k3; rep from *.
Rows 2 and 4—With B, k3, * sl 1 wyif, k3; rep from *.
Row 5—With A, knit.
Row 6—With A, purl.

Repeat Rows 1–6.

Fancy Basket Pattern

Multiple of 4 sts plus 1. Colors A and B.

Row 1 (Wrong side)—With A, purl.
Row 2—With A, knit.
Row 3—With A, p4, * p1 wrapping yarn twice around needle, p3; rep from *, end p1.
Row 4—With B, k4, * sl 1 wyib dropping extra wrap, k3; rep from *, end k1.
Rows 5 and 7—With B, k4, * sl 1 wyif, k3; rep from *, end k1.
Row 6—With B, k4, * sl 1 wyib, k3; rep from *, end k1.
Row 8—With A, k4, * drop sl-st off needle to front of work, k2, pick up dropped st and knit it, k1; rep from *, end k1.
Rows 9, 10, and 11—With A, repeat Rows 1, 2, and 3.
Rows 12, 13, 14, and 15—With B, repeat Rows 4, 5, 6, and 7.
Row 16—With A, k2, * sl 2 wyib, drop sl-st off needle to front of work, sl the same 2 sts back to left-hand needle, pick up dropped st and knit it, k3; rep from *, end k3.

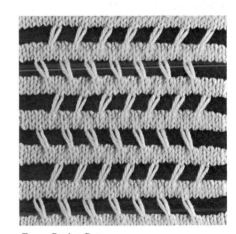

Fancy Basket Pattern

Repeat Rows 1–16.

Belted Stripes

Belted Stripes

This is a simple pattern based on Basket Stitch. The pattern is elongated laterally, so that it gives the illusion of belts of contrasting color woven through a knitted fabric just as ribbons are sometimes woven through a series of eyelets. This pattern can be used very effectively in isolated areas of a garment as trimming, such as near the edges of collars, cuffs, and hem.

Multiple of 12 sts plus 9. Colors A and B.

Rows 1, 3, and 5 (Right side)—With A, knit.

Rows 2 and 4—With A, purl.

Row 6—With A, p3, * p next 3 sts wrapping yarn twice around needle for each st, p9; rep from *, end last repeat p3.

Row 7—With B, k3, * sl 3 wyib dropping extra wraps, k9; rep from *, end last repeat k3.

Rows 8 and 10—With B, k3, * sl 3 wyif, k9; rep from *, end last repeat k3.

Row 9—With B, k3, * sl 3 wyib, k9; rep from *, end last repeat k3.

Rows 11, 13, and 15—With A, knit.

Rows 12 and 14—With A, purl.

Row 16—With A, p9, * p3 wrapping yarn twice for each st, p9; rep from *.

Row 17—With B, k9, * sl 3 wyib dropping extra wraps, k9; rep from *.

Row 18—With B, k9, * sl 3 wyif, k9; rep from *.

Row 19—With B, k9, * sl 3 wyib, k9; rep from *.

Row 20—Repeat Row 18.

Repeat Rows 1–20.

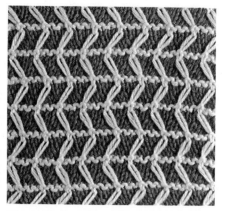

Zigzag Checks

Zigzag Checks

This pattern has another point of interest, beside that of color. The background stitches are drawn into attractive waves behind the slipped stitches of contrasting color, which lends an added dimension to the pattern.

Multiple of 4 sts.

Colors A and B. Color B is the background color. Cast on with A.

NOTE: On wrong side (odd-numbered rows) sl all sl-sts with yarn in front; on right side (even-numbered rows) sl all sl-sts with yarn in back.

Row 1 (Wrong side)—With A, * insert needle into first st knit-wise and wrap yarn twice around point of needle, then knit the st (k1-2 wraps); k3; rep from *.

Row 2—With B, * k3, sl 1 dropping extra wrap; rep from *.

Rows 3 and 5—With B, * sl 1, p3; rep from *.

Row 4—With B, * k3, sl 1; rep from *.

Row 6—With A, * sl 3 sts to right-hand needle, drop next (Color A) st off left-hand needle and leave at front, sl same 3 sts back to left-hand needle, pick up dropped st and knit it; k3; rep from *.

Row 7—With A, * k3, k1-2 wraps; rep from *.

Row 8—With B, * sl 1 dropping extra wrap, k3; rep from *.

Rows 9 and 11—With B, * p3, sl 1; rep from *.

Row 10—With B, * sl 1, k3; rep from *.

Row 12—With A, * drop first (Color A) st off needle and leave at front, k3, then pick up dropped st and knit it; rep from *.

Repeat Rows 1–12.

Staircase Pattern

Because of its strong diagonal line, this pattern is interesting in round knitting, such as for socks or seamless sweaters done on circular needles—the diagonal pattern thus becoming a spiral, the two edge sts omitted.

Multiple of 6 sts plus 2. Colors A and B.

Cast on with Color A.

Row 1 (Right side)—With B, k1, * sl 2 wyib, k4; rep from *, end k1.

Row 2—With B, k1, * p4, sl 2 wyif; rep from *, end k1.

Row 3—With A, k1, * k4, sl 2 wyib; rep from *, end k1.

Row 4—With A, k1, * sl 2 wyif, p4; rep from *, end k1.

Row 5—With B, k3, * sl 2 wyib, k4; rep from *, end sl 2, k3.

Row 6—With B, k1, p2, * sl 2 wyif, p4; rep from *, end sl 2, p2, k1.

Rows 7 and 8—With A, repeat Rows 1 and 2.

Rows 9 and 10—With B, repeat Rows 3 and 4.

Rows 11 and 12—With A, repeat Rows 5 and 6.

Repeat Rows 1–12.

Staircase Pattern

Chain Stripes

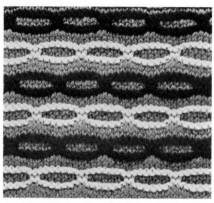

Chain Stripes

Multiple of 8 sts plus 6.

Colors A, B, and C. Color A is the background color.

Row 1 (Right side)—With A, knit.
Row 2—With A, purl.
Rows 3 and 4—With B, knit.
Row 5—With A, k6, * sl 2 wyib, k6; rep from *.
Row 6—With A, p6, * sl 2 wyif, p6; rep from *.
Row 7—With B, repeat Row 5.
Row 8—With B, knit.
Rows 9 and 10—With A, repeat Rows 1 and 2.
Rows 11 and 12—With C, knit.
Row 13—With A, k2, * sl 2 wyib, k6; rep from *, end sl 2, k2.
Row 14—With A, p2, * sl 2 wyif, p6; rep from *, end sl 2, p2.
Row 15—With C, repeat Row 13.
Row 16—With C, knit.

Repeat Rows 1–16.

Bubble Tweed

Bubble Tweed

Here is an interesting tweed with a subtle diagonal line. The pattern moves one stitch to the right every other row.

NOTE: On right-side rows sl all sl-sts with yarn in back. On wrong-side rows sl all sl-sts with yarn in front.

Multiple of 3 sts plus 2. Colors A and B.

Cast on with Color B and purl one row.

Row 1 (Right side)—With A, k1, * sl 1, ssk, lift running thread between st just worked and next st, and knit in back loop of this thread (Make One or M1); rep from *, end k1.
Row 2—With A, p1, * p2, sl 1; rep from *, end p1.
Row 3—With B, k2, * sl 1, ssk, M1; rep from *, end sl 1, k2.
Row 4—With B, p2, * sl 1, p2; rep from *.
Row 5—With A, k3, * sl 1, ssk, M1; rep from *, end sl 1, k1.
Row 6—With A, p1, * sl 1, p2; rep from *, end p1.
Rows 7 and 8—With B, repeat Rows 1 and 2.
Rows 9 and 10—With A, repeat Rows 3 and 4.
Rows 11 and 12—With B, repeat Rows 5 and 6.

Repeat Rows 1–12.

Star Tweed

A soft, thick tweed pattern that can make beautiful and unusual coats and suits. The technique is a little different from most slip-stitch color patterns, but it is quickly mastered and works smoothly and rapidly.

Multiple of 4 sts plus 1. Colors A and B.

Cast on with B and purl one row.

Row 1 (Right side)—With A, k1, * sl 1 wyib, insert needle under running thread between the st just slipped and the next st, and knit this thread; sl 1 wyib, k1, then pass first slipped st over 3 sts; k1; rep from *.
Row 2—With A, purl.
Row 3—With B, k3, * rep from * of Row 1, end k2.
Row 4—With B, purl.

Repeat Rows 1–4.

Star Tweed

Hexagon Pattern

This is a variation of the Checkered Pattern, in which the slipped stitches pull the garter stitch rows out of line upward and downward, to form hexagons. If desired, a third color can be introduced in Rows 13 through 18.

Multiple of 8 sts plus 6. Colors A and B.

Rows 1 and 2—With A, knit. (Odd-numbered rows are right-side rows.)
Rows 3, 5, and 7—With B, k2, * sl 2 wyib, k6; rep from *, end sl 2, k2.
Rows 4, 6, and 8—With B, p2, * sl 2 wyif, p6; rep from *, end sl 2, p2.

(Throughout these six rows the same A sts are slipped.)

Rows 9, 10, 11, and 12—With A, knit.
Rows 13, 15, and 17—With B, k6, * sl 2 wyib, k6; rep from *.
Rows 14, 16, and 18—With B, p6, * sl 2 wyif, p6; rep from *.
Rows 19 and 20—With A, knit.

Repeat Rows 1–20.

Hexagon Pattern

Clouds and Mountains

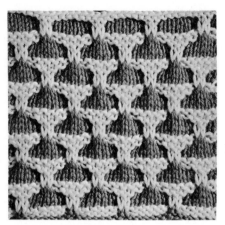

Clouds and Mountains

Intriguingly textured, this pattern works on the same principle as the Hexagon Pattern—that is, by straining the slip-stitches upward over 8 rows so that they distort the rows they span. The result is a "different" kind of check arranged roughly in triangles.

Multiple of 8 sts plus 6. Colors A and B.

Cast on with A and purl one row.

Row 1 (Right side)—With B, knit.
Row 2—With B, k6, * sl 2 wyif, k6; rep from *.
Row 3—With B, k6, * sl 2 wyib, k6; rep from *.
Row 4—With B, repeat Row 2.
Rows 5 and 7—With A, k6, * sl 2 wyib, k6; rep from *.
Rows 6 and 8—With A, p6, * sl 2 wyif, p6; rep from *.
Row 9—With B, knit.
Row 10—With B, k2, * sl 2 wyif, k6; rep from *, end sl 2, k2.
Row 11—With B, k2, * sl 2 wyib, k6; rep from *, end sl 2, k2.
Row 12—With B, repeat Row 10.
Rows 13 and 15—With A, k2, * sl 2 wyib, k6; rep from *, end sl 2, k2.
Rows 14 and 16—With A, p2, * sl 2 wyif, p6; rep from *, end sl 2, p2.

Repeat Rows 1–16.

Tweed Knot Stitch

Tweed Knot Stitch

Tweed Knot Stitch is simply the knit version of Waffle Stitch (which see) worked in two colors. In blocking, this pattern should not be too much stretched, so that the purled "knots" can remain close together for a nubby effect.

Odd number of sts. Colors A and B.

Row 1 (Wrong side)—With A, knit.
Row 2—With A, k1, * k next st in the row below, k1; rep from *.
Row 3—With B, knit.
Row 4—With B, k2, * k next st in the row below, k1; rep from *, end k1.

Repeat Rows 1–4.

Blister Check, or Coin Stitch

In this pattern the drop-stitch technique is used to make a very attractive fabric with the double interest of color and texture.

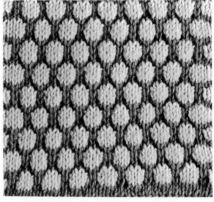

Blister Check, or Coin Stitch

Multiple of 4 sts plus 1.

Colors A and B. Cast on with A and knit one row.

Row 1 (Wrong side)—With A, purl.
Rows 2 and 4—With B, knit.
Rows 3 and 5—With B, purl.
Row 6—With A, k2, * drop next st off needle and unravel 4 rows down, picking up the Color A st from Row 1 below; insert needle into this st and under the 4 loose strands of Color B, and knit, catching the 4 loose strands behind st; k3; rep from *, end last repeat k2.
Row 7—With A, purl.
Rows 8 and 10—With B, knit.
Rows 9 and 11—With B, purl.
Row 12—With A, k4, * drop next st, unravel, and knit Color A st from 5th row below as in Row 6; k3; rep from *, end k1.

Repeat Rows 1–12.

Zebra Chevron

NOTE: On all right-side rows (odd numbers) all sl-sts are slipped with yarn in back. On wrong-side rows (even numbers) all sl-sts are slipped with yarn in front.

Zebra Chevron

Multiple of 24 sts plus 2. Colors A and B.

Cast on with Color A and purl one row.

Row 1 (Right side)—With B, k1, * sl 1, k2; rep from *, end k1.
Row 2—With B, k1, * p2, sl 1; rep from *, end k1.
Row 3—With A, k1, * k1, sl 1, (k2, sl 1) 3 times, k3, (sl 1, k2) 3 times, sl 1; rep from *, end k1.
Row 4—With A, k1, * sl 1, (p2, sl 1) 3 times, p3, (sl 1, p2) 3 times, sl 1, p1; rep from *, end k1.
Row 5—With B, k1, * k2, (sl 1, k2) 3 times, sl 1, k1, sl 1, (k2, sl 1) 3 times, k1; rep from *, end k1.
Row 6—With B, k1, * p1, (sl 1, p2) 3 times, sl 1, pl, sl 1, (p2, sl 1) 3 times, p2; rep from *, end k1.
Rows 7 and 8—With A, repeat Rows 1 and 2.
Rows 9 and 10—With B, repeat Rows 3 and 4.
Rows 11 and 12—With A, repeat Rows 5 and 6.

Repeat Rows 1–12.

Two-Color Cable Rib

This is the Slipped Cable Rib pattern, which looks very effective in two colors.

Two-Color Cable Rib

Multiple of 8 sts plus 2. Colors A and B.

Row 1 (Wrong side)—With A, k2, * p6, k2; rep from *.
Row 2—With A, p2, * sl 1 wyib, k4, sl 1 wyib, p2; rep from *.
Row 3—With B, k2, * sl 1 wyif, p4, sl 1 wyif, k2; rep from *.
Rows 4 and 5—With B, repeat Rows 2 and 3.
Row 6—With B, p2, * drop sl-st off needle to front of work, k2, then pick up sl-st and knit it (taking care that sl-st is not twisted); sl next 2 sts to right-hand needle, drop next sl-st off needle to front of work, then sl the 2 sts back to left-hand needle, pick up dropped st with right needle, replace it on left needle and knit it; k2, p2; rep from *.

Repeat Rows 1–6.

Yarn-Over Check

The technique of making this pattern is interesting and novel. Because of the use of yarn-over stitches, the fabric tends to be loose and fluffy, with a good deal of lateral spread. Care must be taken not to cast on too many stitches.

Yarn-Over Check

Odd number of sts. Colors A and B.

Cast on with Color A and knit one row.

Row 1 (Right side)—With B, p1, * yo, sl 1 wyib, p1; rep from *. (The yo is taken over the top of the needle and held in back of the slipped st, then brought forward again for the next p st.)
Row 2—With B, k1, * yo, sl the sl-st and the yo of previous row together wyib, k1; rep from *.
Row 3—With A, p1, * k3 tog (the sl-st and the two yo sts), p1; rep from *.
Row 4—With A, k1, * yo, sl 1 wyib, k1; rep from *.
Row 5—With A, p1, * yo, sl the sl-st and the yo of previous row wyib, p1; rep from *.
Row 6—With A, k1, * p3 tog (the sl-st and the two yo sts), k1; rep from *.

Repeat Rows 1–6.

Shadow Box Pattern

Although it is one of the simplest of three-color patterns, the Shadow Box is very striking. It uses color, rather than texture, to give the impression of a heavily sculptured surface.

Multiple of 4 sts plus 3.

Colors A, B, and C.

Row 1 (Right side)—With A, knit.
Row 2—With A, k1, * k1 wrapping yarn twice around needle, k3; rep from *, end last repeat k1.
Row 3—With B, k1, * sl 1 wyib dropping extra wrap, k3; rep from *, end last repeat k1.
Row 4—With B, k1, * sl 1 wyif, k3; rep from *, end sl 1, k1.
Row 5—With C, k1, * sl 2 wyib, k2; rep from *, end sl 1, k1.
Row 6—With C, k1, sl 1 wyif, * p2, sl 2 wyif; rep from *, end k1.

Repeat Rows 1–6.

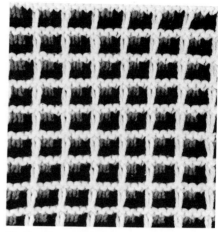

Shadow Box Pattern

Beaded Stripe Pattern

This pattern is excellent for sweaters, and is very effective when worked in fine yarn. Like many of the tweed-type patterns, it is interesting as a sort of optical illusion: it can be seen as dark strings of "beads" on a light background, or as light ones on a dark background.

Multiple of 6 sts plus 5. Colors A and B.

Row 1 (Right side)—With A, knit.
Row 2—With A, k1, * p3, k3; rep from *, end p3, k1.
Row 3—With B, k1, * sl 3 wyib, k3; rep from *, end sl 3, k1.
Row 4—With B, k1, p1, * sl 1 wyif, p5; rep from *, end sl 1, p1, k1.
Row 5—With B, knit.
Row 6—With B, k4, * p3, k3; rep from *, end k1.
Row 7—With A, k4, * sl 3 wyib, k3; rep from *, end k1.
Row 8—With A, k1, p4, * sl 1 wyif, p5; rep from *, end sl 1, p4, k1.

Repeat Rows 1–8.

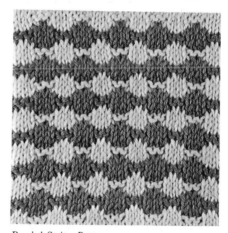

Beaded Stripe Pattern

Striped Quilting Pattern

This delightful pattern makes a honeycomb-like lattice of diamond shapes against a background of striped Garter Stitch. The fabric is dense both vertically and horizontally.

Multiple of 6 sts plus 2. Colors A and B.

Row 1 (Wrong side)—With A, k1, * p1, k4, p1; rep from *, end k1.

Row 2—With B, k1, * sl 1 wyib, k4, sl 1 wyib; rep from *, end k1.

Row 3—With B, k1, * sl 1 wyif, k4, sl 1 wyif; rep from *, end k1.

Row 4—With A, k1, * drop Color A sl-st to front of work, k2, pick up dropped st and knit it; sl 2 wyib, drop Color A sl-st to front of work, sl the same 2 sts back to left-hand needle, pick up dropped st and knit it, k2; rep from *, end k1.

Row 5—With A, k1, * k2, p2, k2; rep from *, end k1.

Row 6—With B, k1, * k2, sl 2 wyib, k2; rep from *, end k1.

Row 7—With B, k1, * k2, sl 2 wyif, k2; rep from *, end k1.

Row 8—With A, k1, * sl 2 wyib, drop Color A sl-st to front of work, sl the same 2 sts back to left-hand needle, pick up dropped st and knit it, k2, drop Color A sl-st to front of work, k2, pick up dropped st and knit it; rep from *, end k1.

Repeat Rows 1–8.

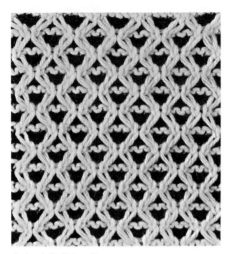

Striped Quilting Pattern

Royal Quilting

Royally beautiful, indeed, is this two-color quilting pattern which can hardly be surpassed for novelty and ingenuity. The fabric is firm, close, and somewhat restrained from excessive curling by the strands of Color A which are carried across the *wrong* side on Rows 4 and 8. On these rows, as well as on Rows 1 and 5 (when the strands are carried on the *right* side), be sure to keep a *very* light tension on the strands so that they do not "squeeze" the pattern. A comparison of this pattern with Quilted Lattice will be instructive, demonstrating the changes that must be made when converting from a one-color to a two-color design.

Royal Quilting is a wonderful pattern for cushion covers, hats, slippers, and garment accents such as collars, cuffs, and pockets, as well as making delightful sweaters and jackets when used all over the garment.

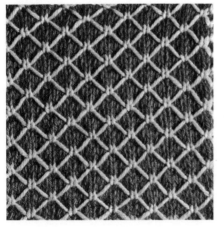

Royal Quilting

Multiple of 6 sts plus 3. Colors A and B.

Row 1 (Wrong side)—With A, k1, p1, * sl 5 wyib, p1; rep from *, end k1.
Row 2—With B, knit.
Row 3—With B, k1, purl to last st, k1.
Row 4—With A, k1, sl 3 wyib, * insert needle under the loose strand of Row 1 and knit the next st bringing st out under strand to catch strand behind st; sl 5 wyib; rep from * to last 5 sts, end knit next st under loose strand, sl 3 wyib, k1.
Row 5—With A, k1, sl 3 wyib, * p1, sl 5 wyib; rep from * to last 5 sts, end p1, sl 3 wyib, k1.
Rows 6 and 7—With B, repeat Rows 2 and 3.
Row 8—With A, k1, * knit next st under loose strand of Row 5, sl 5 wyib; rep from * to last 2 sts, end knit next st under loose strand, k1.

Repeat Rows 1–8.

Criss Cross Pattern

For a test swatch, cast on a minimum of 22 sts.

Multiple of 10 sts plus 2. Colors A and B.

Cast on with Color A and knit one row.

Row 1 (Wrong side)—With A, k3, * k1 wrapping yarn 3 times around needle, k4; rep from *, end last repeat k3.
Row 2—With B, k3, * sl 1 wyib dropping extra wraps, k4; rep from *, end last repeat k3.
Rows 3 and 5—With B, p3, * sl 1 wyif, p4; rep from *, end last repeat p3.
Row 4—With B, k3, * sl 1 wyib, k4; rep from *, end last repeat k3.
Row 6—With A, k3, * drop 1st Color A sl-st off needle to front of work, sl next 4 sts wyib, drop 2nd Color A sl-st off needle to front of work, sl the same 4 sts back to left-hand needle, pick up *2nd* dropped st and knit it, k4 (these are the same 4 Color B sts that were slipped before), then pick up the *1st* dropped st and knit it, k4; rep from *, end last repeat k3.
Rows 7 through 11—Repeat Rows 1 through 5.
Row 12—With A, k1, sl 2 wyib, drop Color A sl-st off needle to front of work, sl the same 2 sts back to left-hand needle, pick up dropped st and knit it, k6, *, rep from * of Row 6 across to last 4 sts, end: drop Color A sl-st off needle to front of work, k2, pick up dropped st and knit it, k1.

Repeat Rows 1–12.

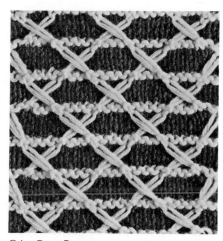

Criss Cross Pattern

Fancy Bricks

This charming three-color version of "Bricks" is done with elongated slip-stitches. Since the slipped stitches must be carried up for six rows, they are loosened by making extra turns around the needle at the base of the stitch. When thus elongated, the slipped stitches will not deform the horizontal rows to which they are attached.

Multiple of 4 sts plus 3.

Colors A, B, and C; Color B is the background color.

Row 1 (Right side)—With A, knit.

Row 2—With A, k3, * insert needle into next st as if to knit, then wrap yarn 3 times around point of needle, then knit the st carrying extra loops on needle; k3; rep from *.

Row 3—With B, k3, * sl 1 wyib dropping extra wraps off needle, k3; rep from *.

Row 4—With B, p3, * sl 1 wyif, p3; rep from *.

Row 5—With C, k3, * sl 1 wyib, k3; rep from *.

Row 6—With C, k3, * sl 1 wyif, k3; rep from *.

Row 7—With B, k3, * sl 1 wyib, k3; rep from *.

Row 8—With B, repeat Row 4.

Row 9—With A, knit.

Row 10—With A, k1, * k1 wrapping yarn 3 times as in row 2, k3; rep from *, end last rep k1.

Row 11—With B, k1, * sl 1 wyib dropping extra wraps, k3; rep from *, end last rep k1.

Row 12—With B, p1, * sl 1 wyif, p3; rep from *, end last rep p1.

Row 13—With C, k1, * sl 1 wyib, k3; rep from *, end last rep k1.

Row 14—With C, k1, * sl 1 wyif, k3; rep from *, end last rep k1.

Row 15—With B, k1, * sl 1 wyib, k3; rep from *, end last rep k1.

Row 16—With B, repeat Row 12.

Repeat Rows 1–16.

Tricolor Basket Plaid

A delightful three-color plaid pattern that looks more complicated than it really is. In this pattern, as in "Fancy Bricks", the slip-stitches are elongated to span six rows. There are four preparatory rows which are omitted from subsequent repeats. To bind off, knit one row plain and then bind off; or finish with four final rows as illustrated.

Fancy Bricks

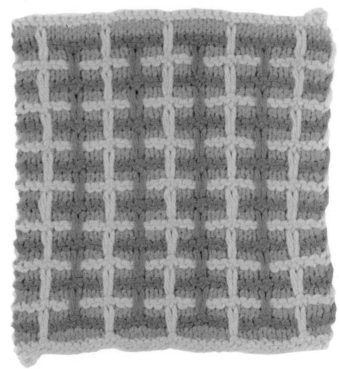

Tricolor Basket Plaid

Navajo Basket

Multiple of 8 sts plus 7.

Colors A, B, and C; Color B is the background color.

Row 1 (Right side)—With A, knit.

Row 2—With A, k3, insert needle into next st as if to knit and wrap yarn 3 times around point of needle, then knit the st carrying extra loops on needle; this is called k1-3 wraps; * k7, k1-3 wraps; rep from *, end k3.

Row 3—With B, k3, sl 1 wyib dropping extra wraps off needle, * k7, sl 1 wyib dropping extra wraps; rep from *, end k3.

Row 4—With B, p3, sl 1 wyif, * p7, sl 1 wyif; rep from *, end p3.

End of preparation rows.

Row 5—With C, k3, sl 1 wyib, * k7, sl 1 wyib; rep from *, end k3.

Row 6—With C, * k3, sl 1 wyif, k3, k1-3 wraps; rep from *, end k3, sl 1 wyif, k3.

Row 7—With B, * k3, sl 1 wyib, k3, sl 1 wyib dropping extra wraps; rep from *, end k3, sl 1 wyib, k3.

Row 8—With B, p3, * sl 1 wyif, p3; rep from *.

Row 9—With A, k7, * sl 1 wyib, k7; rep from *.

Row 10—With A, * k3, k1-3 wraps, k3, sl 1 wyif; rep from *, end k3, k1-3 wraps, k3.

Row 11—With B, * k3, sl 1 wyib dropping extra wraps, k3, sl'1 wyib; rep from *, end k3, sl 1 wyib dropping extra wraps, k3.

Row 12—With B, p3, * sl 1 wyif, p3; rep from *.

Repeat Rows 5–12.

Navajo Basket

This is a pleasing combination of variation Basket Stitch and a two-color Woven Stitch.

Multiple of 4 sts plus 3. Colors A, B, and C.

Row 1 (Right side)—With A, knit.

Row 2—With A, purl.

Row 3—With B, k1, * sl 1 wyif, k1; rep from *.

Row 4—With B, purl.

Row 5—With A, k2, * sl 1 wyif, k1; rep from *, end k1.

Row 6—With A, purl.

Rows 7 and 9—With C, k1, * sl 1 wyib, k3; rep from *, end last rep k1.

Rows 8 and 10—With C, p1, * sl 1 wyif, p3; rep from *, end last rep p1.

Repeat Rows 1–10.

Three-Color Basket Tweed

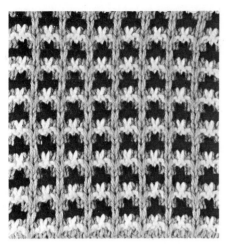

Three-Color Basket Tweed

This is a simple and easy pattern with a remarkably striking effect. For possible variations, try reversing the knits and purls (i.e., purl in Rows 2 and 6, knit in Rows 4 and 8) or working the entire pattern in garter stitch fashion (i.e., knit wrong-side rows) as in Three-and-One Tweed.

Multiple of 4 sts plus 1.

Colors A, B, and C. Cast on with Color A and purl one row.

Row 1 (Right side)—With B, k1, * k3, sl 1 wyib; rep from *, and k4.
Row 2—With B, k1, * k3, sl 1 wyif; rep from *, end k4.
Row 3—With A, k2, * sl 1 wyib, k3; rep from *, end sl 1, k2.
Row 4—With A, p2, * sl 1 wyif, p3; rep from *, end sl 1, p2.
Rows 5 and 6—With C, repeat Rows 1 and 2.
Rows 7 and 8—With A, repeat Rows 3 and 4.

Repeat Rows 1–8.

Motley Check

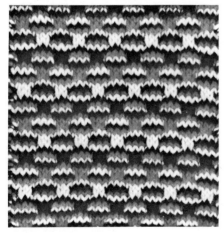

Motley Check

While this pattern is identical in technique to a Simple Check Pattern, the constant alternation of three different strands of color gives it a most unusual appearance. Worked in three strongly contrasting, bright colors, it is gay and brilliant; worked in three colors that are close together in hue or tone, it is a subtle mixture.

Multiple of 6 sts plus 4. Colors A, B, and C.

Cast on with Color C.

Row 1 (Right side)—With A, knit.
Row 2—With B, purl.
Row 3—With C, k1, * sl 2 wyib, k4; rep from *, end sl 2, k1.
Row 4—With A, p1, * sl 2 wyif, p4; rep from *, end sl 2, p1.
Row 5—With B, knit.
Row 6—With C, purl.
Row 7—With A, k4, * sl 2 wyib, k4; rep from *.
Row 8—With B, p4, * sl 2 wyif, p4; rep from *.
Rows 9–24—Repeat Rows 1–8 twice more, changing colors every row.

Repeat Rows 1–24.

Three-and-One Check

This is a pretty variation on the "Bricks" theme. With the addition of extra rows, the bricks take on a rather arched shape.

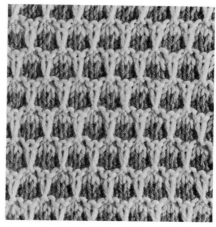

Multiple of 4 sts plus 3. Colors A and B.

Row 1 (Right side)—With A, knit.
Row 2—With A, knit.
Row 3—With B, k1, * sl 1 wyib, k3; rep from *, end sl 1, k1.
Row 4—With B, p1, * sl 1 wyif, p3; rep from *, end sl 1, p1.
Row 5—With A, k1, * sl 1 wyib, k1; rep from *.
Row 6—With A, p1, * sl 1 wyif, p3; rep from *, end sl 1, p1.
Rows 7 and 8—With A, knit.
Row 9—With B, k3, * sl 1 wyib, k3; rep from *.
Row 10—With B, p3, * sl 1 wyif, p3; rep from *.
Row 11—With A, k1, * sl 1 wyib, k1; rep from *.
Row 12—With A, p3, * sl 1 wyif, p3; rep from *.

Repeat Rows 1–12.

Three-and-One Check

Rippled Chevron

This pattern is similar to Zebra Chevron but it is wider, and has a faintly Oriental flavor. Patterns like this can be found in Persian rugs, Turkish mosaic work and the like.

Multiple of 16 sts plus 3. Colors A and B.

Cast on with Color A and purl one row.

Row 1 (Right side)—With B, k1, sl 1 wyib, * k3, sl 1 wyib; rep from *, end k1.
Row 2—With B, k1, sl 1 wyif, * p3, sl 1 wyif; rep from *, end k1.
Row 3—With A, k4, * sl 1 wyib, k3, sl 1 wyib, k1, sl 1 wyib, k3, sl 1 wyib, k5; rep from *, end last repeat k4.
Row 4—With A, k1, p3, * sl 1 wyif, p3, sl 1 wyif, p1, sl 1 wyif, p3, sl 1 wyif, p5; rep from *, end last repeat p3, k1.
Row 5—With B, k3, * sl 1 wyib, k3; rep from *.
Row 6—With B, k1, p2, * sl 1 wyif, p3; rep from *, end sl 1 wyif, p2, k1.
Row 7—With A, k2, * sl 1 wyib, k3, sl 1 wyib, k5, sl 1 wyib, k3, sl 1 wyib, k1; rep from *, end k1.
Row 8—With A, k1, p1, * sl 1 wyif, p3, sl 1 wyif, p5, sl 1 wyif, p3, sl 1 wyif, p1; rep from *, end k1.

Repeat Rows 1–8.

Rippled Chevron

Gull Check

Gull Check

Here is a beautiful pattern in which the Gull Stitch cable can be traced, translated into two colors and repeated continuously across the fabric. It is a good example of a classic pattern subjected to a novel treatment.

Multiple of 7 sts plus 1. Colors A and B.

Row 1 (Wrong side)—With A, k3, * p2, k5; rep from *, end p2, k3.

Rows 2 and 4—With B, k3, * sl 2 wyib, k5; rep from *, end sl 2, k3.

Rows 3 and 5—With B, p3, * sl 2 wyif, p5; rep from *, end sl 2, p3.

Row 6—With A, * k1, sl 2 wyib, drop Color A sl-st off needle to front of work, sl the same 2 sts back to left-hand needle, pick up dropped st and knit it; k2, drop next Color A sl-st off needle to front of work, k2, pick up dropped st and knit it; rep from *, end k1.

Repeat Rows 1–6.

Triple Torch

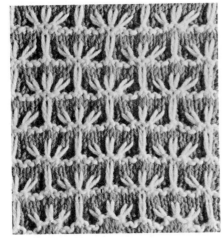

Triple Torch

The directions for this pattern seem complicated, but it is actually simple to work. The knitter can easily grasp the pattern principle in the first 16 rows and thereafter work by looking only at the fabric.

A variation can be made by repeating Rows 1–8 only. This produces a kind of Basket Stitch with wide blocks, the small triple flare being reproduced in each block, one above the other. The last eight rows out of the sixteen only serve to alternate the patterns.

Multiple of 10 sts plus 3. Colors A and B.

Row 1 (Right side)—With A, knit.

Row 2—With A, k1, k1 wrapping yarn twice around needle, * k3, k3 wrapping yarn twice for each st, k3, k1 wrapping yarn twice; rep from *, end k1.

Row 3—With B, k1, sl 1 wyib, * k3, sl 3 wyib, k3, sl 1 wyib; rep from *, end k1. (On this row drop all extra wraps as the wrapped sts are slipped.)

Rows 4 and 6—With B, p1, sl 1 wyif, * p3, sl 3 wyif, p3, sl 1 wyif; rep from *, end p1.

Row 5—With B, repeat Row 3.

Row 7—With B, k1, sl 1 wyib, * k1, sl 2 wyib, drop the *first* st of the group of 3 sl-sts off needle to front of work, sl the same 2 sts back to left-hand needle, pick up dropped st and knit it, k2, sl 1 wyib (this is the 2nd sl-st of the group), drop next (3rd) sl-st off needle to front of work, k2, pick up dropped st and knit it, k1, sl 1 wyib; rep from *, end k1.

Row 8—With B, p1, * sl 1 wyif, p9; rep from *, end sl 1, p1.

Row 9—With A, knit.

Row 10—With A, k1, k2 wrapping yarn twice for each st, * k3, k1 wrapping yarn twice, k3, k3 wrapping yarn twice for each st; rep from *, end last repeat k2 wrapping yarn twice for each st, k1.

Row 11—With B, k1, sl 2 wyib, * k3, sl 1 wyib, k3, sl 3 wyib; rep from *, end last repeat sl 2 wyib, k1. (On this row all extra wraps are dropped as in Row 3.)

Rows 12 and 14—With B, p1, sl 2 wyif, * p3, sl 1 wyif, p3, sl 3 wyif; rep from *, end last repeat sl 2 wyif, p1.

Row 13—With B, repeat Row 11.

Row 15—With B, k1, * sl 1 wyib, drop next sl-st off needle to front of work, k2, pick up dropped st and knit it, k1, sl 1 wyib, k1, sl 2 wyib, drop next sl-st off needle to front of work, sl the same 2 sts back to left-hand needle, pick up dropped st and knit it, k2; rep from *, end sl 1 wyib, k1.

Row 16—With B, p6, sl 1 wyif, * p9, sl 1 wyif; rep from *, end p6.

Repeat Rows 1–16.

Linked Stripe Pattern

This is a very simple pattern that demonstrates how effective an uncomplicated two-color design can be. If Rows 9–16 are omitted, the first eight rows of the pattern will give a kind of check linking solid vertical ribs of Color A.

Multiple of 4 sts. Colors A and B.

NOTE: odd-numbered rows are right-side rows.

Rows 1, 2, 5, and 6—With A, knit.

Rows 3 and 7—With B, k1, * sl 2 wyib, k2; rep from *, end sl 2, k1.

Rows 4 and 8—With B, p1, * sl 2 wyif, p2; rep from *, end sl 2, p1.

Rows 9, 10, 13, and 14—With B, knit.

Rows 11 and 15—With A, k1, * sl 2 wyib, k2; rep from *, end sl 2, k1.

Rows 12 and 16—With A, p1, * sl 2 wyif, p2; rep from *, end sl 2, p1.

Linked Stripe Pattern

Repeat Rows 1–16.

Chickenwire Check

This is a scaled-down version of the classic Hexagon Pattern that gives a somewhat lighter and looser fabric. It is quite pretty when worked in fine yarn.

Chickenwire Check

Multiple of 6 sts plus 3. Colors A and B.

Row 1 (Right side)—With A, knit.
Row 2—With A, purl.
Rows 3, 5, and 7—With B, k1, * sl 1 wyib, k5; rep from *, end sl 1, k1.
Rows 4, 6, and 8—With B, p1, * sl 1 wyif, p5; rep from *, end sl 1, p1.
Rows 9 and 10—With A, repeat Rows 1 and 2.
Rows 11, 13, and 15—With B, k4, * sl 1 wyib, k5; rep from *, end sl 1, k4.
Rows 12, 14, and 16—With B, p4, * sl 1 wyif, p5; rep from *, end sl 1, p4.

Repeat Rows 1–16.

Eccentric Check

Multiple of 6 sts plus 5. Colors A and B.

Row 1 (Right side)—With A, knit.
Row 2—With A, k1, purl to last st, k1.
Row 3—With B, k1, * k4, sl 2 wyib; rep from *, end k4.
Row 4—With B, * k4, sl 2 wyif; rep from *, end k5.
Row 5—With A, k3, * sl 2 wyib, k4; rep from *, end sl 1, k1.
Row 6—With A, k1, sl 1 wyif, * p4, sl 2 wyif; rep from *, end p2, k1.
Row 7—With B, k1, * sl 2 wyib, k4; rep from *, end sl 2, k2.
Row 8—With B, k2, * sl 2 wyif, k4; rep from *, end sl 2, k1.
Rows 9 and 10—With A, repeat Rows 1 and 2.
Row 11—With B, * k4, sl 2 wyib; rep from *, end k5.
Row 12—With B, k5, * sl 2 wyif, k4; rep from *.
Row 13—With A, k1, sl 1 wyib, * k4, sl 2 wyib; rep from *, end k3.
Row 14—With A, k1, p2, * sl 2 wyif, p4; rep from *, end sl 1, k1.
Row 15—With B, k2, * sl 2 wyib, k4; rep from *, end sl 2, k1.
Row 16—With B, k1, * sl 2 wyif, k4; rep from *, end sl 2, k2.

Eccentric Check

Repeat Rows 1–16.

Elongated-Stitch Waves

Due to the loosening effect of the elongated stitches, this fabric will spread. Take the gauge carefully from a blocked test swatch, and beware of casting on too many stitches.

Multiple of 8 sts plus 6. Colors A and B.

Row 1 (Right side)—With A, k1, * k4 wrapping yarn twice around needle for each st, k4; rep from *, end last repeat k1.

Rows 2 and 4—With A, p1, * p4 wrapping yarn twice for each st and dropping the extra wrap of previous row, p4; rep from *, end last repeat p1.

Row 3—With A, k1, * k4 wrapping yarn twice for each st and dropping the extra wrap of previous row, k4; rep from *, end last repeat k1.

Row 5—With B, knit. (All elongated sts are knitted once, and all extra wraps of previous row are dropped.)

Row 6—With B, knit.

Row 7—With A, k5, * k4 wrapping yarn twice for each st, k4; rep from *, end k1.

Rows 8 and 10—With A, p5, * p4 wrapping yarn twice for each st and dropping extra wrap of previous row, p4; rep from *, end p1.

Row 9—With A, k5, * k4 wrapping yarn twice for each st and dropping extra wrap of previous row, k4; rep from *, end k1.

Rows 11 and 12—With B, repeat Rows 5 and 6.

Repeat Rows 1–12.

Elongated-Stitch Waves

Triple L Tweed

This pattern makes a thick fabric, good for coats, suits, afghans, etc. The L-shaped spots of color alternate in an interesting nubby pattern, and seem to be shadowing each other in diagonal lines.

Multiple of 3 sts plus 1. Colors A, B, and C.

Cast on with Color A and knit one row.

Row 1 (Right side)—With B, k3, * sl 1 wyib, k2; rep from *, end k1.

Row 2—With B, k3, * sl 1 wyif, k2; rep from *, end k1.

Row 3—With C, * k2, sl 1 wyib; rep from *, end k1.

Row 4—With C, k1, * sl 1 wyif, k2; rep from *.

Row 5—With A, k1, * sl 1 wyib, k2; rep from *.

Row 6—With A, * k2, sl 1 wyif; rep from *, end k1.

Repeat Rows 1–6.

Triple L Tweed

Dots and Dashes

Dots and Dashes

Multiple of 10 sts plus 7. Colors A and B.

Row 1 (Right side)—With A, knit.

Row 2—With A, purl.

Row 3—With B, k1, * k5, sl 2 wyib, k1, sl 2 wyib; rep from *, end k6.

Row 4—With B, k1, * k5, sl 2 wyif, k1, sl 2 wyif; rep from *, end k6.

Rows 5 and 6—With A, repeat Rows 1 and 2.

Row 7—With B, k1, * sl 2 wyib, k1, sl 2 wyib, k5; rep from *, end last repeat k1.

Row 8—With B, k1, * sl 2 wyif, k1, sl 2 wyif, k5; rep from *, end last repeat k1.

Repeat Rows 1–8.

Fretwork Pattern

Fretwork Pattern

Here is a stunning slip-stitch color design based on the famous Greek Fret, a class of patterns favored by the ancients for architectural ornamentation as well as for that of clothing. Adapted to a knitting pattern, it appears intricate but the technique is a straightforward one.

Multiple of 10 sts plus 2. Colors A and B.

NOTE: On all right-side (odd-numbered) rows slip all sl-sts with yarn in back; on all wrong-side (even-numbered) rows slip all sl-sts with yarn in front.

Row 1 (Right side)—With A, knit.

Row 2—With A, purl.

Row 3—With B, k1, * k8, sl 2; rep from *, end k1.

Row 4 and all subsequent wrong-side rows—Using the same color as in previous row, purl across, slipping wyif all the same sts that were slipped on previous row.

Row 5—With A, k1, * sl 2, k4, sl 2, k2; rep from *, end k1.

Row 7—With B, k1, * k2, sl 2, k4, sl 2; rep from *, end k1.

Row 9—With A, k1, * sl 2, k8; rep from *, end k1.

Row 11—With B, knit.

Row 13—With A, * k4, sl 2, k4; rep from *, end k2.

Row 15—With B, k2, * sl 2, k2, sl 2, k4; rep from *.

Row 17—With A, * k4, sl 2, k2, sl 2; rep from *, end k2.

Row 19—With B, * k6, sl 2, k2; rep from *, end k2.

Row 20—See Row 4.

Repeat Rows 1–20.

Two Color-Reversal Patterns: Night-and-Day Stripe, and Nordic Stripe Pattern

Both of these patterns consist of horizontal stripes, each stripe bearing accents of the opposite color. The first is a variation of Simple Check Pattern, the second a variation of Three-and-One Tweed. Both variations are made by adding more plain knit and purl rows to the basic pattern. Further variations can be obtained by working some of the rows in Garter Stitch (knitting on the wrong side) or by purling Rows 4 and 10 in Nordic Stripe Pattern.

NIGHT-AND-DAY STRIPE

Multiple of 4 sts plus 2. Colors A and B.

Row 1 (Right side)—With A, knit.

Row 2—With A, purl.

Row 3—With B, k1, sl 1 wyib, * k2, sl 2 wyib; rep from *, end k2, sl 1, k1.

Row 4—With B, p1, sl 1 wyif, * p2, sl 2 wyif; rep from *, end p2, sl 1, p1.

Rows 5 and 6—With A, repeat Rows 1 and 2.

Rows 7 and 8—With B, repeat Rows 1 and 2.

Row 9—With A, k2, * sl 2 wyib, k2; rep from *.

Row 10—With A, p2, * sl 2 wyif, p2; rep from *.

Rows 11 and 12—With B, repeat Rows 1 and 2.

Repeat Rows 1–12.

ABOVE: *Night-and-Day Stripe*
BELOW: *Nordic Stripe Pattern*

NORDIC STRIPE PATTERN

Multiple of 4 sts plus 3. Colors A and B.

Row 1 (Right side)—With A, knit.

Row 2—With A, purl.

Row 3—With B, k1, * sl 1 wyib, k3; rep from *, end sl 1, k1.

Row 4—With B, k1, * sl 1 wyif, k3; rep from *, end sl 1, k1.

Row 5—With A, k3, * sl 1 wyib, k3; rep from *.

Row 6—With A, p3, * sl 1 wyif, p3; rep from *.

Rows 7 and 8—With A, repeat Rows 1 and 2.

Rows 9 through 16—Repeat Rows 1 through 8 reversing colors: B for 9 and 10, A for 11 and 12, B for 13, 14, 15, and 16.

Repeat Rows 1–16.

Embroidery Check Pattern

Embroidery Check Pattern

Multiple of 8 sts plus 5. Colors A and B.

Cast on with Color A and purl one row.

Row 1 (Right side)—With B, k5, * sl 3 wyib, k5; rep from *.
Row 2—With B, k2, p1, k2, * sl 3 wyif, k2, p1, k2; rep from *.
Row 3—With A, k2, * sl 1 wyib, k7; rep from *, end sl 1, k2.
Row 4—With A, k1, p1, * sl 1 wyif, p7; rep from *, end sl 1, p1, k1.
Rows 5, 6, and 7—Repeat Rows 1, 2, and 3.
Row 8—With A, k1, purl to last st, k1.
Row 9—With B, k1, * sl 3 wyib, k5; rep from *, end sl 3, k1.
Row 10—With B, k1, * sl 3 wyif, k2, p1, k2; rep from *, end sl 3, k1.
Row 11—With A, k6, * sl 1 wyib, k7; rep from *, end sl 1, k6.
Row 12—With A, k1, p5, * sl 1 wyif, p7; rep from *, end sl 1, p5, k1.
Rows 13, 14, and 15—Repeat Rows 9, 10, and 11.
Row 16—With A, repeat Row 8.

Repeat Rows 1–16.

Tile Pattern

Tile Pattern

This pattern utilizes some rather novel knitting techniques. Elongated slip-stitches are carried two stitches over on the diagonal, giving a roughly octagonal shape to the "tiles". Although each of these octagonal shapes is spanned by four rows of contrasting color in the center, the contrasting color is minimized into four little dots arranged in a square. The quilted effect of a Tile Pattern fabric makes it excellent for heavy ski sweaters, cushions, and hats. The fabric is dense; be sure to cast on enough stitches for width.

Multiple of 12 sts plus 1. Colors A and B.

Cast on with Color A and purl one row.

Row 1 (Preparation row—right side)—With B, k3, * sl 2 wyib, k1, sl 1 wyib, k1, sl 2 wyib, k5; rep from *, end last rep k3.
Row 2—With B, p3, * sl 2 wyif, k1, sl 1 wyif, k1, sl 2 wyif, p5; rep from *, end last rep p3.
Row 3—With A, k1, * sl 2 wyib, k7, sl 2 wyib, k1; rep from *.
Row 4—With A, k1, * sl 2 wyif, p7, sl 2 wyif, k1; rep from *.

Row 5—With B, k3, * sl 2 wyib, k1, sl 1 wyib, k1, sl 2 wyib, k5; rep from *, end last rep k3.

Row 6—With B, p2, * p1 wrapping yarn twice around needle, sl 2 wyif, k1, sl 1 wyif, k1, sl 2 wyif, p1 wrapping yarn twice, p3; rep from *, end last rep p2.

Row 7—With A, k2, * sl 1 wyib dropping extra wrap, k7, sl 1 wyib dropping extra wrap, k3; rep from *, end last rep k2.

Row 8—With A, p2, * sl 1 wyif, p7, sl 1 wyif, p3; rep from *, end last rep p2.

Row 9—With B, k2, * drop next sl-st off needle to front of work, sl 2 wyib, pick up dropped st and knit it, k3, sl 2 wyib, drop next sl-st off needle to front of work, sl the same 2 sts back to left-hand needle, pick up dropped st and knit it, sl 2 wyib (the same 2 sts that were slipped before), k1, sl 1 wyib, k1; rep from *, end last rep k2 instead of k1, sl 1, k1.

Row 10—With B, k2, * sl 2 wyif, p5, sl 2 wyif, k1, sl 1 wyif, k1; rep from *, end last rep k2 instead of k1, sl 1, k1.

Row 11—With A, k4, * sl 2 wyib, k1, sl 2 wyib, k7; rep from *, end last rep k4.

Row 12—With A, p4, * sl 2 wyif, k1, sl 2 wyif, p7; rep from *, end last rep p4.

Row 13—With B, k2, * sl 2 wyib, k5, sl 2 wyib, k1, sl 1 wyib, k1; rep from *, end last rep k2 instead of k1, sl 1, k1.

Row 14—With B, k2, * sl 2 wyif, p1 wrapping yarn twice around needle, p3, p1 wrapping yarn twice, sl 2 wyif, k1, sl 1 wyif, k1; rep from *, end last rep k2 instead of k1, sl 1, k1.

Row 15—With A, k4, * sl 1 wyib dropping extra wrap, k3, sl 1 wyib dropping extra wrap, k7; rep from *, end last rep k4.

Row 16—With A, p4, * sl 1 wyif, p3, sl 1 wyif, p7; rep from *, end last rep p4.

Row 17—With B, k2, * sl 2 wyib, drop next sl-st off needle to front of work, sl the same 2 sts back to left-hand needle, pick up dropped st and knit it, sl 2 wyib (the same 2 sts that were slipped before), k1, sl 1 wyib, k1, drop next sl-st off needle to front of work, sl 2 wyib, pick up dropped st and knit it, k3; rep from *, end last rep k2.

Omitting Row 1 from subsequent repeats, repeat Rows 2–17.

Dotted Block Pattern

Multiple of 7 sts plus 4. Colors A and B.

Row 1 (Wrong side)—With A, knit.

Row 2—With B, k1, * sl 2 wyib, k5; rep from *, end sl 2, k1.

Row 3—With B, k1, * sl 2 wyif, p5; rep from *, end sl 2, k1.

Row 4—With A, k3, * sl 2 wyib, k1, sl 2 wyib, k2; rep from *, end k1.

Row 5—With A, k1, * p2, sl 2 wyif, k1, sl 2 wyif; rep from *, end p2, k1.

Rows 6 and 7—With B, repeat Rows 2 and 3.

Row 8—With A, knit.

Repeat Rows 1–8.

Dotted Block Pattern

Diagonal Stripe

Multiple of 4 sts. Colors A and B.

Cast on with Color A and purl one row.

Row 1 (Right side)—With B, k1, * sl 2 wyib, k2; rep from *, end sl 2, k1.
Row 2—With B, k1, * sl 1 wyif, p3; rep from *, end sl 1, p1, k1.
Row 3—With A, k1, sl 1 wyib, * k2, sl 2 wyib; rep from *, end k2.
Row 4—With A, k1, p1, * sl 1 wyif, p3; rep from *, end sl 1, k1.
Row 5—With B, k1, * k2, sl 2 wyib; rep from *, end k3.
Row 6—With B, k1, p2, * sl 1 wyif, p3; rep from *, end k1.
Row 7—With A, * k2, sl 2 wyib; rep from *, end k2, sl 1, k1.
Row 8—With A, k1, * p3, sl 1 wyif; rep from *, end p2, k1.

Repeat Rows 1-8.

Diagonal Stripe

Dotted Diamond Pattern

This is a really beautiful example of slip-stitch color knitting, a pattern that can make the simplest knitted garment wonderfully striking. A plain sweater, for instance, worked in this pattern, could surely be worn with pride.

Multiple of 20 sts plus 2. Colors A and B.

Cast on with Color A and purl one row.

NOTE: On right-side (odd-numbered) rows all sl-sts are slipped with yarn in back. On wrong-side (even-numbered) rows all sl-sts are slipped with yarn in front.

Row 1 (Right side)—With B, k1, * sl 1, k18, sl 1; rep from *, end k1.
Row 2—With B, k1, * sl 1, p18, sl 1; rep from *, end k1.
Row 3—With A, k1, * k3, sl 2, (k1, sl 1) twice, k2, (sl 1, k1) twice, sl 2, k3; rep from *, end k1.
Row 4—With A, k1, * p3, sl 2, (k1, sl 1) twice, k2, (sl 1, k1) twice, sl 2, p3; rep from *, end k1.
Row 5—With B, k1, * k1, sl 2, k14, sl 2, k1; rep from *, end k1.
Row 6—With B, k1, * p1, sl 2, p14, sl 2, p1; rep from *, end k1.
Row 7—With A, k1, * sl 1, k4, sl 2, k1, sl 1, k2, sl 1, k1, sl 2, k4, sl 1; rep from *, end k1.
Row 8—With A, k1, * sl 1, p4, sl 2, k1, sl 1, k2, sl 1, k1, sl 2, p4, sl 1; rep from *, end k1.
Row 9—With B, k1, * k3, sl 2, k10, sl 2, k3; rep from *, end k1.
Row 10—With B, k1, * p3, sl 2, p10, sl 2, p3; rep from *, end k1.
Row 11—With A, k1, * k1, sl 2, k4, sl 2, k2, sl 2, k4, sl 2, k1; rep from *, end k1.

Dotted Diamond Pattern

Row 12—With A, k1, * k1, sl 2, p4, sl 2, k2, sl 2, p4, sl 2, k1; rep from *, end k1.

Row 13—With B, k1, * k5, sl 2, k6, sl 2, k5; rep from *, end k1.

Row 14—With B, k1, * p5, sl 2, p6, sl 2, p5; rep from *, end k1.

Row 15—With A, k1, * k1, sl 1, k1, sl 2, (k4, sl 2) twice, k1, sl 1, k1; rep from *, end k1.

Row 16—With A, k1, * k1, sl 1, k1, sl 2, (p4, sl 2) twice, k1, sl 1, k1; rep from *, end k1.

Row 17—With B, k1, * k7, sl 2, k2, sl 2, k7; rep from *, end k1.

Row 18—With B, k1, * p7, sl 2, p2, sl 2, p7; rep from *, end k1.

Row 19—With A, k1. * (k1, sl 1) twice, k1, sl 2, k6, sl 2, k1, (sl 1, k1) twice; rep from *, end k1.

Row 20—With A, k1, * (k1, sl 1) twice, k1, sl 2, p6, sl 2, k1, (sl 1, k1) twice; rep from *, end k1.

Row 21—With B, k1, * k9, sl 2, k9; rep from *, end k1.

Row 22—With B, k1, * p9, sl 2, p9; rep from *, end k1.

Rows 23 and 24—With A, repeat Rows 19 and 20.

Rows 25 and 26—With B, repeat Rows 17 and 18.

Rows 27 and 28—With A, repeat Rows 15 and 16.

Rows 29 and 30—With B, repeat Rows 13 and 14.

Rows 31 and 32—With A, repeat Rows 11 and 12.

Rows 33 and 34—With B, repeat Rows 9 and 10.

Rows 35 and 36—With A, repeat Rows 7 and 8.

Rows 37 and 38—With B, repeat Rows 5 and 6.

Rows 39 and 40—With A, repeat Rows 3 and 4.

Repeat Rows 1–40.

Cross-Color Stripe

This pattern may be worked in a straight stockinette version by purling all the stitches that are worked on Rows 2 and 4, slipping the slip-stitches with yarn in front as given. Or, it may be worked in a garter stitch version by knitting these same wrong-side stitches.

Multiple of 14 sts plus 9. Colors A and B.

Cast on with Color A and knit one row.

Row 1 (Right side)—With B, k1, * sl 1 wyib, k5, (sl 1 wyib, k3) twice; rep from *, end sl 1, k5, sl 1, k1.

Row 2—With B, k1, * sl 1 wyif, k5, (sl 1 wyif, p3) twice; rep from *, end sl 1, k5, sl 1, k1.

Row 3—With A, k1, * (k3, sl 1 wyib) twice, k5, sl 1 wyib; rep from *, end k3, sl 1, k4.

Row 4—With A, k1, * (p3, sl 1 wyif) twice, k5, sl 1 wyif; rep from *, end p3, sl 1, p3, k1.

Repeat Rows 1–4.

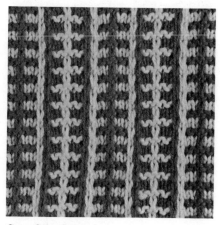

Cross-Color Stripe

Windows

This is a handsome arrangement of a Simple Check Pattern into columns and bands, the checks being grouped into windows of six "panes" each. The pattern is wonderfully simple to work, and yet novel enough to make a most original garment.

Multiple of 10 sts plus 3. Colors A and B.

Row 1 (Right side)—With A, knit.
Row 2—With A, purl.
Row 3—With B, k1, sl 2 wyib, * k3, sl 1 wyib, k3, sl 3 wyib; rep from *, end last rep sl 2, k1.
Row 4—With B, k1, sl 2 wyif, * p3, sl 1 wyif, p3, sl 3 wyif; rep from *, end last rep sl 2, k1.
Row 5—With A, knit.
Row 6—With A, k1, p2, * k7, p3; rep from *, end last rep p2, k1.
Rows 7, 8, 9, 10, 11, and 12—Repeat Rows 3, 4, 5, and 6, then repeat Rows 3 and 4 once more.
Rows 13, 14, 15, and 16—With A, repeat Rows 1 and 2 twice.
Rows 17 and 18—With B, knit.
Rows 19 and 20—With A, repeat Rows 1 and 2.

Repeat Rows 1–20.

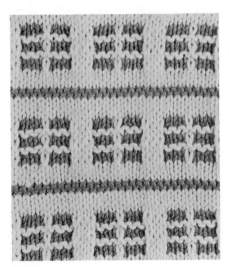

Windows

Harlequin Pattern

Here is a delightful pattern of contrasting diamonds with a nubby garter-stitch texture like that of a Waffle Check or Three-and-One Tweed. The same pattern may be given a smooth texture, if desired, simply by purling the wrong-side rows. Nubby or smooth, Harlequin Pattern is an excellent design for socks, knitted vests, or ties.

Multiple of 10 sts plus 3. Colors A and B.

Cast on with Color A and knit one row.

NOTE: On right-side (odd-numbered) rows slip all sl-sts with yarn in *back*.

Row 1 (Right side)—With B, k1, * sl 1, k9; rep from *, end sl 1, k1.
Row 2 and all other wrong-side rows—Using same color as previous row, repeat the previous row, but slip all sl-sts with yarn in *front*.
Row 3—With A, k3, * (sl 1, k1) 3 times, sl 1, k3; rep from *.
Row 5—With B, k2, * sl 1, k7, sl 1, k1; rep from *, end k1.
Row 7—With A, k4, * (sl 1, k1) twice, sl 1, k5; rep from *, end last repeat k4.

Harlequin Pattern

Row 9—With B, (k1, sl 1) twice, * k5, (sl 1, k1) twice, sl 1; rep from *, end k5, (sl 1, k1) twice.

Row 11—With A, k5, * sl 1, k1, sl 1, k7; rep from *, end last repeat k5.

Row 13—With B, k1, (k1, sl 1) twice, * k3, (sl 1, k1) 3 times, sl 1; rep from *, end k3, (sl 1, k1) twice, k1.

Row 15—With A, k6, * sl 1, k9; rep from *, end last repeat k6.

Rows 17 and 18—With B, repeat Rows 13 and 14.

Rows 19 and 20—With A, repeat Rows 11 and 12.

Rows 21 and 22—With B, repeat Rows 9 and 10.

Rows 23 and 24—With A, repeat Rows 7 and 8.

Rows 25 and 26—With B, repeat Rows 5 and 6.

Rows 27 and 28—With A, repeat Rows 3 and 4.

Repeat Rows 1–28.

Sanquar Check

This is a slip-stitch imitation of the traditional Scottish Sanquar Pattern, which consists of plain light-colored squares alternating with dark-colored squares containing light accents. The original pattern is worked by the usual "Fair Isle" method of color knitting, and the squares are considerably larger than those in this slip-stitch version. Sanquar Check is, however, a crisp and handsome pattern, easy to work, and making a firm, flat fabric.

Sanquar Check

Multiple of 8 sts plus 3. Colors A and B.

Row 1 (Right side)—With A, knit.

Row 2—With A, knit.

Row 3—With B, k3, * (sl 1 wyib, k1) twice, sl 1 wyib, k3; rep from *.

Row 4—With B, p3, * (sl 1 wyif, k1) twice, sl 1 wyif, p3; rep from *.

Row 5—With A, k1, sl 2 wyib, * k5, sl 3 wyib; rep from *, end k5, sl 2, k1.

Row 6—With A, k1, sl 2 wyif, * k5, sl 3 wyif; rep from *, end k5, sl 2, k1.

Rows 7 and 8—With B, repeat Rows 3 and 4.

Rows 9 and 10—With A, repeat Rows 1 and 2.

Row 11—With B, (k1, sl 1 wyib) twice, * k3, (sl 1 wyib, k1) twice, sl 1 wyib; rep from *, end k3, (sl 1, k1) twice.

Row 12—With B, (k1, sl 1 wyif) twice, * p3, (sl 1 wyif, k1) twice, sl 1 wyif; rep from *, end p3, (sl 1, k1) twice.

Row 13—With A, k4, * sl 3 wyib, k5; rep from *, end last rep k4.

Row 14—With A, k4, * sl 3 wyif, k5; rep from *, end last rep k4.

Rows 15 and 16—With B, repeat Rows 11 and 12.

Repeat Rows 1–16.

Swiss Check

Swiss Check

This is an extremely pretty pattern, simple to work, yet having some unusual features. Unlike most other slip-stitch color patterns, Swiss Check works different groups of stitches on the return row of the same color. The result is a very dainty check arranged diagonally in a lattice-like pattern. Be sure to keep yarn stranded *loosely* behind each group of three slipped stitches in Rows 2 and 6.

Multiple of 4 sts plus 1. Colors A and B.

Row 1 (Wrong side)—With A, purl.

Row 2—With B, k1, sl 1 wyib, * k1, sl 3 wyib; rep from *, end k1, sl 1, k1.

Row 3—With B, k1, * p3, sl 1 wyif; rep from *, end p3, k1.

Row 4—With A, k2, * sl 1 wyib, k3; rep from *, end sl 1, k2.

Row 5—With A, purl.

Row 6—With B, k1, * sl 3 wyib, k1; rep from *.

Row 7—With B, k1, p1, * sl 1 wyif, p3; rep from *, end sl 1, p1, k1.

Row 8—With A, k4, * sl 1 wyib, k3; rep from *, end k1.

Repeat Rows 1–8.

Houndstooth Check

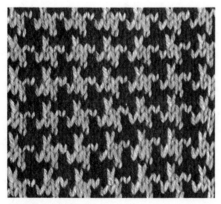

Houndstooth Check

This pattern is one of the simpler ones that change colors all along the row. See the discussion of "Fair Isle" knitting in the Introduction to this section.

Multiple of 4 sts. One dark color (D) and one light (L).

Row 1 (Right side)—K: D1, * L1, D3; rep from * to last 3 sts, end L1, D2.

Row 2—P: * L3, D1; rep from *.

Row 3—K: * L3, D1; rep from *.

Row 4—P: D1, * L1, D3; rep from * to last 3 sts, end L1, D2.

Repeat Rows 1–4.

"Fair Isle" Pattern

This is a classic argyle-type pattern with contrasting diamonds intersected by diagonal lines. It uses the "Fair Isle" method of changing colors all along the row, carrying the unused strands across the back. See the discussion of "Fair Isle" knitting in the Introduction to this section.

"Fair Isle" Pattern

Multiple of 16 sts. One dark color (D) and one light color (L).

Row 1 (Right side)—K: * D1, L7; rep from *.
Row 2—P: * D1, L5, D1, L1, D1, L5, D2; rep from *.
Row 3—K: * D3, L3, D1, L3, D1, L3, D2; rep from *.
Row 4—P: * D3, L1, D1, L5, D1, L1, D4; rep from *.
Row 5—K: * D3, L1, D1, L7, D1, L1, D2; rep from *.
Row 6—P: * D1, L1, D3, L5, D3, L1, D2; rep from *.
Row 7—K: * D1, L1, D5, L3, D5, L1; rep from *.
Row 8—P: * D7, L1; rep from *.
Row 9—Repeat Row 7.
Row 10—Repeat Row 6.
Row 11—Repeat Row 5.
Row 12—Repeat Row 4.
Row 13—Repeat Row 3.
Row 14—Repeat Row 2.

Repeat Rows 1–14.

CHAPTER FIVE

Slip-Stitch Patterns

The slip-stitch technique of pattern formation is one of the most interesting in all knitting. It can be used in a great variety of ways to draw strands up, across, or diagonally over the face of a knitted fabric, and by this means some fascinating patterns can be made. The slip-stitch method is simple to do and speedy, in contrast to some other methods of working stitches, such as cables and twists, which are a little more time-consuming.

Many slip-stitch patterns lend themselves very nicely to contrasting colors, while others do not. Just as the patterns in the Color-Change section can be worked in solid color, so some of the patterns in this section might reward the experimenter in color knitting with some very handsome results. Try them out, play around with them, and experience for yourself the satisfaction of discovering new possibilities.

In general, slip-stitch patterns tend to produce a dense fabric, because the slipped stitches pull the other stitches together. Usually it is a vertical density, so that more rows than the average are required for a given length. Sometimes it is a horizontal density, so that more stitches are required for a given width. Sometimes it is both. Be generous when casting on stitches, and remember that it is easier to let a slip-stitch pattern contract into its own firm texture than to try to stretch it into a larger shape. In any slip-stitch pattern the yarn should be handled easily, never stretched taut while being worked.

Slipped-Stitch Ridges

This is a "basic" pattern, which may be used plain or ornamented and developed in a variety of ways. See also Basket Stitch.

Multiple of 6 sts plus 5.

Rows 1 and 3 (Right side)—K5, * sl 1 wyib, k5; rep from *.
Row 2—P5, * sl 1 wyif, p5; rep from *.
Row 4—Purl.

Repeat Rows 1–4.

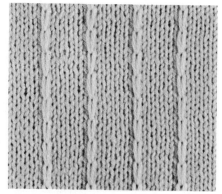

Slipped-Stitch Ridges

Long-Slip Textured Pattern

Because of the slip-stitches extended over three rows, this fabric has considerable tendency to shorten and curl, so that many rows are required for a given length. But it is a cosy fabric, with a deep, soft, honeycomb-like texture, good for warm winter clothing.

Odd number of sts.

Row 1 (Wrong side)—K1, purl to last st, k1.
Row 2—K1, * sl 1 wyib, k1; rep from *.
Row 3—K1, * sl 1 wyif, p1; rep from *, end sl 1, k1.
Row 4—Repeat Row 2.
Row 5—Repeat Row 1.
Row 6—K2, * sl 1 wyib, k1; rep from *, end k1.
Row 7—K1, p1, * sl 1 wyif, p1; rep from *, end k1.
Row 8—Repeat Row 6.

Repeat Rows 1–8.

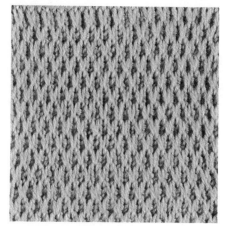

Long-Slip Textured Pattern

Slip-Stitch Honeycomb

This is the only one of the many "honeycombs" which is pure illusion. The strands which give the honeycomb effect are not diagonally linked at all, but only touch one another. It is strictly a horizontal pattern, which fools the eye into seeing a diagonal cross-hatch.

Odd number of sts.

Rows 1 and 3 (Right side)—Knit.
Row 2—K1, * sl 1 wyib, k1; rep from *.
Row 4—K2, * sl 1 wyib, k1; rep from *, end k1.

Repeat Rows 1–4.

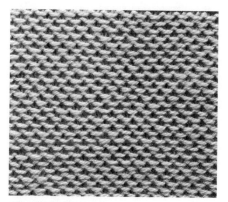

Slip-Stitch Honeycomb

Heel Stitch

ABOVE: *Heel Stitch*
BELOW: *Close Stitch*

Every knitter of socks is familiar with this pattern, which is commonly used to reinforce the heels. But both Heel Stitch and its relative Close Stitch have many other uses. They are good for any article that is going to have to sustain rough wear, such as gloves, cushion covers, chair seats, mats, the soles of knitted slippers, etc. Heel Stitch can be effectively used in making durable coats, jackets, or children's leggings. Done in heavy yarn on small needles it is virtually windproof and creates a very strong fabric.

Odd number of sts.

Row 1 (Wrong side)—Purl.
Row 2—K1, * sl 1 wyib, k1; rep from *.

Repeat Rows 1 and 2.

VARIATION: *CLOSE STITCH*

Work the same as Heel Stitch except in Row 1 *knit* instead of purl. This pattern is particularly good for borders, as it will lie flat with no curl and is very firm. Close Stitch, due to its Garter-Stitch foundation, is vertically nearly twice as dense as Heel Stitch.

Three-and-One Pattern

Three-and-One Pattern

The three-and-one pattern, on a multiple of 4 sts plus 3, is very familiar to anyone who has worked extensively with slip-stitches, as so many slip-stitch patterns use this form. The "basic" given here yields a heavy, dense fabric, with a nubby texture, good for jackets, coats, windbreakers, etc. Because it is so compressed vertically it requires a large number of rows to reach a given length.

Multiple of 4 sts plus 3.

Row 1 (Right side)—K3, * sl 1 wyib, k3; rep from *.
Row 2—K3, * sl wyif, k3; rep from *.
Row 3—K1, * sl 1 wyib, k3; rep from *, end sl 1, k1.
Row 4—K1, * sl 1 wyif, k3; rep from *, end sl 1, k1.

Repeat Rows 1–4.

Woven Stitch

Woven Stitch is one of the most useful and popular of patterns. It is a knitting basic, with dozens of variations, and is adaptable to almost any kind of knitting. Worked plain, it gives a pretty texture; a handsome tweedy effect can be obtained by working it in two colors (see below).

Even number of sts.

Rows 1 and 3 (Wrong side)—Purl.
Row 2—K1, * sl 1 wyif, k1; rep from *, end k1.
Row 4—K1, * k1, sl 1 wyif; rep from *, end k1.

Repeat Rows 1–4.

DOUBLE WOVEN STITCH

Multiple of 4 sts plus 2.

Rows 1 and 3 (Wrong side)—Purl.
Row 2—K1, * sl 2 wyif, k2; rep from *, end k1.
Row 4—K1, * k2, sl 2 wyif; rep from *, end k1.

Repeat Rows 1–4.

WOVEN STITCH IN TWO COLORS

To work either Woven Stitch or Double Woven Stitch in two colors, simply work Rows 1 and 2 in one color, Rows 3 and 4 in the other.

UPPER BAND: *Woven Stitch*
SECOND BAND: *Woven Stitch in Two Colors*
THIRD BAND: *Double Woven Stitch*
LOWER BAND: *Double Woven Stitch in Two Colors*

Double Woven Rib Stitch

The reverse side of this fabric and of its variation, the Single Woven Rib, are also very attractive.

Multiple of 4 sts plus 2.

Row 1 (Right side)—K2, * sl 2 wyif, k2; rep from *.
Row 2—Purl.

Repeat Rows 1 and 2.

VARIATION: SINGLE WOVEN RIB STITCH

Odd number of sts.

Row 1 (Right side)—K1, * sl 1 wyif, k1; rep from *.
Row 2—Purl.

Repeat Rows 1 and 2.

ABOVE: *Double Woven Rib Stitch*
BELOW: *Single Woven Rib Stitch*

Woven Diagonal Herringbone

Woven Diagonal Herringbone

After you have knitted a swatch of this pattern, see how very attractive its wrong side is. You may want to use it inside-out!

Multiple of 6 sts.

NOTE: All slip-stitches are slipped with yarn in front.

Row 1 (Wrong side) and all other wrong-side rows—Purl.
Row 2—* Sl 3, k3; rep from *.
Row 4—K1, * sl 3, k3; rep from *, end sl 3, k2.
Row 6—K2, * sl 3, k3; rep from *, end sl 3, k1.
Row 8—* K3, sl 3; rep from *.
Row 10—Sl 1, * k3, sl 3; rep from *, end k3, sl 2.
Row 12—Sl 2, * k3, sl 3; rep from *, end k3, sl 1.

Repeat Rows 1–12.

VARIATION

To make a zigzag pattern, work Rows 1–12, then Rows 1 and 2 again, then right-side rows backward from 12 to 4; repeat these 24 rows.

Woven Transverse Herringbone

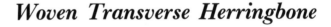

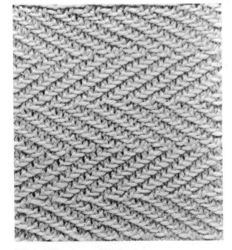

Woven Transverse Herringbone

This is a very dense, close-woven pattern, compressed both horizontally and vertically. The gauge must be carefully checked. This Herringbone is suitable for color knitting; rows 1–12 make upward diagonals to the left, rows 13–24 make upward diagonals to the right, and thus it is possible to work the former in one color and the latter in another.

Multiple of 4 sts plus 2.

Row 1 (Right side)—K2, * sl 2 wyif, k2; rep from *.
Row 2—P1, * sl 2 wyib, p2; rep from *, end p1.
Row 3—Sl 2 wyif, * k2, sl 2 wyif; rep from *.
Row 4—P3, * sl 2 wyib, p2; rep from *, end last rep p1.
Rows 5 through 12—Repeat first 4 rows twice more.
Row 13—Repeat Row 3.
Row 14—Repeat Row 2.
Row 15—Repeat Row 1.
Row 16—Repeat Row 4.
Rows 17 through 24—Repeat Rows 13 through 16 twice more.

Repeat Rows 1–24.

Woven Diamond Pattern

Like many woven patterns, this one has a very attractive wrong side, on which a subtle, shadowy image of the pattern appears in purl stitches.

NOTE: All slip-stitches are slipped with yarn in front.

Multiple of 16 sts plus 2.

Row 1 (Wrong side)—and all other wrong-side rows: Purl.
Row 2—K1, * k3, sl 2, k3, sl 1, k3, sl 2, k2; rep from *, end k1.
Row 4—K1, * k2, sl 2, k3, sl 3, k3, sl 2, k1; rep from *, end k1.
Row 6—K1, * (k1, sl 2, k3, sl 2) twice; rep from *, end k1.
Row 8—K1, sl 2, * (k3, sl 2) twice, k3, sl 3; rep from *; end last repeat sl 1, k1 instead of sl 3.
Row 10—K1, * sl 1, k3, sl 2, k5, sl 2, k3; rep from *, end k1.
Row 12—Repeat Row 8.
Row 14—Repeat Row 6.
Row 16—Repeat Row 4.

Repeat Rows 1–16.

Woven Diamond Pattern

Mock Ribbing

Mock Ribbing is a good all-purpose pattern, equally attractive in heavy or fine yarn. Superficially it resembles ribbing, but it has little elasticity and makes a fairly flat fabric; the reason for this is that the strands woven in front of the knit stitches prevent them from lifting forward as in ordinary ribbing. The reverse side of the fabric shows a pretty ribbed effect similar to the Broken Rib pattern.

Odd number of sts.

Row 1 (Wrong side)—K1, * p1, k1; rep from *.
Row 2—P1, * sl 1 wyif, p1; rep from *.

Repeat Rows 1 and 2.

VARIATION: *DOUBLE MOCK RIBBING*

Multiple of 4 sts plus 2.

Row 1 (Wrong side)—K2, * p2, k2; rep from *.
Row 2—P2, * sl 2 wyif, p2; rep from *.

Repeat Rows 1 and 2.

ABOVE: *Mock Ribbing*
BELOW: *Double Mock Ribbing*

SLIP-STITCH PATTERNS   97

Little Herringbone

Little Herringbone

This pattern makes a thick, dense fabric calculated to keep the wearer warm. It is well suited to heavy jackets, coats, and afghans. Check gauge, and be sure to cast on enough stitches for proper width. In small areas it is good for borders, such as neckbands and cuffs.

Odd number of sts.

Row 1 (Wrong side)—* P2 tog and leave sts on needle; p first st again, drop both sts together from left-hand needle; rep from *, end p1.

Row 2—* Sl 1 wyib, k1, then with left-hand needle raise up sl-st slightly, pull right-hand needle through raised st like a psso but do not drop raised st from left-hand needle; knit in *back* loop of raised st and drop from needle; rep from *, end k1.

Repeat Rows 1 and 2.

Twisted Slip-Stitch

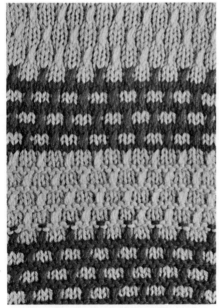

UPPER BAND: *Twisted Slip-Stitch*
SECOND BAND: *Twisted Slip-Stitch in Two Colors*
THIRD BAND: *Variation Twisted Slip-Stitch*
LOWER BAND: *Variation Twisted Slip-Stitch in Two Colors*

This pattern, or its variation (see below), may be worked in two colors. Rows 1, 4, 5, and 8 are done with the contrasting color.

Multiple of 4 sts plus 1.

Row 1 (Wrong side)—P2, * p1 wrapping yarn twice around needle, p3; rep from *, end p1 wrapping yarn twice, p2.

Row 2—K2, * sl 1 knitwise wyib dropping extra wrap, k3; rep from *, end sl 1, k2.

Row 3—P2, * sl 1 purlwise wyif, p3; rep from *, end sl 1, p2.

Row 4—K2, * sl 1 knitwise wyib, k3; rep from *, end sl 1, k2.

Row 5—P4, * p1 wrapping yarn twice, p3; rep from *, end p1.

Row 6—K4, * sl 1 knitwise wyib dropping extra wrap, k3; rep from *, end k1.

Row 7—P4, * sl 1 purlwise wyif, p3; rep from *, end p1.

Row 8—K4, * sl 1 knitwise wyib, k3; rep from *, end k1.

Repeat Rows 1–8.

VARIATION

Work same as above, except in Rows 1 and 5 *knit* instead of purl. The same stitches are given extra wraps as knitted.

Diagonal Weave

This is a dense pattern, perfect for heavy outdoor clothing, with a fascinating texture that looks far more complicated than it really is. Take care, however, not to twist the dropped slip-stitches when they are retrieved. The pattern is delightful when worked in two colors. The contrasting color is introduced in Rows 2, 3, 6, and 7.

Multiple of 4 sts plus 1.

Row 1 (Wrong side)—Purl.
Row 2—K1, * sl 1 wyib, k3; rep from *.
Row 3—* P3, sl 1 wyif; rep from *, end p1.
Row 4—K1, * drop sl-st off needle to front of work, k2, then pick up dropped st and knit it; k1; rep from *.
Row 5—Purl.
Row 6—K5, * sl 1 wyib, k3; rep from *.
Row 7—* P3, sl 1 wyif; rep from *, end p5.
Row 8—K3, * sl next 2 sts wyib, drop sl-st off needle to front of work, sl the same 2 sts back to left-hand needle, then pick up dropped st and knit it; k3; rep from *, end k2.

Repeat Rows 1–8.

Diagonal Weave

Fabric Stitch

Both versions of this pattern are very dense, and must be worked on large needles lest the stitches become too tight. Fabric Stitch produces a fabric that is firm, close, flat, and sturdy, therefore ideal for sports wear and "hard use" articles like cushion covers and slippers. Worked on large needles in heavy cotton yarn, and surrounded by a fringed edging, either version makes delightful place mats. Double Fabric Stitch, because of its thickness and body, is good for hot-dish mats and potholders.

SPECIAL NOTE: The first row alone of Fabric Stitch makes a unique double-thick stockinette fabric with the knit stitches facing out on both sides, the two layers being entirely unconnected except at the edges. This is known as Double Knitting. To try it out, use good-sized needles, cast on an *even* number of stitches, knit the first row plain, and then work every subsequent row as follows: K2, * k1, sl 1 wyif; rep from *, end k2. Double Knitting can be closed at the top, as well as the other three

ABOVE: *Fabric Stitch*
BELOW: *Double Fabric Stitch*

edges, by casting off in the usual way; or, it can be left open at the top, forming a pouch or pocket, by casting off every alternate stitch with a separate needle. Or, a "drawstring" can be made by running a strand through alternate stitches.

Odd number of sts.

Row 1 (Right side)—K1, * sl 1 wyif, k1; rep from *.
Row 2—K1, p1, * sl 1 wyib, p1; rep from *, end k1.

Repeat Rows 1 and 2.

DOUBLE FABRIC STITCH

(*See illustration, page 99*)

Multiple of 4 sts.

Row 1 (Right side)—K1, * sl 2 wyif, k2; rep from *, end sl 2 wyif, k1.
Row 2—K1, p2, * sl 2 wyib, p2; rep from *, end k1.

Repeat Rows 1 and 2.

Mock Honeycomb

Mock Honeycomb

This is a "mock" honeycomb because it does not require the use of the cable needle, as does the true Aran Honeycomb. Mock Honeycomb is, instead, a variety of smocking, with strands drawn across the surface of the fabric in honeycomb pattern. It is especially good for bulky sweaters.

Multiple of 4 sts plus 1.

Rows 1, 3, and 5 (Wrong side)—Purl.
Rows 2 and 4—K1, * sl 3 wyif (holding yarn loosely), k1, rep from *.
Row 6—K2, * insert needle *under* the long loose strands of 2 previous rows and knit the next st; k3; rep from *, end k2 instead of k3.
Rows 7, 9, and 11—Purl.
Rows 8 and 10—K3, * sl 3 wyif, k1; rep from *, end k2.
Row 12—K4, * insert needle *under* the loose strands of 2 previous rows and knit the next st, k3; rep from *, end k1.

Repeat Rows 1–12.

Butterfly Stitch

Multiple of 10 sts plus 9.

Rows 1, 3, 5, 7, and 9 (Right side)—K2, * sl 5 wyif, k5; rep from *, end sl 5, k2.

Rows 2, 4, 6, and 8—Purl.

Row 10—P4, * on the next st (which is at the center of the slipped group) insert right-hand needle down through the 5 loose strands, bring needle up and transfer the 5 strands to left-hand needle, purl the 5 strands and the next st together as one st; p9; rep from *, end last repeat p4.

Rows 11, 13, 15, 17, and 19—K7, * sl 5 wyif, k5; rep from *, end sl 5, k7.

Rows 12, 14, 16, and 18—Purl.

Row 20—P9, * insert needle down through 5 loose strands, bring them up and purl them together with next st as before; p9; rep from *.

Repeat Rows 1–20.

Butterfly Stitch

Little Butterfly or Bowknot Stitch

"Bowknot Stitch" is often used as a name for this pattern, although it is something of a misnomer, as the real Bowknot Stitch is something else. "Little Butterfly" is to be preferred, since the pattern is worked in much the same manner as the Butterfly. Note, however, the slight difference in the method of gathering the strands.

Multiple of 10 sts plus 7.

Rows 1, 3, and 5 (Right side)—K1, * k5, sl 5 wyif, rep from *, end k6.

Rows 2 and 4—Purl.

Row 6—P8, * insert right-hand needle from below under the 3 loose strands on right side of work; yarn over needle and draw up a loop (gathering loop); purl the next st and sl gathering loop over purled st; p9; rep from *, end last repeat p8.

Rows 7, 9, and 11—K1, * sl 5 wyif, k5; rep from *, end sl 5, k1.

Rows 8 and 10—Purl.

Row 12—P3, * lift 3 loose strands with gathering loop, purl the next st and slip loop over purled st as in Row 6; p9; rep from *, end last repeat p3.

Repeat Rows 1–12.

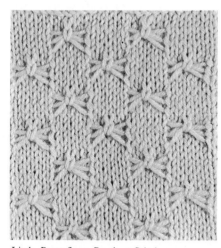

Little Butterfly or Bowknot Stitch

Quilted Lattice

Quilted Lattice

Here is a very beautiful pattern which gives the impression that embossed strands have been woven diagonally through the finished knitting—a process that would require great care indeed! But such a process is quite unnecessary, for the strands are, instead, slipped and knitted in as you go. The Quilted Lattice is fun to work and, when finished, very impressive!

Multiple of 6 sts plus 3.

Row 1 (Wrong side) and all other wrong-side rows—Purl.

Row 2—K2, * sl 5 wyif, k1; rep from *, end k1.

Row 4—K4, * insert needle under loose strand and knit next st, bringing st out under strand; k5; rep from *, end last repeat k4.

Row 6—K1, sl 3 wyif, * k1, sl 5 wyif; rep from *, end k1, sl 3 wyif, k1.

Row 8—K1, * k next st under loose strand, k5; rep from *, end last repeat k1.

Repeat Rows 1–8.

English Diamond Quilting Pattern

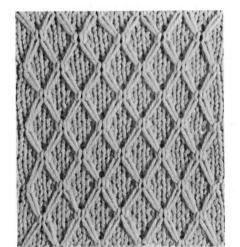

English Diamond Quilting Pattern

Here is a pattern that is really stunning in its individuality and its clean, sharp lines. It is wonderful for coats, suits, and medium-weight sweaters; for best results it should be worked in medium or heavy yarn, not fine yarn. Knitting worsted is ideal.

Multiple of 6 sts plus 2.

NOTE: On right-side (even-numbered) rows, sl all sl-sts with yarn in back; on wrong side (odd-numbered rows) sl all sl-sts with yarn in front.

Row 1 (Wrong side)—P1, * yo, p5, yo, p1; rep from *, end p1.

Row 2—K1, * sl 1, drop yo off needle, k4, sl 1, drop yo; rep from *, end k1.

Row 3—P1, * sl 1, p4, sl 1; rep from *, end p1.

Row 4—K1, * sl 1, k4, sl 1; rep from *, end k1.

Row 5—Repeat Row 3.

Row 6—K1, * drop next st to front of work, k2, pick up dropped st and knit it; sl 2, drop next st to front of work, sl same 2 sts back to left-hand needle, pick up dropped st and knit it, k2; rep from *, end k1.

Row 7—P1, * p2, (yo, p1) twice, p2; rep from *, end p1.

Row 8—K1, * k2, (sl 1, drop yo) twice, k2; rep from *, end k1.

Row 9—P1, * p2, sl 2, p2; rep from *, end p1.

Row 10—K1, * k2, sl 2, k2; rep from *, end k1.
Row 11—Repeat Row 9.
Row 12—K1, * sl 2, drop next st to front of work, sl same 2
sts back to left-hand needle, pick up dropped st and knit it;
k2, drop next st to front of work, k2, pick up dropped st and
knit it; rep from *, end k1.

Repeat Rows 1–12.

Little Tent Pattern

The elements of this pattern are plain to be seen: a portion
of Quilted Lattice, arranged vertically between panels of Garter
Stitch. It is a good pattern for deep-textured sweaters done in
heavy yarn.

Multiple of 8 sts plus 1.

Rows 1 and 3 (Wrong side)—K2, * p5, k3; rep from *, end p5,
k2.
Row 2—K2, * sl 5 wyif, k3; rep from *, end sl 5 wyif, k2.
Row 4—K4, * insert needle under loose strand and knit next st,
bringing st out under strand; k7; rep from *, end last repeat
k4.

Repeat Rows 1–4.

Little Tent Pattern

Shadow Check

This fabric has an absolutely fascinating wrong side. It presents a series of deep-textured horizontal corrugations, and could
well be used in any garment where a novel texture is desired.

Odd number of sts.

Row 1 (Right side)—Purl.
Row 2—K1, * p1, k1; rep from *.
Row 3—P1, * yo, sl 1 wyib, p1; rep from *. (The yo is taken
over the top of the needle and held in back of the slipped
stitch, then brought forward again for the next purl stitch.)
Row 4—K1, * sl 1 wyif dropping yo of previous row, k1; rep
from *. (The yo is dropped in front of the slipped stitch, mak-
ing 2 strands woven across each sl-st as it is slipped.)
Row 5—P1, * sl 1 wyib, p1; rep from *.
Row 6—K1, * sl 1 wyif, k1; rep from *.

Repeat Rows 1–6.

ABOVE: *Shadow Check, right side*
BELOW: *Shadow Check, wrong side*

Floating Hexagon Pattern

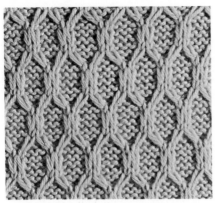

Floating Hexagon Pattern

This pattern shows a honeycomb formation embossed in very high relief upon a garter-stitch background. Its charm lies in the fact that the hexagons really do appear to "float" on the background, with no obvious attachment to it. This is an excellent pattern for sweaters and hats. If used for dresses it should be worked in fine yarn.

Multiple of 6 sts plus 2.

Row 1 (Wrong side)—K3, * p2 wrapping yarn twice around needle for each p st, k4; rep from *, end last repeat k3.

Row 2—K3, * sl 2 wyib dropping extra wraps, k4; rep from *, end last repeat k3.

Rows 3 and 5—K3, * sl 2 wyif, k4; rep from *, end last repeat k3.

Row 4—K3, * sl 2 wyib, k4; rep from *, end last repeat k3.

Row 6—K1, * sl 2 wyib, drop next st at front of work, sl same 2 sts back to left needle, pick up dropped st and knit it, k2; drop next st at front of work, k2, pick up dropped st and knit it; rep from *, end k1.

Row 7—K1, * p1 wrapping yarn twice, k4, p1 wrapping yarn twice; rep from *, end k1.

Row 8—K1, * sl 1 wyib dropping extra wrap, k4, sl 1 wyib dropping extra wrap; rep from *, end k1.

Rows 9 and 11—K1, * sl 1 wyif, k4, sl 1 wyif; rep from *, end k1.

Row 10—K1, * sl 1 wyib, k4, sl 1 wyib; rep from *, end k1.

Row 12—Knit.

Rows 13 through 17—Repeat Rows 7 through 11.

Row 18—K1, * drop next st at front of work, k2, pick up dropped st and knit it; sl next 2 sts wyib, drop next st at front of work, sl same 2 sts back to left needle, pick up dropped st and knit it; k2; rep from *, end k1.

Rows 19 through 23—Repeat Rows 1 through 5.

Row 24—Knit.

Repeat Rows 1–24.

Checked Basket Stitch

This pattern is an "evolutionary intermediate", which is a fancy way of saying that it stands in between one pattern and another in their progressive development. Basket Stitch is here alternated and turned into a check, by working on the half-drop principle. The third step in the series is Clouds and Mountains, which is a Checked Basket Stitch somewhat enlarged and worked in two colors.

This pattern also takes to color contrast very nicely. It is done by working Rows 3 through 6 and Rows 9 through 12 in the contrasting color.

Multiple of 6 sts plus 4.

Row 1 (Right side)—Knit.
Row 2—Purl.
Rows 3 and 5—K1, * sl 2 wyib, k4; rep from *, end sl 2, k1.
Rows 4 and 6—K1, * sl 2 wyif, k4; rep from *, end sl 2, k1.
Row 7—Knit.
Row 8—Purl.
Rows 9 and 11—K4, * sl 2 wyib, k4; rep from *.
Rows 10 and 12—K4, * sl 2 wyif, k4; rep from *.

Repeat Rows 1–12.

Checked Basket Stitch

Little Birds

Here is an easy spot-pattern, derived from Mock Gull Stitch, which is a very pleasant way of ornamenting a plain stockinette fabric. The "birds" can, of course, be arranged at other positions on the fabric if the knitter wishes.

Multiple of 14 sts plus 8.

Row 1 (Wrong side)—Purl.
Row 2—Knit.
Row 3—Purl.
Row 4—K10, * sl 2 wyib, k12; rep from *, end last repeat k10.
Row 5—P10, * sl 2 wyif, p12; rep from *, end last repeat p10.
Row 6—K8, * sl 2 wyib, drop first sl-st to front of work, sl same 2 sts back to left-hand needle, pick up dropped st and knit it, k2, drop next sl-st to front of work, k2, pick up dropped st and knit it, k8; rep from *.
Rows 7, 8, and 9—Repeat Rows 1, 2, and 3.
Row 10—K3, * sl 2 wyib, k12; rep from *, end last repeat k3.
Row 11—P3, * sl 2 wyif, p12; rep from *, end last repeat p3.
Row 12—K1, * rep from * of Row 6; end last repeat k1.

Repeat Rows 1–12.

Little Birds

Slipped Cable Rib

When is a cable not a cable? When it is done like this (or as a Cross-Stitch Cable, Yarn-Over Cable, etc.) This mock cable is a good approximation of a little Horseshoe Cable, done without cabling.

LEFT: *Slipped Cable Rib*
RIGHT: *Mock Gull Stitch*

Multiple of 8 sts plus 2.

Row 1 (Wrong side)—K2, * p6, k2; rep from *.
Row 2—P2, * sl 1 wyib, k4, sl 1 wyib, p2; rep from *.
Row 3—K2, * sl 1 wyif, p4, sl 1 wyif, k2; rep from *.
Row 4—Repeat Row 2.
Row 5—Repeat Row 3.
Row 6—P2, * drop sl-st off needle to front of work, k2, then pick up sl-st and knit it; sl next 2 sts, drop sl-st to front of work, sl the same 2 sts back onto left-hand needle, pick up dropped sl-st and knit it; k2, p2; rep from *.

Repeat Rows 1–6.

VARIATION: *MOCK GULL STITCH*

This pattern, which is the reverse of a Slipped Cable Rib, is so similar to the beautiful classic Gull Stitch (so popular in Aran sweaters) that only a really experienced eye can tell the difference.

Multiple of 8 sts plus 2.

Row 1 (Wrong side)—K2, * p6, k2; rep from *.
Row 2—P2, * k2, sl 2 wyib, k2, p2; rep from *.
Row 3—K2, * p2, sl 2 wyif, p2, k2; rep from *.
Row 4—Repeat Row 2.
Row 5—Repeat Row 3.
Row 6—P2, * sl next 2 sts, drop 1 sl-st to front of work, sl the same 2 sts back onto left-hand needle, pick up dropped sl-st and knit it; k2; drop next sl-st to front of work, k2, pick up dropped sl-st and knit it; p2; rep from *.

Repeat Rows 1–6.

Crochet-Knit Cross Stitch

Stitches that are elongated and crossed in this manner may be crossed either to the right or to the left. Both methods of crossing the stitches are given, as some knitters may find one more convenient, and some the other. If desired, the two methods can be alternated (i.e., the Right Cross being used in

Row 2, the Left Cross in Row 4) to produce a diagonal basket-weave effect.

Multiple of 4 sts plus 2.

METHOD I (Right Cross):

Rows 1 and 3 (Wrong side)—K1, purl to last st wrapping yarn twice around needle for each purl st, end k1.

Row 2—K1, * sl 4 wyib dropping extra wraps to form 4 long sts; sl same 4 sts back to left needle; insert point of right needle purlwise into 3rd and 4th sts and lift these sts together over the first 2 sts, placing them nearest the point of left needle in position to be knitted first; then knit all 4 sts; rep from *, end k1.

Row 4—K3, * slip, cross, and knit next 4 sts as before; rep from *, end k3.

Repeat Rows 1-4.

METHOD II (Left Cross):

Work same as Method I except: in Rows 2 and 4 cross each group of 4 sts as follows: sl 4 wyib dropping extra wraps, then insert left needle into 1st and 2nd sts, pass them over 3rd and 4th sts and onto left needle like a psso; then sl remaining 2 sts also back onto left needle in position to be knitted first; then knit all 4 sts.

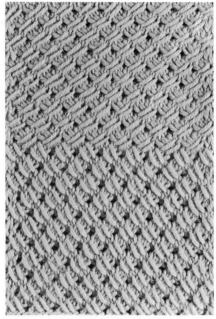

ABOVE: *Crochet-Knit Cross Stitch, right cross*
BELOW: *Crochet-Knit Cross Stitch, left cross*

Slipped Diagonal Rib

Multiple of 4 sts plus 2.

Row 1 (Wrong side)—K1, * k3, p1; rep from *, end k1.
Row 2—K1, * sl 1 wyib, p3; rep from *, end k1.
Row 3—K1, * k3, sl 1 wyif; rep from *, end k1.
Row 4—K1, * drop sl-st to front of work, p2, pick up dropped st and knit it, p1; rep from *, end k1.
Row 5—K2, * p1, k3; rep from *.
Row 6—K1, * p2, sl 1 wyib, p1; rep from *, end k1.
Row 7—K2, * sl 1 wyif, k3; rep from *.
Row 8—K1, p2, * drop sl-st to front of work, p2, pick up dropped st and knit it, p1; rep from * to last 3 sts, end drop sl-st to front of work, p1, pick up dropped st and purl it, k1.

Repeat Rows 1-8.

Slipped Diagonal Rib

Cross-Stitch Cable

Cross-Stitch Cable

Here is one of the "easy cables"—that is, a cable made without the cable needle. It is simply a Cross Stitch arranged in cable formation. It can be used like any cable, in single or multiple decorative panels.

Panel of 8 sts.

Row 1 (Right side)—P2, k4, p2.
Row 2—K2, p4 wrapping yarn twice around needle for each purl st, k2.
Row 3—P2, sl 4 wyib dropping extra wraps, then with point of left-hand needle pass the first 2 sts over the second 2; return the sts on right-hand needle to left-hand needle and knit all 4 sts in this crossed order; p2.
Row 4—K2, p4, k2.

Repeat Rows 1–4.

Slipped Cables

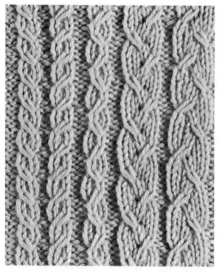

Slipped Cables

LEFT TO RIGHT:
1. Simple Slipped Cable, Left Twist
2. Simple Slipped Cable, Right Twist
3. Slipped Zigzag Cable
4. Slipped Plait Cable
5. Reverse Slipped Plait Cable

The slip-stitch method of making cables is a useful one, and yields several pretty cable effects that cannot be obtained by alternate methods. Simple Slipped Cables resemble twisted Mock Cables but are a little neater and flatter. In all Slipped Cables the left twist is worked by dropping a stitch, knitting the stitches beyond, and then picking up the dropped stitch; the right twist is worked by slipping stitches temporarily in order to release and drop the crossing stitch, then proceeding in reverse order.

1. SIMPLE SLIPPED CABLE, LEFT TWIST

Panel of 7 sts.

Row 1 (Wrong side)—K2, p3, k2.
Row 2—P2, sl 1 wyib, k2, p2.
Row 3—K2, p2, sl 1 wyif, k2.
Row 4—P2, drop sl-st to front of work, k2, pick up dropped st and knit it, p2.

Repeat Rows 1–4.

2. SIMPLE SLIPPED CABLE, RIGHT TWIST

Panel of 7 sts.

Row 1 (Wrong side)—K2, p3, k2.
Row 2—P2, k2, sl 1 wyib, p2.
Row 3—K2, sl 1 wyif, p2, k2.
Row 4—P2, sl 2 wyib, drop sl-st to front of work, sl the same 2 sts back to left-hand needle, pick up dropped st and knit it, k2, p2.

Repeat Rows 1–4.

3. SLIPPED ZIGZAG CABLE

Panel of 7 sts.

Rows 1–4—Work as (1), Left Twist, above.
Rows 5–8—Work as (2), Right Twist, above.

Repeat Rows 1–8.

4. SLIPPED PLAIT CABLE

Panel of 9 sts.

Row 1 (Wrong side)—K2, p5, k2.
Row 2—P2, k2, sl 1 wyib, k2, p2.
Row 3—K2, p2, sl 1 wyif, p2, k2.
Row 4—P2, k2, drop sl-st to front of work, k2, pick up dropped st and knit it, p2.
Rows 5, 6, and 7—Repeat Rows 1, 2, and 3.
Row 8—P2, sl 2 wyib, drop sl-st to front of work, sl the same 2 sts back to left-hand needle, pick up dropped st and knit it, k4, p2.

Repeat Rows 1–8.

5. REVERSE SLIPPED PLAIT CABLE

Panel of 9 sts.

Row 1 (Wrong side)—K2, p5, k2.
Row 2—P2, sl 1 wyib, k4, p2.
Row 3—K2, p4, sl 1 wyif, k2.
Row 4—P2, drop sl-st to front of work, k2, pick up dropped st and knit it, k2, p2.
Row 5—Repeat Row 1.
Row 6—P2, k4, sl 1 wyib, p2.
Row 7—K2, sl 1 wyif, p4, k2.
Row 8—P2, k2, sl 2 wyib, drop sl-st to front of work, sl the same 2 sts back to left-hand needle, pick up dropped st and knit it, k2, p2.

Repeat Rows 1–8.

Banded Crescent Pattern

Banded Crescent Pattern

Multiple of 3 sts.

Row 1 (Wrong side)—Knit.

Rows 2 and 3—Purl.

Row 4—K2, * sl 1 wyib, k2; rep from *, end k1.

Row 5—P3, * sl 1 wyif, p2; rep from *.

Row 6—K2, * drop sl-st off needle to front of work, k2, pick up dropped st and knit it; rep from *, end k1.

Row 7—Purl.

Row 8—K2, * yo, k2 tog, k1; rep from *, end k1.

Row 9—Purl.

Row 10—K4, * sl 1 wyib, k2; rep from *, end sl 1, k1.

Row 11—P1, * sl 1 wyif, p2; rep from *, end p2.

Row 12—K2, * sl 2 wyib, drop next sl-st off needle to front of work, sl the same 2 sts back to left-hand needle, pick up dropped st and knit it, k2; rep from *, end k1.

Repeat Rows 1–12.

Slipped Hourglass

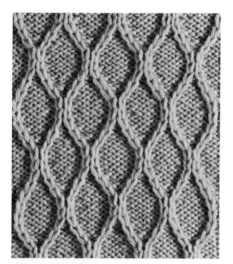

Slipped Hourglass

This pattern, which is similar to the standard cabled Hourglass, is made by an unusual method. The knit stitches forming the lattice are large and open, since in effect they are worked only half as many times as the purled background stitches. The latter will contract, of course, forming a rather dense fabric.

Multiple of 8 sts plus 2.

Notes: Right Slip (RS)—Sl 1 purl st wyib, drop next (knitted) sl-st off needle to front of work, sl same purl st back to left-hand needle, pick up dropped st and knit it, p1. Left Slip (LS)—Drop (knitted) sl-st off needle to front of work, p1, pick up dropped st and knit it.

Rows 1 and 3 (Right side)—P1, * p3, k2, p3; rep from *, end p1.

Row 2 and all other wrong-side rows—Knit all knit sts, sl all purl sts wyif. (Thus Rows 2 and 4: K1, * k3, sl 2 wyif, k3; rep from *, end k1. Etc.)

Row 5—P1, * p2, RS, LS, p2; rep from *, end p1.

Row 7—P1, * p1, RS, p2, LS, p1; rep from *, end p1.

Row 9—P1, * RS, p4, LS; rep from *, end p1.

Rows 11 and 13—P1, * k1, p6, k1; rep from *, end p1.

Row 15—P1, * LS, p4, RS; rep from *, end p1.

Row 17—P1, * p1, LS, p2, RS, p1; rep from *, end p1.

Row 19—P1, * p2, LS, RS, p2; rep from *, end p1.

Row 20—See Row 2.

Repeat Rows 1–20.

Looking-Glass Pattern

The slip-cross method of working this pattern is a somewhat faster substitute for using the cable needle to cross stitches on right-side rows. Care must be taken not to let the dropped stitches shorten up so much that they cannot be retrieved. For any knitter who finds this method uncomfortable, the cable needle is recommended for extra security. The technique then would be similar to that of the Tree of Life cable.

Looking-Glass Pattern

Multiple of 16 sts plus 2.

NOTES: Left Purl Slip (LPS)—Drop (knitted) sl-st off needle to front of work, *purl* the next st, pick up dropped st and knit it. Left Knit Slip (LKS)—Drop (knitted) sl-st off needle to front of work, *knit* the next st, pick up dropped st and knit it. Right Purl Slip (RPS)—Sl 1 wyib, drop next st off needle to front of work, sl the same st back to left-hand needle, pick up dropped st and knit it, *p1*. Right Knit Slip (RKS)—Sl 1 wyib, drop next st off needle to front of work, sl the same st back to left-hand needle, pick up dropped st and knit it, *k1*. On wrong-side (even-numbered) rows slip all sl-sts with yarn in *front*.

Row 1 (Right side)—K1, * p4, k8, p4; rep from *, end k1.
Row 2—K1, * k4, sl 1, p6, sl 1, k4; rep from *, end k1.
Row 3—K1, * k1, p3, LPS, k4, RPS, p3, k1; rep from *, end k1.
Row 4—K1, * sl 1, k4, sl 1, p4, sl 1, k4, sl 1; rep from *, end k1.
Row 5—K1, * LKS, p3, LPS, k2, RPS, p3, RKS; rep from *, end k1.
Row 6—K1, * p1, sl 1, k4, sl 1, p2, sl 1, k4, sl 1, p1; rep from *, end k1.
Row 7—K1, * k1, LKS, p3, LPS, RPS, p3, RKS, k1; rep from *, end k1.
Row 8—K1, * p2, sl 1, k4, p2, k4, sl 1, p2; rep from *, end k1.
Row 9—K1, * k2, LKS, p8, RKS, k2; rep from *, end k1.
Row 10—K1, * p3, sl 1, k8, sl 1, p3; rep from *, end k1.
Row 11—K1, * k4, p8, k4; rep from *, end k1.
Row 12—Repeat Row 10.
Row 13—K1, * k2, RPS, p3, k2, p3, LPS, k2; rep from *, end k1.
Row 14—K1, * p2, sl 1, k4, sl 2, k4, sl 1, p2; rep from * end k1.
Row 15—K1, * k1, RPS, p3, RKS, LKS, p3, LPS, k1; rep from *, end k1.
Row 16—K1, * p1, sl 1, k4, sl 1, p2, sl 1, k4, sl 1, p1; rep from *, end k1.
Row 17—K1, * RPS, p3, RKS, k2, LKS, p3, LPS; rep from *, end k1.
Row 18—K1, * p1, k4, sl 1, p4, sl 1, k4, p1; rep from *, end k1.
Row 19—K1, * p4, RKS, k4, LKS, p4; rep from *, end k1.
Row 20—Repeat Row 2.

Repeat Rows 1–20.

Indian Cross Stitch

Indian Cross Stitch

Both sides of this interesting fabric will show the same pattern. It is very nice for scarves, baby blankets, and stoles—wherever a loose, open pattern is desired.

Multiple of 8 sts.

Rows 1–4—Knit.

Row 5—K1, * insert needle into next st and wrap yarn 4 times around the point of needle, then knit the st withdrawing all the wraps along with the needle. Repeat from * on every st across row to last st, ending k1.

Row 6—* Sl 8 sts wyib, dropping all extra wraps, thus forming 8 long sts on right-hand needle. Then insert left-hand needle into the first 4 of these 8 long sts and pass them over the second 4. Then return all sts to left-hand needle and knit the 8 sts in this crossed order, the 2nd 4 first and the original first 4 next. Rep from * on each group of 8 sts.

Rows 7–10—Knit.

Row 11—Repeat Row 5.

Row 12—Sl 4 sts dropping extra wraps, then cross 2 over 2 as in Row 6 and knit these 4; * sl 8, cross, and knit as in Row 6; rep from * on each group of 8 sts across row to last 4 sts, end by crossing 2 over 2.

Repeat Rows 1–12.

Slipped Double Cables

All three of these Double Cables are worked with a single central stitch, which may be omitted if desired, making each panel 10 stitches wide instead of 11. If the central stitch is thus omitted, then version 2, the "Opening" Double Cable, becomes a true Gull Stitch absolutely indistinguishable from the one worked with a cable needle; and version 1, the "Closing" Double Cable, is a true Reverse Gull Stitch.

1. "CLOSING" DOUBLE CABLE

Panel of 11 sts.

Row 1 (Wrong side)—K2, p7, k2.

Row 2—P2, sl 1 wyib, k5, sl 1 wyib, p2.

Row 3—K2, sl 1 wyif, p5, sl 1 wyif, k2.

Row 4—P2, drop sl-st to front of work, k2, pick up dropped st and knit it, k1, sl 2 wyib, drop sl-st to front of work, sl the same 2 sts back to left-hand needle, pick up dropped st and knit it, k2, p2.

Repeat Rows 1–4.

Slipped Double Cables
LEFT: *"Closing" Double Cable*
CENTER: *"Opening" Double Cable*
RIGHT: *Slipped Chain Cable*

2. "OPENING" DOUBLE CABLE

Panel of 11 sts.

Row 1 (Wrong side)—K2, p7, k2.
Row 2—P2, k2, sl 1 wyib, k1, sl 1 wyib, k2, p2.
Row 3—K2, p2, sl 1 wyif, p1, sl 1 wyif, p2, k2.
Row 4—P2, sl 2 wyib, drop sl-st to front of work, sl the same 2 sts back to left-hand needle, pick up dropped st and knit it, k3, drop sl-st to front of work, k2, pick up dropped st and knit it, p2.

Repeat Rows 1–4.

3. SLIPPED CHAIN CABLE

Rows 1–4—Work as (1), Closing Double Cable, above.
Rows 5–8—Work as (2), Opening Double Cable, above.

Repeat Rows 1–8.

CHAPTER SIX

Twist Stitch Patterns

The principle of twist stitches is a simple one: it is a method of twisting two or more stitches around each other in cable fashion, but without using the cable needle. It is always done by skipping a stitch or stitches, knitting the stitch beyond them and leaving it on the needle, then going back and knitting the skipped stitch or stitches and dropping the entire set of twisted stitches from the left-hand needle together. Many beautiful pattern effects can be made with this method.

Whenever stitches are crossed over one another, by any means, the fabric is pulled together horizontally. Therefore twist stitches, like cables, tend to make a piece narrower than the same number of stitches knitted in stockinette stitch. When doing any twist stitch be sure to check the gauge and cast on a sufficient number of stitches for the desired width.

Little Mock Cables: Classic Mock Cable, Tamerna Stitch, and Mock Wave Cable

These two-stitch twist patterns have a multitude of uses. On either side of a large cable, or any other panel pattern with a purled background, they make very nice borders to give the panel a fancy finish. Repeated continuously all the way across a fabric, they make beautiful ribbings. Used as accents in a plain fabric, with varying numbers of knit stitches between panels, they give a cable effect without the use of the cable needle.

I. CLASSIC MOCK CABLE

The method of twisting the stitches (to the right) given here is the one most commonly used. But a preferable method can be seen in Baby Cable Ribbing and the second half of Mock Wave Cable.

Panel of 6 sts.

Rows 1 and 3 (Wrong side)—K2, p2, k2.
Row 2—P2, k2, p2.
Row 4—P2, skip 1 st and knit the second st, leaving it on needle; then knit the skipped st and sl both sts from needle together; p2.

Repeat Rows 1–4.

LEFT: *Classic Mock Cable*
CENTER: *Tamerna Stitch*
RIGHT: *Mock Wave Cable*

II. TAMERNA STITCH

This is a Classic Mock Cable in the other direction—twisting the stitches to the left instead of to the right.

Panel of 6 sts.

Rows 1 and 3 (Wrong side)—K2, p2, k2.
Row 2—P2, k2, p2.
Row 4—P2, take right needle behind left needle, skip 1 st and knit the second st in *back* loop, then knit the skipped st in front loop, sl both sts from needle together; p2.

Repeat Rows 1–4.

III. MOCK WAVE CABLE

In this pattern the stitches are twisted left and right with the same stitch remaining on top, after the manner of the Wave Cable. Note the "k2 tog" type twist in the second half of the pattern. This is the same as the Baby Cable Ribbing twist, and is neater than the classic method of knitting the second and then the first stitch.

Panel of 6 sts.

Rows 1–4—Same as Tamerna Stitch.
Rows 5 and 7—K2, p2, k2.
Row 6—P2, k2, p2.
Row 8—P2, k2 tog but do not sl from needle; then insert right needle between the sts just knitted tog, and knit the 1st st again, then sl both sts from needle together; p2.

Repeat Rows 1–8.

TWIST STITCH PATTERNS   115

Twist-Three and Twist-Four Mock Cables

LEFT: *Twist-Three Mock Cable*
RIGHT: *Twist-Four Mock Cable*

These pretty little cables can be used in any place where an ordinary small cable might be. They can be worked all over the fabric, in wide panels of several cables together, or in single panels.

TWIST-THREE MOCK CABLE

Panel of 7 sts.

Rows 1 and 3 (Wrong side)—K2, p3, k2.
Row 2—P2, k3, p2.
Row 4—P2, knit into 3rd st on left-hand needle, then into 2nd st, then into 1st st, then sl all 3 sts from needle together; p2.

Repeat Rows 1–4.

TWIST-FOUR MOCK CABLE

Panel of 8 sts.

Rows 1, 3, and 5 (Wrong side)—K2, p4, k2.
Rows 2 and 4—P2, k4, p2.
Row 6—P2, knit into 4th st on left-hand needle, then into 3rd st, then into 2nd st, then into 1st st, then sl all 4 sts from needle together; p2.

Repeat Rows 1–6.

Bavarian Block Pattern

Bavarian Block Pattern

Multiple of 14 sts plus 4.

NOTE: "Tw 2": Twist Two as follows: knit second st on left-hand needle, knit first st on left-hand needle, slip both sts from needle together.

Rows 1 and 2—Knit.
Rows 3, 5, and 7 (Right side)—* P1, Tw 2, p1, k10-b; rep from *, end p1, Tw 2, p1.
Rows 4, 6, and 8—* K1, p2, k1, p10-b; rep from *, end k1, p2, k1.
Rows 9 and 10—Knit.
Rows 11, 13, and 15—* K7-b, p1, Tw 2, p1, k3-b; rep from *, end k4-b.
Rows 12, 14, and 16—* P7-b, k1, p2, k1, p3-b; rep from *, end p4-b.

Repeat Rows 1–16.

Bavarian Check Pattern

In this pattern, checks of two-stitch twisted ribbing are contrasted with twisted stockinette stitch.

Multiple of 18 sts plus 10.

NOTE: "Tw 2": Twist Two as follows: knit second st on left-hand needle, knit first st on left-hand needle, slip both sts from needle together.

Rows 1, 3, 5, 7, and 9 (Right side)—* (P1, Tw 2) 3 times, p1, k8-b, rep from *, end (p1, Tw 2) 3 times, p1.

Rows 2, 4, 6, 8, and 10—* (K1, p2) 3 times, k1, p8-b; rep from *, end (k1, p2) 3 times, k1.

Rows 11, 13, 15, 17, and 19—P1, * k8-b, (p1, Tw 2) 3 times, p1; rep from *, end k8-b, p1.

Rows 12, 14, 16, 18, and 20—K1, * p8-b, (k1, p2) 3 times, k1; rep from *, end p8-b, k1.

Repeat Rows 1–20.

Bavarian Check Pattern

Twisted Check Pattern

This is a boldly-textured pattern that can be varied in several ways. For a smaller check, omit Rows 5, 6, 11, and 12. For an elongated check, work three twist rows in succession instead of two.

Multiple of 4 sts plus 2.

Row 1 (Right side)—Knit.
Row 2—Purl.
Row 3—P2, * skip 1 st and knit into the 2nd st, then knit into the skipped st, then sl both sts from needle together (Twist Two, Tw 2), p2; rep from *.
Row 4—K2, * p2, k2; rep from *.
Rows 5 and 6—Repeat Rows 3 and 4.
Row 7—Knit.
Row 8—Purl.
Row 9—Tw 2, * p2, Tw 2; rep from *.
Row 10—P2, * k2, p2; rep from *.
Rows 11 and 12—Repeat Rows 9 and 10.

Repeat Rows 1–12.

Twisted Check Pattern

Twisted Basket

Twisted Basket

A very pleasing allover texture pattern, of Irish origin.

Multiple of 8 sts plus 5.

NOTE: "Tw 3": Twist Three as follows: skip 2 and knit 3rd st on left-hand needle, knit 2nd st, then knit 1st st and slip all three from needle together.

Row 1 (Right side)—P5, * Tw 3, p5; rep from *.
Row 2—K5, * p3, k5; rep from *.
Row 3—Repeat Row 1.
Row 4—Repeat Row 2.
Row 5—P1, * Tw 3, p5; rep from *, end Tw 3, p1.
Row 6—K1, * p3, k5; rep from *, end p3, k1.
Row 7—Repeat Row 5.
Row 8—Repeat Row 6.

Repeat Rows 1–8.

Plaited Basket Stitch

Plaited Basket Stitch

In this pattern all stitches are twisted on both right-side and wrong-side rows, and the result is a wonderful and unusual texture that resembles a diagonal basketweave. The fabric is dense and firm, excellent for such articles as cushion covers, potholders, and mats, as well as garments. Unless a very small, tight "weave" is desired, the pattern should be worked with large needles.

Odd number of sts.

Row 1 (Right side)—K2, * insert needle from back to front between first and second sts on left-hand needle, knit the second st, then knit the first st, then sl both sts from needle together; rep from *, end k1.
Row 2—P2, * skip next st and purl the second st, then purl the skipped st, then sl both sts from needle together; rep from *, end p1.

Repeat Rows 1 and 2.

Twist Zigzag

Multiple of 9 sts plus 3.

Row 1 (Wrong side) and all other wrong-side rows:—Purl.

Row 2—K3, * (insert right-hand needle from back to front between first and second sts, k the second st, then k the first st and slip both sts from needle together—this is Back Twist Two or BTT) 3 times, k3; rep from *.

Row 4—K4, * (BTT) 3 times, k3; rep from *, end last rep k2.

Row 6—BTT, * k3, (BTT) 3 times, rep from *, end k1.

Row 8—K1, BTT, * k3, (BTT) 3 times, rep from *.

Row 10—K1, make two-stitch twist in the usual way by knitting into second st and then first st and slipping both sts together—this is Tw 2; * k3, (Tw 2) 3 times, rep from *.

Row 12—Tw 2, * k3, (Tw 2) 3 times, rep from *, end k1.

Row 14—K4, * (Tw 2) 3 times, k3; rep from *, end last rep k2.

Row 16—K3, * (Tw 2) 3 times, k3; rep from *.

Repeat Rows 1–16.

Twist Zigzag

Rickrack Pattern

This is a good-looking, deeply textured fabric for sport sweaters, coats, and tweedy suits. Because its basis is Garter Stitch, it will lie flat and widen out well.

Multiple of 4 sts.

Row 1 (Right side)—K1, * take needle behind work, skip 1 st and knit the 2nd st through *back* loop, leave on needle; then knit the skipped st through front in the usual manner; then sl both sts from needle together; k2; rep from *, end last repeat k1.

Row 2—K1, * with yarn in front, skip 1 st and purl the 2nd st, then purl the skipped st, then sl both sts from needle together; k2; rep from *, end last repeat k1.

Repeat Rows 1 and 2.

Rickrack Pattern

Two-Color Twisted Ladder

Two-Color Twisted Ladder

Here is a delightful pattern from France, notable for its ease of working and its striking interplay of color and texture. The little twisted columns are like pilasters on a wall, standing in high relief with apparently little connection to the background. Having a garter-stitch basis, the fabric is dense and flat, and will not require much blocking.

Multiple of 5 sts plus 4. Colors A and B.

Row 1 (Right side)—With A, k1, * skip 1 st and knit into 2nd st, then knit into skipped st, then sl both sts from needle together; k3; rep from *, end last repeat k1.
Row 2—With A, k1, * p2, k3; rep from *, end p2, k1.
Row 3—With B, k1, * sl 2 wyib, k3; rep from *, end sl 2, k1.
Row 4—With B, k1, * sl 2 wyif, k3; rep from *, end sl 2, k1.

Repeat Rows 1–4.

Diagonal Stitch

Diagonal Stitch

Here is the pattern that is the basis for many pretty twist designs: Baby Cable Ribbing, Spiral Columns, etc. It is very effective in vertical panels of any width whatever, as well as being a useful allover pattern.

Even number of sts.

Rows 1 and 3 (Wrong side)—Purl.
Row 2—* K2 tog but do not sl from needle; insert right-hand needle between the sts just knitted tog, and knit the first st again; then sl both sts from needle together; rep from *.
Row 4—K1, * rep from * of Row 2 to last st, end k1.

Repeat Rows 1–4.

Twist-Stitch Diamond Pattern

This pattern of two knit-stitch diamonds, one within the other, on a purl-stitch ground, could equally well be done by crossing the sts over each other with the cable needle: a back cross for Right Twist and a front cross for Left Twist. The advantage of using the cable needle is that it does not warp the stitches quite so much, and gives a neater and flatter appearance. The advantage of using the twist method is that it is faster and more convenient to work.

CENTER PANEL:
Twist-Stitch Diamond Pattern
SIDE PANELS: *Spiral Columns*

Panel of 14 sts.

Row 1 (Right side)—P6, * skip 1 st and knit 2nd st, then knit the 1st st, slip both sts together from left-hand needle, * p6.
Row 2—K6, p2, k6.
Row 3—P5, skip 1 st and k 2nd st, then *purl* 1st st and slip both sts together from left-hand needle (*Right Twist*); skip the next st and purl into *back* loop of 2nd st, k the 1st st and slip both sts together from left-hand needle (*Left Twist*); p5.
Row 4—K5, p1, k2, p1, k5.
Row 5—P4, *RT*, p2, *LT*, p4.
Row 6—K4, p1, k4, p1, k4.
Row 7—P3, *RT*, p1, repeat from * to * of Row 1, p1, *LT*, p3.
Row 8—K3, p1, k2, p2, k2, p1, k3.
Row 9—P2, *RT*, p1, *RT*, *LT*, p1, *LT*, p2.
Row 10—(K2, p1) 4 times, k2.
Row 11—P1, *RT*, p1, *RT*, p2, *LT*, p1, *LT*, p1.
Row 12—K1, p1, k2, p1, k4, p1, k2, p1, k1.
Row 13—P1, k1, p2, k1, p4, k1, p2, k1, p1.
Row 14—Repeat Row 12.
Row 15—P1, *LT*, p1, *LT*, p2, *RT*, p1, *RT*, p1.
Row 16—Repeat Row 10.
Row 17—P2, *LT*, p1, *LT*, *RT*, p1, *RT*, p2.
Row 18—Repeat Row 8.
Row 19—P3, *LT*, p1, *LT*, p1, *RT*, p3.
Row 20—Repeat Row 6.
Row 21—P4, *LT*, p2, *RT*, p4.
Row 22—Repeat Row 4.
Row 23—P5, *LT*, *RT*, p5.
Row 24—Repeat Row 2.

Repeat Rows 1–24.

Spiral Columns

Panel of 10 sts.

Row 1 (Wrong side)—K2, p6, k2.
Row 2—P2, * k2 tog but do not drop from left-hand needle; k the first st again and slip both together from needle; rep from * twice more, end p2.
Row 3—K2, p6, k2.
Row 4—P2, k1, * k2 tog and k first st again as in row 2; rep from * once more; end k1, p2.

Repeat Rows 1–4.

Lace Ladder and Twist

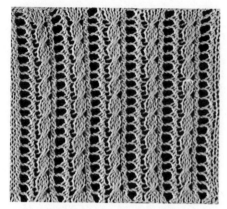

Lace Ladder and Twist

In this traditional Italian design, two simple patterns are effectively combined: a garter-stitch lace ladder and a three-stitch twist.

Multiple of 7 sts plus 6.

Row 1 (Right side)—K1, * k2 tog, (yo) twice, ssk, k3; rep from *, end last repeat k1.

Row 2—K1, * k1, (k1-b, k1) into the 2 yo's of previous row; k1, p3; rep from *, end k1, (k1-b, k1) into 2 yo's, k2.

Row 3—K1, * k2 tog, (yo) twice, ssk, skip next 2 sts and knit into 3rd st, then knit into 2nd st, then knit into 1st st, then sl all 3 sts from needle together; rep from *, end k2 tog, (yo) twice, ssk, k1.

Row 4—Repeat Row 2.

Repeat Rows 1–4.

Quartered Diamonds

Quartered Diamonds

A number of novel knitting techniques are displayed in this interesting pattern. Notice the difference in the method of twisting stitches so that they travel diagonally, between this pattern and others. Since the Diamonds are arranged in panel fashion, this is a very good pattern for fancy sweaters incorporating cables and other panel patterns. The Quartered Diamond pattern may be worked in a single panel of 18 stitches.

Multiple of 17 sts plus 1.

NOTES: KD (Knit Double stitch): insert needle from front to back into the stitch below next stitch, which will be formed of double strands, and draw through a loop; then knit the next stitch and pass the loop over the stitch just knitted.

PD (Purl Double stitch): insert needle from back to front into the stitch below next stitch, which will be formed of double strands, wrap yarn as if to purl and draw a loop out backward; then purl the next stitch and pass the loop over the stitch just purled.

BT (Back Twist): insert needle from front between 1st and 2nd stitches and knit the 2nd stitch in *back* loop; then knit the 1st stitch in front loop and sl both sts from needle together.

FT (Front Twist): skip 1 st and knit the 2nd st in *back* loop; then knit the skipped st in *back* loop; then sl both sts from needle together.

Row 1 (Right side)—KD, * p4, (BT) twice, (FT) twice, p4, KD; rep from *.

Row 2—PD, * k4, p1, k1, p1, k2, p1, k1, p1, k4, PD; rep from *.

Row 3—KD, * p3, (BT) twice, p2, (FT) twice, p3, KD; rep from *.

Row 4—PD, * k3, p1, k1, p1, k4, p1, k1, p1, k3, PD; rep from *.

Row 5—KD, * p2, (BT) twice, p4, (FT) twice, p2, KD; rep from *.

Row 6—PD, * k2, p1, k1, p2, k4, p2, k1, p1, k2, PD; rep from *.

Row 7—KD, * p1, (BT) twice, FT, p2, BT, (FT) twice, p1, KD; rep from *.

Row 8—PD, * (k1, p1) twice, (k2, p1) 3 times, k1, p1, k1, PD; rep from *.

Row 9—KD, * (BT) twice, p2, FT, BT, p2, (FT) twice, KD; rep from *.

Row 10—PD, * p1-b, k1, p1-b, k4, with right-hand needle behind left-hand needle skip next st and purl the 2nd st through back loop, then purl the skipped st through back loop, then sl both sts from needle together; k4, p1-b, k1, p1-b, PD; rep from *.

Row 11—KD, * (FT) twice, p2, BT, FT, p2, (BT) twice, KD; rep from *.

Row 12—Repeat Row 8.

Row 13—KD, * p1, (FT) twice, BT, p2, FT, (BT) twice, p1, KD; rep from *.

Row 14—Repeat Row 6.

Row 15—KD, * p2, (FT) twice, p4, (BT) twice, p2, KD; rep from *.

Row 16—Repeat Row 4.

Row 17—KD, * p3, (FT) twice, p2, (BT) twice, p3, KD; rep from *.

Row 18—Repeat Row 2.

Row 19—KD, * p4, (FT) twice, (BT) twice, p4, KD; rep from *.

Row 20—PD, * k5, p1-b, k1, with right-hand needle behind left-hand needle skip next st and purl the 2nd st through back loop, then purl the skipped st through back loop, then sl both sts from needle together; p2, k5, PD; rep from *.

Repeat Rows 1–20.

Banded Rib

This pattern is useful as a soft, thick ribbing accent, or as a fancy-textured fabric. It may be added to a plain garment in either vertical or horizontal bands.

Multiple of 4 sts.

Rows 1 and 3 (Right side)—K1, * p2, k2; rep from *, end p2, k1.

Row 2—P1, k1, * skip next 3 sts and insert needle into front of 4th st and draw through a loop; then knit 1st st on left-hand needle, purl next 2 sts on left-hand needle, then drop the original 4th st off needle (this st has already been knitted with the long loop); rep from *, end k1, p1.

Row 4—P1, * k2, p2; rep from *, end k2, p1.

Repeat Rows 1–4.

Banded Rib

Twist-Stitch Waves

The handsome simplicity of this pattern makes it good for an entire garment, when the garment is desired in an all-over purl-stitch lightly ornamented. On the other hand, a single panel of Twist-Stitch Waves can be used very successfully in a more complicated creation, like a fisherman sweater, in combination with cables and other patterns. If two single panels of Twist-Stitch Waves are to be placed on either side of a common center, then one of the panels should be started on Row 1 and the other started on Row 17 so that the right and left diagonals will balance.

Multiple of 8 sts plus 2.

NOTE: RT (Right Twist): skip 1 st and knit the 2nd st, leave on needle; then purl the skipped st, sl both sts from needle together. LT (Left Twist): skip 1 st and purl into *back* of 2nd st, leave on needle; then knit the skipped st, sl both sts from needle together.

Row 1 (Wrong side)—K1, * k7, p1; rep from *, end k1.
Row 2—P1, * LT, p6; rep from *, end p1.
Row 3—K1, * k6, p1, k1; rep from *, end k1.
Row 4—P1, * p1, LT, p5; rep from *, end p1.
Row 5—K1, * k5, p1, k2; rep from *, end k1.
Row 6—P1, * p2, LT, p4; rep from *, end p1.
Row 7—K1, * k4, p1, k3; rep from *, end k1.
Row 8—P1, * p3, LT, p3; rep from *, end p1.
Row 9—K1, * k3, p1, k4; rep from *, end k1.
Row 10—P1, * p4, LT, p2; rep from *, end p1.
Row 11—K1, * k2, p1, k5; rep from *, end k1.
Row 12—P1, * p5, LT, p1; rep from *, end p1.
Row 13—K1, * k1, p1, k6; rep from *, end k1.
Row 14—P1, * p6, LT; rep from *, end p1.
Row 15—K1, * p1, k7; rep from *, end k1.
Row 16—P1, * p7, k1; rep from *, end p1.
Rows 17, 19, 21, 23, 25, 27, 29, and 31—Repeat Rows 15, 13, 11, 9, 7, 5, 3, and 1.
Row 18—P1, * p6, RT; rep from *, end p1.
Row 20—P1, * p5, RT, p1; rep from *, end p1.
Row 22—P1, * p4, RT, p2; rep from *, end p1.
Row 24—P1, * p3, RT, p3; rep from *, end p1.
Row 26—P1, * p2, RT, p4; rep from *, end p1.
Row 28—P1, * p1, RT, p5; rep from *, end p1.
Row 30—P1, * RT, p6; rep from *, end p1.
Row 32—P1, * k1, p7; rep from *, end p1.

Repeat Rows 1–32.

Twist-Stitch Waves

Twist-Stitch Lattice

Although a lattice done by the twist-stitch method is not quite as tidy as that done by the cable method (see Basic Lattice), it is adequate, and useful for those who are not experienced with cabling. For best results a smallish needle should be used, to make a close fabric. Twists tend to open the stitches a little, which might leave holes when an over-large needle is used.

Multiple of 8 sts plus 2.

NOTE: RT (Right Twist): skip 1 st and knit the 2nd st, then purl the skipped st, then sl both sts from needle together. LT (Left Twist): skip 1 st and purl the 2nd st through *back* loop, then knit the skipped st, then sl both sts from needle together.

Row 1 (Wrong side)—K4, * p2, k6; rep from *, end last repeat k4.
Row 2—P3, * RT, LT, p4; rep from *, end last repeat p3.
Row 3—K3, * p1, k2, p1, k4; rep from *, end last repeat k3.
Row 4—P2, * RT, p2, LT, p2; rep from *.
Row 5—K2, * p1, k4, p1, k2; rep from *.
Row 6—P1, * RT, p4, LT; rep from *, end p1.
Row 7—K1, * p1, k6, p1; rep from *, end k1.
Row 8—P1, k1, * p6, skip 1 st and knit the 2nd st, then knit skipped st through *back* loop, then sl both sts from needle together; rep from *, end p6, k1, p1.
Rows 9, 11, 13, and 15—Repeat Rows 7, 5, 3, and 1.
Row 10—P1, * LT, p4, RT; rep from *, end p1.
Row 12—P2, * LT, p2, RT, p2; rep from *.
Row 14—P3, * LT, RT, p4; rep from *, end last repeat p3.
Row 16—P4, * skip 1 st and knit the 2nd st through *back* loop, then knit the skipped st, then sl both sts from needle together; p6; rep from *, end last repeat p4.

Repeat Rows 1–16.

Twist-Stitch Lattice

Purl-Twist Fabric

This stitch makes a very prettily textured fabric with a close weave, suitable for coats, suits, gloves, cushions, and other firmly-knit articles.

Even number of sts.

Rows 1 and 3 (Right side)—Knit.
Row 2—* P2 tog, but do not sl from needle; then purl 1st st again, and sl both sts from needle together; rep from *.
Row 4—P1, * rep from * of Row 2 across to last st, end p1.

Repeat Rows 1–4.

Purl-Twist Fabric

TWIST STITCH PATTERNS   125

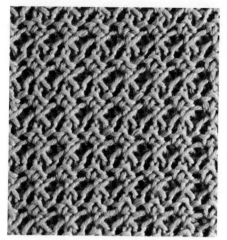

Twist Brioche

Twist Brioche

This variation on the classic Brioche produces a soft mesh in which the strands are intricately woven. The fabric looks the same on both sides, thus it is good for articles that show both sides, such as scarves and stoles. It is composed of a standard Brioche interrupted by one twist row (Row 3) which is worked on each side alternately. Like all Brioche patterns it is very elastic and lacy when worked in fine yarn.

Even number of sts.

Rows 1 and 2—K1, * yo, sl 1 wyib, k2 tog; rep from *, end k1. (In Row 2 the sts knitted together will include the yo of previous row.)

Row 3—K1, * k1, skip 1 st, knit the yo st of previous row and leave on needle; then knit the st before the yo and sl both sts from needle together; rep from *, end k1.

Repeat Rows 1–3.

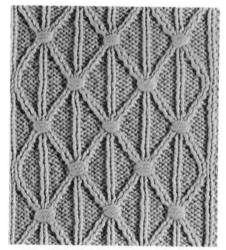

Ribbed Cluster Diamond Pattern

Ribbed Cluster Diamond Pattern

A cable needle is required for the Cluster Stitch in Rows 10 and 20, but the rest of this pattern is worked in twist stitches. Of course, if the knitter prefers, the entire pattern may be worked as a Cable Pattern with the traveling stitches moved along by the cable needle instead of by twists.

Multiple of 12 sts plus 1.

Row 1 (Wrong side)—P2, * k4, p1, k4, p3; rep from *, end last repeat p2.

Row 2—K1, * skip 1 st and purl into *back* of 2nd st, then knit skipped st through front, sl both sts from needle together (Left Twist, LT); p3, k1, p3, skip 1 st and knit the second st, then purl skipped st, sl both sts from needle together (Right Twist, RT); k1; rep from *.

Row 3—P1, * k1, p1, (k3, p1) twice, k1, p1; rep from *.

Row 4—K1, * p1, LT, p2, k1, p2, RT, p1, k1; rep from *.

Row 5—P1, * k2, p1; rep from *.

Row 6—K1, * p2, LT, p1, k1, p1, RT, p2, k1; rep from *.

Row 7—P1, * k3, (p1, k1) twice, p1, k3, p1; rep from *.

Row 8—K1, * p3, LT, k1, RT, p3, k1; rep from *.

Row 9—P1, * k4, p3, k4, p1; rep from *.

Row 10—K1, * p4, knit next 3 sts and transfer these 3 sts to dpn; then wrap yarn 4 times around these sts under dpn in a counterclockwise direction (looking down from top), then return the 3 sts to right-hand needle (Cluster 3); p4, k1; rep from *.

Rows 11, 13, 15, 17, and 19—Repeat Rows 9, 7, 5, 3, and 1.

Row 12—K1, * p3, RT, k1, LT, p3, k1; rep from *.

Row 14—K1, * p2, RT, p1, k1, p1, LT, p2, k1; rep from *.

Row 16—K1, * p1, RT, p2, k1, p2, LT, p1, k1; rep from *.

Row 18—K1, * RT, p3, k1, p3, LT, k1; rep from *.

Row 20—K2, * p4, k1, p4, Cluster 3; rep from *, end p4, k1, p4, k2.

Repeat Rows 1–20.

CHAPTER SEVEN

Fancy Texture Patterns

This is a catch-all category if ever there was one. These patterns have little similarity to each other, except that all of them create a knitted fabric that is "different". No one method of knitting can be described here, but each pattern has its own technique which must be discussed individually. Some are done with increases and decreases, some with other specialized knitting actions. To understand how to use each pattern in a garment, and to visualize the sort of garment it would enhance, one simply must try out the patterns—make them and study them. About the only thing they have in common is that all of them are novel, interesting to work, and fun to use.

Ribbon Stitch, or Ruching

Ribbon Stitch, or Ruching

The "ribbon" may be worked in a contrasting color. For best results work Rows 7 through 13 inclusive in the contrasting color, breaking off the strands to change colors. This pattern is prettiest when worked in fine yarn on small needles.

Any number of sts.

Row 1 (Wrong side) and all other wrong-side rows—Purl.
Rows 2, 4, 6, 10, and 12—Knit.
Row 8—Knit into front and back of each st (thus doubling the number of sts). At the end of this row change to needles one size smaller.
Row 14—K2 tog across row. (Original number of sts restored.) At the end of this row change back to original needles.

Repeat Rows 1–14.

Waffle Stitch, or Rose Fabric

In all four versions of this pattern care must be taken not to cast on too tightly or too many stitches, because the pattern spreads laterally to make a wider piece than might be expected. Check gauge.

NOTE: For all four versions, odd number of sts.

I. SEED STITCH VERSION

Row 1 (Wrong side)—K2, * p1, k1; rep from *, end k1.
Row 2—K1, * k next st in the row below, k1; rep from *.
Row 3—K1, * p1, k1; rep from *.
Row 4—K2, * k next st in the row below, k1; rep from *, end k1.

Repeat Rows 1–4.

II. REVERSE SEED STITCH VERSION

Row 1 (Wrong side)—P2, * k1, p1; rep from *, end p1.
Rows 2 and 4—As above in Version I.
Row 3—P1, * k1, p1; rep from *.

Repeat Rows 1–4.

III. PURL VERSION

As Version I, above, except Rows 1 and 3—purl.

IV. KNIT VERSION

(*Also known as Honeycomb Stitch*)

As Version I, above, except Rows 1 and 3—knit.

Waffle Stitch, or Rose Fabric
UPPER BAND: *Seed Stitch version*
SECOND BAND: *Reverse Seed Stitch version*
THIRD BAND: *Purl version*
LOWER BAND: *Knit version (Honeycomb Stitch)*

Trinity, Cluster or Bramble Stitch

This famous pattern is also (erroneously) called Bobble Pattern, and it probably has a few other names as well. It is one of the best of the "knobbly" texture patterns and is often used in panels to help embellish fancy-knit garments like fisherman sweaters.

Multiple of 4 sts.

Row 1 (Right side)—Purl.
Row 2—* (K1, p1, k1) all in the same st; p3 tog; rep from *.
Row 3—Purl.
Row 4—* P3 tog, (k1, p1, k1) all in the same st; rep from *.

Repeat Rows 1–4.

Trinity, Cluster or Bramble Stitch

FANCY TEXTURE PATTERNS   129

Allover Cross Stitch

This is a beautiful and unusual pattern which gives a soft, thick texture with a "lacy" quality, as the sts are bundled together leaving small spaces between.

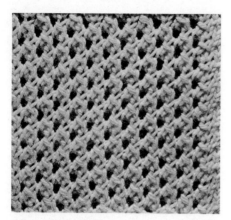
Allover Cross Stitch

Multiple of 4 sts plus 3.

Row 1 (Wrong side)—Purl.

Row 2—K2, k into the next st *in the row below,* then sl the st itself onto right-hand needle; k2 tog, psso, * k into the next st *in the row below,* k the st itself, k again into the row below at left of st (3 sts made from 1); sl 1, k2 tog, psso; rep from * to last 2 sts, k into the next st in the row below, k the st itself, k1.

Row 3—Purl.

Row 4—K1, k2 tog, * k the next st 3 times as in Row 2, sl 1, k2 tog, psso; rep from * to last 4 sts, k into the next st 3 times as in Row 2, sl 1, k1, psso, k1.

Repeat Rows 1–4.

Coral Knot Stitch

This unique and beautiful pattern, while not technically an eyelet or a lace, is definitely openwork, since the running threads are lifted in Row 2 to leave holes beneath them. In addition to these rows of holes the pattern shows a nubby texture. It has a great deal of lateral spread and the knitter must be careful not to cast on too many stitches. Used in large areas it may tend to go slightly bias.

Coral Knot Stitch

Even number of sts.

Row 1 (Right side)—K1, * k2 tog; rep from * across row knitting tog every 2 sts, end k1.

Row 2—K1, * k1, insert needle under running thread between st just worked and the next st, and knit this thread; rep from *, end k1.

Row 3—Knit.

Row 4—Purl.

Repeat Rows 1–4.

Grecian Plait Stitch

Since this pattern is worked on the same principle as Threaded Stitch, i.e., passing the second stitch over the first as the knitting is done, one would think the two patterns would be similar in appearance. But this is not at all the case. The Grecian Plait Stitch makes a fascinating fabric that looks like many tiny braids set close together, with open spaces at the points where the stitches are crossed.

Even number of sts.

NOTE: Two needle sizes are used, one needle to be 4 sizes larger than the other. Cast on large needle. There is one preparatory row.

SPECIAL NOTE ON METHOD: the object of the knitting action on all right-side rows (except preparatory row) is to pass the second stitch over the first, either before or while knitting it. This may be accomplished in several ways. One way is as follows: insert point of right-hand needle as if to purl into second stitch, lift this stitch over first stitch, then lay it down upon the left-hand needle in *front* of (that is, nearer to the needle point) the first stitch; then knit this second stitch from this position; then knit the other stitch.

A second method, perhaps a little easier to work, is as follows: insert point of right-hand needle into the second stitch as if to knit, then take the tip of right-hand needle *around* the first stitch on its right, to the back; catch yarn and knit; then slip the second stitch off left-hand needle *over* the first stitch, being careful not to let the first stitch come off with it. Then knit the first stitch.

Either way this action is done, it is called "knit second st over, k first st."

Row 1 (Preparatory row, right side)—with small needle, knit.
Row 2—With large needle, purl.
Row 3—* K 2nd st over, k 1st st (see special note); rep from * across.

Repeat Rows 2 and 3.

GRECIAN PLAIT STITCH–VARIATION

Quite a different texture effect may be had by working the Grecian Plait Stitch in alternating fashion. This would require four pattern rows: Rows 2 and 3 of Grecian Plait Stitch plus two more:

Row 4—With large needle, purl.
Row 5—With small needle, k1, * k 2nd st over, k 1st st (see special note on Grecian Plait Stitch); rep from * across to last st, end k1.

Repeat Rows 2–5.

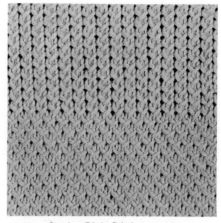

ABOVE: *Grecian Plait Stitch*
BELOW: *Grecian Plait Stitch variation*

Threaded Stitch

ABOVE: *Threaded Stitch*
BELOW: *Threaded Stitch variation*

Also called Flecked Stitch, Diaper Stitch, Threaded Cross Stitch, etc. This pattern gives a charming diagonal-weave texture, the stitches being drawn upward to right and left crossing under and over one another. There is one preparatory row which is not to be included in subsequent repeats.

Even number of sts.

NOTE: Two needle sizes are used, one needle to be 3 to 4 sizes larger than the other. Cast on larger needle.

Row 1 (Preparatory row, right side)—With small needle, knit.
Row 2—With large needle, purl.
Row 3—With small needle, * insert tip of right-hand needle through first st as if to purl, k the second st and leave on needle, then k the first st through back loop, slip both sts together from left-hand needle; rep from *.
Row 4—With large needle, purl.
Row 5—With small needle, k1, * k second st through first st, then k first st in back loop as before; rep from * across to last st, k1.

Repeat Rows 2–5.

VARIATION

The texture is altered to one which has less of a diagonally-woven quality by leaving out Rows 4 and 5, and repeating Rows 2 and 3 only.

Little Knot Stitch

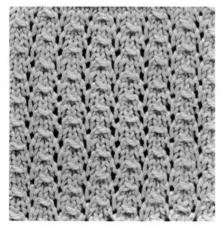

Little Knot Stitch

This pattern derives from Coral Knot Stitch and lifts the running threads in the same way. But its name is rather misleading, since there are no knots left and the surface of the fabric is, on the contrary, rather smooth.

Multiple of 6 sts plus 2.

Rows 1 and 3 (Wrong side)—Purl.
Row 2—K1, * k3, insert needle under the running thread between the st just worked and the next st, and knit this thread; sl 1—k2 tog—psso, knit running thread as before; rep from *, end k1.
Row 4—K1, * knit the running thread as before, sl 1—k2 tog—psso, knit the running thread, k3; rep from *, end k1.

Repeat Rows 1–4.

Peppercorn Stitch

In practice, the knitting action forming the "peppercorn" is not precisely a slipping of the stitch, since the right-hand needle need not be completely removed from the stitch. Simply insert the left-hand needle into the front of the stitch and knit, drawing through a new loop which is then worked in the same way.

Peppercorn Stitch

Multiple of 4 sts plus 3.

Rows 1 and 3 (Wrong side)—Purl.

Row 2—K3, * k next st, then (sl the st just knitted back onto left needle and knit it again through back loop) 3 times, k3; rep from *.

Row 4—K1, * k next st 4 times as in Row 2, k3; rep from *, end last repeat k1.

Repeat Rows 1–4.

Bowknot Stitch

Simple and easy to work, this pattern is charming for little girls' dresses and sweaters, and babies' wear. The "bowknots" are formed of purl welts drawn together by gathering loops.

Bowknot Stitch

Multiple of 18 sts plus 9.

Row 1 (Right side)—K9, * p9, k9; rep from *.

Row 2—P9, * k9, p9; rep from *.

Rows 3 and 5—Knit.

Rows 4 and 6—Purl.

Rows 7 and 8—Repeat Rows 1 and 2.

Row 9—K13, * insert needle into front of next st 9 rows below, and draw up a loop; slip this loop onto left-hand needle and knit it tog with next st; k17; rep from *, end last repeat k13.

Row 10—Purl.

Row 11—P9, * k9, p9; rep from *.

Row 12—K9, * p9, k9; rep from *.

Rows 13 and 15—Knit.

Rows 14 and 16—Purl.

Rows 17 and 18—Repeat Rows 11 and 12.

Row 19—K4, * draw up a loop from 9th row below and knit it tog with next st as before; k17; rep from *, end last repeat k4.

Row 20—Purl.

Repeat Rows 1–20.

Raindrop Stitch

Raindrop Stitch

This is a quiet and subtle pattern with just a hint of texture.

Multiple of 4 sts plus 1.

Rows 1 and 3 (Wrong side)—Purl.

Row 2—K1, * k into next st in the row below, keeping the original st on needle; then sl the new st on to left needle and knit it again; then knit the original st and pass the new st over it; k3; rep from *.

Row 4—K3, * rep from * of Row 2, end last repeat k1.

Repeat Rows 1–4.

Smocking

Smocking

This highly embossed pattern is ideal for panels in very fancy cable sweaters. It is easier to work than the traditional Aran Honeycomb but can be successfully used in its place.

Multiple of 8 sts plus 2.

Rows 1 and 3 (Wrong side)—K2, * p2, k2; rep from *.

Row 2—P2, * k2, p2; rep from *.

Row 4—P2, * insert right-hand needle from front between 6th and 7th sts on left-hand needle and draw through a loop; sl this loop onto left-hand needle and knit it together with the 1st st on left-hand needle; k1, p2, k2, p2; rep from *.

Rows 5 and 7—Repeat Rows 1 and 3.

Row 6—Repeat Row 2.

Row 8—P2, k2, p2, * draw loop from between 6th and 7th sts as before and knit it together with 1st st, then k1, p2, k2, p2; rep from *, end k2, p2.

Repeat Rows 1–8.

VARIATION SMOCKING

Multiple of 6 sts plus 2.

Row 1 (Right side)—* P2, k4; rep from *, end p2.

Row 2—* K2, p4; rep from *, end k2.

Row 3—* P2, [keeping yarn in back, insert right-hand needle from front to back between 4th and 5th st on left-hand needle and draw up a loop; k4, then sl the top thread of loop over the 4 sts]; rep from *, end p2.

Row 4—* K2, p4; rep from *, end k2.

Row 5—K3, p2, * k4, p2; rep from *, end k3.

Row 6—P3, k2, * p4, k2; rep from *, end p3.

Row 7—K1, [keeping yarn in back, insert right-hand needle from front to back between 2nd and 3rd st on left-hand

Variation Smocking

needle and draw up a loop; k2, then sl the top thread of loop over the 2 sts], * p2, repeat from [to] of Row 3 over the next 4 sts; rep from * to last 5 sts, end p2, repeat from [to] of Row 7 over the next 2 sts, k1.

Row 8—P3, k2, * p4, k2; rep from *, end p3.

Repeat Rows 1–8.

Loop Stitch

It is very handy to know this technique of knitting a row of loop fringe across a fabric. Its decorative possibilities are endless. A few rows of such fringe can make an edging for coat collars and cuffs, or borders for stoles, blankets, pillow covers, jackets, and hats. A very deep fringed border or an all-over fringed fabric can be made simply by repeating the pattern rows as often as desired. Loop rugs can be made by this method, as can shag mats and bathroom accessories.

Loop Stitch

Any number of sts.

Rows 1, 2, 3, and 4—Knit.

Row 5 (Wrong side)—* Holding 3rd finger of left hand over yarn behind work, k1 (so that yarn forms a loop around finger) but do not sl this st from needle; then transfer the st just worked back onto left-hand needle and k2 tog-b (the st just knitted, and the original st); then remove finger from loop to make another loop in the next st as before; rep from * in every st.

Row 6—K-b every st across row.

Repeat Rows 1–6.

Drop-Stitch Pattern

The reverse side of this fabric is extremely pretty, showing deep-textured rows of puffs. The pattern is very good for soft, loose garments such as bedjackets and robes, or in fine yarn for dressy sweaters.

Drop-Stitch Pattern

Multiple of 3 sts plus 2.

Rows 1, 3, and 5 (Wrong side)—K2, * p1, k2; rep from *.

Rows 2 and 4—P2, * k1, p2; rep from *.

Row 6—P2, * drop next st off needle and unravel it 4 rows down, so that there are 4 loose strands behind st; then insert right-hand needle from front into 5th st down and also under the 4 loose strands, and knit, drawing the st up and catching strands behind it; p2; rep from *.

Repeat Rows 1–6.

Horizontal Ridged Herringbone

Horizontal Ridged Herringbone

This fascinating knitting technique gives a pattern of horizontal embossed ridges, between which the stitches lie slanted back and forth in herringbone fashion. In practice it will be found that when a stitch is to be slipped back to the left-hand needle, it is convenient simply to insert the point of the left-hand needle into the front of this stitch from the left, then all that remains is to pick up the next stitch in its back loop with the right-hand needle, so the two stitches can be knitted together. When finishing a row, be sure that it is this *returned* stitch that is knitted plain. Thus in Row 4 the left-hand needle is completely cleared and the last stitch returned and knitted once more for the final "k1".

Odd number of sts.

Rows 1 and 3 (Wrong side)—K1, purl to last st, k1.
Row 2—K2, * k2 tog-b but do not sl from needle; insert right-hand needle between the sts just knitted tog and k the 2nd st again; then sl both sts off needle together; then sl the last st worked back to left-hand needle and repeat from *; end k2.
Row 4—K1, * rep from * of Row 2, end k1.

Repeat Rows 1–4.

Powder Puff

Powder Puff

Multiple of 10 sts plus 2.

Row 1 (Wrong side)—K2, * p5, k2, p1, k2; rep from *.
Row 2—P2, * insert needle under running thread between st just worked and the next st, and knit this thread; k1; knit running thread, p2, ssk, k1, k2 tog, p2; rep from *.
Row 3—K2, * p3, k2; rep from *.
Row 4—P2, * k running thread, k3, k running thread, p2, sl 2 knitwise—k1—p2sso, p2; rep from *.
Row 5—K2, * p1, k2, p5, k2; rep from *.
Row 6—P2, * ssk, k1, k2 tog, p2, k running thread, k1, k running thread, p2; rep from *.
Row 7—Repeat Row 3.
Row 8—P2, * sl 2 knitwise—k1—p2sso, p2, k running thread, k3, k running thread, p2; rep from *.

Repeat Rows 1–8.

Pineapple Stitch

Multiple of 6 sts plus 2.

Row 1 (Right side)—K1, * sl 3 wyib, k2 tog, pass 3 sl-sts over, one at a time; purl loosely into front, back, front, back, and front of next st (5 sts from 1); rep from *, end k1.

Row 2—P1, * k5, p1; rep from *, end p1.

Rows 3 and 5—K1, * k1, p5; rep from *, end k1.

Rows 4 and 6—Repeat Row 2.

Row 7—K1, * inc by purling 5 times into next st as in Row 1, sl 3 wyib, k2 tog, pass 3 sl-sts over as in Row 1; rep from *, end k1.

Row 8—P1, * p1, k5; rep from *, end p1.

Rows 9 and 11—K1, * p5, k1; rep from *, end k1.

Rows 10 and 12—Repeat Row 8.

Repeat Rows 1–12.

Pineapple Stitch

Indian Pillar Stitch

This pattern should be worked loosely with large needles, in which case it will give a pretty lace-like fabric. The wrong side is most attractive, showing twisted columns decorated with little bands of purl; and this is often presented as the right side. So the choice of sides is up to the knitter. In the variation below, however, the right side is definitely the more successful.

Multiple of 4 sts plus 3.

Row 1 (Right side)—K2, * p3 tog, then knit the same 3 sts tog, then purl the same 3 sts tog again, then sl all 3 sts from needle, k1; rep from *, end k1.

Row 2—Purl.

Repeat Rows 1 and 2.

VARIATION

Indian Pillar Stitch is readily converted into a very beautiful allover pattern by the simple expedient of adding two more rows in order to alternate the motifs.

Multiple of 4 sts plus 3.

Rows 1 and 2—Same as Rows 1 and 2, above.

Row 3—K4, * p3 tog, knit the same 3 tog, purl the same 3 tog, then sl all 3 sts from needle, k1; rep from *, end k3.

Row 4—Purl.

Repeat Rows 1–4.

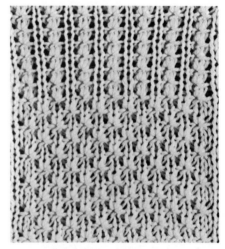

ABOVE: *Indian Pillar Stitch*
BELOW: *Variation*

FANCY TEXTURE PATTERNS   137

Bells and Bell-Ropes

Here is a charming allover pattern based on the Embossed Bell Motif. In Bells and Bell-Ropes the little bells are less bold, since they are formed at the bottom out of a single stitch instead of a number of cast-on stitches. An attractive novelty sweater could be worked in this pattern and trimmed with the Embossed Bell Motif as shown.

Multiple of 8 sts plus 7.

Row 1 (Wrong side)—K3, * p1-b, k3; rep from *.
Row 2—P3, * k1-b, p3; rep from *.
Row 3—K3, p1-b, k3, * (k1, p1, k1, p1, k1) in next st making 5 sts from 1; k3, p1-b, k3; rep from *.
Row 4—P3, k1-b, p3, * k5, p3, k1-b, p3; rep from *.
Row 5—K3, p1-b, k3, * p5, k3, p1-b, k3; rep from *.
Row 6—P3, k1-b, p3, * ssk, k1, k2 tog, p3, k1-b, p3; rep from *.
Row 7—K3, p1-b, k3, * p3, k3, p1-b, k3; rep from *.
Row 8—P3, k1-b, p3, * sl 1—k2 tog—psso, p3, k1-b, p3; rep from *.
Rows 9 and 10—Repeat Rows 1 and 2.
Row 11—K3, make 5 sts from 1, k3, * p1-b, k3, make 5 sts from 1, k3; rep from *.
Row 12—P3, k5, p3, * k1-b, p3, k5, p3; rep from *.
Row 13—K3, p5, k3, * p1-b, k3, p5, k3; rep from *.
Row 14—P3, ssk, k1, k2 tog, p3, * k1-b, p3, ssk, k1, k2 tog, p3; rep from *.
Row 15—K3, p3, k3, * p1-b, k3, p3, k3; rep from *.
Row 16—P3, sl 1—k2 tog—psso, p3, * k1-b, p3, sl 1—k2 tog—psso, p3; rep from *.

Repeat Rows 1–16.

Embossed Bell Motif

This cheerful pattern makes rows of little bells across the fabric. It is fun to use for borders, children's knitwear, etc. It always adds a touch of novelty.

Multiple of 8 sts plus 4.

Row 1 (Right side)—Purl.
Row 2—Knit.
Row 3—P4, * cast on 8 sts, p4, rep from *.
Row 4—K4, * p8 (the 8 cast-on sts), k4; rep from *.
Row 5—P4, * k8, p4, rep from *.
Row 6—K4, * p8, k4; rep from *.
Row 7—P4, * ssk, k4, k2 tog, p4; rep from *.
Row 8—K4, * p6, k4; rep from *.

ABOVE: *Bells and Bell-Ropes*
BELOW: *Embossed Bell Motif*

Row 9—P4, * ssk, k2, k2 tog, p4; rep from *.
Row 10—K4, * p4, k4; rep from *.
Row 11—P4, * ssk, k2 tog, p4; rep from *.
Row 12—K4, * p2, k4; rep from *.
Row 13—P4, * k2 tog, p4; rep from *.
Row 14—K4, * p1, k4; rep from *.
Row 15—P4, * k2 tog, p3; rep from *.
Row 16—Knit.

Repeat Rows 1–16.

Embossed Diamond Stitch

These diamonds are formed by increases, and thus the pattern has a tendency to spread out laterally and requires comparatively few stitches for a desired width, especially when the panel is repeated as an all-over pattern. When using the panel in this way, with two or three or more repetitions, be sure to use the *entire* panel, rather than fusing the 6 purl sts between diamonds into 3, as is usually done in cable patterns.

Panel of 7 sts.

Row 1 (Wrong side)—Knit.
Row 2—Purl.
Row 3—Knit.
Row 4—P3, k1, p3.
Row 5—K3, purl into front, back, and front again of next st, k3.
Row 6—P3, k3, p3.
Row 7—K3, purl into front and back of next st, p1, purl into front and back of next st, k3.
Row 8—P3, k5, p3.
Row 9—K3, p into front and back of next st, p3, p into front and back of next st, k3.
Row 10—P3, k7, p3.
Row 11—K3, p into front and back of next st, p5, p into front and back of next st, k3.
Row 12—P3, k9, p3.
Row 13—K3, p2 tog, p5, p2 tog-b, k3.
Row 14—P3, k7, p3.
Row 15—K3, p2 tog, p3, p2 tog-b, k3.
Row 16—P3, k5, p3.
Row 17—K3, p2 tog, p1, p2 tog-b, k3.
Row 18—P3, k3, p3.
Row 19—K3, p3 tog, k3.
Row 20—P3, k1, p3.

Repeat Rows 1–20.

Embossed Diamond Stitch

CENTER PANEL: *Carillon Pattern*
SIDE PANELS: *Willow Buds*

Willow Buds

This is a nubby pattern which, when used in a single panel, makes a nice border for cables, diamonds, and other wider panel patterns. It is derived, of course, from the Indian Pillar Stitch.

Panel of 5 sts.

Row 1 (Wrong side)—K1, p3, k1.
Row 2—P1, p3 tog but do not drop from needle; k same 3 sts tog inserting needle through fronts; p same 3 sts tog again and slip all 3 from needle; p1.
Row 3—K1, p3, k1.
Row 4—P1, k3, p1.

Repeat Rows 1–4.

Carillon Pattern

This is a very handsome arrangement of Bells and Bell-Ropes in a panel. Being a narrow vertical pattern it will combine nicely with cables and other vertical embossed patterns. Innumerable other variations on Bells and Bell-Ropes are possible, with the "ropes" being spaced at varying distances and the "bells" at varying positions upon them.

Panel of 17 sts.

Row 1 (Wrong side)—K2, (k1, p1, k1, p1, k1) in next st making 5 sts from 1, (k2, p1-b) 3 times, k2, make 5 sts from 1, k2.
Row 2—P2, k5, (p2, k1-b) 3 times, p2, k5, p2.
Row 3—K2, p5, (k2, p1-b) 3 times, k2, p5, k2.
Row 4—P2, ssk, k1, k2 tog, (p2, k1-b) 3 times, p2, ssk, k1, k2 tog, p2.
Row 5—K2, p3, (k2, p1-b) 3 times, k2, p3, k2.
Row 6—P2, sl 1—k2 tog—psso, (p2, k1-b) 3 times, p2, sl 1—k2 tog—psso, p2.
Row 7—K2, (p1-b, k2, make 5 sts from 1, k2) twice, p1-b, k2.
Row 8—P2, (k1-b, p2, k5, p2) twice, k1-b, p2.
Row 9—K2, (p1-b, k2, p5, k2) twice, p1-b, k2.
Row 10—P2, (k1-b, p2, ssk, k1, k2 tog, p2) twice, k1-b, p2.
Row 11—K2, (p1-b, k2, p3, k2) twice, p1-b, k2.
Row 12—P2, (k1-b, p2, sl 1—k2 tog—psso, p2) twice, k1-b, p2.
Row 13—K2, (p1-b, k2) twice, make 5 sts from 1, (k2, p1-b) twice, k2.
Row 14—P2, (k1-b, p2) twice, k5, (p2, k1-b) twice, p2.
Row 15—K2, (p1-b, k2) twice, p5, (k2, p1-b) twice, k2.
Row 16—P2, (k1-b, p2) twice, ssk, k1, k2 tog, (p2, k1-b) twice, p2.

Row 17—K2, (p1-b, k2) twice, p3, (k2, p1-b) twice, k2.
Row 18—P2, (k1-b, p2) twice, sl 1—k2 tog—psso, (p2, k1-b) twice, p2.

Repeat Rows 1–18.

Parquet Pattern

This is a pattern of very highly embossed diamonds, in which the increases in one motif are compensated for by the decreases in the next.

Multiple of 18 sts plus 1.

NOTE: M1 (Make One) is done *purlwise* in this pattern: i.e., lift the running thread between the st just worked and the next st, and purl into the back of this thread.

Row 1 (Right side)—K1, * p3, k11, p3, k1; rep from *.
Row 2—P1, * M1, k3, p2 tog, p7, p2 tog-b, k3, M1, p1; rep from *.
Row 3—K2, * p3, k9, p3, k3; rep from *, end last repeat k2.
Row 4—P2, * M1, k3, p2 tog, p5, p2 tog-b, k3, M1, p3; rep from *, end last repeat p2.
Row 5—K3, * p3, k7, p3, k5; rep from *, end last repeat k3.
Row 6—P3, * M1, k3, p2 tog, p3, p2 tog-b, k3, M1, p5; rep from *, end last repeat p3.
Row 7—K4, * p3, k5, p3, k7; rep from *, end last repeat k4.
Row 8—P4, * M1, k3, p2 tog, p1, p2 tog-b, k3, M1, p7; rep from *, end last repeat p4.
Row 9—K5, * p3, k3, p3, k9; rep from *, end last repeat k5.
Row 10—P5, * M1, k3, p3 tog, k3, M1, p9; rep from *, end last repeat p5.
Row 11—K6, * p3, k1, p3, k11; rep from *, end last repeat k6.
Row 12—P4, * p2 tog-b, k3, M1, p1, M1, k3, p2 tog, p7; rep from *, end last repeat p4.
Row 13—K5, * p3, k3, p3, k9; rep from *, end last repeat k5.
Row 14—P3, * p2 tog-b, k3, M1, p3, M1, k3, p2 tog, p5; rep from *, end last repeat p3.
Row 15—K4, * p3, k5, p3, k7; rep from *, end last repeat k4.
Row 16—P2, * p2 tog-b, k3, M1, p5, M1, k3, p2 tog, p3; rep from *, end last repeat p2.
Row 17—K3, * p3, k7, p3, k5; rep from *, end last repeat k3.
Row 18—P1, * p2 tog-b, k3, M1, p7, M1, k3, p2 tog, p1; rep from *.
Row 19—K2, * p3, k9, p3, k3; rep from *, end last repeat k2.
Row 20—P2 tog-b, * k3, M1, p9, M1, k3, p3 tog; rep from *, end last repeat *p2 tog* instead of p3 tog.

Repeat Rows 1–20.

Parquet Pattern

Chevron Fantastic

Chevron Fantastic

This pattern is particularly effective in variegated or ombre yarns; the shading of colors displays the alternating bias slant of the stitches very well. Horizontal stripes in contrasting colors also make a striking chevron effect.

Multiple of 8 sts plus 10.

Row 1 (Right side)—K1, k1 and leave st on needle, k into the head of the st below the one just knitted, and sl both sts from needle together; k2, * k2 tog-b, put the resulting st back on left-hand needle and pass the *next* st over it and off needle; then return the st to right-hand needle; k2, knit into the head of st *below* the next st, then knit the next st through back loop, then knit again into the head of same st below (the "same" st is now the 3rd st down); k2; rep from *, end k2 tog-b and pass the next st over, k2, k into the st below next st, then k the next st itself.

Row 2—Purl.

Repeat Rows 1 and 2.

Double Wing Pattern

ABOVE: *Double Wing Pattern*
BELOW: *Double Wing, Openwork Version*

This is a subtle but very effective pattern of contrasting purl stitches and gently curved knit stitches.

Multiple of 16 sts.

Row 1 (Right side)—Knit.
Row 2—* K4, p8, k4; rep from *.
Row 3—* P3, k2 tog, k3, lift running thread between the st just worked and the next st, and knit into the *back* and *front* of this thread; k3, ssk, p3; rep from *.
Row 4—* K3, p10, k3; rep from *.
Row 5—* P2, k2 tog, k3, lift running thread and knit into the back of this thread (Make One, M1); k2, M1, k3, ssk, p2; rep from *.
Row 6—* K2, p12, k2; rep from *.
Row 7—* P1, k2 tog, k3, M1, k4, M1, k3, ssk, p1; rep from *.
Row 8—* K1, p14, k1; rep from *.
Row 9—* K2 tog, k3, M1, k6, M1, k3, ssk; rep from *.
Row 10—Purl.

Repeat Rows 1–10.

DOUBLE WING, OPENWORK VERSION

Work exactly as above, with these exceptions:

Row 3—* P3, k2 tog, k3, (yo) twice, k3, ssk, p3; rep from *.

Row 4—K3, p4, purl into front and back of double yo, p4, k3; rep from *.

Work the rest of the pattern as above but with a "yo" in place of every "M1". Now you can see the close family resemblance between this pattern and Pine Trees!

Herringbone

This pattern is really a simplified version of Chevron Fantastic. Having the unobtrusive, trim, tailored look of the true herringbone weave, it is a very good pattern for suits and coats.

Multiple of 7 sts plus 1.

Rows 1 and 3 (Wrong side)—Purl.

Row 2—* K2 tog, k2, increase in next st as follows: place point of right-hand needle behind left-hand needle, insert point of right-hand needle from the top down through the (purled) head of st *below* next st, and knit; then knit the st above; k2; rep from *, end k1.

Row 4—K1, * k2, increase in next st as above, k2, k2 tog; rep from *.

Herringbone

Repeat Rows 1–4.

Welting Fantastic

This striking pattern is a form of Chevron Fantastic, traversed by horizontal welts. Although the welts are worked straight across, the chevron formation of the background causes them to wave up and down, following the alternate bias of the stitches. In this case the welts are worked in Garter Stitch. They may be done as plain purl welts simply by purling instead of knitting Rows 2 and 4 on the right side of the fabric; but this is somewhat less successful. Plain purl welts more than three rows wide tend to be loose, and roll up too much; welts worked in Garter Stitch are trimmer and give a more manageable fabric.

Welting Fantastic

Welting Fantastic is very effective when the welts are knitted in a contrasting color. The contrast should be used in Rows 1, 2, 3, 4, 5, and 12 of each pattern repeat.

Multiple of 11 sts.

NOTE: Odd-numbered rows are wrong-side rows.

Rows 1 through 5—Knit.
Row 6—* K2 tog, k2, knit into front and back of each of the next 2 sts, k3, ssk; rep from *.
Rows 7, 9, and 11—Purl.
Rows 8, 10, and 12—Repeat Row 6.

Repeat Rows 1–12.

Popcorns and Bobbles

ABOVE: *Popcorns*
BELOW: *Bobbles*

Popcorns and Bobbles are not alike, although they are all too frequently confused with each other. Both are puffy knot-like formations made out of a single stitch. But there *is* a difference, and it is this: Bobbles are "turned", and Popcorns are not. "Turning" means that the work is turned around to the other side, and a few stitches worked backward over the most recent ones. In most bobble patterns the work is turned 4 times for each bobble. A popcorn, on the other hand, is made by increasing in one stitch, leaving it, and decreasing the extra stitches on the return row. Thus a popcorn requires two rows to make, being started on a wrong-side row and completed on the following right-side row. A bobble is completed all at once on the same right-side row.

It is impossible to give all the arrangements of Popcorns and Bobbles that can be made. Their number is enormous. Since each motif is formed out of a single stitch, they can be scattered over the fabric in any sort of design: in vertical columns, horizontal rows, diagonal rows, spot-patterns, diamonds, clumps or clusters, stars, squares, circles, or what have you. They can be made as isolated accents in the midst of other patterns, or to simulate buttons, or to decorate collars and cuffs. Their background can be anything at all—knit stitches, purl stitches, Seed Stitch, Moss Stitch, cables, twists, ribbings—even lace. For the sake of simplicity they are shown here as spot-patterns on Garter Stitch, but it must be remembered that this is only a basic demonstration.

POPCORNS

For an alternate way of making Popcorns, see Aran Diamonds with Popcorns.

Multiple of 6 sts plus 5.

NOTE: Odd-numbered rows are wrong-side rows.

Rows 1 through 4—Knit.

Row 5—K5, * (k1, p1, k1, p1) loosely in next st, k5; rep from *.

Row 6—K5, * sl 3, k1, pass 3rd, 2nd, and 1st of sl-sts separately over the last knitted st, completing Popcorn; k5; rep from *.

Rows 7 through 10—Knit.

Row 11—K8, * (k1, p1, k1, p1) loosely in next st, k5; rep from *, end k3.

Row 12—K8, * sl 3, k1, pass sl-sts over to complete Popcorn, k5; rep from *, end k3.

Repeat Rows 1–12.

BOBBLES

Bobbles are more versatile than Popcorns. For one thing, they can be made much larger; for another, there are many different ways of working them. For alternate methods of working Bobbles, see Blackberry Bobble Pattern, Openwork Bobble Pattern, Fancy Bobble Cable, Ribbed Lattice with Bobbles, and Cathedral Pattern.

Multiple of 6 sts plus 5.

NOTE: Odd-numbered rows are wrong-side rows.

Rows 1 through 5—Knit.

Row 6—K5, * (yo, k1) 3 times into the next st, forming 6 bobble sts; turn work around and sl 1, p5 across these 6 sts; turn again and sl 1, k5; turn again and (p2 tog) 3 times; turn again and sl 1—k2 tog—psso, completing bobble; k5; rep from *.

Row 7—K5, * p1-b, k5; rep from *.

Rows 8 through 11—Knit.

Row 12—K8, * Make Bobble in next st as in Row 6, k5; rep from *, end k3.

Repeat Rows 1–12.

On subsequent repeats, always purl into the *back* of each bobble st on the return row, as in Row 7.

Blackberry Bobble Pattern

Here is a delightful pattern of bobbles grouped close together to form clusters. Each "blackberry" is a cluster of six bobbles. The bobbles are smallish, being turned only twice. If larger bobbles are desired, two more turnings may be added.

This pattern is fun to use in hats, mittens, and children's sweaters; also, it is very good for bedspreads. Touches of embroidery can be added to simulate leaves around the upper portion of each "berry"; or, leaves of felt can be sewn to the fabric.

Blackberry Bobble Pattern

Multiple of 20 sts plus 1.

NOTE: Throughout pattern, MB (Make Bobble) as follows: (k1, yo, k1, yo, k1) into the same st, forming 5 bobble sts; turn work around and p5 across the bobble sts; turn again and k5, then pass the 4th, 3rd, 2nd, and 1st sts separately over the last st knitted, completing bobble.

Row 1 (Right side)—K1, * (p4, k1) twice, p4, MB, p4, k1; rep from *.
Row 2—P1, * k4, p1-b (into bobble st); (k4, p1) 3 times; rep from *.
Row 3—K1, * (p4, k1) twice, p3, MB, p1, MB, p3, k1; rep from *.
Row 4—P1, * k3, p1-b, k1, p1-b, k3, p1, (k4, p1) twice; rep from *.
Row 5—K1, * (p4, k1) twice, p2, MB, (p1, MB) twice, p2, k1; rep from *.
Row 6—P1, * k2, p1-b, (k1, p1-b) twice, k2, p1, (k4, p1) twice; rep from *.
Row 7—K1, * p4, MB, (p4, k1) 3 times; rep from *.
Row 8—P1, * (k4, p1) twice, k4, p1-b, k4, p1; rep from *.
Row 9—K1, * p3, MB, p1, MB, p3, k1, (p4, k1) twice; rep from *.
Row 10—P1, * (k4, p1) twice, k3, p1-b, k1, p1-b, k3, p1; rep from *.
Row 11—K1, * p2, MB, (p1, MB) twice, p2, k1, (p4, k1) twice; rep from *.
Row 12—P1, * (k4, p1) twice, k2, (p1-b, k1) twice, p1-b, k2, p1; rep from *.

Repeat Rows 1–12.

Openwork Bobble Pattern

Still another method of making bobbles is demonstrated by this pattern, which is a form of Openwork Diamonds. The bobbles are formed of knit stitches against a purled background, which could be reversed if desired.

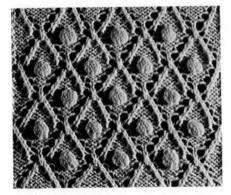

Openwork Bobble Pattern

Multiple of 10 sts plus 1.

Row 1 (Right side)—P1, * yo, ssk, p5, k2 tog, yo, p1; rep from *.
Row 2—K1, * k1, p1, k5, p1, k2; rep from *.
Row 3—P1, * p1, yo, ssk, p3, k2 tog, yo, p2; rep from *.
Row 4—K1, * k2, p1, k3, p1, k3; rep from *.
Row 5—P1, * p2, yo, ssk, p1, k2 tog, yo, p3; rep from *.
Row 6—K1, * k3, p1, k1, p1, k4; rep from *.
Row 7—P1, * p3, yo, sl 2 knitwise—k1—p2sso, yo, p3, Make Bobble (MB) in next st as follows: (k1, yo, k1, yo, k1) into same st, turn and p5, turn and k5, turn and p5, turn and ssk, k1, k2 tog, turn and p3 tog, turn and with yarn in back sl bobble st onto right-hand needle; rep from *, end last repeat p4.
Row 8—K1, * k3, p3, k3, p1-b into bobble st; rep from *, end last repeat k4.

Row 9—P1, * p2, k2 tog, yo, p1, yo, ssk, p3; rep from *.

Row 10—K1, * k2, p1, k3, p1, k3; rep from *.

Row 11—P1, * p1, k2 tog, yo, p3, yo, ssk, p2; rep from *.

Row 12—K1, * k1, p1, k5, p1, k2; rep from *.

Row 13—P1, * k2 tog, yo, p5, yo, ssk, p1; rep from *.

Row 14—K1, * p1, k7, p1, k1; rep from *.

Row 15—K2 tog, * yo, p3, MB in next st, p3, yo, sl 2 knitwise
—k1—p2sso; rep from *, end yo, p3, MB, p3, yo, ssk.

Row 16—P1, * p1, k3, p1-b into bobble st, k3, p2; rep from *.

Repeat Rows 1–16.

CHAPTER EIGHT

Patterns Made with Yarn-Over Stitches

So many lovely knitted patterns, including all laces and eyelets, are done with yarn-over stitches that it is important for anyone aspiring to master the art of knitting to learn this simple operation. It consists of taking the yarn over the top of the right-hand needle before making the next stitch, thus putting one more strand on the needle between stitches. A yarn-over therefore constitutes an increase. For those who are unaccustomed to using yarn-over stitches, it may be encouraging to know that making a yarn-over is the least complicated action in all knitting, faster and simpler even than working a single knit stitch. It is done in one quick flick.

Having been placed on the needle, the yarn-over is treated as a separate stitch on the return row. Its usual, though not invariable, purpose is to leave a hole in the fabric. Since it is an increase, it must be compensated for by a decrease: "k2 tog" or "ssk" being the usual forms. Two yarn-overs at once can be compensated for by a "sl 1—k2 tog—psso" or a "k3 tog." Sometimes these compensatory decreases are performed immediately before or after the yarn-over, sometimes a few stitches earlier or later, sometimes not until some other row is being worked.

The patterns in this section are neither laces nor eyelets, though some of them are lace-like fabrics created by openwork. Others are quite solid, using their yarn-overs in some way other than to make holes. Still other patterns, like those of the Brioche family, have a dual nature: they are solid when worked in heavy yarn, and lace-like when worked in fine yarn. Like Fancy Texture Patterns (which some of them really are), the patterns in this section have not much in common except variety. You should experiment with them, using differing sizes of needles and yarns, and discover their possibilities for yourself.

Dewdrop Pattern

This is a nice, easy little English pattern making a pretty openwork that the beginner can quickly master. It has the added virtue of being a flat, non-curling fabric, and thus can be used without blocking. Note that in the first 3 rows of the first half, and the first 3 rows of the second half, the right and wrong sides exchange places.

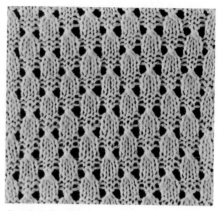

Dewdrop Pattern

Multiple of 6 sts plus 1.

Rows 1 and 3 (Wrong side)—K2, * p3, k3; rep from *, end p3, k2.

Row 2—P2, * k3, p3; rep from *, end k3, p2.

Row 4—K2, * yo, sl 1—k2 tog—psso, yo, k3; rep from *, end yo, sl 1—k2 tog—psso, yo, k2.

Rows 5 and 7—P2, * k3, p3; rep from *, end k3, p2.

Row 6—K2, * p3, k3; rep from *, end p3, k2.

Row 8—K2 tog, * yo, k3, yo, sl 1—k2 tog—psso; rep from *, end yo, k3, yo, ssk.

Repeat Rows 1–8.

Fuchsia Pattern

This is a popular pattern in traditional knitting, known in some form or another throughout Europe. This particular version is German. It is so simple to work that any beginner could make a deceptively fancy-looking garment with it. In a fine yarn it makes pretty baby dresses or little girls' party clothes.

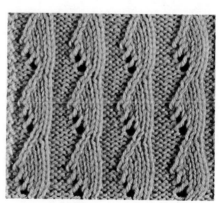

Fuchsia Pattern

Multiple of 6 sts.

Row 1 (Right side)—* P2, k2, yo, p2; rep from *.

Row 2—* K2, p3, k2; rep from *.

Row 3—* P2, k3, yo, p2; rep from *.

Row 4—* K2, p4, k2; rep from *.

Row 5—* P2, k4, yo, p2; rep from *.

Row 6—* K2, p5, k2; rep from *.

Row 7—* P2, k3, k2 tog, p2; rep from *.

Row 8—Repeat Row 4.

Row 9—* P2, k2, k2 tog, p2; rep from *.

Row 10—Repeat Row 2.

Row 11—* P2, k1, k2 tog, p2; rep from *.

Row 12—* K2, p2, k2; rep from *.

Repeat Rows 1–12.

Mrs. Hunter's Pattern

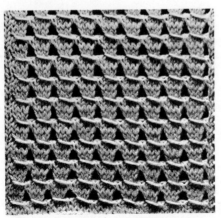

Mrs. Hunter's Pattern

The "Mrs. Hunter" who originated this pattern was a member of the famous Hunter family of the Isle of Unst, the most northerly of the Shetland Islands. The Hunters began and developed the art of Shetland lace knitting, and have created lace shawls for the British royal family from the time of Queen Victoria to the present.

Note the close kinship between Mrs. Hunter's pattern and the Yarn-Over Cable, which undoubtedly was derived from it.

Multiple of 4 sts plus 2.

Row 1 (Right side)—Knit.
Row 2—Purl.
Row 3—K1, * sl 1, k3, psso the 3 knit sts; rep from *, end k1.
Row 4—P1, * p3, yo; rep from *, end p1.

Repeat Rows 1–4.

Puff Stitch

Puff Stitch

This is a novel texture pattern with considerable horizontal elasticity.

Multiple of 6 sts plus 2.

Row 1 (Right side)—P2, * (k1, p1) twice in next st (forming 4 puff sts), p2, k1, p2; rep from *.
Row 2—K2, * p1, k2; (k1, yo) 3 times and k1 on the 4 puff sts; k2; rep from *.
Row 3—P2, * (k1, drop yo) 3 times and k1 on the 4 puff sts; p2, k1, p2; rep from *.
Row 4—Repeat Row 2.
Row 5—Repeat Row 3.
Row 6—K2, * p1, k2, p4 tog (completing puff), k2; rep from *.
Row 7—P2, * k1, p2, (k1, p1) twice in next st, p2; rep from *.
Row 8—K2, * (k1, yo) 3 times and k1 on 4 puff sts, k2, p1, k2; rep from *.
Row 9—P2, * k1, p2, (k1, drop yo) 3 times and k1 on the 4 puff sts; p2; rep from *.
Row 10—Repeat Row 8.
Row 11—Repeat Row 9.
Row 12—K2, * p4 tog (completing puff), k2, p1, k2; rep from *.

Repeat Rows 1–12.

Laburnum Stitch

Multiple of 5 sts plus 2.

NOTE: In this pattern the (yo) twice is performed in reverse: i.e., up the back of the needle and over forward, then around and over forward again, instead of the usual way.

Row 1 (Right side)—P2, * sl 1 wyif, yarn to back, k2 tog, psso, (yo) twice in reverse, p2; rep from *.

Row 2—K2, * purl into back and then into front of (yo) twice of previous row, p1, k2; rep from *.

Row 3—P2, * k3, p2; rep from *.

Row 4—K2, * p3, k2; rep from *.

Repeat Rows 1–4.

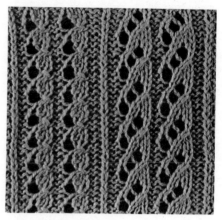

LEFT: *Laburnum Stitch*
RIGHT: *Waterfall Pattern*

Waterfall Pattern

This pretty design is done on the same principle as the Fuchsia Pattern, and is equally simple to work. If desired, two purl stitches may be inserted between motifs instead of three, making a multiple of 5 plus 2.

Multiple of 6 sts plus 3.

Row 1 (Wrong side)—K3, * p3, k3; rep from *.

Row 2—P3, * k3, yo, p3; rep from *.

Row 3—K3, * p4, k3; rep from *.

Row 4—P3, * k1, k2 tog, yo, k1, p3; rep from *.

Row 5—K3, * p2, p2 tog, k3; rep from *.

Row 6—P3, * k1, yo, k2 tog, p3; rep from *.

Repeat Rows 1–6.

Madeira Mesh

This is a Spanish pattern of great antiquity. When done in fine yarn it gives a lovely cobwebby effect.

Multiple of 6 sts plus 7.

Rows 1 through 6—K2, * yo, p3 tog, yo, k3; rep from *, end yo, p3 tog, yo, k2.

Rows 7 through 12—K2, * k3, yo, p3 tog, yo; rep from *, end k5.

Repeat Rows 1–12.

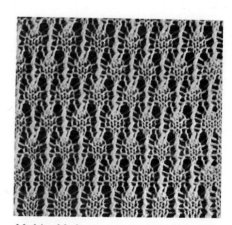

Madeira Mesh

PATTERNS MADE WITH YARN-OVER STITCHES   151

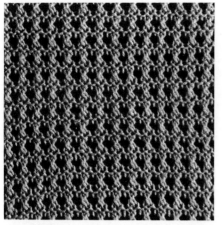

Open Honeycomb Stitch

Open Honeycomb Stitch

A lace-like mesh pattern could hardly be any more simple than this. Yet this pattern has its own little touch of ingenuity: the purled rows help to compensate for the one-way pull of so many similar decreases, thus preventing the fabric from going too far on the bias. Since the basis of the pattern is a purled garter stitch, it is quite loose and stretches very readily.

Odd number of sts.

Row 1 (Right side)—Purl.
Row 2—Purl.
Row 3—K1, * yo, ssk; rep from *.
Row 4—Purl.

Repeat Rows 1–4.

Barred Knit Pattern

Barred Knit Pattern

This is a "basic idea" pattern. The technique of passing a yarn-over stitch over subsequent knit stitches to form a horizontal bar is one that is capable of much variation. See also Barred Braid Cable.

Multiple of 6 sts plus 5.

Row 1 (Wrong side) and all other wrong-side rows—Purl.
Rows 2, 4, and 6—K4, * yo, k3, pass yo over last 3 knit sts, k3; rep from *, end k1.
Rows 8, 10, and 12—K1, * yo, k3, pass yo over last 3 knit sts, k3; rep from *, end yo, k3, pass yo over 3 knit sts, k1.

Repeat Rows 1–12.

Embossed Leaf Pattern

Embossed Leaf Pattern

Here is a handsome traditional German pattern, good for bedspreads, fancy blouses, scarves, or hats. The "leaves" stand out in very high relief, to make a most interesting fabric.

Multiple of 8 sts plus 7.

Row 1 (Right side)—P7, * k1, p7; rep from *.
Row 2—K7, * p1, k7; rep from *.
Row 3—P7, * lift running thread between st just worked and the next st, and knit into *back* of this thread (Make One or M1); k1, M1, p7; rep from *.
Row 4—K7, * p3, k7; rep from *.

Row 5—P7, * (k1, yo) twice, k1, p7; rep from *.
Row 6—K7, * p5, k7; rep from *.
Row 7—P7, * k2, yo, k1, yo, k2, p7; rep from *.
Row 8—K7, * p7, k7; rep from *.
Row 9—P7, * k2, sl 2 knitwise—k1—p2sso, k2, p7, rep from *.
Row 10—Repeat Row 6.
Row 11—P7, * k1, sl 2 knitwise—k1—p2sso, k1, p7; rep from *.
Row 12—Repeat Row 4.
Row 13—P7, * sl 2 knitwise—k1—p2sso, p7; rep from *.
Row 14—Repeat Row 2.
Row 15—P3, * k1, p7; rep from *, end k1, p3.
Row 16—K3, * p1, k7; rep from *, end p1, k3.
Row 17—P3, * M1, k1, M1, p7; rep from *, end M1, k1, M1, p3.
Row 18—K3, * p3, k7; rep from *, end p3, k3.
Row 19—P3, * (k1, yo) twice, k1, p7; rep from *, end (k1, yo) twice, k1, p3.
Row 20—K3, * p5, k7; rep from *, end p5, k3.
Row 21—P3, * k2, yo, k1, yo, k2, p7; rep from *, end k2, yo, k1, yo, k2, p3.
Row 22—K3, * p7, k7; rep from *, end p7, k3.
Row 23—P3, * k2, sl 2 knitwise—k1—p2sso, k2, p7; rep from *, end k2, sl 2 knitwise—k1—p2sso, k2, p3.
Row 24—Repeat Row 20.
Row 25—P3, * k1, sl 2 knitwise—k1—p2sso, k1, p7; rep from *, end k1, sl 2 knitwise—k1—p2sso, k1, p3.
Row 26—Repeat Row 18.
Row 27—P3, * sl 2 knitwise—k1—p2sso, p7; rep from *, end sl 2 knitwise—k1—p2sso, p3.
Row 28—Repeat Row 16.

Repeat Rows 1–28.

Daisy Stitch

This beautiful fabric is a relative of Trinity Stitch, although both technique and appearance are different. Daisy Stitch is definitely feminine, dressy, and decorative. It can be used in many ways to make delightful garments for women and girls, or pretty baby blankets. It makes a flat, shapely piece, requiring little or no blocking.

Multiple of 4 sts plus 1.

Rows 1 and 3 (Right side)—Knit.
Row 2—K1, * p3 tog, yo (wrapping yarn completely around needle), p same 3 sts tog again, k1; rep from *.
Row 4—K1, p1, k1, * p3 tog, yo, p same 3 sts tog again, k1; rep from *, end p1, k1.

Repeat Rows 1–4.

Daisy Stitch

Yarn-Over Cable

Yarn-Over Cable

This delightfully unusual pattern gives a cable effect without actual cabling, each twist having an eyelet at the center. When repeated over many stitches it makes a handsome ribbed appearance. Stitches are slipped with yarn in back. Note that the stitch count does not remain constant every row.

Multiple of 5 sts plus 2.

Row 1 (Right side)—P2, * sl 1, k2, psso the 2 k sts, p2; rep from *.
Row 2—K2, * p1, yo, p1, k2; rep from *.
Row 3—P2, * k3, p2; rep from *.
Row 4—K2, * p3, k2; rep from *.

Repeat Rows 1–4.

Open Star Stitch

Open Star Stitch

This is another of those lovely, soft, lacy knitting patterns that resemble crochet. The Open Star Stitch stretches very readily, and should be stretched in order to show to best advantage.

Multiple of 3 sts plus 3 edge sts.

Row 1 (Wrong side)—K2, * yo, k3; then insert point of left-hand needle from left to right into the top of the *first* of these 3 k sts, and lift it over the other two and off the right-hand needle, as in psso; rep from *, end k1.
Row 2—Knit, including all yo's.
Row 3—K1, * k3, take first st over the other 2 as before, yo; rep from *, end k2.
Row 4—Knit.

Repeat Rows 1–4.

Palm-Tree Puff

Multiple of 10 sts plus 4.

Row 1 (Right side)—P4, * k1, p4, yo, k1, yo, p4; rep from *.
Row 2—K4, * yo, p3, yo, k4, p1, k4; rep from *.
Row 3—P4, * k1, p4, yo, k5, yo, p4; rep from *.

Row 4—K4, * yo, p7, yo, k4, p1, k4; rep from *.
Row 5—P4, * k1, p4, yo, k9, yo, p4; rep from *.
Row 6—K4, * p2 tog, p7, p2 tog-b, k4, p1, k4; rep from *.
Row 7—P4, * k1, p4, ssk, k5, k2 tog, p4; rep from *.
Row 8—K4, * p2 tog, p3, p2 tog-b, k4, p1, k4; rep from *.
Row 9—P4, * k1, p4, ssk, k1, k2 tog, p4; rep from *.
Row 10—K4, * p3 tog, k4, p1, k4; rep from *.
Row 11—P4, * yo, k1, yo, p4, k1, p4; rep from *.
Row 12—K4, * p1, k4, yo, p3, yo, k4; rep from *.
Row 13—P4, * yo, k5, yo, p4, k1, p4; rep from *.
Row 14—K4, * p1, k4, yo, p7, yo, k4; rep from *.
Row 15—P4, * yo, k9, yo, p4, k1, p4; rep from *.
Row 16—K4, * p1, k4, p2 tog, p7, p2 tog-b, k4; rep from *.
Row 17—P4, * ssk, k5, k2 tog, p4, k1, p4; rep from *.
Row 18—K4, * p1, k4, p2 tog, p3, p2 tog-b, k4; rep from *.
Row 19—P4, * ssk, k1, k2 tog, p4, k1, p4; rep from *.
Row 20—K4, * p1, k4, p3 tog, k4; rep from *.

Repeat Rows 1–20.

CENTER PANEL: *Palm-Tree Puff*
SIDE PANELS: *Quilted Leaf Pattern*

Quilted Leaf Pattern

This pattern is very pretty for a vertical panel accent, or it may be repeated all over the knitted article in stripes, with single knit stitches between the panels, cable fashion. It is very handsome for light knitted blankets and throws, baby articles, etc.

Panel of 9 sts.

Rows 1 and 3 (Right side)—Purl.
Rows 2 and 4—Knit.
Row 5—P2, p2 tog, yo, k1-b, yo, p2 tog, p2.
Row 6—K4, p1-b, k4.
Row 7—P1, p2 tog, yo, k3-b, yo, p2 tog, p1.
Row 8—K3, p3-b, k3.
Row 9—P2 tog, yo, k5-b, yo, p2 tog.
Row 10—K2, p5-b, k2.
Row 11—P1, yo, k2-b, sl 1—k2 tog—psso, k2-b, yo, p1.
Row 12—Repeat Row 10.
Row 13—P2, yo, k1-b, sl 1—k2 tog—psso, k1-b, yo, p2.
Row 14—Repeat Row 8.
Row 15—P3, yo, sl 1—k2 tog—psso, yo, p3.
Row 16—Repeat Row 6.

Repeat Rows 1–16.

Slip-Stitch Mesh

Slip-Stitch Mesh

This is a very easy pattern to work, and a pretty texture for fancy summer sweaters or stoles. The fabric is soft and thick, with a "crochet" look. A most interesting effect can be obtained by introducing a strongly contrasting second color in Rows 3 and 4: the contrasting color will be almost completely concealed, remaining only as a tiny accent around the lower and left-hand edges of the windowlike openings.

Even number of sts.

Row 1 (Right side)—Purl.
Row 2—Knit.
Row 3—K2, * sl 1 wyib, k1; rep from *.
Row 4—* K1, sl 1 wyif; rep from *, end k2.
Row 5—K1, * yo, k2 tog; rep from *, end k1.
Row 6—Purl.

Repeat Rows 1–6.

Shell Cross Stitch

Shell Cross Stitch

This is a pretty texture pattern of Italian origin. It makes use of what might be called the "temporary yarn-over"—that is, a yarn-over made only in order to elongate a stitch, and dropped on the return row. The same kind of yarn-over can be found, for example, in the English Diamond Quilting Pattern.

Multiple of 4 sts plus 2.

Row 1 (Wrong side)—Purl.
Row 2—K1, * yo, k1; rep from * to last st, end k1.
Row 3—Purl, dropping all yo's off needle.
Row 4—K1, * knit into 4th st on left-hand needle, then into 3rd st on left-hand needle; then knit the 1st st on left-hand needle and sl this st from needle; then knit the 2nd st and sl all 3 sts from needle together; rep from *, end k1.
Row 5—Purl.
Row 6—K2, * yo, k1; rep from * to last 2 sts, end k2.
Row 7—Purl, dropping all yo's off needle.
Row 8—K3, * knit 4th and 3rd sts, knit 1st st and sl from needle, knit 2nd st and sl all 3 sts together as in Row 4; rep from *, end k3.

Repeat Rows 1–8.

Brioche Stockinette

This pattern gives a loose, soft weave good for scarves, bed-jackets and robes.

Odd number of sts.

NOTE: When slipping sts, slip all sts *as if to knit.*

Row 1 (Right side)—Sl 1, * yo, sl 1, k1; rep from *.
Row 2—Sl 1, * p2 tog (yo st and next st), p1; rep from *, end p2 tog, k1.
Row 3—Sl 1, * k1, yo, sl 1; rep from *, end k2.
Row 4—Sl 1, * p1, p2 tog; rep from *, end p1, k1.

Repeat Rows 1–4.

Brioche Stockinette

Double Brioche or Three-Dimensional Honeycomb

This fabric has a soft, fluffy texture with a very interesting appearance. It is delightful for baby blankets, sweaters, or (in fine yarn) for scarves. Knitted in fine yarn on large needles it resembles a lace.

KNIT VERSION

NOTE: There are two preparatory rows. All sl-sts are slipped with yarn in back. Bind off on the right side, knitting together the k1 and yo of last row as one stitch.

Even number of sts.

Row 1 (Wrong side)—* K1, yo, sl 1; rep from *.
Row 2—K1, * sl the yo st, k2; rep from *, end sl yo st, k1.
Row 3—* Yo, sl 1, k2 tog (the yo st and next st); rep from *.
Row 4—* K2, sl the yo st; rep from *.
Row 5—* K2 tog (the yo st and next st), yo, sl 1; rep from *.
Row 6—K1, * sl the yo st, k2; rep from *, end sl yo st, k1.

Repeat Rows 3–6.

*Double Brioche or
Three-Dimensional Honeycomb*

PURL VERSION

NOTE: There are two preparatory rows. On right side (odd-numbered rows) sl all sl-sts with yarn in back; on wrong side (even-numbered rows) sl all sl-sts with yarn in front. This version looks the same as Knit Version, but just a trifle looser.

PATTERNS MADE WITH YARN-OVER STITCHES   157

Even number of sts.

Row 1 (Right side)—* Yo, sl 1, k1; rep from *.
Row 2—P1, * sl the yo st, p2; rep from *, end sl yo st, p1.
Row 3—* P2 tog (st and yo), yo, sl 1; rep from *. (Be careful that the last yo remains on the needle, wrapping around it as the work is turned.)
Row 4—* Skip 1 st and sl the yo over this st, then p the st, p1; rep from *.
Row 5—* Yo, sl 1, p2 tog (st and yo); rep from *.
Row 6—P1, * sl yo st over the st, p2; rep from *, end sl yo st, p1.

Repeat Rows 3–6.

Syncopated Brioche Stitch

Syncopated Brioche Stitch

The fascinating Syncopated Brioche is a fluffy lace pattern when worked in fine yarn on large needles, and a soft texture pattern when worked in medium-weight yarn, with a solid appearance. It combines Brioche Stitch (see Ribbings) with the so-called Turkish Brioche, which is simply Brioche Stitch worked backward. The result has a broken-rib checked effect. The fabric is reversible.

Even number of sts.

Row 1 (Preparation row)—* Yo, sl 1 wyib, k1; rep from *.
Row 2—* Yo, sl 1 wyib, k2 tog; rep from *.
Rows 3, 4, 5, 6, and 7—Repeat Row 2.
Rows 8—* Sl 1 wyif, yo, p2 tog; rep from *.
Rows 9, 10, 11, 12, and 13—Repeat Row 8.

Repeat Rows 2–13.

Waffle Brioche or Plaited Brioche

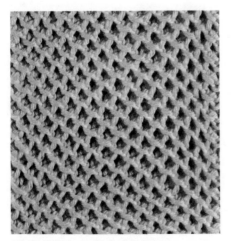

Waffle Brioche or Plaited Brioche

If this pattern is not familiar to you, it can be rather tricky to begin. But once learned, it works easily and quickly. It is a pattern well worth learning; its lovely soft texture is adaptable to dozens of things: scarves, cosy sweaters, babies' wear, dresses. It is very pretty when done in fine yarn.

Remember that all slipped stitches, whether a stitch or a yo, are done as if to knit. On the repeats of Rows 1 and 3, the two sts that are knitted together through their back loops are a yo and a stitch, not two knitted sts. On the repeats of Rows 2 and 4, care must be taken to knit the two knitted sts from the previous row and *not* the yo. The second of these two sts will be slightly behind the yo, which sometimes will have to be pushed aside to get the needle point to the front loop of the stitch. Work loosely.

Multiple of 3 sts plus 2.

NOTE: All sl-sts are slipped knitwise and with yarn in back.

Row 1 (Wrong side)—K1, * yo, sl 1, k2 tog-b; rep from *, end k1.

Row 2—K3, * sl 1, k2; rep from *, end sl 1, k1. (All slipped sts are the yo's of previous row.)

Row 3—K1, * k2 tog-b, yo, sl 1; rep from *, end k1.

Row 4—K2, * sl 1, k2; rep from *. (All slipped sts are the yo's of previous row.)

Repeat Rows 1–4.

Tunisian Rib Stitch

Tunisian Rib Stitch is a Westernization of true Tunisian knitting, which is a special technique, sometimes awkward for Western hands and habits. (See Tunisian Knitting, below). The rib version, however, can be done quite easily by our customary methods. The extra stitch inserted into the pattern holds down the base of the yo stitches and makes them easy to catch on the return row. Tunisian Rib Stitch is dense in the vertical dimension, and hence good for jackets, coats, ski sweaters, and other articles requiring a fabric with warmth and body.

Odd number of sts.

Row 1 (Wrong side)—K1, * yo, sl 1 wyib, k1; rep from *.

Row 2—K1, * k the yo and sl-st of previous row tog through back loops; k1; rep from *.

Repeat Rows 1 and 2.

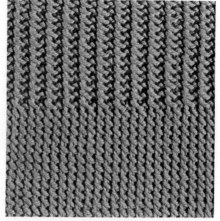

ABOVE: *Tunisian Rib Stitch*
BELOW: *Tunisian Knitting*

Tunisian Knitting

This Eastern method of knitting is fascinating to learn, and once learned it is not difficult. But at first the technique requires concentration, and a few adjustments of tension in yarn and fingers; for it is strange to the Western knitter. Practice is required. The wrong side of a piece of Tunisian knitting is especially interesting. It is a firm and sturdy fabric that looks more like crochet than knitting.

Any number of sts.

Row 1 (Wrong side)—Slip first st knitwise, wyib. Then bring yarn to front between needles and slip next st knitwise, holding yarn in front. * Then take yarn over right needle (yo) and around under needle to front again, as a yo is done before a purl st. Then slip next st knitwise, holding yarn in front. Repeat from * across row. (No sts are knitted on this row;

all sts are slipped knitwise, with the yarn weaving around the needle.) After slipping the last st with the yarn held in front, make the same yo as before, taking the yarn over to the back and under to the front of the needle. This last yo will be loose, and must be held on the needle while the work is turned.

Row 2—Insert right needle purlwise down into the upside-down loop of the last, loose yo of the previous row (which passes under the needle to the back), and * knit the yo together with the next st through *back* loops. Repeat from * across the row, knitting each st together with the yo that lies ahead of it, through the back loops. The last st will be without a yo. K-b the last st.

Repeat Rows 1 and 2.

Candle Flames

This fascinating pattern is based on the well-known Fern or Leaf-Patterned Lace, which consists of eyelets arranged on either side of a single knit stitch and has literally dozens of variations. But "Candle Flames" is a little different. It could perhaps be considered an eyelet pattern, since it does include a bit of openwork, but it is more like a solid-fabric pattern with an embossed design. It is therefore not included among Eyelets but placed in this catchall category of novelty yarn-over patterns.

Candle Flames

Multiple of 12 sts plus 2.

NOTE: In this pattern the number of sts varies from row to row. Accurate count of sts may be made on Rows 12 or 24.

Row 1 (Right side)—* P2, yo, k1, yo, p2, k2, k2 tog, k3; rep from *, end p2.
Row 2—* K2, p6, k2, p3; rep from *, end k2.
Row 3—* P2, k1, (yo, k1) twice, p2, k2, k2 tog, k2; rep from *, end p2.
Row 4—* (K2, p5) twice; rep from *, end k2.
Row 5—* P2, k2, yo, k1, yo, k2, p2, k2, k2 tog, k1; rep from *, end p2.
Row 6—* K2, p4, k2, p7; rep from *, end k2.
Row 7—* P2, k3, yo, k1, yo, k3, p2, k2, k2 tog; rep from *, end p2.
Row 8—* K2, p3, k2, p9; rep from *, end k2.
Row 9—* P2, k2, k2 tog, k5, p2, k1, k2 tog; rep from *, end p2.
Row 10—* K2, p2, k2, p8; rep from *, end k2.
Row 11—* P2, k2, k2 tog, k4, p2, k2 tog; rep from *, end p2.
Row 12—* K2, p1, k2, p7; rep from *, end k2.
Row 13—* P2, k2, k2 tog, k3, p2, yo, k1, yo; rep from *, end p2.
Row 14—* K2, p3, k2, p6; rep from *, end k2.

Row 15—* P2, k2, k2 tog, k2, p2, (k1, yo) twice, k1; rep from *, end p2.
Row 16—* (K2, p5) twice; rep from *, end k2.
Row 17—* P2, k2, k2 tog, k1, p2, k2, yo, k1, yo, k2; rep from *, end p2.
Row 18—* K2, p7, k2, p4; rep from *, end k2.
Row 19—* P2, k2, k2 tog, p2, k3, yo, k1, yo, k3; rep from *, end p2.
Row 20—* K2, p9, k2, p3; rep from *, end k2.
Row 21—* P2, k1, k2 tog, p2, k2, k2 tog, k5; rep from *, end p2.
Row 22—* K2, p8, k2, p2; rep from *, end k2.
Row 23—* P2, k2 tog, p2, k2, k2 tog, k4; rep from *, end p2.
Row 24—* K2, p7, k2, p1; rep from *, end k2.

Repeat Rows 1–24.

Filigree Pattern

As given, this pattern uses twisted stitches, but they may be worked plain if desired, or alternatively, crossed only on the right-side rows.

Multiple of 14 sts plus 3.

Row 1 (Right side)—K1, * p2, ssk, k3-b, yo, k1-b, yo, k3-b, k2 tog, p1; rep from *, end p1, k1.
Row 2—K2, * k1, p4-b, p1, p1-b, p1, p4-b, k2; rep from *, end k1.
Row 3—K1, * p2, ssk, k2-b, yo, k3-b, yo, k2-b, k2 tog, p1; rep from *, end p1, k1.
Row 4—K2, * k1, (p3-b, p1) twice, p3-b, k2; rep from *, end k1.
Row 5—K1, * p2, ssk, k1-b, yo, k5-b, yo, k1-b, k2 tog, p1; rep from *, end p1, k1.
Row 6—K2, * k1, p2-b, p1, p5-b, p1, p2-b, k2; rep from *, end k1.
Row 7—K1, * k1-b, yo, k3-b, k2 tog, p3, ssk, k3-b, yo; rep from *, end k1-b, k1.
Row 8—K1, p1-b, * p1, p4-b, k3, p4-b, p1, p1-b; rep from *, end k1.
Row 9—K1, * k2-b, yo, k2-b, k2 tog, p3, ssk, k2-b, yo, k1-b; rep from *, end k1-b, k1.
Row 10—K1, p1-b, * p1-b, p1, p3-b, k3, p3-b, p1, p2-b; rep from *, end k1.
Row 11—K1, * k3-b, yo, k1-b, k2 tog, p3, ssk, k1-b, yo, k2-b; rep from *, end k1-b, k1.
Row 12—K1, p1-b, * p2-b, p1, p2-b, k3, p2-b, p1, p3-b; rep from *, end k1.

Repeat Rows 1–12.

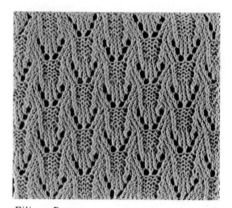

Filigree Pattern

Openwork Hourglass

There are two ways of working this pattern. The first, with all knit stitches showing on the right side, is smoother and more lace-like; the second, with purl stitches to set off the hourglass shapes of the decreases, has a rougher texture and greater depth.

I. KNIT VERSION

Multiple of 6 sts plus 2.

Row 1 (Right side)—K2, * yo, ssk, k2 tog, yo, k2; rep from *.
Row 2—Purl.
Row 3—K2, * k2 tog, (yo) twice, ssk, k2; rep from *.
Row 4—P3, * (k1, p1) into the double yo, p4; rep from *, end last repeat p3.
Row 5—K1, * k2 tog, yo, k2, yo, ssk; rep from *, end k1.
Row 6—Purl.
Row 7—K1, yo, * ssk, k2, k2 tog, (yo) twice; rep from *, end ssk, k2, k2 tog, yo, k1.
Row 8—P6, * (k1, p1) into the double yo, p4; rep from *, end p2.

Repeat Rows 1–8.

II. PURL VERSION

Multiple of 6 sts plus 2.

Row 1 (Right side)—P2, * yo, ssk, k2 tog, yo, p2; rep from *.
Row 2—K2, * p4, k2; rep from *.
Row 3—P2, * k2 tog, (yo) twice, ssk, p2; rep from *.
Row 4—K2, * p1, (k1, p1) into the double yo, p1, k2; rep from *.
Row 5—P1, * k2 tog, yo, p2, yo, ssk; rep from *, end p1.
Row 6—K1, * p2, k2, p2; rep from *, end k1.
Row 7—P1, yo, * ssk, p2, k2 tog, (yo) twice; rep from *, end ssk, p2, k2 tog, yo, p1.
Row 8—K1, p2, * k2, p1, (k1, p1) into the double yo, p1; rep from *, end k2, p2, k1.

Repeat Rows 1–8.

Openwork Hourglass
ABOVE: *Knit version*
BELOW: *Purl version*

Umbrella Pattern

Here is an ingenious pattern from Germany. The decreases are hidden in the purl stitches between the ribs of the "umbrella", so that these ribs converge smoothly. The pattern is novel enough to be a successful single-panel feature in a plain garment, when not used as an allover pattern.

Multiple of 18 sts plus 1.

Row 1 (Wrong side)—* P1, (p1, k3) 4 times, p1; rep from *, end p1.

Row 2—* K1, yo, k1, p2 tog, p1, (k1, p3) twice, k1, p1, p2 tog, k1, yo; rep from *, end k1.

Row 3—* P3, k2, (p1, k3) twice, p1, k2, p2; rep from *, end p1.

Row 4—* K2, yo, k1, p2, (k1, p1, p2 tog) twice, k1, p2, k1, yo, k1; rep from *, end k1.

Row 5—* P3, (p1, k2) 4 times, p3; rep from *, end p1.

Row 6—* K3, yo, k1, p2 tog, (k1, p2) twice, k1, p2 tog, k1, yo, k2; rep from *, end k1.

Row 7—* P5, k1, (p1, k2) twice, p1, k1, p4; rep from *, end p1.

Row 8—* K4, yo, k1, p1, (k1, p2 tog) twice, k1, p1, k1, yo, k3; rep from *, end k1.

Row 9—* P5, (p1, k1) 4 times, p5; rep from *, end p1.

Row 10—* K5, yo, ssk, (k1, p1) twice, k1, k2 tog, yo, k4; rep from *, end k1.

Row 11—* P8, k1, p1, k1, p7; rep from *, end p1.

Row 12—* K8, p1, k1, p1, k7; rep from *, end k1.

Repeat Rows 1–12.

Umbrella Pattern

Wave and Shield Pattern

This graceful, lacy fabric with its pretty curves and its combination of knit and purl textures is quite easy to work, and remarkably effective in evening wear or fancy fine-yarn sweaters. It is less open than a true lace but has the same general quality.

Multiple of 14 sts plus 1.

Row 1 (Right side)—K1, * yo, k2, p3, p3 tog, p3, k2, yo, k1; rep from *.

Row 2—* P4, k7, p3; rep from *, end p1.

Row 3—K1, * k1, yo, k2, p2, p3 tog, p2, k2, yo, k2; rep from *.

Row 4—* P5, k5, p4; rep from *, end p1.

Row 5—K1, * k2, yo, k2, p1, p3 tog, p1, k2, yo, k3; rep from *.

Row 6—* P6, k3, p5; rep from *, end p1.

Row 7—K1, * k3, yo, k2, p3 tog, k2, yo, k4; rep from *.

Row 8—* P7, k1, p6; rep from *, end p1.

Row 9—P2 tog, * p3, k2, yo, k1, yo, k2, p3, p3 tog; rep from *, end last repeat p2 tog.

Row 10—* K4, p7, k3; rep from *, end k1.

Row 11—P2 tog, * p2, k2, yo, k3, yo, k2, p2, p3 tog; rep from *, end last repeat p2 tog.

Row 12—* K3, p9, k2; rep from *, end k1.

Row 13—P2 tog, * p1, k2, yo, k5, yo, k2, p1, p3 tog; rep from *, end last repeat p2 tog.

Wave and Shield Pattern

PATTERNS MADE WITH YARN-OVER STITCHES   163

Row 14—* K2, p11, k1; rep from *, end k1.
Row 15—P2 tog, * k2, yo, k7, yo, k2, p3 tog; rep from *, end last repeat p2 tog.
Row 16—* K1, p13; rep from *, end k1.

Repeat Rows 1–16.

Pine Trees, Version I

Even the most cursory examination will reveal that this pattern is simply the first half of Wave and Shield Pattern without its second half. It lacks the graceful waving curves of the Wave and Shield, therefore, and instead forms abruptly truncated triangles.

Multiple of 14 sts plus 1.

Row 1 (Right side)—K1, * yo, k2, p3, p3 tog, p3, k2, yo, k1; rep from *.
Row 2—* P4, k7, p3; rep from *, end p1.
Row 3—K1, * k1, yo, k2, p2, p3 tog, p2, k2, yo, k2; rep from *.
Row 4—* P5, k5, p4; rep from *, end p1.
Row 5—K1, * k2, yo, k2, p1, p3 tog, p1, k2, yo, k3; rep from *.
Row 6—* P6, k3, p5; rep from *, end p1.
Row 7—K1, * k3, yo, k2, p3 tog, k2, yo, k4; rep from *.
Row 8—* P7, k1, p6; rep from *, end p1.
Row 9—K1, * k4, yo, k1, sl 1—k2 tog—psso, k1, yo, k5; rep from *.
Row 10—Purl.
Row 11—K1, * k5, yo, sl 1—k2 tog—psso, yo, k6; rep from *.
Row 12—Purl.

Repeat Rows 1–12.

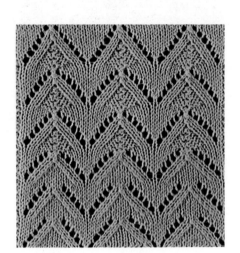

ABOVE: *Pine Trees, Version I*
BELOW: *Pine Trees, Version II*

Pine Trees, Version II

In Version II the decreases are moved away from the center of the pattern, the purl stitches are eliminated, and the pattern comes very close to a Lace Chevron.

Multiple of 14 sts plus 1.

Row 1 (Wrong side) and all other wrong-side rows—Purl.
Row 2—K1, * yo, k1, ssk, k7, k2 tog, k1, yo, k1; rep from *.
Row 4—K1, * k1, yo, k1, ssk, k5, k2 tog, k1, yo, k2; rep from *.
Row 6—K1, * k2, yo, k1, ssk, k3, k2 tog, k1, yo, k3; rep from *.
Row 8—K1, * k3, yo, k1, ssk, k1, k2 tog, k1, yo, k4; rep from *.
Row 10—K1, * k4, yo, k1, sl 1—k2 tog—psso, k1, yo, k5; rep from *.

Repeat Rows 1–10.

Crochet-Knit Shell Pattern

This does resemble a dainty crocheted shell. It is loose and lacy, and to be most successful it should be knitted with very fine yarn and needles. Several repeats of the pattern rows will make a lovely border for collars, cuffs, gauntlets of lace or openwork gloves, or the hem of an overblouse—the number of rows worked depending upon the depth of border wanted.

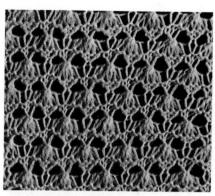

Crochet-Knit Shell Pattern

Multiple of 6 sts plus 3.

Row 1 (Wrong side)—K1, * yo, k1; rep from *, end k1.
Row 2—Knit, dropping all yo's of previous row off needle.
Row 3—K1, k3 tog, * (yo) twice, k1, (yo) twice, sl 2—k3 tog— p2sso; rep from *, end (yo) twice, k1, (yo) twice, k3 tog, k1.
Row 4—K1, * k1, k into front and back of double yo; rep from *, end k2.
Rows 5 and 6—Repeat Rows 1 and 2.
Row 7—K1, * k1, (yo) twice, sl 2—k3 tog—p2sso, (yo) twice; rep from *, end k2.
Row 8—Repeat Row 4.

Repeat Rows 1–8.

Veil Stitch

This is not so much a pattern as a fancy way of knitting. Essentially it is an elongated garter stitch, with the base of each stitch twisted by the manner in which the yarn is passed over and around the needles. Its usefulness is not limited to the making of veils; a few rows of Veil Stitch make very attractive horizontal insertions in a solid fabric, and as an allover mesh with plenty of stretch it is good for gloves, stockings, and other openwork articles. The directions seem more complicated than they really are. Once the technique is learned, and the fingers "understand" the action, the knitting goes quickly.

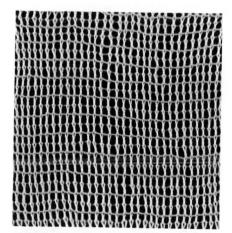

Veil Stitch

Any number of sts.

Every stitch on every row is worked as follows: insert needle into the stitch as if to knit, then bring yarn from under the right-hand needle forward between the crossed needle points (i.e., to a "purl position" beneath the left-hand needle); then up in front of, and over the top of, the *left-* hand needle; then to the back over the top of the right-hand needle, then down in back and under the right-hand needle. Then knit the stitch, bringing out the last strand that was passed under the right-hand needle, and passing the point of the right-hand needle, as it is removed from the stitch, beneath and clear of the crossed strands still on the left-hand needle. As the stitch is completed, these strands are dropped off the left-hand needle to form the twisted base of the stitch.

Shell Mesh

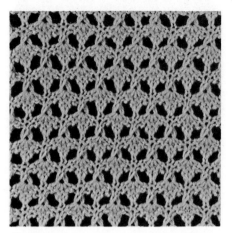

Shell Mesh

This pattern is similar to the Crochet-Knit Shell Pattern, but with a few significant differences. The loose and wavy quality of the crochet-knit version disappears here, to be replaced by a square filet-like effect. The mesh is firmer, and therefore applicable to a wider variety of uses. The pattern is worked from the wrong side instead of from the right side, and it goes more quickly and easily.

Multiple of 6 sts plus 1.

Row 1 (Wrong side)—Knit.

Row 2—Knit.

Row 3—P1, * (yo) twice, sl 2 wyif, p3 tog, p2sso, (yo) twice, p1; rep from *.

Row 4—K1, * (k1, p1) into double yo, k1, (p1, k1) into next double yo, k1; rep from *.

Rows 5 and 6—Knit.

Row 7—P3 tog, * (yo) twice, p1, (yo) twice, sl 2 wyif, p3 tog, p2sso; rep from *, end (yo) twice, p1, (yo) twice, p3 tog.

Row 8—K1, * (p1, k1) into double yo, k1, (k1, p1) into next double yo, k1; rep from *.

Repeat Rows 1–8.

Diagonal Demi-Brioche

This pattern is similar to other Brioche patterns in that the pattern row incorporates a slip-stitch and a yo. But there the resemblance ends. The slip-stitches which are passed over two subsequent stitches make a diagonal texture pattern.

Diagonal Demi-Brioche works well in two colors. It will make either of two differently shaped horizontal stripes, depending on which rows take the contrasting color. If the contrasting yarn is introduced in Rows 3 and 4, then the stripes will look scalloped, neatly overlapping like fish scales. If, instead, the contrasting yarn is introduced in Rows 2 and 3, then the stripes will look rather spiky. In both cases the diagonal line will become less evident because of the strong horizontal contrast.

ABOVE: *Diagonal Demi-Brioche*
CENTER: *Contrasting color in Rows 3 and 4*
BELOW: *Contrasting color in Rows 2 and 3*

Even number of sts.

Rows 1 and 3 (Wrong side)—Purl.

Row 2—* Sl 1 wyib, yo, k1, pass sl-st over the yo and knit st; rep from *.

Row 4—K1, * rep from * of Row 2 across to last st, k1.

Repeat Rows 1–4.

Crested Medallion

The oval "medallions" here are made with contrasting color, and the yarn-overs constitute increases which are not compensated for until four rows later, where decreases are worked to restore the original number of stitches. Each of the decreases includes a Color A slip-stitch carried from four rows below, and an adjacent Color B stitch from the preceding row.

Crested Medallion

Multiple of 12 sts plus 3. Colors A and B.

Note: on right-side (even-numbered) rows sl all sl-sts with yarn in back; on wrong-side (odd-numbered) rows sl all sl-sts with yarn in front.

Row 1 (Wrong side)—With A, knit.
Row 2—With B, k6, * (sl 1, yo) twice, sl 1, k9; rep from *, end last repeat k6. (On this row care must be taken to keep the 2 yo's strictly positioned between the 3 sl-sts. The central arrangement will be a double yo in Color B sts divided by a slipped Color A st.)
Row 3—With B, p6, * sl 1, purl the 1st yo, sl 1, knit the next yo, sl 1, p9; rep from *, end last repeat p6. (Be sure each Color A sl-st is slipped onto right-hand needle *before* the following yo is worked.)
Row 4—With B, k6, * (sl 1, k1) twice, sl 1, k9; rep from *, end last repeat k6.
Row 5—With B, p6, * (sl 1, p1) twice, sl 1, p9; rep from *, end last repeat p6.
Row 6—With A, k5, * k2 tog, k3, ssk, k7; rep from *, end last repeat k5.
Row 7—With A, knit.
Row 8—With B, k1, sl 1, yo, sl 1, * k9, (sl 1, yo) twice, sl 1; rep from *, end k9, sl 1, yo, sl 1, k1.
Row 9—With B, (p1, sl 1) twice, * p9, sl 1, purl the 1st yo, sl 1, knit the next yo, sl 1; rep from *, end p9, (sl 1, p1) twice.
Row 10—With B, (k1, sl 1) twice, * k9, (sl 1, k1) twice, sl 1; rep from *, end k9, (sl 1, k1) twice.
Row 11—With B, (p1, sl 1) twice, * p9, (sl 1, p1) twice, sl 1; rep from *, end p9, (sl 1, p1) twice.
Row 12—With A, k3, * ssk, k7, k2 tog, k3; rep from *.

Repeat Rows 1–12.

CHAPTER NINE

Eyelet Patterns

The distinction between Eyelet Patterns and Lace is a subtle one, and rather arbitrary since there are a number of patterns that could be classified either way. Broadly speaking, the Eyelet Pattern is less open than Lace. Lace is an openwork fabric, while the Eyelet Pattern is a solid fabric pierced by openings arranged in various ways. But this definition will not hold true for every pattern in either category.

Eyelet Patterns are charming in dresses, blouses, fancy sweaters, dressy gloves, head scarves, baby clothes and the like. Their outstanding quality is daintiness, and thus they should be worked in fine yarn so that the pattern is kept small. As in a lace, or any other pattern formed of openings, the fabric will have some tendency to spread. It may be stretched into a larger shape, but it must never be compressed, lest the openings that make the pattern be lost. Therefore the knitter must beware of casting on too many stitches or making the article too big. When in doubt cast on fewer stitches rather than more. To take your gauge from a test swatch, first block the swatch while it is stretched tight.

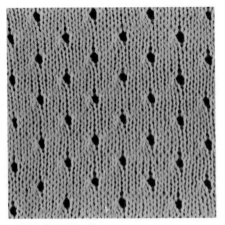

Simple Eyelet Pattern

Simple Eyelet Pattern

Simple eyelets are formed either by "yo, k2 tog" or by "yo, ssk". The former is given here, but the latter may be used if a slightly more open eyelet is desired.

Multiple of 8 sts.

Row 1 (Right side)—Knit.
Row 2 and all other wrong-side rows—Purl.
Row 3—* K6, yo, k2 tog, rep from *.
Row 5—Knit.
Row 7—K2, * yo, k2 tog, k6; rep from *, end last rep k4.
Row 8—Purl.

Repeat Rows 1–8.

Zigzag Eyelet Pattern

Multiple of 11 sts plus 2.

Row 1 (Wrong side) and all other wrong-side rows—Purl.
Row 2—K6, * yo, ssk, k9; rep from *, end last rep k5.
Row 4—K7, * yo, ssk, k9; rep from *, end last rep k4.
Row 6—K3, * k2 tog, yo, k3, yo, ssk, k4; rep from *, end last rep k3.
Row 8—* K2, k2 tog, yo, k5, yo, ssk; rep from *, end k2.
Row 10—K1, * k2 tog, yo, k9; rep from *, end k1.
Row 12—* K2 tog, yo, k9; rep from *, end k2.

Repeat Rows 1–12.

Zigzag Eyelet Pattern

Cloverleaf Eyelet Pattern

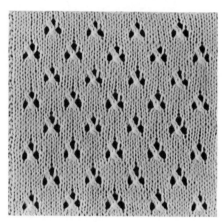

This is a pretty, crisp little eyelet that can be substituted for Stockinette Stitch in almost any garment. It is a good allover pattern for fine-yarn sweaters, dresses, etc.

Multiple of 8 sts plus 7.

Row 1 (Wrong side) and all other wrong-side rows—Purl.
Row 2—Knit.
Row 4—K2, yo, sl 1—k2 tog—psso, yo, * k5, yo, sl 1—k2 tog—psso, yo; rep from *, end k2.
Row 6—K3, yo, ssk, * k6, yo, ssk; rep from *, end k2.
Row 8—Knit.
Row 10—K1, * k5, yo, sl 1—k2 tog—psso, yo; rep from *, end k6.
Row 12—K7, * yo, ssk, k6; rep from *.

Repeat Rows 1–12.

Cloverleaf Eyelet Pattern

Traveling Ribbed Eyelet

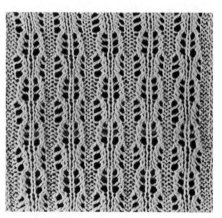

Multiple of 7 sts plus 6.

Row 1 (Wrong side)—and all other wrong-side rows—K2, * k2, p5; rep from *, end k4.
Rows 2, 4, and 6—K2, * p2, yo, ssk, k1, k2 tog, yo; rep from *, end p2, k2.
Row 8—K2, * p2, k5; rep from *, end p2, k2.
Rows 10, 12, and 14—K2, * p2, k2 tog, yo, k1, yo, ssk; rep from *, end p2, k2.
Row 16—Repeat Row 8.

Repeat Rows 1–16.

Traveling Ribbed Eyelet

Cloverleaf Eyelet Rib

The Cloverleaf Eyelet is beautifully adapted to vertical patterns, such as the Cloverleaf Eyelet Rib and Cloverleaf Eyelet Cable. In this Rib variation, the pattern could be widened by working on a multiple of 7 sts plus 2, inserting 2 purl sts between ribs instead of one.

LEFT: *Cloverleaf Eyelet Rib*
RIGHT: *Cloverleaf Eyelet Cable*

Multiple of 6 sts plus 1.

Rows 1, 3, and 5 (Wrong side)—K1, * p5, k1; rep from *.
Row 2—P1, * k1, yo, sl 1—k2 tog—psso, yo, k1, p1; rep from *.
Row 4—P1, * k2, yo, ssk, k1, p1; rep from *.
Row 6—P1, * k5, p1; rep from *.

Repeat Rows 1–6.

Cloverleaf Eyelet Cable

Because of the slant of the decreases, the Cloverleaf Eyelet in vertical arrangement can be made to resemble a dainty little cable done in openwork. This cable pattern also makes a very attractive fancy ribbing when worked on a multiple of 5 sts plus 2—i.e., three cable sts with 2 purl sts in between.

Panel of 7 sts.

Rows 1, 3, and 5 (Wrong side)—K2, p3, k2.
Row 2—P2, yo, sl 1—k2 tog—psso, yo, p2.
Row 4—P2, k1, yo, ssk, p2.
Row 6—P2, k3, p2.

Repeat Rows 1–6.

Raindrops

An embossed design of knit stitches on a purled ground, with eyelets setting off the knit-stitch "drops". There are many possibilities for varying this pattern.

Multiple of 6 sts plus 5.

NOTE: Stitch count does not remain constant. Accurate count may be taken on rows 6 or 12.

Row 1 (Right side)—P5, * k1, yo, p5; rep from *.
Rows 2 and 4—K5, * p2, k5; rep from *.
Rows 3 and 5—P5, * k2, p5; rep from *.
Row 6—K5, * p2 tog, k5; rep from *.

Row 7—P2, * k1, yo, p5; rep from *, end k1, yo, p2.
Rows 8 and 10—K2, * p2, k5; rep from *, end p2, k2.
Rows 9 and 11—P2, * k2, p5; rep from *, end k2, p2.
Row 12—K2, * p2 tog, k5; rep from *, end p2 tog, k2.

Repeat Rows 1–12.

Bluebell Pattern

If this pattern is worked upside down, as in a garment knitted from the top, it is best described as Tulip Pattern.

Multiple of 6 sts plus 5.

Row 1 (Right side)—P2, * k1, p5; rep from *, end k1, p2.
Row 2—K2, * p1, k5; rep from *, end p1, k2.
Row 3—P5, * yo, k1, yo, p5; rep from *.
Rows 4, 6, and 8—K5, * p3, k5; rep from *.
Rows 5 and 7—P5, * k3, p5; rep from *.
Row 9—P5, * sl 1—k2 tog—psso, p5; rep from *.
Rows 10 and 12—K5, * p1, k5; rep from *.
Row 11—P5, * k1, p5; rep from *.
Row 13—P2, * yo, k1, yo, p5; rep from *, end yo, k1, yo, p2.
Rows 14, 16, and 18—K2, * p3, k5; rep from *, end p3, k2.
Rows 15 and 17—P2, * k3, p5; rep from *, end k3, p2.
Row 19—P2, * sl 1—k2 tog—psso, p5; rep from *, end sl 1—k2 tog—psso, p2.
Row 20—Repeat Row 2.

Repeat Rows 1–20.

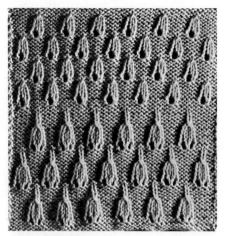

ABOVE: *Raindrops*
BELOW: *Bluebell Pattern*

Quatrefoil Eyelet

Multiple of 8 sts.

Row 1 (Wrong side) and all other wrong-side rows—Purl.
Row 2—Knit.
Row 4—K3, * yo, ssk, k6, * rep from * to *, end last rep k3 instead of k6.
Row 6—K1, * k2 tog, yo, k1, yo, ssk, k3; * rep from * to *, end last rep k2 instead of k3.
Row 8—Repeat Row 4.
Row 10—Knit.
Row 12—K7, repeat from * to * of Row 4, end k1.
Row 14—K5, repeat from * to * of Row 6, end k3.
Row 16—Repeat Row 12.

Repeat Rows 1–16.

Quatrefoil Eyelet

Eyelet Check

Eyelet Check

In this pattern, eyelets are placed in small purled checks on a knit-stitch ground. There are many variations to this, due to the fact that the eyelet checks may be placed various distances from each other, and may be worked in diamonds or other shapes.

Multiple of 8 sts plus 3.

Row 1 (Right side)—K2, * p3, k5; rep from *, end k1.
Row 2—P1, * p5, k3; rep from *, end p2.
Row 3—K2, * p1, yo, p2 tog, k5; rep from *, end k1.
Row 4—P1, * p5, k3; rep from *, end p2.
Row 5—K2, * p3, k5; rep from *, end k1.
Row 6—Purl.
Row 7—K1, * k5, p3; rep from *, end k2.
Row 8—P2, * k3, p5; rep from *, end p1.
Row 9—K1, * k5, p1, yo, p2 tog; rep from *, end k2.
Row 10—P2, * k3, p5; rep from *, end p1.
Row 11—K1, * k5, p3; rep from *, end k2.
Row 12—Purl.

Repeat Rows 1–12.

Diamond Eyelet Pattern

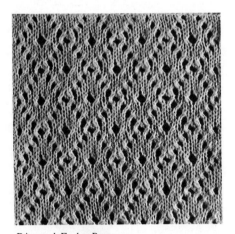

Diamond Eyelet Pattern

This lovely eyelet pattern could be called a type of lace. But note that the openings are divided not by a single strand, but by the entire decrease.

Multiple of 10 sts plus 4.

Row 1 (Right side)—K2, yo, ssk, * k1, k2 tog, (yo) twice, ssk; rep from * to last 5 sts, k1, k2 tog, yo, k2.
Row 2 and all other wrong-side rows—Purl. Throughout rows 2 and 10, purl into the front and back of every "(yo) twice" of previous row.
Row 3—K2, * k2 tog, yo, k6, yo, ssk; rep from *, end k2.
Row 5—K3, * k2 tog, yo, k4, yo, ssk, k2; rep from *, end k1.
Row 7—K4, * k2 tog, yo, k2, yo, ssk, k4; rep from *.
Row 9—K2, yo, ssk, * k1, k2 tog, (yo) twice, ssk; rep from * to last 5 sts, k1, k2 tog, yo, k2.
Row 11—K5, * yo, ssk, k2 tog, yo, k6; rep from *, end last rep k5.
Row 13—K4, * yo, ssk, k2, k2 tog, yo, k4; rep from *.
Row 15—K3, * yo, ssk, k4, k2 tog, yo, k2; rep from *, end k1.
Row 16—Purl.

Repeat Rows 1–16.

Hourglass Eyelet Pattern

The wrong side of this pattern is an amusing little surprise. After working a swatch look at the wrong side, and see if you, too, think of . . . baby elephants!

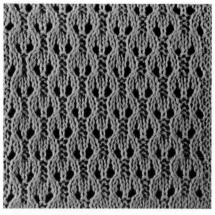

Multiple of 6 sts plus 1.

Row 1 (Right side)—K6, * p1, k5; rep from *, end k1.
Row 2—K1, * p5, k1; rep from *.
Row 3—K1, * yo, ssk, p1, k2 tog, yo, k1; rep from *.
Row 4—K1, p2, * k1, p5; rep from * to last 4 sts, end k1, p2, k1.
Row 5—K3, * p1, k5; rep from *, end last repeat k3.
Row 6—Repeat Row 4.
Row 7—K1, * k2 tog, yo, k1, yo, ssk, p1; rep from *, end last repeat k1 instead of p1.
Row 8—Repeat Row 2.

Repeat Rows 1–8.

Hourglass Eyelet Pattern

Crown of Glory

The Crown of Glory is a traditional Shetland pattern, which is best worked in fine yarn on small needles because of the very large eyelets caused by the three yarn-overs in Row 3, which form the bottom opening of each "crown". Note that the number of stitches does not remain constant through Rows 1–7, but accurate count may be taken on Rows 8–12.

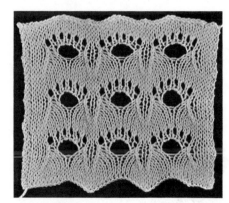

Multiple of 14 sts plus 5.

Row 1 (Right side)—K3, * ssk, k9, k2 tog, k1; rep from *, end k2.
Row 2—P2, * p1, p2 tog, p7, p2 tog-b, rep from *, end p3.
Row 3—K3, * ssk, k2, (yo) 3 times, k3, k2 tog, k1; rep from *, end k2.
Row 4—P2, * p1, p2 tog, p2; make 5 sts out of the large loop formed by 3 yo's of previous row by working (k1, p1) twice, k1 into it; p1, p2 tog-b; rep from *, end p3.
Row 5—K3, * ssk, k6, k2 tog, k1; rep from *, end k2.
Row 6—P2, * p1, p2 tog, p6; rep from *, end p3.
Row 7—K3, * k1, (yo, k1) 6 times, k1; rep from *, end k2.
Row 8—Purl.
Rows 9 and 11—Knit.
Rows 10 and 12—Purl.

Repeat Rows 1–12.

Crown of Glory

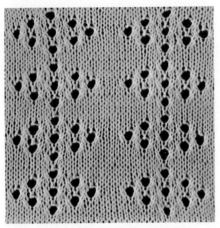

Embroidery Eyelet Pattern

Embroidery Eyelet Pattern

Multiple of 21 sts plus 3.

Row 1 (Wrong side) and all other wrong-side rows—Purl. Special note: throughout pattern, p1 and k1 into every yo.
Row 2—Knit.
Row 4—K10, * k2 tog, yo, ssk, k17; rep from *, end last rep k10.
Row 6—K6, * k2 tog, yo, ssk, k4, k2 tog, yo, ssk, k9; rep from *, end last rep k6.
Row 8—K3, * k2 tog, yo, ssk, k3; rep from * across.
Row 10—Repeat Row 6.
Row 12—Repeat Row 4.

Repeat Rows 1–12.

Eyelets for Threading: Dimple Eyelet and Ridged Ribbon Eyelet

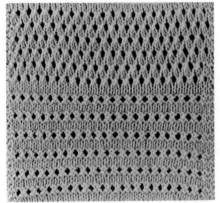

ABOVE: *Dimple Eyelet*
BELOW: *Ridged Ribbon Eyelet*

These two eyelet patterns are not only quite pretty when used unadorned, but also useful where ribbon or some other decorative strand is to be threaded through the fabric. Both patterns make long horizontal rows of holes, and look very nice when a narrow velvet or satin ribbon, or a strand of heavier yarn in a contrasting color, is woven through them. Dimple Eyelet is particularly useful for a gathering ribbon, as around the neckline of a blouse or the hem of a sleeve. Ridged Ribbon Eyelet, having purled ridges above and below the line of openings, makes a frame into which the threaded ribbon is seated. The number of stockinette rows in between eyelet rows is optional.

DIMPLE EYELET

Even number of sts.

Row 1 (Right side)—Knit.
Row 2—Purl.
Row 3—P1, * yo in reverse, i.e., bring yarn over needle from back to front instead of the usual direction; p2 tog; rep from *, end p1.
Row 4—Purl, purling all yo sts through *back* loops.
Rows 5 and 6—Repeat Rows 1 and 2.
Row 7—P2, * yo in reverse, p2 tog; rep from *.
Row 8—Purl, purling all yo sts through *back* loops.

Repeat Rows 1–8.

RIDGED RIBBON EYELET

Odd number of sts.

Row 1 (Right side)—Knit.
Row 2—Purl.
Rows 3 and 4—Knit.
Row 5—* K2 tog, yo; rep from *, end k1.
Row 6—Knit.

Repeat Rows 1–6.

Crochet-Knit Traveling Eyelet

This is a traditional Italian pattern. Note that the number of sts is decreased by one in each pattern repeat on Rows 1 and 3, and restored to the original number on Rows 2 and 4.

Multiple of 6 sts plus 8.

Row 1 (Right side)—K1, yo, ssk, k2, * k2 tog, yo, ssk, k2; rep from * to last 3 sts, end k2 tog, yo, k1.
Row 2—K1, p1, * p4, purl into front and back of next st (yo of previous row); rep from * to last 6 sts, p5, k1.
Row 3—K2, * k2 tog, yo, ssk, k2; rep from *.
Row 4—K1, p2, * purl into front and back of next st, p4; rep from * to last 4 sts, p into front and back of next st, p2, k1.

Repeat Rows 1–4.

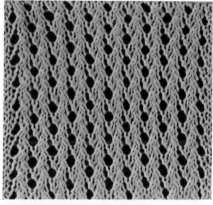

Crochet-Knit Traveling Eyelet

Eyelet Puff

Because this pattern includes so many increases, it has a great tendency to spread out laterally; the knitter must beware of casting on too many stitches. In fine yarn, this is a pleasing pattern for stoles and fancy blouses.

Multiple of 4 sts plus 3.

Row 1 (Wrong side) and all other wrong-side rows—Purl.
Row 2—K3, * yo, p1, yo, k3; rep from *.
Row 4—K4, yo, p1, yo, * k5, yo, p1, yo; rep from *, end k4.
Row 6—K5, yo, p1, yo, * k7, yo, p1, yo; rep from *, end k5.
Row 8—K6, yo, p1, yo, * k9, yo, p1, yo; rep from *, end k6.
Row 10—K3, * k4 tog through back loops, p1, k4 tog through front loops, k3; rep from *.
Row 12—K3, * p3 tog, k3; rep from *.

Repeat Rows 1–12.

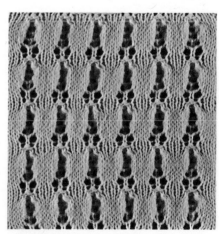

Eyelet Puff

EYELET PATTERNS 175

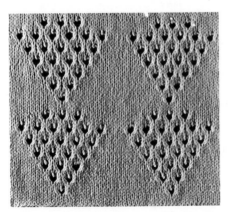

Peacock's Tail

Peacock's Tail

This pattern is a handsome arrangement of picot eyelets in a solid stockinette fabric, in the same manner as Picot Eyelet Diamond. These eyelets can be placed in an infinite number of other designs, according to the whim of the knitter. After becoming familiar with the method of working picot eyelets, try an arrangement of your own. The design can easily be planned on graph paper. Remember that four stitches (counting the decreases) must be allotted to each eyelet.

Panel of 28 sts.

Rows 1 and 3 (Right side)—Knit.
Rows 2 and 4—Purl.
Row 5—K12, k2 tog, (yo) twice, ssk, k12.
Row 6 and all subsequent wrong-side rows—Purl, working (p1, k1) into every double yo of the preceding row.
Rows 7, 11, 15, 19, 23, and 27—Knit.
Row 9—K10, (k2 tog, yo twice, ssk) twice, k10.
Row 13—K8, (k2 tog, yo twice, ssk) 3 times, k8.
Row 17—K6, (k2 tog, yo twice, ssk) 4 times, k6.
Row 21—K4, (k2 tog, yo twice, ssk) 5 times, k4.
Row 25—K2, (k2 tog, yo twice, ssk) 6 times, k2.
Row 29—Repeat Row 13.
Row 30—Purl, working (p1, k1) into each double yo.

Repeat Rows 1–30.

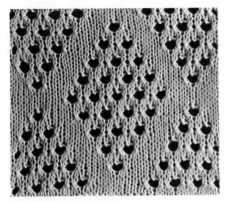

Picot Eyelet Diamond

Picot Eyelet Diamond

A picot eyelet is one that is heart-shaped rather than round. It is created by working (p1, k1) into a double yarn-over instead of the usual (k1, p1). This attractive pattern places picot eyelets in alternating diamonds, set off by solid borders.

Multiple of 28 sts plus 12.

Row 1 (Right side)—Knit.
Row 2—Purl. Special note: throughout pattern purl all wrong-side rows, purling once into every single yo and working (p1, k1) into every (yo) twice.
Row 3—K2, * (k2 tog, yo twice, ssk) 3 times, (k4, k2 tog, yo twice, ssk) twice; rep from * to last 10 sts, end (k2 tog, yo twice, ssk) twice, k2.
Row 5—Knit.

Row 7—K2, yo, ssk, * (k2 tog, yo twice, ssk) twice, k4, (k2 tog, yo twice, ssk) twice, k4, k2 tog, yo twice, ssk; rep from * to last 8 sts, end k2 tog, yo twice, ssk, k2 tog, yo, k2.

Row 9—Knit.

Row 11—K2, * (k2 tog, yo twice, ssk) twice, k4, (k2 tog, yo twice, ssk) 3 times, k4; rep from * to last 10 sts, end (k2 tog, yo twice, ssk) twice, k2.

Row 13—Knit.

Row 15—K4, * k2 tog, yo twice, ssk, k4, (k2 tog, yo twice, ssk) 4 times, k4; rep from * to last 8 sts, end k2 tog, yo twice, ssk, k4.

Row 17—Knit.

Row 19—K2, * k8, (k2 tog, yo twice, ssk) 5 times; rep from *, end k10.

Row 21—Knit.

Row 23—Repeat Row 15.

Row 25—Knit.

Row 27—Repeat Row 11.

Row 29—Knit.

Row 31—Repeat Row 7.

Row 33—Knit.

Row 35—Repeat Row 3.

Row 37—Knit.

Row 39—K2, yo, ssk, * (k2 tog, yo twice, ssk) 3 times, k8, (k2 tog, yo twice, ssk) twice; rep from * to last 8 sts, end k2 tog, yo twice, ssk, k2 tog, yo, k2.

Row 40—Purl (once into each single yo, [p1, k1] into each double yo).

Repeat Rows 1–40.

Checkered Fleurette

This is an adaptation of the French lace pattern, Fleurette, to the eyelet form. The substitution of purled decreases for knitted ones in the motifs is interesting, and gives the pattern a hint of texture.

Multiple of 12 sts plus 5.

Row 1 (Wrong side) and all other wrong-side rows—Purl.

Row 2—K6, p2 tog, yo, k1, yo, p2 tog, * k7, p2 tog, yo, k1, yo, p2 tog; rep from *, end k6.

Rows 4 and 6—K6, yo, p2 tog, k1, p2 tog, yo, * k7, yo, p2 tog, k1, p2 tog, yo; rep from *, end k6.

Row 8—Repeat Row 2.

Row 10—K2, * k1, yo, p2 tog, k7, p2 tog, yo; rep from *, end k3.

Rows 12 and 14—K2, * k1, p2 tog, yo, k7, yo, p2 tog; rep from *, end k3.

Row 16—Repeat Row 10.

Repeat Rows 1–16.

Checkered Fleurette

Rosebud Pattern

Rosebud Pattern

This is a pretty, easy-to-work pattern that would make an adorable party dress for a little girl . . . or for a big girl. It is also very nice for baby clothes, scarves, and knitted tablecloths. For the same type of eyelet incorporated into a highly developed lace pattern, see Rose Trellis Lace.

Multiple of 16 sts plus 9.

Row 1 (Wrong side) and all other wrong-side rows—Purl.

Row 2—K10, * k2 tog, yo, k1, yo, ssk, k11; rep from *, end last repeat k10.

Row 4—K9, * k2 tog, yo, k3, yo, ssk, k9; rep from *.

Row 6—K10, * yo, ssk, yo, k3 tog, yo, k11; rep from *, end last repeat k10.

Row 8—K11, * yo, sl 1—k2 tog—psso, yo, k13; rep from *, end last repeat k11.

Row 10—K2, * k2 tog, yo, k1, yo, ssk, k11; rep from *, end last repeat k2.

Row 12—K1, * k2 tog, yo, k3, yo, ssk, k9; rep from *, end last repeat k1.

Row 14—K2, * yo, ssk, yo, k3 tog, yo, k11; rep from *, end last repeat k2.

Row 16—K3, * yo, sl 1—k2 tog—psso, yo, k13; rep from *, end last repeat k3.

Repeat Rows 1–16.

Cat's Eye

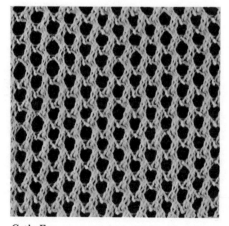

Cat's Eye

Cat's Eye is a simple Shetland all-over lace pattern derived from the picot eyelet. In fine yarn on medium-sized needles, it makes a very open mesh. Note that the yo's are worked on right-side rows and the corresponding decreases are delayed until the subsequent wrong-side rows.

Multiple of 4 sts.

Row 1 (Right side)—K4, * (yo) twice, k4; rep from *.

Row 2—P2, * p2 tog, (p1, k1) into 2 yo's of previous row, p2 tog; rep from *, end p2.

Row 3—K2, yo, * k4, (yo) twice; rep from *, end k4, yo, k2.

Row 4—P3, * (p2 tog) twice, (p1, k1) into 2 yo's; rep from *, end (p2 tog) twice, p3.

Repeat Rows 1–4.

Shetland Eyelet Pattern

This is a lace fabric in actuality, the only true eyelets being the ones on the edges of the pattern, formed by the first and last yarn-overs in Row 6. From these, however, the pattern takes its name. The remainder is a simple Shetland lace. Note the opening "k2 tog, yo, k1, yo, ssk" in the first pattern row. This is a standard opening which occurs again and again in Shetland lace, like a standard gambit in chess.

The Shetland Eyelet Pattern makes a very pretty vertical insertion, such as might be used to dress up an otherwise plain sweater. Try one panel on either side of the front bands of a fine-yarn cardigan. On the other hand, when repeated throughout the fabric on a multiple of 9 stitches, it makes an attractive allover lace.

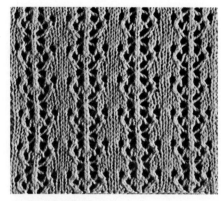

Shetland Eyelet Pattern

Panel of 9 sts.

Row 1 (Wrong side) and all other wrong-side rows—Purl.
Row 2—K2, k2 tog, yo, k1, yo, ssk, k2.
Row 4—K1, k2 tog, yo, k3, yo, ssk, k1.
Row 6—K1, yo, ssk, yo, sl 2 knitwise—k1—p2sso, yo, k2 tog, yo, k1.
Row 8—K3, yo, sl 2 knitwise—k1—p2sso, yo, k3.

Repeat Rows 1–8.

Grand Eyelet Lace

The "grand" eyelet is an extra-large one, as in Crown of Glory, usually made by a (yo) twice or (yo) 3 times. In this pattern the eyelet is enlarged instead by working three more stitches from it. The fabric is reversible.

Multiple of 4 sts plus 4 edge sts.

SPECIAL NOTE: Row 3 should be worked very loosely. For this single row it is best to use a needle 3 or 4 sizes larger than the needles used for the rest of the work.

Row 1—P2, * yo, p4 tog; rep from *, end p2.
Row 2—K2, * k1, (k1, p1, k1) into the yo of previous row; rep from *, end k2.
Row 3—Knit.

Repeat Rows 1–3.

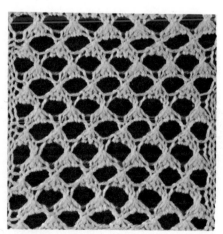

Grand Eyelet Lace

Dice Patterns

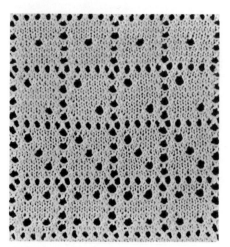

Dice Patterns

<small>UPPER BAND:</small> *Snake Eyes*
<small>SECOND BAND:</small> *Deuce*
<small>THIRD BAND:</small> *Trey*
<small>LOWER BAND:</small> *Four-Spot*

These patterns make a pretty novelty fabric consisting of garter-stitch blocks divided by rows and columns of eyelets. Each block contains one or more eyelets arranged in imitation of the spots on the face of a die. Any of the six possible arrangements can be used, depending on how Rows 5, 6, 9, 10, 13, and 14 are worked. Rows 5 and 6 control the lower third of each die, Rows 9 and 10 the middle third, and Rows 13 and 14 the upper third. If desired, all these rows may be knitted plain. The result then is a pattern of "blank" or solid garter-stitch blocks. Five-Spot and Boxcars, being simple combinations of the other four, are not illustrated.

Multiple of 10 sts plus 6.

I. SNAKE EYES (BASIC DICE PATTERN)

Row 1—(Right side)—K2, * yo, k2 tog; rep from * to last 2 sts, end k2.
Row 2—Knit.
Row 3—K1, * k2 tog, yo, ssk, k6; rep from *, end last repeat k1.
Row 4—K2, * (k1, p1) into the yo of previous row, k8; rep from *, end last repeat k2.
Rows 5 and 6—Knit.
Rows 7 and 8—Repeat Rows 3 and 4.
Row 9—K6, * k2 tog, yo, ssk, k6; rep from *.
Row 10—K7, * (k1, p1) into the yo, k8; rep from *, end last repeat k7.
Rows 11 through 16—Repeat Rows 3 through 8 once more.

Repeat Rows 1–16.

II. DEUCE

Work the same as I, with the following exceptions:
Row 5—K4, * k2 tog, yo, ssk, k6; rep from *, end k2.
Row 6—K9, * (k1, p1) into the yo, k8; rep from *, end last repeat k5.
Rows 9 and 10—Knit.
Row 13—K8, * k2 tog, yo, ssk, k6; rep from *, end last repeat k4.
Row 14—K5, * (k1, p1) into the yo, k8; rep from *, end k1.

III. TREY

Work the same as I, with the following exceptions:
Rows 5 and 6—Repeat Rows 5 and 6 of II.
Rows 13 and 14—Repeat Rows 13 and 14 of II.

IV. FOUR-SPOT

Work the same as I, with the following exceptions:
Row 5—K4, * (k2 tog, yo, ssk) twice, k2; rep from *, end k2.
Row 6—K5, * (k1, p1) into the yo, k2, (k1, p1) into the yo, k4; rep from *, end k1.
Rows 9 and 10—Knit.
Rows 13 and 14—Repeat Rows 5 and 6.

V. FIVE-SPOT

Work the same as I, with the following exceptions:
Rows 5 and 6—Repeat Rows 5 and 6 of IV.
Rows 13 and 14—Repeat Rows 5 and 6 of IV.

VI. BOXCARS

Work the same as I, with the following exceptions:
Rows 5, 9, and 13—Repeat Row 5 of IV.
Rows 6, 10, and 14—Repeat Row 6 of IV.

Eyelet Honeycomb

Multiple of 8 sts plus 6.

Row 1 (Wrong side)—Knit.
Row 2—Purl.
Row 3—K2, * sl 2 wyif, p6; rep from *, end sl 2, k2.
Row 4—K2, * sl 2 wyib, k1, k2 tog, (yo) twice, ssk, k1; rep from *, end sl 2, k2.
Row 5—K2, * sl 2 wyif, p2, (p1, k1) into the double yo, p2; rep from *, end sl 2, k2.
Row 6—K2, * sl 2 wyib, k6; rep from *, end sl 2, k2.
Rows 7 and 8—Repeat Rows 1 and 2.
Row 9—K2, p4, * sl 2 wyif, p6; rep from *, end sl 2, p4, k2.
Row 10—K3, yo, ssk, k1, * sl 2 wyib, k1, k2 tog, (yo) twice, ssk, k1; rep from *, end sl 2, k1, k2 tog, yo, k3.
Row 11—K2, p4, * sl 2 wyif, p2, (p1, k1) into the double yo, p2; rep from *, end sl 2, p4, k2.
Row 12—K6, * sl 2 wyib, k6; rep from *.

Repeat Rows 1–12.

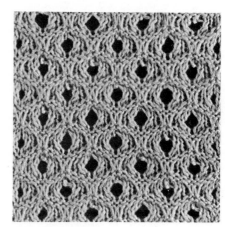

Eyelet Honeycomb

Grand Eyelet Lattice

Grand Eyelet Lattice

Multiple of 8 sts.

Row 1 (Wrong side)—Purl.

Row 2—* (K2 tog) twice, (yo) twice, (ssk) twice; rep from *.

Row 3—* P2 tog-b, (p1, k1) 3 times into the double yo, p2 tog; rep from *.

Row 4—K1, * k6 (the 6 new sts above the yo), k2 tog but do not slip from needle; insert right-hand needle between the sts just knitted tog and knit the 1st st again, then sl both sts from needle together; rep from *, end k7.

Row 5—Purl.

Row 6—K4, * (k2 tog) twice, (yo) twice, (ssk) twice; rep from *, end k4.

Row 7—P4, * p2 tog-b, (p1, k1) 3 times into the double yo, p2 tog; rep from *, end p4.

Row 8—K3, * k2 tog and knit 1st st again as in Row 4, k6; rep from *, end last repeat k3.

Repeat Rows 1–8.

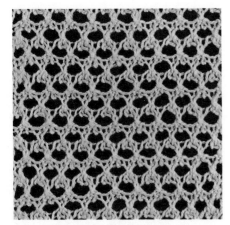

Cane Stitch, or Grand Picot Eyelet

Cane Stitch, or Grand Picot Eyelet

Having a 3-row pattern, this fabric looks the same on both sides. Thus it is particularly good for articles both sides of which will be seen, such as scarves and stoles. It has much vertical elasticity, and can take a good deal of stretching when blocked.

Multiple of 3 sts plus 4 edge sts.

Row 1—K2, * sl 1—k2 tog—psso, (yo) twice; rep from *, end k2.

Row 2—K2, * (p1, k1) into the double yo, p1; rep from *, end k2.

Row 3—Knit.

Repeat Rows 1–3.

CHAPTER TEN

Lace

Lace knitting is justly called "the height of the knitter's art." No education in knitting is complete without it. There is such a world of variety in lace patterns, and they take so many forms, that you might think every possible shape or design has already been used! But that, in lace knitting, is never true.

Bewildered by this world of variety, beginners sometimes confuse it with difficulty, and assume that all lace patterns demand great care and skill in working. Of course, this is hardly the case. Most lace patterns are faster and less tedious to knit than, say, the average cable pattern; and many are even childishly simple. Only a very few laces are truly complicated. But the one great virtue of lace is that the finished result nearly always *looks* more complicated than it really is. One has only to follow directions accurately in order to experience the joy of seeing a lovely lace pattern take shape under one's hands.

Many beginners are afraid to use lace in their garments because, when yarn-over stitches are involved, it is easier to lose track of the increases and decreases in shaping. But this difficulty is quickly overcome by restricting the lace at first to vertical panels placed in or near the center, well away from the edges of the piece where the shaping will take place. Then as you gain confidence in lace knitting, such panels can be extended and combined with panels of different patterns. The most exquisite examples of lace knitting consist of such combinations: perhaps ten or twelve different patterns placed side by side in panel arrangement across the whole width of the garment. Just as cable patterns are combined at will in the fisherman sweater, so lace patterns can be combined at will to make a dress, blouse, sweater, curtain, scarf, or any other article absolutely unique, a treasure of artistry in knitting.

Most lace is interchangeable with stockinette stitch, but it must be remembered that lace is likely to be a little looser, due to the holes left by the yarn-over stitches. The more "open" the lace, the looser it will be, and thus fewer stitches are required for width. A lace pattern can be stretched a great deal in blocking, but it must *not* be compressed or shrunk, for then the openwork pattern will be lost. When making lace it is well to keep in mind that fewer stitches are better than too many.

Lace is best worked in fine yarn with small needles, for it is meant to look dainty and delicate. But the needles must not be too small in proportion to the weight of the yarn, for then the work will become too tight to show the openwork properly. Experiment with different yarns and needles to see which are best suited to your personal gauge and tension in lace making.

More than any other type of knitting, lace offers the greatest scope for individual ingenuity and creativity. The knitters of the past knew this, and took advantage of it; that is why so many different lace patterns exist today. To the knitter, the working of lace is not only a source of delight but also a source of ideas. Practically any lace pattern can be subjected to little variations that change its appearance, sometimes very markedly. Once you have thoroughly learned any lace pattern, possible variations continue to pop into your head as you work. A little playing around with these ideas will often produce the most satisfying event in all knitting experience: a brand-new, original pattern, all your own!

Faggoting

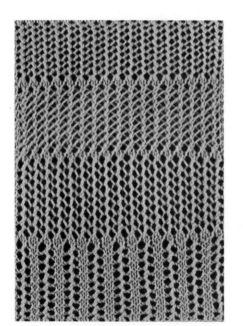

UPPER BAND: *Basic Faggoting Stitch*
SECOND BAND: *Turkish Stitch*
THIRD BAND: *Purse Stitch*
LOWER BAND: *Feather Faggot*

Faggoting is a basic lace stitch. It is, in fact, lace reduced to its two bare essentials: (1) a yarn-over stitch and (2) a decrease. Typically, faggoting consists of just these two operations and the pattern has only one row. In spite of this simple structure there are a surprising number of different types of faggoting.

Faggoting may be used as a vertical insertion, to set off other patterns. Or it may be used as an allover fabric, in which case it resembles a form of netting and has great elasticity. Thus it is very good for fancy stockings or tights, openwork gloves, dress sleeves and the like.

BASIC FAGGOTING STITCH

Even number of sts.

K1, * yo, ssk; rep from *, end k1.   Repeat this row.

What kind of a decrease is used does make a difference, as can be seen from the next type of faggoting which is known as Turkish Stitch. Turkish Stitch is done just like Basic Faggoting except for the decrease, yet its appearance is quite different. Turkish Stitch may be worked in heavy yarn to make a nearly solid fabric with a pleasingly textured appearance and a lot of stretch.

TURKISH STITCH

Even number of sts.

K1, * yo, k2 tog; rep from *, end k1.   Repeat this row.

Still another difference is shown by still another decrease. In Purse Stitch, the decrease is purled, thus the fabric is looser and more open than Basic Faggoting because of the greater distance a yarn-over must travel (i.e., all the way around the needle) when the next stitch is to be purled. Purse Stitch is extremely elastic.

PURSE STITCH

Even number of sts.

K1, * yo, p2 tog; rep from *, end k1.   Repeat this row.

If two more stitches are added to the Purse Stitch pattern, there will be little vertical garter-stitch ribs between open faggoting. The result is called Feather Faggot.

FEATHER FAGGOT

Multiple of 4 sts.

* K1, yo, p2 tog, k1; rep from *.   Repeat this row.

Herringbone Faggoting

Although the interlocking strands of plain Faggoting form a herringbone design, this design becomes more pronounced when some extra stitches are added to make vertical ribs between the openwork. These ribs also give a little added firmness to the fabric. Half Herringbone Faggot adds one stitch for a small rib.

HALF HERRINGBONE FAGGOT OR FAGGOTING RIB STITCH

Multiple of 3 sts.

* K1, yo, k2 tog; rep from *.   Repeat this row.

When two stitches are added, the rib is more pronounced and obviously dual. Herringbone Faggot is one of the commonest forms in which Faggoting is seen.

UPPER BAND: *Half Herringbone Faggot*
SECOND BAND: *Herringbone Faggot*
THIRD BAND: *Reverse Herringbone Faggot*
LOWER BAND: *Double Herringbone Faggot*

LACE   185

HERRINGBONE FAGGOT

Multiple of 4 sts.

* K2 tog, yo, k2; rep from *.   Repeat this row.

You have to look hard to see the difference between Herringbone Faggot and Reverse Herringbone Faggot, but the difference is there, in the slant of the yarn-over stitches and the structure of the ribs. They are similar enough, however, to look alike to anyone but an expert, so the question of which type to use is really just a matter of convenience to the knitter.

REVERSE HERRINGBONE FAGGOT

Multiple of 4 sts.

* K2, yo, k2 tog; rep from *.   Repeat this row.

In the Double Herringbone Faggot the pattern is expanded to five stitches, the rib reduced back to the narrow one of Half Herringbone Faggot, and the herringbone design formed twice in every pattern repeat. Of course one could go on indefinitely playing around with these patterns, producing also a six-stitch pattern with a double herringbone *and* a double rib, and so on; but a few samples of the many possibilities are enough for general purposes.

DOUBLE HERRINGBONE FAGGOT

Multiple of 5 sts.

* K1, (yo, k2 tog) twice; rep from *.   Repeat this row.

Faggot Beading

This series of patterns plainly shows one of the routes by which true lace develops from a faggoting stitch, and should be studied carefully. Two particular things about Faggot Beading display its ancestral relationship to a real lace pattern. First, the pattern is expanded to two or more rows, which makes possible a greater degree of variation. Second, the openwork is formed only on the right-side rows, and thus consists of a double twisted strand spanning the space, rather than two single strands arranged in herringbone fashion as in older types of faggoting. This double twisted strand is characteristic of most lace patterns, and can give a more open quality to the fabric than the herringbone design, which requires considerable stretching.

Two types of Faggot Beading are given, which are very simple patterns but have a problem: they tend to pull the fabric on the bias because the decreases are made always on the same side of the yarn-overs. A third type is also given, which solves this problem, though not by the method used in most other lace patterns.

GARTER STITCH FAGGOT BEADING

This pattern retains the Garter Stitch foundation of other faggoting patterns, with knit stitches on the wrong side although the openwork is formed only on the right side.

Multiple of 3 sts.

Row 1 (Right side)—* K1, yo, k2 tog; rep from *.
Row 2—Knit.

Repeat Rows 1 and 2.

STOCKINETTE STITCH FAGGOT BEADING

This type of beading presents a smoother appearance than the Garter Stitch type because, like most other lace patterns, the wrong-side rows are purled. It is very close in form to the Lace Trellis, and makes a bias fabric in the same manner, which somewhat limits its utility.

Multiple of 3 sts.

Row 1 (Right side)—* K1, (yo) twice, k2 tog; rep from *.
Row 2—Purl, purling each first yo once and dropping each second yo off needle.

Repeat Rows 1 and 2.

VANDYKE FAGGOT

In this beautiful type of faggoting the bias problem is solved in a unique way—not by pairing decreases in the same row, as most lace patterns do (i.e., a "k2 tog" counteracted by a "ssk"), but by reversing the decreases in every other row. Thus in Row 1 the decrease is located to the left of the yo, in Row 3 to its right. As a result the ribs are drawn first to one side and then to the other in a wavy line. (See also Vertical Lace Trellis).

Multiple of 3 sts.

Row 1 (Right side)—* K1, (yo) twice, k2 tog; rep from *.
Row 2—Purl, purling each first yo once and dropping each second yo off needle.
Row 3—* K2 tog, (yo) twice, k1; rep from *.
Row 4—Repeat Row 2.

Repeat Rows 1–4.

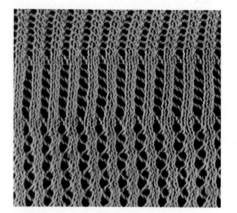

ABOVE: *Garter Stitch Faggot Beading*
CENTER: *Stockinette Stitch Faggot Beading*
BELOW: *Vandyke Faggot*

Faggoting and Beehive Lace Pattern

Faggoting and Beehive Lace Pattern

This is a simple and beautiful lace with vertical panels of faggoting stitch alternating with panels of German Beehive Stitch. In the same manner faggoting may be inserted into any other lace pattern which develops vertical panels.

Multiple of 7 sts plus 4.

Row 1 (Right side)—* K2, yo, ssk, yo, sl 1—k2 tog—psso, yo; rep from *, end k2, yo, ssk.
Row 2—* K2, yo, k2 tog, p3; rep from *, end k2, yo, k2 tog.
Row 3—* K2, yo, ssk, k3; rep from *, end k2, yo, ssk.
Row 4—Repeat Row 2.

Repeat Rows 1–4.

Lace Ladders

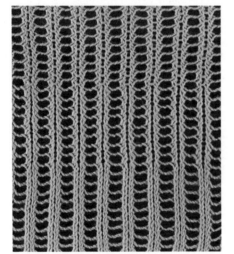

ABOVE: *Garter Stitch Lace Ladder*
CENTER: *Feathered Lace Ladder*
BELOW: *Stockinette Lace Ladder*

The Lace Ladder makes use of paired decreases, which eliminates the bias tendency of Faggot Beading and results in a fine crisp design with the ribs going straight up. Lace Ladders are very useful. They make excellent insertions wherever something a little bolder than Faggoting is desired—for example, to decorate robes and beach wear, knitted tablecloths and throws, fancy stockings. They have the advantage of being simple to work, and add width to a knitted piece by opening up the fabric.

GARTER STITCH LACE LADDER

Multiple of 4 sts.

Row 1 (Right side)—* K2 tog, (yo) twice, ssk; rep from *.
Row 2—* K1, (k1, p1) into double yo, k1; rep from *.

Repeat Rows 1 and 2.

FEATHERED LACE LADDER

Multiple of 4 sts.

In this pattern the wrong-side rows are purled, although the rest is the same as the Garter Stitch version. Note that the "rungs" of the ladders are twisted less tightly and in the opposite direction. The "feathered" effect in the ribs is caused by the way the decreases are placed (see Feather Pattern).

Row 1 (Right side)—* K2 tog, (yo) twice, ssk; rep from *.
Row 2—* P1, (p1, k1) into double yo, p1; rep from *.

Repeat Rows 1 and 2.

STOCKINETTE LACE LADDER

Multiple of 4 sts.

When the decreases are reversed, the rough feathered effect gives way to smooth ribs in which the decrease stitches are quite concealed.

Row 1 (Right side)—* Ssk, (yo) twice, k2 tog; rep from *.
Row 2—* P1, (p1, k1) into double yo, p1; rep from *.

Repeat Rows 1 and 2.

Lace Butterfly

A half-drop variation on a Lace Ladder brings us to the traditional Italian Lace Butterfly, which can be worked in either of two ways: (1) as a panel, and (2) as an allover pattern.

(1) LACE BUTTERFLY, PANEL VERSION

Panel of 10 sts.

Rows 1 and 3 (Right side)—K3, k2 tog, (yo) twice, ssk, k3.
Rows 2 and 4—P4, (k1-b, k1) into double yo, p4.
Rows 5 and 7—K1, k2 tog, (yo) twice, ssk, k2 tog, (yo) twice, ssk, k1.
Rows 6 and 8—P2, (k1-b, k1) into double yo, p2, (k1-b, k1) into double yo, p2.

Repeat Rows 1–8.

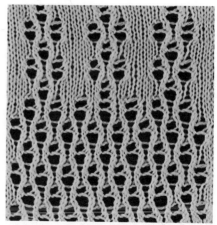

ABOVE: *Lace Butterfly, panel version*
BELOW: *Lace Butterfly, allover version*

(2) LACE BUTTERFLY, ALLOVER VERSION

Multiple of 4 sts.

Rows 1 and 3 (Right side)—* K2 tog, (yo) twice, ssk; rep from *.
Rows 2 and 4—* P1, (k1-b, k1) into double yo, p1; rep from *.
Rows 5 and 7—K2, * k2 tog, (yo) twice, ssk; rep from *, end k2.
Rows 6 and 8—P3, * (k1-b, k1) into double yo, p2; rep from *, end p1.

Repeat Rows 1–8.

Lace Trellis

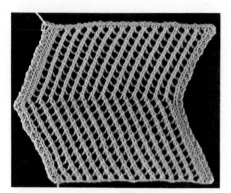

ABOVE: *Lace Trellis, right bias*
BELOW: *Lace Trellis, left bias*

This is the basic lace stitch, upon which nearly all lace patterns are built. It is simply faggoting on the right side, backed by purl rows on the wrong side. Worked plain, it makes an openwork mesh that will pull the fabric on the bias, either to the right or left, depending upon whether the yarn-over is made before the decrease or after it. Therefore the trellis may be worked in either of two ways.

Even number of sts.

I. To produce a right bias:

Row 1—K1, * yo, k2 tog; rep from *, end k1.
Row 2—Purl.

Repeat Rows 1 and 2.

II. To produce a left bias:

Row 1—K1, * ssk, yo; rep from *, end k1.
Row 2—Purl.

Repeat Rows 1 and 2.

Zigzag Lace Trellis

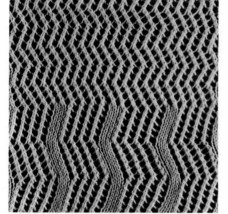

ABOVE: *Zigzag Lace Trellis*
BELOW: *Rib Fantastic*

This pattern clearly shows how the Lace Trellis forms a bias fabric. By alternating the two methods of making the trellis, the lace mesh is drawn first to the right and then to the left to form zigzags. Practice with this striking pattern will induce a better understanding of lace and its formation in general.

Even number of sts.

Row 1 (Wrong side) and all other wrong-side rows—Purl.
Rows 2, 4, and 6—K1, * yo, k2 tog; rep from *, end k1.
Rows 8, 10, and 12—K1, * ssk, yo; rep from *, end k1.

Repeat Rows 1–12.

Rib Fantastic

Here is the Zigzag Lace Trellis with a rib of solid knit stitches inserted. Although the rib is knitted straight up, it is pulled into zigzag form along with the bias lace stitches.

Multiple of 11 sts plus 12.

Row 1 (Wrong side) and all other wrong-side rows—Purl.

Even-numbered rows from 2 through 12—K2, * (yo, k2 tog) 4 times, k3; rep from *, end (yo, k2 tog) 4 times, k2.

Even-numbered rows from 14 through 24—K2, * (ssk, yo) 4 times, k3; rep from *, end (ssk, yo) 4 times, k2.

Repeat Rows 1–24.

Vertical Lace Trellis

In this very valuable basic lace, the bias pull of ordinary Lace Trellis is eliminated in the same way as in Vandyke Faggot: a row in which the decreases precede the yo's is alternated with a row in which the decreases follow the yo's. The structure of the lace is therefore much the same as Vandyke Faggot but on a smaller scale. Alone, Vertical Lace Trellis makes a pretty openwork design; in combination with other pattern arrangements it has great versatility; see Lace Check and Cathedral Pattern.

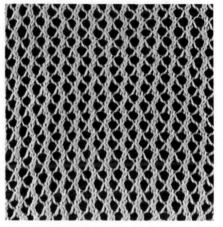

Vertical Lace Trellis

Odd number of sts.

Rows 1 and 3 (Wrong side)—Purl.

Row 2—K1, * yo, k2 tog; rep from *.

Row 4—* Ssk, yo; rep from *, end k1.

Repeat Rows 1–4.

Lace Check

Here is one example of a Vertical Lace Trellis used in the building of larger designs. This lace, in contrast to most others, has a tailored quality due to the sharply geometrical arrangement of the checks.

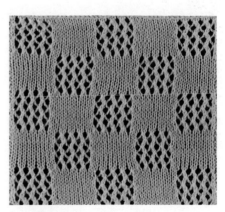

Lace Check

Multiple of 18 sts plus 9.

Row 1 (Wrong side) and all other wrong-side rows—Purl.

Rows 2, 6, and 10—K1, * (yo, k2 tog) 4 times, k10; rep from *, end (yo, k2 tog) 4 times.

Rows 4, 8, and 12—* (Ssk, yo) 4 times, k10; rep from *, end last repeat k1.

Rows 14, 18, and 22—* K10, (yo, k2 tog) 4 times; rep from *, end k9.

Rows 16, 20, and 24—K9, * (ssk, yo) 4 times, k10; rep from *.

Repeat Rows 1–24.

Ploughed Acre

This handsome openwork rib with the bucolic name is one of the very simplest of Shetland lace patterns, based on a Lace Ladder.

Multiple of 10 sts plus 2.

Row 1 (Wrong side)—Purl.
Row 2—K2, * yo, k2 tog, k4, ssk, yo, k2; rep from *.

Repeat Rows 1 and 2.

VARIATION: *CHECKERED ACRE*

The simple Ploughed Acre pattern is easily varied, and is given an eyelet-like quality by the simple expedient of staggering the pattern every eighth row. The ladder effect is retained by the decreases, which still fall above one another in vertical lines.

Multiple of 10 sts plus 2.

Row 1 (Wrong side) and all other wrong-side rows—Purl.
Rows 2, 4, 6, and 8—K2, * yo, k2 tog, k4, ssk, yo, k2; rep from *.
Rows 10, 12, 14, and 16—K3, * ssk, yo, k2, yo, k2 tog, k4; rep from *, end last repeat k3.

Repeat Rows 1–16.

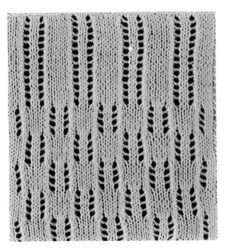

ABOVE: *Ploughed Acre*
BELOW: *Checkered Acre*

Pearl-Barred Scallop Pattern

In this pretty and easy-to-work pattern, the rows of purl stitches do deserve their ancient name of "pearls". They resemble strings of seed pearls applied in embroidery on an old-fashioned lace. The pattern is in fact an old-fashioned one, and was used by Victorian knitters for bureau scarves, tray cloths, antimacassars and the like. But it has much charm, and could be elegantly adapted to today's dresses, blouses, baby clothes, or evening stoles.

Multiple of 14 sts plus 1.

Rows 1, 3, 5, 7, and 9 (Wrong side)—Purl.
Rows 2, 4, 6, 8, and 10—K1, * yo, k3, ssk, yo, sl 1—k2 tog—psso, yo, k2 tog, k3, yo, k1; rep from *.
Row 11—Knit.
Row 12—Purl.

Repeat Rows 1–12.

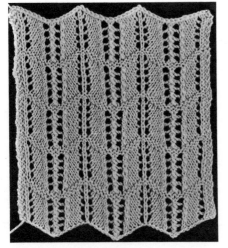

Pearl-Barred Scallop Pattern

Arrowhead Lace

Arrowhead Lace consists of panels of Lace Trellis placed so that the left bias and the right bias counteract each other. The panels can be made wider simply by adding four more stitches to each repeat for each extra diagonal rib desired (i.e., one extra "yo, ssk" on the right-hand side, and one extra "k2 tog, yo" on the left-hand side; or two extra of each, etc.) Arrowhead Lace makes a beautiful, crisp-looking insertion in stockinette fabric, or a mesh-like allover pattern.

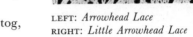

Multiple of 10 sts plus 1.

Rows 1 and 3 (Wrong side)—Purl.
Row 2—K1, * (yo, ssk) twice, k1, (k2 tog, yo) twice, k1; rep from *.
Row 4—K2, * yo, ssk, yo, sl 2 knitwise—k1—p2sso, yo, k2 tog, yo, k3; rep from *, end last repeat k2.

Repeat Rows 1–4.

LEFT: *Arrowhead Lace*
RIGHT: *Little Arrowhead Lace*

VARIATION: *LITTLE ARROWHEAD LACE*

This is Arrowhead Lace in its smallest possible dimensions.

Multiple of 6 sts plus 1.

Rows 1 and 3 (Wrong side)—Purl.
Row 2—K1, * yo, ssk, k1, k2 tog, yo, k1; rep from *.
Row 4—K2, * yo, sl 2 knitwise—k1—p2sso, yo, k3; rep from *, end last repeat k2.

Repeat Rows 1–4.

English Mesh Lace

This is a pretty and popular pattern which resembles a miniature Fern Lace.

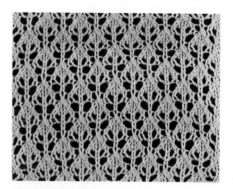

Multiple of 6 sts plus 1.

Row 1 (Wrong side) and all other wrong-side rows—Purl.
Row 2—K1, * yo, ssk, k1, k2 tog, yo, k1; rep from *.
Row 4—K1, * yo, k1, sl 1—k2 tog—psso, k1, yo, k1; rep from *.
Row 6—K1, * k2 tog, yo, k1, yo, ssk, k1; rep from *.
Row 8—K2 tog, * (k1, yo) twice, k1, sl 1—k2 tog—psso; rep from * to last 5 sts, end (k1, yo) twice, k1, ssk.

Repeat Rows 1–8.

English Mesh Lace

Feather Pattern

"Feathering" is the working of decreases so that they fall opposite to the slant of the stitches and thus become more prominent, giving a rough texture to the fabric. The classic Feather Pattern produces a scalloped edge, because the decreases fall directly over one another. The Expanded Feather Pattern is modified with decreases traveling toward the center; this takes up the slack of the fabric and produces a straight edge.

Multiple of 7 sts plus 1.

Row 1 (Wrong side)—Purl.
Row 2—K1, * yo, k1, ssk, k2 tog, k1, yo, k1; rep from *.

Repeat Rows 1 and 2.

SIDE PANELS: *Feather Pattern*
CENTER PANEL: *Expanded Feather Pattern*

Expanded Feather Pattern

Multiple of 12 sts plus 1.

Row 1 (Wrong side) and all other wrong-side rows—Purl.
Row 2—K1, * yo, ssk, k7, k2 tog, yo, k1; rep from *.
Row 4—K1, * yo, k1, ssk, k5, k2 tog, k1, yo, k1; rep from *.
Row 6—K1, * yo, k2, ssk, k3, k2 tog, k2, yo, k1; rep from *.
Row 8—K1, * yo, k3, ssk, k1, k2 tog, k3, yo, k1; rep from *.
Row 10—K1, * yo, k4, sl 1—k2 tog—psso, k4, yo, k1; rep from *.

Repeat Rows 1–10.

Diagonal Faggoting Stripe Pattern

Even more than other simple lace patterns, this one is extremely adaptable. It can lend itself to all sorts of designs: (A) Either diagonal may be worked plain, to give a fabric with attractive openwork stripes all going in the same direction or (in circular knitting) in a spiral. (B) An insertion of some other vertical pattern—six or eight plain knit stitches, a cable, or another lace in a narrow panel—may be placed between 1, 2, 3 or more repeats of the plain diagonal fabric to add interest and break the diagonal lines. (C) On either side of a common center, such as on the front of a blouse, both diagonals should be used, one on the left, the other on the right, to give symmetry. (D) If the center is kept small, say a single knit stitch, then the diagonal patterns on either side will form chevrons. If the Left Diagonal is used on the left side of the garment and the Right Diagonal on the right side, the chevrons will converge toward the center. If the Left Diagonal is used on the right side of the garment and the Right Diagonal on the left side, the chevrons will open out from the center.

(E) Still another possible variation is to alternate the Left and Right Diagonals to make vertical zigzags. To do this, work one diagonal through Row 16, omit Rows 17, 18, 19, and 20, and begin the other diagonal. This ensures that the stripes will meet cleanly as in the illustration. For a continuous zigzag pattern, work Rows 1–16 of Left Diagonal, then Rows 1–16 of Right Diagonal, then Rows 1–16 of Left Diagonal again, and so on. (F) The chevron and zigzag designs may be combined, so that the stripes alternately converge and diverge on either side. I.e., Left Diagonal on left side and Right Diagonal on right side for the first 16 rows; then Right Diagonal on the left side and Left Diagonal on the right side for the next 16 rows, etc.

Diagonal Faggoting Stripe Pattern
ABOVE: *Right diagonal*
BELOW: *Left diagonal*

RIGHT DIAGONAL

Multiple of 10 sts plus 2.

Row 1 (Wrong side) and all other wrong-side rows: Purl.
Row 2—K1, * k6, (k2 tog, yo) twice; rep from *, end k1.
Row 4—* K6, (k2 tog, yo) twice; rep from *, end k2.
Row 6—K5, * (k2 tog, yo) twice, k6; rep from *, end last repeat k3.
Row 8—K4, * (k2 tog, yo) twice, k6; rep from *, end last repeat k4.
Row 10—K3, * (k2 tog, yo) twice, k6; rep from *, end last repeat k5.
Row 12—K2, * (k2 tog, yo) twice, k6; rep from *.
Row 14—K1, * (k2 tog, yo) twice, k6; rep from *, end k1.
Row 16—* (K2 tog, yo) twice, k6; rep from *, end k2.
Row 18—K1, k2 tog, yo, * k6, (k2 tog, yo) twice; rep from *, end k6, k2 tog, yo, k1.
Row 20—K2 tog, yo, * k6, (k2 tog, yo) twice; rep from *, end k6, k2 tog, yo, k2.

Repeat Rows 1–20.

LEFT DIAGONAL

Multiple of 10 sts plus 2.

Row 1 (Wrong side) and all other wrong-side rows: Purl.
Row 2—K1, * (yo, ssk) twice, k6; rep from *, end k1.
Row 4—K2, * (yo, ssk) twice, k6; rep from *.
Row 6—K3, * (yo, ssk) twice, k6; rep from *, end last repeat k5.
Row 8—K4, * (yo, ssk) twice, k6; rep from *, end last repeat k4.
Row 10—K5, * (yo, ssk) twice, k6; rep from *, end last repeat k3.
Row 12—* K6, (yo, ssk) twice; rep from *, end k2.
Row 14—K1, * k6, (yo, ssk) twice; rep from *, end k1.
Row 16—K2, * k6, (yo, ssk) twice; rep from *.
Row 18—K1, yo, ssk, * k6, (yo, ssk) twice; rep from *, end k6, yo, ssk, k1.
Row 20—K2, yo, ssk, * k6, (yo, ssk) twice; rep from *, end k6, yo, ssk.

Repeat Rows 1–20.

Star Rib Mesh

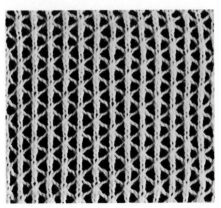

Star Rib Mesh

Here is a stunning mesh pattern that is useful wherever an openwork is wanted, either in panels or in an allover fabric. It has, as well as clear-cut lace geometry, a three-dimensional quality; the vertical ribs stand out strongly against the crisscross background. In this pattern the central decrease (sl 2 knitwise—k1—p2sso) is definitely preferable to the usual sl 1—k2 tog—psso, as the latter will not produce a clean vertical rib and thus the sharpness of the pattern is lost.

Multiple of 4 sts plus 1.

Rows 1 and 3 (Wrong side)—Purl.
Row 2—K1, * yo, sl 2 knitwise—k1—p2sso, yo, k1; rep from *.
Row 4—Ssk, yo, k1, * yo, sl 2 knitwise—k1—p2sso, yo, k1; rep from *, end yo, k2 tog.

Repeat Rows 1–4.

Three Simple Lace Stripe Patterns: Arches and Columns, Little Leaf Stripe, and Broad Leaf Stripe

1. ARCHES AND COLUMNS

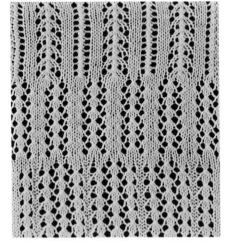

ABOVE: *Arches and Columns*
CENTER: *Little Leaf Stripe*
BELOW: *Broad Leaf Stripe*

Multiple of 14 sts plus 1.

Rows 1 and 3 (Wrong side)—Purl.
Row 2—K2 tog, yo, * k3, yo, k1, sl 1—k2 tog—psso, k1, yo, k3, yo, sl 1—k2 tog—psso, yo; rep from * to last 13 sts, end k3, yo, k1, sl 1—k2 tog—psso, k1, yo, k3, yo, ssk.
Row 4—K2 tog, yo, * k4, yo, sl 1—k2 tog—psso, yo; rep from * to last 6 sts, end k4, yo, ssk.

Repeat Rows 1–4.

2. LITTLE LEAF STRIPE

Multiple of 8 sts plus 1.

Rows 1 and 3 (Wrong side)—Purl.
Row 2—K1, * k2 tog, yo, k3, yo, ssk, k1; rep from *.
Row 4—K3, * yo, sl 1—k2 tog—psso, yo, k5; rep from *, end last repeat k3.

Repeat Rows 1–4.

3. BROAD LEAF STRIPE

Multiple of 11 sts plus 3.

Rows 1 and 3 (Wrong side)—P6, k2, * p9, k2; rep from *, end p6.
Row 2—K3, * yo, sl 1—k2 tog—psso, yo, p2, yo, sl 1—k2 tog—psso, yo, k3; rep from *.
Row 4—K6, p2, * k3, yo, sl 1—k2 tog—psso, yo, k3, p2; rep from *, end k6.

Repeat Rows 1–4.

Bird's Eye

Bird's Eye is a true Shetland mesh, and can be found in the oldest and finest Shetland shawls. It has a Garter Stitch foundation, since Garter Stitch is characteristic of many original Shetland patterns. Hence Bird's Eye should be worked in very fine yarn, unless the nubby effect of Garter Stitch is particularly desired as a pattern feature. Compare this pattern with Cat's Eye, Grand Eyelet Lace and Cane Stitch.

Multiple of 4 sts.

Row 1 (Wrong side)—* K2 tog, (yo) twice, k2 tog; rep from *.
Row 2—* K1, (k1, p1) into 2 yo's of previous row, k1; rep from *.
Row 3—K2, * k2 tog, (yo) twice, k2 tog; rep from * to last 2 sts, end k2.
Row 4—K2, * k1, (k1, p1) into 2 yo's of previous row, k1; rep from * to last 2 sts, end k2.

Repeat Rows 1–4.

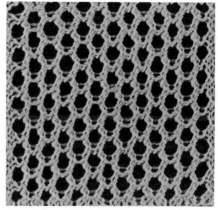
Bird's Eye

Herringbone Lace

This is one of the simplest of the vertical-zigzag lace patterns. The decreases are worked at a distance (2 stitches) from the yo's, which gives the zigzag ribs an alternating bias slant, and tends to form a scalloped or wavy side edge. If a pronounced wavy edge is desired for decorative purposes, this tendency can be intensified by adding more rows in each half of the pattern.

Compare Herringbone Lace with Marriage Lines, and notice how the solid portions of the fabric differ. In Herringbone Lace

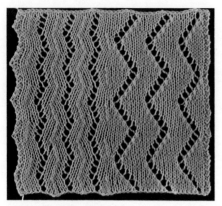

LEFT: *Herringbone Lace*
RIGHT: *Marriage Lines*

the stitches lie in alternate diagonals, drawn left and right by the decreases. In Marriage Lines the stitches run straight up.

Multiple of 6 sts plus 2.

Row 1 (Wrong side) and all other wrong-side rows—Purl.
Rows 2, 4, and 6—* Ssk, k2, yo, k2; rep from *, end k2.
Rows 8, 10, and 12—K1, * k2, yo, k2, k2 tog; rep from *, end k1.

Repeat Rows 1–12.

Marriage Lines

Marriage Lines is a simple zigzag lace pattern, originally Dutch, but popular in various forms throughout most of Europe. It is usually done in panels alternating with panels of Moss Stitch or twisted ribbing, but it may be used as an allover pattern simply by repeating the panels without a break; or, it is pleasing as a vertical border to set off some other lace pattern.

Panel of 7 sts.

Row 1 (Wrong side) and all other wrong-side rows—Purl.
Row 2—K1, yo, k2 tog, k4.
Row 4—K2, yo, k2 tog, k3.
Row 6—K3, yo, k2 tog, k2.
Row 8—K4, yo, k2 tog, k1.
Row 10—K5, yo, k2 tog.
Row 12—K4, ssk, yo, k1.
Row 14—K3, ssk, yo, k2.
Row 16—K2, ssk, yo, k3.
Row 18—K1, ssk, yo, k4.
Row 20—Ssk, yo, k5.

Repeat Rows 1–20.

Madeira Vandyke or Zigzag Lace

This pattern is a somewhat more sophisticated version of the alternating-diagonal motif seen in such patterns as Marriage Lines and Herringbone Lace. Like many Spanish laces, this one employs decreases and yarn-overs on both sides of the fabric, which gives the more delicate effect of openings divided by a single strand instead of two twisted strands. Also, the decreases form a more obvious feature of the design on the surface of the fabric, as in Traveling Vine, etc.

Multiple of 8 sts plus 4.

Row 1 (Right side)—K2, * k6, k2 tog, yo; rep from *, end k2.
Row 2—P2, * p1, yo, p2 tog, p5; rep from *, end p2.
Row 3—K2, * k4, k2 tog, yo, k2; rep from *, end k2.
Row 4—P2, * p3, yo, p2 tog, p3; rep from *, end p2.
Row 5—K2, * k2, k2 tog, yo, k4; rep from *, end k2.
Row 6—P2, * p5, yo, p2 tog, p1; rep from *, end p2.
Row 7—K2, * k2 tog, yo, k6; rep from *, end k2.
Row 8—P2, * p6, p2 tog-b, yo; rep from *, end p2.
Row 9—K2, * k1, yo, ssk, k5; rep from *, end k2.
Row 10—P2, * p4, p2 tog-b, yo, p2; rep from *, end p2.
Row 11—K2, * k3, yo, ssk, k3; rep from *, end k2.
Row 12—P2, * p2, p2 tog-b, yo, p4; rep from *, end p2.
Row 13—K2, * k5, yo, ssk, k1; rep from *, end k2.
Row 14—P2, * p2 tog-b, yo, p6; rep from *, end p2.

Repeat Rows 1–14.

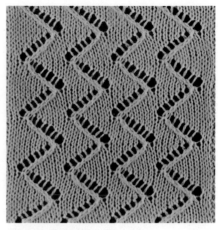

Madeira Vandyke or Zigzag Lace

Madeira Wave Stitch

This very lovely old Spanish lace pattern is based on the simple lace chevron, but adds vertical, short panels of faggoting which give an impression of Gothic windows. It is ideal for a border, but may also be repeated up the entire length of a knitted piece with very striking results.

Multiple of 12 sts plus 5.

Row 1 (Right side)—K2, * yo, ssk, k10; rep from *, end yo, ssk, k1.
All even-numbered rows from 2 through 12—Purl.
Row 3—K2, * k1, yo, ssk, k7, k2 tog, yo; rep from *, end k3.
Row 5—K2, * k2, yo, ssk, k5, k2 tog, yo, k1; rep from *, end k3.
Row 7—K2, * k3, yo, ssk, k3, k2 tog, yo, k2; rep from *, end k3.
Row 9—K2, * k4, yo, ssk, k1, k2 tog, yo, k3; rep from *, end k3.
Row 11—K2, * k5, yo, sl 1—k2 tog—psso, yo, k4; rep from *, end k3.
Rows 13, 15, 17, 19, 21, 23, 25, and 27—K2, * k2, yo, ssk; rep from *, end k3.
Rows 14, 16, 18, 20, 22, 24, 26, and 28—K2, p1, * p2, yo, p2 tog; rep from *, end k2.
Rows 29 through 40—Repeat Rows 1–12.
Row 41—K2, * k6, yo, ssk, k4; rep from *, end k3.
Row 42—Purl.

Repeat Rows 1–42.

Madeira Wave Stitch

Triple Chevron

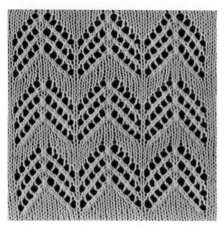

Triple Chevron

This is a beautiful Italian lace, especially well suited to horizontal borders or insertions—for example, as one or two lace bands around a skirt, across a yoke, around sleeves, etc.

Multiple of 12 sts plus 5.

Row 1 (Wrong side)—and all other wrong-side rows: Purl.
Row 2—K2, * k1, yo, ssk, k7, k2 tog, yo; rep from *, end k3.
Row 4—K2, * k2, yo, ssk, k5, k2 tog, yo, k1; rep from *, end k3.
Row 6—K2, * k1, (yo, ssk) twice, k3, (k2 tog, yo) twice; rep from *, end k3.
Row 8—K2, * k2, (yo, ssk) twice, k1, (k2 tog, yo) twice, k1; rep from *, end k3.
Row 10—K2, * k1, (yo, ssk) twice, yo, sl 2 knitwise—k1—p2sso, yo, (k2 tog, yo) twice; rep from *, end k3.
Row 12—Repeat Row 8.
Row 14—K2, * k3, yo, ssk, yo, sl 2 knitwise—k1—p2sso, yo, k2 tog, yo, k2; rep from *, end k3.
Row 16—K2, * k4, yo, ssk, k1, k2 tog, yo, k3; rep from *, end k3.
Row 18—K2, * k5, yo, sl 2 knitwise—k1—p2sso, yo, k4; rep from *, end k3.

Repeat Rows 1–18.

Four Vertical Insertions: Cat's Paw, Gull Wings, Holland Lace, and Pique Lace

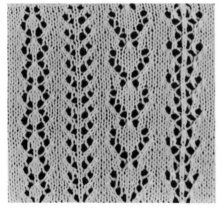

LEFT TO RIGHT:
1. *Cat's Paw*   2. *Gull Wings*
3. *Holland Lace*   4. *Pique Lace*

Many lace patterns can be adapted to vertical insertions, and these are fun to work with. Different vertical insertions can be combined side by side in the same garment, just as different cables are combined in a fisherman sweater, and they can be packed together very closely to produce a lace garment of magnificent and intricate beauty. Lace knitting of this sort is hand knitting at its finest; no machine knitting could even begin to reproduce it. To work many lace insertions together, simply chart your work as in a fisherman sweater (see Special Note on Designing Fisherman Sweaters), using markers if necessary to keep the panels in order.

These four are simple insertions which may be used singly, combined with other patterns, or any one of them can be repeated over the whole fabric for an allover lace.

1. CAT'S PAW

This is a pretty lace of Shetland origin. Note the typical opening in Row 2.

Panel of 7 sts.

Row 1 (Wrong side) and all other wrong-side rows—Purl.
Row 2—K1, k2 tog, yo, k1, yo, ssk, k1.
Row 4—K2 tog, yo, k3, yo, ssk.
Row 6—K2, yo, sl 1—k2 tog—psso, yo, k2.

Repeat Rows 1–6.

2. GULL WINGS

This one is a very simple Dutch lace.

Panel of 7 sts.

Row 1 (Wrong side) and all other wrong-side rows—Purl.
Row 2—K1, k2 tog, yo, k1, yo, ssk, k1.
Row 4—K2 tog, yo, k3, yo, ssk.

Repeat Rows 1–4.

3. HOLLAND LACE

Another Dutch pattern, with somewhat larger motifs.

Panel of 9 sts.

Row 1 (Wrong side) and all other wrong-side rows—Purl.
Row 2—K2, k2 tog, yo, k1, yo, ssk, k2.
Row 4—K1, k2 tog, yo, k3, yo, ssk, k1.
Rows 6 and 8—K2 tog, yo, k5, yo, ssk.
Row 10—K3, yo, sl 2 knitwise—k1—p2sso, yo, k3.

Repeat Rows 1–10.

4. PIQUE LACE

Also Dutch, this pattern is often worked in combination with panels of Moss Stitch.

Panel of 9 sts.

Rows 1, 3, and 5 (Wrong side)—Purl.
Row 2—K3, yo, sl 2 knitwise—k1—p2sso, yo, k3.
Row 4—K2, ssk, yo, k1, yo, k2 tog, k2.
Row 6—K1, ssk, yo, sl 2 knitwise—k1—p2sso, yo, k2 tog, k1.
Row 7—P2, purl into front and back of yo, p1, purl into front and back of yo; p2.
Row 8—(Ssk, yo) twice, k1, (yo, k2 tog) twice.

Repeat Rows 1–8.

ABOVE: *Lace Chevron*
BELOW: *Lace Chevron, Continental Style*

Lace Chevron

Multiple of 10 sts plus 1.

Row 1 (Wrong side) and every other wrong-side row—Purl.
Row 2—* K5, yo, ssk, k3; rep from *, end k1.
Row 4—* K3, k2 tog, yo, k1, yo, ssk, k2; rep from *, end k1.
Row 6—* K2, k2 tog, yo, k3, yo, ssk, k1; rep from *, end k1.
Row 8—* K1, k2 tog, yo, k5, yo, ssk; rep from *, end k1.
Row 10—K2 tog, yo, k7, * yo, sl 1—k2 tog—psso, yo, k7; rep from *, end yo, ssk.

Repeat Rows 1–10.

Lace Chevron, Continental Style

In this version of the Lace Chevron, yarn-overs and decreases are made on every row, both right and wrong sides, in the manner of Spanish and Shetland laces. This produces a chevron that is twice as broad and half as high, in proportion, as the standard chevron. The lace is more delicate, being formed of single strands instead of twisted ones.

Multiple of 20 sts plus 1.

Row 1 (Right side)—K1, * yo, ssk, k15, k2 tog, yo, k1; rep from *.
Row 2—P2, * yo, p2 tog, p13, p2 tog-b, yo, p3; rep from *, end last repeat p2.
Row 3—K3, * yo, ssk, k11, k2 tog, yo, k5; rep from *, end last repeat k3.
Row 4—P4, * yo, p2 tog, p9, p2 tog-b, yo, p7; rep from *, end last repeat p4.
Row 5—K5, * yo, ssk, k7, k2 tog, yo, k9; rep from *, end last repeat k5.
Row 6—P6, * yo, p2 tog, p5, p2 tog-b, yo, p11; rep from *, end last repeat p6.
Row 7—K7, * yo, ssk, k3, k2 tog, yo, k13; rep from *, end last repeat k7.
Row 8—P8, * yo, p2 tog, p1, p2 tog-b, yo, p15; rep from *, end last repeat p8.
Row 9—K9, * yo, sl 1—k2 tog—psso, yo, k17; rep from *, end last repeat k9.
Row 10—Purl.

Repeat Rows 1–10.

Christmas Trees

Here is a fanciful pattern based on the multiple chevron. The directions as given are for an allover fabric with staggered motifs. For a single horizontal band or border, work Rows 1 through 28 only. For a vertical panel with motifs aligned directly above one another, work Rows 1 through 28, then 6 rows of stockinette stitch, then Rows 1 through 28 again, etc.

Multiple of 16 sts plus 1.

Row 1 (Wrong side) and all other wrong-side rows—Purl.

Row 2—K1, * k5, k2 tog, yo, k1, yo, ssk, k6; rep from *.

Row 4—K1, * k4, k2 tog, yo, k3, yo, ssk, k5; rep from *.

Row 6—K1, * k3, (k2 tog, yo) twice, k1, (yo, ssk) twice, k4; rep from *.

Row 8—K1, * k2, (k2 tog, yo) twice, k3, (yo, ssk) twice, k3; rep from *.

Row 10—K1, * k1, (k2 tog, yo) 3 times, k1, (yo, ssk) 3 times, k2; rep from *.

Rows 12, 14, 16, 18, 20, 22, 24, and 26—Repeat Rows 8, 6, 4, 6, 8, 6, 4, and 2.

Row 28—K1, * k6, k2 tog, yo, k8; rep from *.

Row 30—K1, * yo, ssk, k11, k2 tog, yo, k1; rep from *.

Row 32—K1, * k1, yo, ssk, k9, k2 tog, yo, k2; rep from *.

Row 34—K1, * (yo, ssk) twice, k7, (k2 tog, yo) twice, k1; rep from *.

Row 36—K1, * k1, (yo, ssk) twice, k5, (k2 tog, yo) twice, k2; rep from *.

Row 38—K1, * (yo, ssk) 3 times, k3, (k2 tog, yo) 3 times, k1; rep from *

Rows 40, 42, 44, 46, 48, 50, 52, and 54—Repeat Rows 36, 34, 32, 34, 36, 34, 32, and 30.

Row 56—K15, * k2 tog, yo, k14; rep from * to last 2 sts, end k2.

Repeat Rows 1–56.

Christmas Trees

Diagonal Madeira Lace

This is the simplest of the Spanish diagonal lace patterns (see Diagonal Spanish Lace, Madeira Diamond Stitch), and it makes a very beautiful mesh with a strong diagonal line formed largely by the "psso" of the double decrease. This pattern makes exquisite vertical insertions. Like most diagonal patterns it is ideal for circular knitting, as in seamless blouses or skirts.

Multiple of 4 sts.

Row 1 (Wrong side) and all other wrong-side rows—Purl.

Row 2—K2, * yo, sl 1—k2 tog—psso, yo, k1; rep from *, end k2.

Row 4—K2, * k1, yo, sl 1—k2 tog—psso, yo; rep from *, end k2.

Row 6—K1, k2 tog, * yo, k1, yo, sl 1—k2 tog—psso; rep from * to last 5 sts, end yo, k1, yo, ssk, k2.

Row 8—K2, k2 tog, * yo, k1, yo, sl 1—k2 tog—psso; rep from* to last 4 sts, end yo, k1, yo, ssk, k1.

Repeat Rows 1–8.

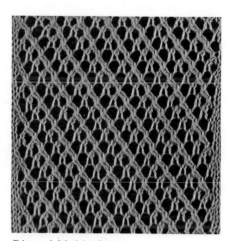

Diagonal Madeira Lace

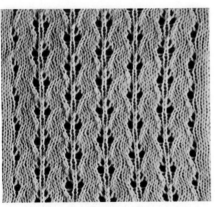

Traveling Leaf Pattern

Traveling Leaf Pattern

Here is a simple but very effective French lace. Much of its beauty lies in the solid part of the fabric, where the stitches are gently waved left and right as the leaf motifs alternate.

Multiple of 12 sts plus 5.

Row 1 (Wrong side) and all other wrong-side rows—Purl.

Rows 2 and 4—K2, * k1, yo, k3, k2 tog, k1, ssk, k3, yo; rep from *, end k3.

Rows 6 and 8—K2, * k1, ssk, k3, yo, k1, yo, k3, k2 tog; rep from *, end k3.

Repeat Rows 1–8.

Frost Flowers

Frost Flowers

"Frost Flowers" is not the correct name for this lace, unless the author happens to be an unusually good guesser. But it is quite an old pattern, dating from at least the early nineteenth century, and therefore probably has its own quaint name by which it is, or used to be, known. In spite of its rather complicated appearance it is a simple lace, consisting essentially of only four rows, which are repeated three times and then alternated on the half-drop principle. On going once through the pattern these rows are quickly learned.

Multiple of 34 sts plus 2.

Row 1 (Right side)—K1, * k3, k2 tog, k4, yo, p2, (k2, yo, ssk) 3 times, p2, yo, k4, ssk, k3; rep from *, end k1.

Row 2—K1, * p2, p2 tog-b, p4, yo, p1, k2, (p2, yo, p2 tog) 3 times, k2, p1, yo, p4, p2 tog, p2; rep from *, end k1.

Row 3—K1, * k1, k2 tog, k4, yo, k2, p2, (k2, yo, ssk) 3 times, p2, k2, yo, k4, ssk, k1; rep from *, end k1.

Row 4—K1, * p2 tog-b, p4, yo, p3, k2, (p2, yo, p2 tog) 3 times, k2, p3, yo, p4, p2 tog; rep from *, end k1.

Rows 5 through 12—Repeat Rows 1 through 4 twice more.

Row 13—K1, * yo, ssk, k2, yo, ssk, p2, yo, k4, ssk, k6, k2 tog, k4, yo, p2, k2, yo, ssk, k2; rep from *, end k1.

Row 14—K1, * yo, p2 tog, p2, yo, p2 tog, k2, p1, yo, p4, p2 tog, p4, p2 tog-b, p4, yo, p1, k2, p2, yo, p2 tog, p2; rep from *, end k1.

Row 15—K1, * yo, ssk, k2, yo, ssk, p2, k2, yo, k4, ssk, k2, k2 tog, k4, yo, k2, p2, k2, yo, ssk, k2; rep from *, end k1.

Row 16—K1, * yo, p2 tog, p2, yo, p2 tog, k2, p3, yo, p4, p2 tog, p2 tog-b, p4, yo, p3, k2, p2, yo, p2 tog, p2; rep from *, end k1.

Rows 17 through 24—Repeat Rows 13 through 16 twice more.

Repeat Rows 1–24.

Feather and Fan Stitch, or Old Shale

This famous old Shetland pattern, with its deep scallops, is probably familiar to every knitter in one or another of its innumerable forms. Because it is so extremely simple, it can be varied in dozens of ways. The number of stitches to a repeat can be greater or smaller; the bands of purl across the pattern can be spaced differently, or placed on another row, or broader, or not there at all; the row count can vary, and so on. It is said that in the Shetland Islands no two families of knitters work the pattern alike. But the basic principle of the pattern row is always the same: half decreases, grouped together, and half increases, likewise grouped together.

Sometimes the pattern is called Shell or Old Shell. It is believed that the name "Old Shale" came from a resemblance to the undulating print of waves upon shale sands.

The uses of Feather and Fan Stitch are many. Its scalloped edge makes a very nice finish for sleeves, necklines, and hems, even when the garment itself is knitted in some other pattern. It makes beautiful baby clothes and dressy skirts. In its home territory, it is often used in the renowned Shetland shawls.

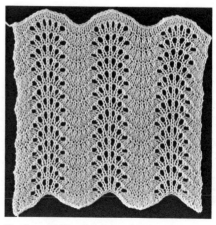

Feather and Fan Stitch, or Old Shale

Multiple of 18 sts.

Row 1 (Right side)—Knit.
Row 2—Purl.
Row 3—* (K2 tog) 3 times, (yo, k1) 6 times, (k2 tog) 3 times; rep from *.
Row 4—Knit.

Repeat Rows 1–4.

Crest of the Wave

Here is a variation on the much-varied Feather and Fan Stitch that is a little bit different from the usual very simple ones. This pattern too comes from Shetland and is used in making delicate lace shawls. Easy and uncomplicated though it is, it is very pretty and would be an asset to any lace garment.

Multiple of 12 sts plus 1.

NOTE: Odd-numbered rows are right-side rows.

Rows 1 through 4—Knit.
Rows 5, 7, 9, and 11—K1, * (k2 tog) twice, (yo, k1) 3 times, yo, (ssk) twice, k1; rep from *.
Row 6, 8, 10, and 12—Purl.

Repeat Rows 1–12.

Crest of the Wave

Fan Shell

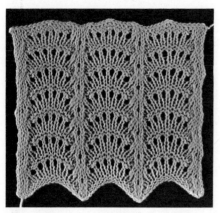

Fan Shell

This is another of the many variations on Feather and Fan. In this pattern the increases are delayed to Row 6, while the decreases are made on preceding rows.

Multiple of 15 sts plus 4.

Row 1 (Wrong side)—P4, * k11, p4; rep from *.
Row 2—K4, * p11, k4; rep from *.
Row 3—P2, * p2 tog, p11, p2 tog-b; rep from *, end p2.
Row 4—K2, * ssk, k9, k2 tog; rep from *, end k2.
Row 5—P2, * p2 tog, p7, p2 tog-b; rep from *, end p2.
Row 6—K4, * (yo, k1) 5 times, yo, k4; rep from *.

Repeat Rows 1–6.

Razor Shell

Razor Shell is a simple Shetland pattern forming lace ribs. It can be made in a variety of widths, on multiples of 4, 6, 8, 10, 12 or more stitches; or in a combination of these—for instance, a wide rib alternating with a narrow one, etc. The tiniest version, a multiple of 4, when repeated across a fabric makes a Lace Rib Mesh. The most commonly used traditional forms are the wide 10- or 12-stitch ribs.

Odd as it may seem at first glance, Razor Shell is the ancestor of the very popular Fern Lace. The intermediary between them is the Fir Cone pattern (which see); this holds the key to the series and shows how one pattern progresses to the next.

Razor Shell
LEFT TO RIGHT:
1. *Four-Stitch Rib*
2. *Six-Stitch Rib*
3. *Eight-Stitch Rib*
4. *Ten-Stitch Rib*
5. *Twelve-Stitch Rib*

1. FOUR-STITCH RIB

Multiple of 4 sts plus 1.

Row 1 (Wrong side)—Purl.
Row 2—K1, * yo, sl 1—k2 tog—psso, yo, k1; rep from *.

Repeat Rows 1 and 2.

2. SIX-STITCH RIB

Multiple of 6 sts plus 1.

Row 1 (Wrong side)—Purl.
Row 2—K1, * yo, k1, sl 1—k2 tog—psso, k1, yo, k1; rep from *.

Repeat Rows 1 and 2.

3. EIGHT-STITCH RIB

Multiple of 8 sts plus 1.

Row 1 (Wrong side)—Purl.
Row 2—K1, * yo, k2, sl 1—k2 tog—psso, k2, yo, k1; rep from *.

Repeat Rows 1 and 2.

4. TEN-STITCH RIB

Multiple of 10 sts plus 1.

Row 1 (Wrong side)—Purl.
Row 2—K1, * yo, k3, sl 1—k2 tog—psso, k3, yo, k1; rep from *.

Repeat Rows 1 and 2.

5. TWELVE-STITCH RIB

Multiple of 12 sts plus 1.

Row 1 (Wrong side)—Purl.
Row 2—K1, * yo, k4, sl 1—k2 tog—psso, k4, yo, k1; rep from *.

Repeat Rows 1 and 2.

Fir Cone

The Shetland Fir Cone pattern is particularly fascinating because it represents an intermediate stage in the evolution of another pattern, the popular Fern or Leaf-Patterned Lace. The series begins with Razor Shell, one of the simplest Shetland lace stitches; next, a half-drop variation of Razor Shell gives the Fir Cone, which produces gracefully curved lines because the central decreases draw the stitches out of position in vertical waves. This effect is pretty, but the pattern has a tendency to pucker and must be carefully blocked. To overcome this difficulty, the decreases are moved out to the sides of each pattern repeat and there form diagonals—and voila! Fern Lace!

Fir Cone

Multiple of 10 sts plus 1.

Row 1 (Wrong side) and all other wrong-side rows—Purl.
Rows 2, 4, 6, and 8—K1, * yo, k3, sl 1—k2 tog—psso, k3, yo, k1; rep from *.
Rows 10, 12, 14, and 16—K2 tog, * k3, yo, k1, yo, k3, sl 1—k2 tog—psso; rep from *, end k3, yo, k1, yo, k3, ssk.

Repeat Rows 1–16.

Fern or Leaf-Patterned Lace

Fern or Leaf-Patterned Lace

There are many versions of this popular English lace pattern. The classic version is a bit larger (12 sts plus 1, 20 rows) but the slightly daintier variation given here is most satisfactory.

Multiple of 10 sts plus 1.

Row 1 (Wrong side) and all other wrong-side rows—Purl.

Row 2—K3, * k2 tog, yo, k1, yo, ssk, k5; rep from *, end last rep k3.

Row 4—K2, * k2 tog, (k1, yo) twice, k1, ssk, k3; rep from *, end last rep k2.

Row 6—K1, * k2 tog, k2, yo, k1, yo, k2, ssk, k1; rep from *.

Row 8—K2 tog, * k3, yo, k1, yo, k3, sl 1—k2 tog—psso; rep from * to last 9 sts, end k3, yo, k1, yo, k3, ssk.

Row 10—K1, * yo, ssk, k5, k2 tog, yo, k1; rep from *.

Row 12—K1, * yo, k1, ssk, k3, k2 tog, k1, yo, k1; rep from *.

Row 14—K1, * yo, k2, ssk, k1, k2 tog, k2, yo, k1; rep from *.

Row 16—K1, * yo, k3, sl 1—k2 tog—psso, k3, yo, k1; rep from *.

Repeat Rows 1–16.

Elfin Lace

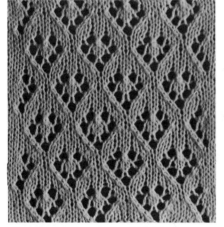

Elfin Lace

Multiple of 8 sts plus 9.

Row 1 (Wrong side) and all other wrong-side rows—Purl.

Row 2—K2, * yo, ssk, k6; rep from *, end last repeat k5.

Row 4—K3, * yo, ssk, k3, k2 tog, yo, k1; rep from *, end yo, ssk, k4.

Row 6—K4, * yo, ssk, k1, k2 tog, yo, k3; rep from *, end yo, ssk, k3.

Row 8—K2, k2 tog, * yo, k5, yo, sl 2 knitwise—k1—p2sso; rep from *, end yo, k5.

Row 10—K6, * yo, ssk, k6; rep from *, end yo, ssk, k1.

Row 12—K4, k2 tog, * yo, k1, yo, ssk, k3, k2 tog; rep from *, end yo, k3.

Row 14—K3, * k2 tog, yo, k3, yo, ssk, k1; rep from *, end k2 tog, yo, k4.

Row 16—K5, * yo, sl 2 knitwise—k1—p2sso, yo, k5; rep from *, end yo, k2 tog, k2.

Repeat Rows 1–16.

Horseshoe Pattern

The Horseshoe Pattern is one of the basic Shetland lace stitches. Its gracefully curved lines are frequently seen in dressy sweaters and blouses, and its popularity owes much to the fact that it is simple and easy to work.

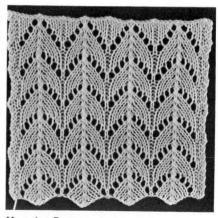

Multiple of 10 sts plus 1.

Rows 1 and 3 (Wrong side)—Purl.
Row 2—K1, * yo, k3, sl 1—k2 tog—psso, k3, yo, k1; .rep from *.
Row 4—P1, * k1, yo, k2, sl 1—k2 tog—psso, k2, yo, k1, p1; rep from *.
Rows 5 and 7—K1, *p9, k1; rep from *.
Row 6—P1, * k2, yo, k1, sl 1—k2 tog—psso, k1, yo, k2, p1; rep from *.
Row 8—P1, * k3, yo, sl 1—k2 tog—psso, yo, k3, p1; rep from *.

Repeat Rows 1–8.

Horseshoe Pattern

Shell Lace

Here, the famous Horseshoe Pattern is varied in the simplest possible way—with a half-drop—to make a quite different lace. Shell Lace is easy to work, and very attractive as an allover fabric. A discerning eye may notice in it an element of the Grapevine Pattern, to which it is related in form if not in technique.

Multiple of 11 sts plus 1.

Row 1 (Wrong side) and all other wrong-side rows—Purl.
Row 2—K2 tog, * k5, yo, k1, yo, k2, sl 1—k2 tog—psso; rep from * to last 2 sts, end last repeat ssk.
Row 4—K2 tog, * k4, yo, k3, yo, k1, sl 1—k2 tog—psso; rep from * to last 2 sts, end last repeat ssk.
Row 6—K2 tog, * k3, yo, k5, yo, sl 1—k2 tog—psso; rep from * to last 2 sts, end last repeat ssk.
Row 8—K2 tog, * k2, yo, k1, yo, k5, sl 1—k2 tog—psso; rep from * to last 2 sts, end last repeat ssk.
Row 10—K2 tog, * k1, yo, k3, yo, k4, sl 1—k2 tog—psso; rep from * to last 2 sts, end last repeat ssk.
Row 12—K2 tog, * yo, k5, yo, k3, sl 1—k2 tog—psso; rep from * to last 2 sts, end last repeat ssk.

Repeat Rows 1–12.

Shell Lace

Trellis Shell

This pattern is a variation on a variation; a more open version of Shell Lace. From Horseshoe Pattern to Shell Lace to Trellis Shell is an interesting progression, showing clearly how lace patterns can be derived from one another.

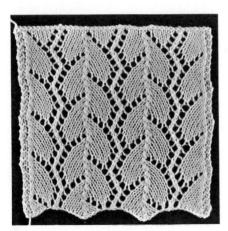

Trellis Shell

Multiple of 13 sts plus 1.

Row 1 (Wrong side) and all other wrong-side rows—Purl.

Row 2—K2 tog, * k5, yo, k2 tog, yo, k1, yo, k2, sl 1—k2 tog—psso; rep from * to last 2 sts, end last repeat ssk.

Row 4—K2 tog, * k4, yo, k2 tog, yo, k3, yo, k1, sl 1—k2 tog—psso; rep from * to last 2 sts, end last repeat ssk.

Row 6—K2 tog, * k3, yo, k2 tog, yo, k5, yo, sl 1—k2 tog—psso; rep from * to last 2 sts, end last repeat ssk.

Row 8—K2 tog, * k2, yo, k1, yo, ssk, yo, k5, sl 1—k2 tog—psso; rep from * to last 2 sts, end last repeat ssk.

Row 10—K2 tog, * k1, yo, k3, yo, ssk, yo, k4, sl 1—k2 tog—psso; rep from * to last 2 sts, end last repeat ssk.

Row 12—K2 tog, * yo, k5, yo, ssk, yo, k3, sl 1—k2 tog—psso; rep from * to last 2 sts, end last repeat ssk.

Repeat Rows 1–12.

Twin Leaf Lace

Twin Leaf Lace

Panel of 23 sts.

Row 1 (Right side)—K8, k2 tog, yo, k1, p1, k1, yo, ssk, k8.
Row 2—P7, p2 tog-b, p2, yo, k1, yo, p2, p2 tog, p7.
Row 3—K6, k2 tog, k1, yo, k2, p1, k2, yo, k1, ssk, k6.
Row 4—P5, p2 tog-b, p3, yo, p1, k1, p1, yo, p3, p2 tog, p5.
Row 5—K4, k2 tog, k2, yo, k3, p1, k3, yo, k2, ssk, k4.
Row 6—P3, p2 tog-b, p4, yo, p2, k1, p2, yo, p4, p2 tog, p3.
Row 7—K2, k2 tog, k3, yo, k4, p1, k4, yo, k3, ssk, k2.
Row 8—P1, p2 tog-b, p5, yo, p3, k1, p3, yo, p5, p2 tog, p1.
Row 9—K2 tog, k4, yo, k5, p1, k5, yo, k4, ssk.
Row 10—P11, k1, p11.
Row 11—K11, p1, k11.
Row 12—P11, k1, p11.

Repeat Rows 1–12.

Diagonal Fern Lace

In this variation, the "fern" motifs are staggered in panels divided by garter stitch.

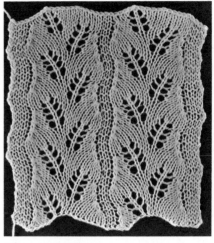

Multiple of 18 sts plus 2.

Row 1 (Wrong side) and all other wrong-side rows—Purl.

Row 2—P2, * k9, yo, k1, yo, k3, sl 1—k2 tog—psso, p2; rep from *.

Row 4—P2, * k10, yo, k1, yo, k2, sl 1—k2 tog—psso, p2; rep from *.

Row 6—P2, * k3 tog, k4, yo, k1, yo, k3, (yo, k1) twice, sl 1—k2 tog—psso, p2; rep from *.

Row 8—P2, * k3 tog, k3, yo, k1, yo, k9, p2; rep from *.

Row 10—P2, * k3 tog, k2, yo, k1, yo, k10, p2; rep from *.

Row 12—P2, * k3 tog, (k1, yo) twice, k3, yo, k1, yo, k4, sl 1—k2 tog—psso, p2; rep from *.

Repeat Rows 1–12.

Diagonal Fern Lace

Mrs. Montague's Pattern

Mrs. Montague was a Lady of the Chamber to Queen Elizabeth I of England. She made stockings for the Queen in this pattern, said to have been copied from a French design. A pair of these stockings still exists today in the museum at Hatfield House.

Ladies, wouldn't it be fun to wear a dress or sweater made in the same lace pattern as Queen Bess's stockings?

Mrs. Montague's Pattern

Multiple of 16 sts plus 1.

Row 1 (Wrong side) and all other wrong-side rows—Purl.

Row 2—K1, * k4, yo, ssk, k3, k2 tog, yo, k5; rep from *.

Row 4—K1, * yo, ssk, k3, yo, ssk, k1, k2 tog, yo, k3, k2 tog, yo, k1; rep from *.

Row 6—K1, * k1, yo, ssk, k3, yo, sl 1—k2 tog—psso, yo, k3, k2 tog, yo, k2; rep from *.

Row 8—K1, * k2, yo, ssk, k7, k2 tog, yo, k3; rep from *.

Row 10—K1, * k1, k2 tog, yo, k9, yo, ssk, k2; rep from *.

Row 12—K1, * k2 tog, yo, k3, k2 tog, yo, k1, yo, ssk, k3, yo, ssk, k1; rep from *.

Row 14—K2 tog, * yo, k3, k2 tog, yo, k3, yo, ssk, k3, yo, sl 1—k2 tog—psso; rep from *, end last repeat ssk instead of sl 1—k2 tog—psso.

Row 16—K1, * k3, k2 tog, yo, k5, yo, ssk, k4; rep from *.

Repeat Rows 1–16.

Diamond Medallion Pattern

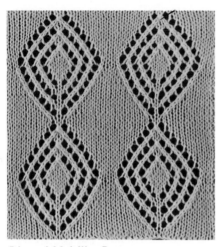

Diamond Medallion Pattern

This is an elaboration of Mrs. Montague's Pattern; and not a very elaborate elaboration, although it may look so at first glance. The diamonds are simply framed by a triple Lace Trellis slanting first outward and then inward. Though easy to work, the pattern has a lot of sparkle.

Panel of 19 sts.

Row 1 (Wrong side) and all other wrong-side rows—Purl.
Row 2—Knit.
Row 4—K7, k2 tog, yo, k1, yo, ssk, k7.
Row 6—K6, k2 tog, yo, k3, yo, ssk, k6.
Row 8—K5, (k2 tog, yo) twice, k1, (yo, ssk) twice, k5.
Row 10—K4, (k2 tog, yo) twice, k3, (yo, ssk) twice, k4.
Row 12—K3, (k2 tog, yo) 3 times, k1, (yo, ssk) 3 times, k3.
Row 14—K2, (k2 tog, yo) 3 times, k3, (yo, ssk) 3 times, k2.
Row 16—K1, (k2 tog, yo) 3 times, k5, (yo, ssk) 3 times, k1.
Row 18—K2, (yo, ssk) 3 times, k3, (k2 tog, yo) 3 times, k2.
Row 20—K3, (yo, ssk) 3 times, k1, (k2 tog, yo) 3 times, k3.
Row 22—K4, (yo, ssk) twice, yo, sl 1—k2 tog—psso, yo, (k2 tog, yo) twice, k4.
Row 24—K5, (yo, ssk) twice, k1, (k2 tog, yo) twice, k5.
Row 26—K6, yo, ssk, yo, sl 1—k2 tog—psso, yo, k2 tog, yo, k6.
Row 28—K7, yo, ssk, k1, k2 tog, yo, k7.
Row 30—K8, yo, sl 1—k2 tog—psso, yo, k8.

Repeat Rows 1–30.

Openwork Diamonds and Openwork Leaf Pattern

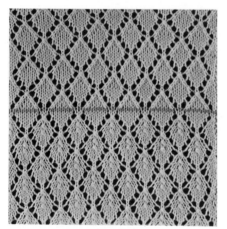

ABOVE: *Openwork Diamonds*
BELOW: *Openwork Leaf Pattern*

These two patterns are presented together because they are similar, with a subtle difference between them that is seldom understood; and they are often confused, Openwork Diamonds being referred to as Leaf Pattern and vice versa. The difference lies in the position of the decreases. In Openwork Diamonds, the decreases are placed at the edges of the diamond motifs, which results in a hard, clear outline with a geometrical quality. In Openwork Leaf Pattern, the decreases are located in the center of each motif. This gives a softer and more naturalistic effect, subtly altering the shape of the motif so that it does resemble a leaf more than a diamond. The difference is plainly shown in the illustration.

Both patterns are frequently used, so it is important for the knitter to comprehend their structure in order to choose between them.

OPENWORK DIAMONDS

If the stitches interposed between the diamond motifs of Mrs. Montague's Pattern are eliminated, the diamonds will abut to form a continuous pattern. This is a very old type of lace. It occurs in many variations, with the diamonds being made either larger or smaller. The version given here, with diamonds five stitches wide, is about average.

Multiple of 8 sts plus 1.

Row 1 (Wrong side) and all other wrong-side rows—Purl.
Row 2—K1, * k1, k2 tog, yo, k1, yo, ssk, k2; rep from *.
Row 4—K1, * k2 tog, yo, k3, yo, ssk, k1; rep from *.
Row 6—K2 tog, * yo, k5, yo, sl 1—k2 tog—psso; rep from *, end last repeat ssk instead of sl 1—k2 tog—psso.
Row 8—K1, * yo, ssk, k3, k2 tog, yo, k1; rep from *.
Row 10—K1, * k1, yo, ssk, k1, k2 tog, yo, k2; rep from *.
Row 12—K1, * k2, yo, sl 1—k2 tog—psso, yo, k3; rep from *.

Repeat Rows 1–12.

OPENWORK LEAF PATTERN

The directions for this pattern are often given in a needlessly complicated form. The manipulation of the yo's at a distance from the central decreases seems confusing to many writers on knitting. Here, the directions are pared down to the utmost possible simplicity and so it is better to learn this version.

Multiple of 8 sts plus 1.

Row 1 (Wrong side) and all other wrong-side rows—Purl.
Row 2—K1, * yo, k2, sl 1—k2 tog—psso, k2, yo, k1; rep from *.
Row 4—K1, * k1, yo, k1, sl 1—k2 tog—psso, k1, yo, k2; rep from *.
Row 6—K1, * k2, yo, sl 1—k2 tog—psso, yo, k3; rep from *.
Row 8—K2 tog, * k2, yo, k1, yo, k2, sl 1—k2 tog—psso; rep from *, end last repeat ssk instead of sl 1—k2 tog—psso.
Row 10—K2 tog, * k1, yo, k3, yo, k1, sl 1—k2 tog—psso; rep from *, end last repeat ssk instead of sl 1—k2 tog—psso.
Row 12—K2 tog, * yo, k5, yo, sl 1—k2 tog—psso; rep from *, end last repeat ssk instead of sl 1—k2 tog—psso.

Repeat Rows 1–12.

Trellis-Framed Openwork Diamonds

Trellis-Framed Openwork Diamonds

In this lovely pattern the classic Diamonds are "opened up" with insertions of Zigzag Trellis. A single panel worked vertically makes zigzag lines of lace which can add much beauty to a garment (each side of a cardigan's front bands, for instance) for very little expenditure of effort.

Multiple of 12 sts plus 1.

Row 1 (Wrong side) and all other wrong-side rows—Purl.
Row 2—K1, * k1, (k2 tog, yo) twice, k1, (yo, ssk) twice, k2; rep from *.
Row 4—K1, * (k2 tog, yo) twice, k3, (yo, ssk) twice, k1; rep from *.
Row 6—K2 tog, * yo, k2 tog, yo, k5, yo, ssk, yo, sl 1—k2 tog—psso; rep from *, end last repeat ssk instead of sl 1—k2 tog—psso.
Row 8—K1, * (yo, ssk) twice, k3, (k2 tog, yo) twice, k1; rep from *.
Row 10—K1, * k1, (yo, ssk) twice, k1, (k2 tog, yo) twice, k2; rep from *.
Row 12—K1, * k2, yo, ssk, yo, sl 1—k2 tog—psso, yo, k2 tog, yo, k3; rep from *.

Repeat Rows 1–12.

Trellis-Framed Leaf Pattern

Trellis-Framed Leaf Pattern

Like its parent the Openwork Leaf Pattern, this lace is basically a simple construction of only six pattern rows. It is often presented in an unnecessarily complex form. The author has seen it given in 40 rows, with decreases awkwardly juggled from side to side among the edge stitches! Often, too, the trellis inserted between the leaf motifs is improperly paired. Since it is an exquisite pattern, very popular among lace knitters, the reader is well advised to use it as given here. Sometimes it is called Medallion Leaf Pattern.

Multiple of 12 sts plus 1.

Row 1 (Wrong side) and all other wrong-side rows—Purl.
Rows 2, 4, and 6—K2 tog, * k2, yo, ssk, yo, k1, yo, k2 tog, yo, k2, sl 1—k2 tog—psso; rep from *, end last repeat ssk instead of sl 1—k2 tog—psso.
Row 8—K2 tog, * k1, yo, k2 tog, yo, k3, yo, ssk, yo, k1, sl 1—k2 tog—psso; rep from *, end last repeat ssk instead of sl 1—k2 tog—psso.
Row 10—K2 tog, * yo, k2 tog, yo, k5, yo, ssk, yo, sl 1—k2 tog—psso; rep from *, end last repeat ssk instead of sl 1—k2 tog—psso.

Rows 12, 14, and 16—K1, * yo, k2 tog, yo, k2, sl 1—k2 tog—psso, k2, yo, ssk, yo, k1; rep from *.

Row 18—K2, * yo, ssk, yo, k1, sl 1—k2 tog—psso, k1, yo, k2 tog, yo, k3; rep from *, end last repeat k2.

Row 20—K3, * yo, ssk, yo, sl 1—k2 tog—psso, yo, k2 tog, yo, k5; rep from *, end last repeat k3.

Repeat Rows 1–20.

Miniature Leaf Pattern

Several kinds of small-patterned lace go by this name. Three versions are given here. Version I is essentially a scaled-down Openwork Diamonds. Note that the double decrease in Rows 4 and 8 is "sl 2 knitwise—k1—p2sso" instead of the usual "sl 1—k2 tog—psso". Version II is the "smallest-of-all" lace, the solution to the problem of how small a lace motif can be made without turning into a mesh or a form of trellis. The answer, of course, is that the lace motif must be at least three stitches wide; to bring it down to two stitches is to turn it into a simple decrease. Version III, an Italian pattern, is somewhat more sophisticated in technique than the other two. The motifs are formed on the right and wrong sides alternately, and the shapes are reminiscent of the Shetland Bead Stitch.

Miniature Leaf Pattern
ABOVE: *Version I*
CENTER: *Version II*
BELOW: *Version III*

VERSION I

Multiple of 6 sts plus 1.

Row 1 (Wrong side) and all other wrong-side rows—Purl.

Row 2—K1, * k2 tog, yo, k1, yo, ssk, k1; rep from *.

Row 4—K2 tog, * yo, k3, yo, sl 2 knitwise—k1—p2sso; rep from *, end last repeat ssk instead of sl 2—k1—p2sso.

Row 6—K1, * yo, ssk, k1, k2 tog, yo, k1; rep from *.

Row 8—K2, * yo, sl 2 knitwise—k1—p2sso, yo, k3; rep from *, end last repeat k2.

Repeat Rows 1–8.

VERSION II

Multiple of 6 sts plus 2.

Rows 1 and 3 (Wrong side)—Purl.

Row 2—K1, * k3, yo, sl 1—k2 tog—psso, yo; rep from *, end k1.

Row 4—K1, * yo, sl 1—k2 tog—psso, yo, k3; rep from *, end k1.

Repeat Rows 1–4.

VERSION III

Multiple of 6 sts plus 3.

Row 1 (Right side)—K1, * k1, yo, ssk, k1, k2 tog, yo; rep from *, end k2.
Row 2—K1, * p2, yo, p3 tog, yo, p1; rep from *, end p1, k1.
Row 3—Knit.
Row 4—K1, * p1, p2 tog-b, yo, p1, yo, p2 tog; rep from *, end p1, k1.
Row 5—K1, k2 tog, * yo, k3, yo, sl 1—k2 tog—psso; rep from *, end yo, k3, yo, ssk, k1.
Row 6—Purl.

Repeat Rows 1–6.

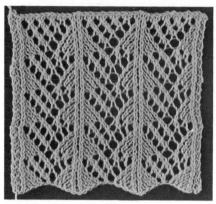

Fan Lace

Fan Lace

Multiple of 11 sts.

Row 1 (Wrong side) and all other wrong-side rows—Purl.
Row 2—* Ssk, k3-b, yo, k1, yo, k3-b, k2 tog; rep from *.
Row 4—* Ssk, k2-b, yo, k1, yo, ssk, yo, k2-b, k2 tog; rep from *.
Row 6—* Ssk, k1-b, yo, k1, (yo, ssk) twice, yo, k1-b, k2 tog; rep from *.
Row 8—* Ssk, yo, k1, (yo, ssk) three times, yo, k2 tog; rep from *.

Repeat Rows 1–8.

Beech Leaf Pattern

This is one of the loveliest of lace patterns. It bears little resemblance to the other "leaf"-theme laces but is more similar to the Openwork Diamond patterns, in that the "leaves" are formed of solid fabric stitches set off by openings around their edges. Note that the number of stitches does not remain constant in every row.

Multiple of 14 sts plus 1.

Row 1 (Right side)—* K1, yo, k5, yo, sl 1—k2 tog—psso, yo, k5, yo; rep from *, end k1.
Row 2—Purl.
Row 3—* K1, yo, k1, k2 tog, p1, ssk, k1, yo, p1, yo, k1, k2 tog, p1, ssk, k1, yo; rep from *, end k1.
Row 4—P1, * (p3, k1) 3 times, p4; rep from *.
Row 5—* K1, yo, k1, k2 tog, p1, ssk, k1, p1, k1, k2 tog, p1, ssk, k1, yo; rep from *, end k1.

Row 6—P1, * p3, k1, (p2, k1) twice, p4; rep from *.

Row 7—* (K1, yo) twice, k2 tog, p1, ssk, p1, k2 tog, p1, ssk, yo, k1, yo; rep from *, end k1.

Row 8—P1, * p4, (k1, p1) twice, k1, p5; rep from *.

Row 9—* K1, yo, k3, yo, sl 1—k2 tog—psso, p1, k3 tog, yo, k3, yo; rep from *, end k1.

Row 10—Purl.

Repeat Rows 1–10.

LEFT: *Beech Leaf Pattern*
RIGHT: *Drooping Elm Leaf*

Drooping Elm Leaf

This pattern represents an adaptation of the well-known Beech Leaf, in which the leaves are staggered instead of being twinned. Note that in Rows 3 and 4 there is one stitch less for each pattern repeat, and in Row 5 the original number of stitches is restored.

Multiple of 15 sts plus 1.

Row 1 (Right side)—* K1, yo, k1, ssk, p1, k2 tog, k1, yo, p1, ssk, p1, k2 tog, yo, k1, yo; rep from *, end k1.

Row 2—P1, * p4, k1, p1, k1, p3, k1, p4; rep from *.

Row 3—* K1, yo, k1, ssk, p1, k2 tog, k1, p1, sl 1—k2 tog—psso, yo, k3, yo; rep from *, end k1.

Row 4—P1, * p6, k1, p2, k1, p4; rep from *.

Row 5—* (K1, yo) twice, ssk, p1, (k2 tog) twice, yo, k5, yo; rep from *, end k1.

Row 6—P1, * p7, k1, p1, k1, p5; rep from *.

Row 7—* K1, yo, k3, yo, sl 1—k2 tog—psso, p1, yo, k1, ssk, p1, k2 tog, k1, yo; rep from *, end k1.

Row 8—P1, * (p3, k1) twice, p7; rep from *.

Row 9—* K1, yo, k5, yo, ssk, k1, ssk, p1, k2 tog, k1, yo; rep from *, end k1.

Row 10—P1, * p3, k1, p2, k1, p8; rep from *.

Repeat Rows 1–10.

Split Leaf Pattern

Here the diamond-shaped leaves are split in the center by a purled rib, with the decreases "feathered" on either side, producing a formation like that of Beech Leaf Pattern. Like Beech Leaf, the Split Leaf is an English lace.

Split Leaf Pattern

Multiple of 12 sts plus 1.

Row 1 (Right side)—P1, * k2 tog, k3, yo, k1, yo, k3, ssk, p1; rep from *.

Rows 2, 4, 6, and 8—K1, * p11, k1; rep from *.

Row 3—P1, * k2 tog, k2, yo, k3, yo, k2, ssk, p1; rep from *.

Row 5—P1, * k2 tog, k1, yo, k5, yo, k1, ssk, p1; rep from *.

Row 7—P1, * k2 tog, yo, k7, yo, ssk, p1; rep from *.

Row 9—K1, * yo, k3, ssk, p1, k2 tog, k3, yo, k1; rep from *.

Rows 10, 12, and 14—P6, * k1, p11; rep from *, end k1, p6.

Row 11—K2, * yo, k2, ssk, p1, k2 tog, k2, yo, k3; rep from *, end last repeat k2.

Row 13—K3, * yo, k1, ssk, p1, k2 tog, k1, yo, k5; rep from *, end last repeat k3.

Row 15—K4, * yo, ssk, p1, k2 tog, yo, k7; rep from *, end last repeat k4.

Row 16—P6, * k1, p11; rep from *, end k1, p6.

Repeat Rows 1–16.

Vine Lace

Vine Lace

Here is one of those beautifully simple lace patterns that give very pretty results for very little effort. Both pattern rows are the same; they simply alternate position by one stitch. The cast-on edge will be lightly scalloped.

Multiple of 9 sts plus 4.

Rows 1 and 3 (Wrong side)—Purl.

Row 2—K3, * yo, k2, ssk, k2 tog, k2, yo, k1; rep from *, end k1.

Row 4—K2, * yo, k2, ssk, k2 tog, k2, yo, k1; rep from *, end k2.

Repeat Rows 1–4.

Vine Lace Zigzag

Examine Vine Lace, and you will see that its basic construction principle is a "yo, k1, yo" moved one stitch over on every other row so that the central "k1" falls above a previous "yo". This pattern is based on the same principle, except that instead of moving back and forth, the "yo, k1, yo" structure keeps going in the same direction for ten rows before reversing.

The same arrangement can be found in the beautiful Traveling Vine.

If only the first ten rows of Vine Lace Zigzag are used, the result is a rather pretty pattern of crescent shapes.

Multiple of 11 sts plus 1.

Row 1 (Wrong side) and all other wrong-side rows—Purl.
Row 2—K1, * k2 tog, k4, (yo, k1) twice, ssk, k1; rep from *.
Row 4—K1, * k2 tog, k3, yo, k1, yo, k2, ssk, k1; rep from *.
Row 6—K1, * k2 tog, k2, yo, k1, yo, k3, ssk, k1; rep from *.
Row 8—K1, * k2 tog, (k1, yo) twice, k4, ssk, k1; rep from *.
Row 10—K1, * k2 tog, yo, k1, yo, k5, ssk, k1; rep from *.
Row 12—Repeat Row 8.
Row 14—Repeat Row 6.
Row 16—Repeat Row 4.
Row 18—Repeat Row 2.
Row 20—K1, * k2 tog, k5, yo, k1, yo, ssk, k1; rep from *.

Repeat Rows 1–20.

Vine Lace Zigzag

Traveling Vine

Here is a subtle and graceful lace, of French origin. Part of its charm lies in the fact that the decrease stitches are placed apart from the yo's for which they compensate, and used to form small corded ribs that are gently curved to left and right. Note that on all right-side rows one extra stitch is added to each pattern repeat, and on all wrong-side rows the extra stitch is taken off.

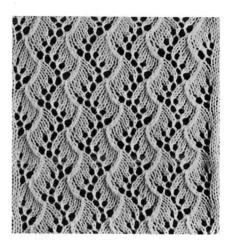

Multiple of 8 sts plus 4.

Row 1 (Right side)—K2, * yo, k1-b, yo, ssk, k5; rep from *, end k2.
Row 2—P6, * p2 tog-b, p7; rep from *, end last rep p5.
Row 3—K2, * yo, k1-b, yo, k2, ssk, k3; rep from *, end k2.
Row 4—P4, * p2 tog-b, p7; rep from *.
Row 5—K2, * k1-b, yo, k4, ssk, k1, yo; rep from *, end k2.
Row 6—P3, * p2 tog-b, p7; rep from *, end p1.
Row 7—K2, * k5, k2 tog, yo, k1-b, yo; rep from *, end k2.
Row 8—P5, * p2 tog, p7; rep from *, end last rep p6.
Row 9—K2, * k3, k2 tog, k2, yo, k1-b, yo; rep from *, end k2.
Row 10—* P7, p2 tog; rep from *, end p4.
Row 11—K2, * yo, k1, k2 tog, k4, yo, k1-b; rep from *, end k2.
Row 12—P1, * p7, p2 tog; rep from *, end p3.

Repeat Rows 1–12.

Traveling Vine

Scroll Pattern

Scroll Pattern

This lovely pattern is a variant of the French Traveling Vine, with the same trick of separating increases and decreases so that the groups of stitches are drawn into soft, undulating curves. Unlike Traveling Vine, the Scroll Pattern does retain the same number of stitches on every row.

Multiple of 10 sts plus 2.

Row 1 (Right side)—K1, * yo, k8, k2 tog; rep from *, end k1.
Row 2—P1, * p2 tog, p7, yo, p1; rep from *, end p1.
Row 3—K1, * k2, yo, k6, k2 tog; rep from *, end k1.
Row 4—P1, * p2 tog, p5, yo, p3; rep from *, end p1.
Row 5—K1, * k4, yo, k4, k2 tog; rep from *, end k1.
Row 6—P1, * p2 tog, p3, yo, p5; rep from *, end p1.
Row 7—K1, * k6, yo, k2, k2 tog; rep from *, end k1.
Row 8—P1, * p2 tog, p1, yo, p7; rep from *, end p1.
Row 9—K1, * k8, yo, k2 tog; rep from *, end k1.
Row 10—P1, * yo, p8, p2 tog-b; rep from *, end p1.
Row 11—K1, * ssk, k7, yo, k1; rep from *, end k1.
Row 12—P1, * p2, yo, p6, p2 tog-b; rep from *, end p1.
Row 13—K1, * ssk, k5, yo, k3; rep from *, end k1.
Row 14—P1, * p4, yo, p4, p2 tog-b; rep from *, end p1.
Row 15—K1, * ssk, k3, yo, k5; rep from *, end k1.
Row 16—P1, * p6, yo, p2, p2 tog-b; rep from *, end p1.
Row 17—K1, * ssk, k1, yo, k7; rep from *, end k1.
Row 18—P1, * p8, yo, p2 tog-b; rep from *, end p1.

Repeat Rows 1–18.

Grapevine Pattern

Note that in this pattern stitches are decreased on Rows 2 and 8, and increased on Rows 6 and 12.

Multiple of 8 sts plus 6.

Row 1 (Wrong side) and all other wrong-side rows—Purl.
Row 2—K2, * k2 tog, k1, yo, k1, ssk, k2; rep from *, end k4.
Row 4—K1, k2 tog, k1, yo, * k1, yo, k1, ssk, k2 tog, k1, yo; rep from *, end k2.
Row 6—K3, yo, * k3, yo, k1, ssk, k1, yo; rep from *, end k3.
Row 8—K5, * k2 tog, k1, yo, k1, ssk, k2; rep from *, end k2.
Row 10—K4, * k2 tog, k1, (yo, k1) twice, ssk; rep from *, end k3.
Row 12—K3, k2 tog, * k1, yo, k3, yo, k1, k2 tog; rep from *, end k2.

Repeat Rows 1–12.

Grapevine Pattern

Trellis Grapevine

This expanded version of the Grapevine dates from the early 18th century, when the advent of fine cotton yarns ushered in the heyday of "white" lace knitting.

Trellis Grapevine

Multiple of 12 sts plus 6.

Row 1 (Wrong side) and all other wrong-side rows—Purl.

Row 2—K2, * k2 tog, k1, (yo, ssk) twice, yo, k1, ssk, k2; rep from *, end k4.

Row 4—K1, k2 tog, k1, yo, * k1, (yo, ssk) twice, yo, k1, ssk, k2 tog, k1, yo; rep from *, end k2.

Row 6—K3, yo, * k3, (yo, ssk) twice, yo, k1, ssk, k1, yo; rep from *, end k3.

Row 8—K5, * k2 tog, k1, yo, (k2 tog, yo) twice, k1, ssk, k2; rep from *, end k2.

Row 10—K4, * k2 tog, k1, yo, (k2 tog, yo) twice, k1, yo, k1, ssk; rep from *, end k3.

Row 12—K3, k2 tog, * k1, yo, (k2 tog, yo) twice, k3, yo, k1, k2 tog; rep from *, end k2.

Repeat Rows 1–12.

Fleurette

This charming old French lace pattern has a delicate, mesh-like quality which makes it ideal for dressy or evening wear. Note that one stitch is increased in each pattern repeat on Rows 4 and 10, and decreased back to the original number of stitches on Rows 6 and 12.

Fleurette

Multiple of 6 sts plus 5.

Row 1 (Wrong side) and all other wrong-side rows—Purl.

Row 2—K2, * k1, yo, ssk, k1, k2 tog, yo; rep from *, end k3.

Row 4—K4, * yo, k3; rep from *, end k1.

Row 6—K2, k2 tog, * yo, ssk, k1, k2 tog, yo, sl 2 knitwise—k1—p2sso; rep from *, end yo, ssk, k1, k2 tog, yo, ssk, k2.

Row 8—K2, * k1, k2 tog, yo, k1, yo, ssk; rep from *, end k3.

Row 10—Repeat Row 4.

Row 12—K2, * k1, k2 tog, yo, sl 2 knitwise—k1—p2sso, yo, ssk; rep from *, end k3.

Repeat Rows 1–12.

Madeira Cascade

Madeira Cascade

This is an old pattern; there are, therefore, many versions of it. In other variations the proportions of the motifs differ, but their general shape remains the same. It is a good pattern for blouses, especially since it forms a scalloped border at the lower edge.

Multiple of 20 sts plus 5.

Row 1 (Right side)—Purl.

Row 2—Knit.

Row 3—K2, * k1, yo, k8, sl 1—k2 tog—psso, k8, yo; rep from *, end k3.

Wrong-side rows from 4 through 18—Purl.

Row 5—K2, * k2, yo, k7, sl 1—k2 tog—psso, k7, yo, k1; rep from *, end k3.

Row 7—K2, k2 tog, * yo, k1, yo, k6, sl 1—k2 tog—psso, k6, yo, k1, yo, sl 1—k2 tog—psso; rep from * to last 4 sts, end last repeat yo, ssk, k2 instead of yo, sl 1—k2 tog—psso.

Row 9—K2, * k4, yo, k5, sl 1—k2 tog—psso, k5, yo, k3; rep from *, end k3.

Row 11—K2, * k1, yo, sl 1—k2 tog—psso, yo, k1, yo, k4, sl 1—k2 tog—psso, k4, yo, k1, yo, sl 1—k2 tog—psso, yo; rep from *, end k3.

Row 13—K2, * k6, yo, k3, sl 1—k2 tog—psso, k3, yo, k5; rep from *, end k3.

Row 15—K2, k2 tog, * yo, k1, yo, sl 1—k2 tog—psso, yo, k1, yo, k2, sl 1—k2 tog—psso, k2, (yo, k1, yo, sl 1—k2 tog—psso) twice; rep from * to last 4 sts, end last repeat yo, ssk, k2 instead of yo, sl 1—k2 tog—psso.

Row 17—K2, * k8, yo, k1, sl 1—k2 tog—psso, k1, yo, k7; rep from *, end k3.

Row 19—K2, * (k1, yo, sl 1—k2 tog—psso, yo) 5 times; rep from *, end k3.

Row 20—Knit.

Repeat Rows 1–20.

Lace Diamond Chain

This is a fairly wide vertical-panel pattern of great beauty.

Panel of 18 sts.

Row 1 (Wrong side) and all other wrong-side rows—Purl.

Row 2—K6, yo, ssk, k2, yo, ssk, k6.

Row 4—K4, k2 tog, yo, k1, yo, ssk, k2, yo, ssk, k5.

Row 6—K3, k2 tog, yo, k3, yo, ssk, k2, yo, ssk, k4.

Row 8—(K2, k2 tog, yo) twice, k1, yo, ssk, k2, yo, ssk, k3.

Row 10—K1, k2 tog, yo, k2, k2 tog, yo, k3, (yo, ssk, k2) twice.

Row 12—K3, yo, ssk, k2, yo, ssk, yo, k2 tog, yo, k2, k2 tog, yo, k2 tog, k1.

Row 14—K4, yo, ssk, k2, yo, sl 1—k2 tog—psso, yo, k2, k2 tog, yo, k3.

Row 16—K5, yo, ssk, k2, yo, ssk, k1, k2 tog, yo, k4.

Repeat Rows 1–16.

CENTER PANEL: *Lace Diamond Chain*
SIDE PANELS: *Shetland Fern Stitch*

Shetland Fern Stitch

Here is one of the loveliest of traditional Shetland lace patterns. Because of its popularity it has been much varied, but most of the variations constitute an enlargement of the pattern rather than a difference in the actual working of it. The version given here is basic.

Panel of 15 sts.

Row 1 (Right side)—K7, yo, ssk, k6.
Rows 2, 4, 6, 8, and 10—Purl.
Row 3—K5, k2 tog, yo, k1, yo, ssk, k5.
Row 5—K4, k2 tog, yo, k3, yo, ssk, k4.
Row 7—K4, yo, ssk, yo, sl 1—k2 tog—psso, yo, k2 tog, yo, k4.
Row 9—K2, k2 tog, yo, k1, yo, ssk, k1, k2 tog, yo, k1, yo, ssk, k2.
Row 11—K2, (yo, ssk) twice, k3, (k2 tog, yo) twice, k2.
Row 12—P3, (yo, p2 tog) twice, p1, (p2 tog-b, yo) twice, p3.
Row 13—K4, yo, ssk, yo, sl 1—k2 tog—psso, yo, k2 tog, yo, k4.
Row 14—P5, yo, p2 tog, p1, p2 tog-b, yo, p5.
Row 15—K6, yo, sl 1—k2 tog—psso, yo, k6.
Row 16—Purl.

Repeat Rows 1–16.

Ogee Lace

In its form this lace pattern copies the s-shaped curve of the architectural ogee, the central or open portion of the s-curve being decorated with openwork flowers.

Multiple of 24 sts plus 1.

Row 1 (Right side)—* K2, yo, k2 tog, k1, k2 tog, k3, yo, ssk, yo, p1, yo, k2, yo, ssk, (k1, ssk) twice, yo, k1; rep from *, end k1.
Row 2—P1, * p7, yo, p2 tog, p5, yo, p2 tog, p8; rep from *.
Row 3—* K1, yo, k2 tog, k1, k2 tog, k3, yo, ssk, (k1, yo) twice, k3, yo, (ssk, k1) twice, ssk, yo; rep from *, end k1.
Row 4—P1, * p6, (yo, p2 tog, p7) twice; rep from *.
Row 5—* K3, k2 tog, k3, yo, ssk, k1, (yo, k3) twice, yo, ssk, k1, ssk, k2; rep from *, end k1.
Row 6—P1, * p5, yo, p2 tog, p9, yo, p2 tog, p6; rep from *.
Row 7—* K2, k2 tog, k3, yo, ssk, k3, yo, k1, yo, k5, yo, (ssk, k1) twice; rep from *, end k1.
Row 8—P1, * p4, yo, p2 tog, p11, yo, p2 tog, p5; rep from *.
Row 9—* K1, k2 tog, k3, yo, ssk, (k3, yo) twice, k5, yo, ssk, k1, ssk; rep from *, end k1.
Row 10—P1, * p3, yo, p2 tog, p13, yo, p2 tog, p4; rep from *.

Ogee Lace

Row 11—Ssk, * k3, yo, ssk, k1, ssk, yo, k2, yo, k1, yo, k2, yo, k2 tog, k3, yo, ssk, k1, sl 1—k2 tog—psso; rep from *, end last rep ssk instead of sl 1—k2 tog—psso.

Row 12—P1, * p2, yo, p2 tog, p15, yo, p2 tog, p3; rep from *.

Row 13—Ssk, * k2, yo, ssk, k5, yo, k3, yo, k7, yo, ssk, sl 1—k2 tog—psso; rep from *, end last rep ssk instead of sl 1—k2 tog—psso.

Row 14—P1, * p1, yo, p2 tog, p17, yo, p2 tog, p1, k1; rep from *.

Row 15—* P1, yo, k2, yo, (ssk, k1) twice, ssk, yo, k3, yo, k2 tog, k1, k2 tog, k3, yo, ssk, yo; rep from *, end p1.

Row 16—P1, * p2, yo, p2 tog, p15, yo, p2 tog, p3; rep from *.

Row 17—* K1, yo, k3, yo, (ssk, k1) twice, ssk, yo, k1, yo, k2 tog, k1, k2 tog, k3, yo, ssk, k1, yo; rep from *, end k1.

Row 18—P1, * p3, yo, p2 tog, p13, yo, p2 tog, p4; rep from *.

Row 19—* K2, yo, k3, yo, ssk, k1, ssk, k5, k2 tog, k3, yo, ssk, k1, yo, k1; rep from *, end k1.

Row 20—P1, * p4, yo, p2 tog, p11, yo, p2 tog, p5; rep from *.

Row 21—* K1, yo, k5, yo, ssk, k1, ssk, k3, k2 tog, k3, yo, ssk, k3, yo; rep from *, end k1.

Row 22—P1, * p5, yo, p2 tog, p9, yo, p2 tog, p6; rep from *.

Row 23—* K2, yo, k5, yo, (ssk, k1) twice, k2 tog, k3, yo, ssk, k3, yo, k1; rep from *, end k1.

Row 24—P1, * p6, yo, p2 tog, p7, yo, p2 tog, p7; rep from *.

Row 25—* K1, yo, k2, yo, k2 tog, k3, yo, ssk, k1, sl 1—k2 tog—psso, k3, yo, ssk, k1, ssk, yo, k2, yo; rep from *, end k1.

Row 26—P1, * p7, yo, p2 tog, p5, yo, p2 tog, p8; rep from *.

Row 27—* K2, yo, k7, yo, ssk, sl 1—k2 tog—psso, k2, yo, ssk, k5, yo, k1; rep from *, end k1.

Row 28—P1, * p8, yo, p2 tog, p1, k1, p1, yo, p2 tog, p9; rep from *.

Repeat Rows 1–28.

Persian Lace

This graceful though not very "open" lace features purl-stitch medallions whose shape is reminiscent of the "onion" domes of Eastern temples. These medallions may be further enriched by touches of embroidery.

Multiple of 8 sts plus 2.

Rows 1 and 3—K1, p3, * k2, p6; rep from * to last 6 sts, k2, p3, k1. (Right side)

Rows 2 and 4—K4, p2, * k6, p2; rep from *, end k4.

Row 5—K1, p2, * k2 tog, yo, ssk, p4; rep from *, end last rep p3.

Row 6—K3, * p1, k into front and back of next st, p1, k4; rep from *, end last rep k3.

Row 7—K1, p1, * k2 tog, yo, k2, yo, ssk, p2; rep from *.

Row 8—K2, * p6, k2; rep from *.

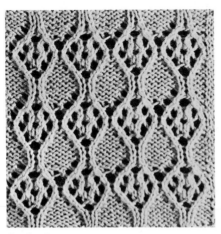

Persian Lace

Row 9—K1, * (k2 tog, yo) twice, ssk, yo, ssk; rep from *, end k1.

Row 10—K1, p3, * k into front and back of next st, p6; rep from *, end last rep p4.

Row 11—K1, * (yo, ssk) twice, k2 tog, yo, k2 tog; rep from *, end yo, k1.

Row 12—K1, k1-b, p6, * k into front and back of next st, p6; rep from * to last 2 sts, k1-b, k1.

Row 13—K1, p1, * yo, sl 1—k2 tog—psso, yo, k3 tog, yo, p2; rep from *.

Row 14—K2, * k1-b, p1, k into front and back of next st, p1, k1-b, k2; rep from *.

Row 15—K1, p2, * yo, ssk, k2 tog, yo, p4; rep from *, end last rep p2, k1 instead of p4.

Row 16—K3, * k1-b, p2, k1-b, k4; rep from *, end last rep k3.

Omit Rows 1 and 2, Repeat Rows 3–16.

Triple Flower Pattern

A very pretty lace panel can be made by repeating only the first eight rows of this pattern: that is, the "stem" and the two lower "leaves"—omitting the triple flower above. The entire pattern is fun when worked into a garment that is made from the top down. Turn the "flower" upside down and what do you see? An old-fashioned ceiling chandelier, a street lamp, or a pawn-shop sign?

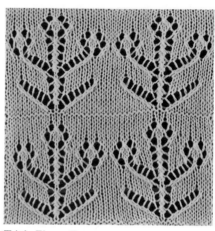

Triple Flower Pattern

Panel of 21 sts.

Row 1 (Wrong side)—Purl.

Row 2—K8, k2 tog, yo, k1, yo, ssk, k8.

Row 3—P7, p2 tog-b, yo, p3, yo, p2 tog, p7.

Row 4—K6, k2 tog, yo, k1, yo, sl 1—k2 tog—psso, yo, k1, yo, ssk, k6.

Row 5—P5, p2 tog-b, yo, p7, yo, p2 tog, p5.

Row 6—K4, k2 tog, yo, k3, yo, sl 1—k2 tog—psso, yo, k3, yo, ssk, k4.

Row 7—P3, p2 tog-b, yo, p11, yo, p2 tog, p3.

Row 8—K2, k2 tog, yo, k5, yo, sl 1—k2 tog—psso, yo, k5, yo, ssk, k2.

Rows 9 through 15—Repeat Rows 1 through 7.

Row 16—K1, k2 tog, yo, k1, yo, ssk, k3, yo, sl 1—k2 tog—psso, yo, k3, k2 tog, yo, k1, yo, ssk, k1.

Rows 17, 19, 21, 23, 25, and 27—Purl.

Row 18—K2 tog, yo, k3, yo, ssk, k2, yo, sl 1—k2 tog—psso, yo, k2, k2 tog, yo, k3, yo, ssk.

Row 20—K2, yo, sl 1—k2 tog—psso, yo, k3, k2 tog, yo, k1, yo, ssk, k3, yo, sl 1—k2 tog—psso, yo, k2.

Row 22—K7, k2 tog, yo, k3, yo, ssk, k7.

Row 24—K9, yo, sl 1—k2 tog—psso, yo, k9.

Row 26—Knit.

Row 28—Purl.

Repeat Rows 1–28.

Rose Trellis Lace

Rose Trellis Lace

This extraordinarily beautiful lace pattern is a joy to work even though the pattern rows are numerous. For a test swatch, cast on at least 42 sts, or else the rosettes at the intersections of the diamonds will not be seen. *Note* that there is a yo before the ending sts of Rows 3, 21, and 39. The number of sts remains the same throughout.

Multiple of 20 sts plus 2.

Row 1 (Right side)—K1, * yo, k3 tog, yo, k2, yo, ssk, yo, k3 tog, yo, k1, yo, ssk, yo, k3 tog, yo, k2, yo, ssk; rep from *, end k1.

Row 2 and all other wrong-side rows—Purl.

Row 3—K1, ssk, * yo, k4, yo, sl 1—k2 tog—psso, yo, k3, yo, sl 1—k2 tog—psso, yo, k4, yo, sl 1—k2 tog—psso; rep from * to last 6 sts, end last rep k6 instead of k4, yo, sl 1—k2 tog—psso.

Row 5—K2, * (yo, ssk) twice, k3, yo, ssk, yo, k3 tog, yo, k3, (k2 tog, yo) twice, k1; rep from *.

Row 7—* K3, (yo, ssk) twice, k3, yo, sl 1—k2 tog—psso, yo, k3, (k2 tog, yo) twice; rep from *, end k2.

Row 9—K4, * (yo, ssk) twice, k7, (k2 tog, yo) twice, k5; rep from *, end last rep k3.

Row 11—K5, * (yo, ssk) twice, k5, (k2 tog, yo) twice, k7; rep from *, end last rep k4.

Row 13—K6, * (yo, ssk) twice, k3, (k2 tog, yo) twice, k9; rep from *, end last rep k5.

Row 15—K2, * yo, ssk, k3, (yo, ssk) twice, k1, (k2 tog, yo) twice, k3, k2 tog, yo, k1; rep from *.

Row 17—* (K3, yo, ssk) twice, yo, sl 1—k2 tog—psso, yo, k2 tog, yo, k3, k2 tog, yo; rep from *, end k2.

Row 19—K1, * yo, k3 tog, yo, k1, yo, k3, k3 tog, yo, k1, yo, sl 1—k2 tog—psso, k3, yo, k1, yo, ssk; rep from *, end k1.

Row 21—K1, ssk, * yo, k3, yo, k1, k3 tog, yo, k3, yo, sl 1—k2 tog—psso, k1, yo, k3, yo, sl 1—k2 tog—psso; rep from * to last 5 sts, end last rep k5 instead of k3, yo, sl 1—k2 tog—psso.

Row 23—K2, * (yo, ssk, yo, k3 tog, yo, k2) twice, yo, ssk, yo, k3 tog, yo, k1; rep from *.

Row 25—* K3, yo, sl 1—k2 tog—psso, (yo, k4, yo, sl 1—k2 tog—psso) twice, yo; rep from *, end k2.

Row 27—K1, * yo, k3 tog, yo, k3, (k2 tog, yo) twice, k1, (yo, ssk) twice, k3, yo, ssk; rep from *, end k1.

Row 29—K1, ssk, * yo, k3, (k2 tog, yo) twice, k3, (yo, ssk) twice, k3, yo, sl 1—k2 tog—psso; rep from * to last 5 sts, end last rep k5 instead of k3, yo, sl 1—k2 tog—psso.

Row 31—K5, * (k2 tog, yo) twice, k5, (yo, ssk) twice, k7; rep from *, end last rep k4.

Row 33—K4, * (k2 tog, yo) twice, k7, (yo, ssk) twice, k5; rep from *, end last rep k3.

Row 35—* K3, (k2 tog, yo) twice, k9, (yo, ssk) twice; rep from *, end k2.

Row 37—K2, * (k2 tog, yo) twice, k3, k2 tog, yo, k1, yo, ssk, k3, (yo, ssk) twice, k1; rep from *.

Row 39—K1, k2 tog, * yo, (k2 tog, yo, k3) twice, yo, ssk, k3, yo, ssk, yo, sl 1—
k2 tog—psso; rep from * to last 2 sts, end last rep ssk instead of sl 1—k2 tog—
psso.

Row 41—K2, * yo, sl 1—k2 tog—psso, k3, yo, k1, yo, ssk, yo, k3 tog, yo, k1, yo,
k3, k3 tog, yo, k1; rep from *.

Row 43—* K3, yo, sl 1—k2 tog—psso, k1, yo, k3, yo, sl 1—k2 tog—psso, yo, k3,
yo, k1, k3 tog, yo; rep from *, end k2.

Row 44—Purl.

Repeat Rows 1–44.

Tulip-Bud Pattern

Two versions of this grand old pattern are given, Version I
being an earlier and Version II a later development. Version II
is clearly more sophisticated, yet Version I has a certain primi-
tive charm which is lacking in the later pattern. In Version I
the stiffness and angularity of the openwork "leaves" show a
simpler approach to a problem that is much more gracefully
solved in Version II. The garter stitch ground of Version I is
characteristic of earlier methods, but in this pattern it is necessary to support the embossed bud, which could not stand so well
upon a ground of stockinette stitch. Version II's bud, therefore,
is lost along with the garter stitch ground, and becomes a flat
diamond outlined by openwork.

Version I is particularly well suited to bedspreads, fancy baby
blankets, and the like. Version II is better for dresses, stoles, lace
mats, and other articles requiring a flatter fabric.

Tulip-Bud Pattern, Version I

VERSION I

Panel of 37 sts.

Row 1 (Wrong side)—K18, p1, k18.
Row 2—K16, k2 tog, yo, k1, yo, ssk, k16.
Row 3—K16, p5, k16.
Row 4—K15, k2 tog, yo, k3, yo, ssk, k15.
Row 5—K15, p7, k15.
Row 6—K14, (k2 tog, yo) twice, k1, (yo, ssk) twice, k14.
Row 7—K14, p9, k14.
Row 8—K13, (k2 tog, yo) twice, k3, (yo, ssk) twice, k13.
Row 9—K13, p4, k1, p1, k1, p4, k13.
Row 10—K12, (k2 tog, yo) twice, k5, (yo, ssk) twice, k12.
Row 11—K12, p4, k2, p1, k2, p4, k12.
Row 12—K11, (k2 tog, yo) twice, k3, yo, k1, yo, k3, (yo, ssk)
twice, k11. (39 sts)
Row 13—K11, p4, k3, p3, k3, p4, k11.

Tulip-Bud Pattern, Version II

Row 14—K3, yo, ssk, k5, (k2 tog, yo) twice, k5, yo, k1, yo, k5, (yo, ssk) twice, k5, k2 tog, yo, k3. (41 sts)

Row 15—K3, p2, k5, p4, k4, p5, k4, p4, k5, p2, k3.

Row 16—K4, yo, ssk, k3, (k2 tog, yo) twice, k7, yo, k1, yo, k7, (yo, ssk) twice, k3, k2 tog, yo, k4. (43 sts)

Row 17—K4, p2, k3, p4, k5, p7, k5, p4, k3, p2, k4.

Row 18—K5, yo, ssk, k1, (k2 tog, yo) twice, k9, yo, k1, yo, k9, (yo, ssk) twice, k1, k2 tog, yo, k5. (45 sts)

Row 19—K5, p2, k1, p4, k6, p9, k6, p4, k1, p2, k5.

Row 20—K6, yo, sl 1—k2 tog—psso, yo, k2 tog, yo, k7, ssk, k5, k2 tog, k7, yo, ssk, yo, k3 tog, yo, k6. (43 sts)

Row 21—K6, p5, k7, p7, k7, p5, k6.

Row 22—K18, ssk, k3, k2 tog, k18. (41 sts)

Row 23—K18, p5, k18.

Row 24—K18, ssk, k1, k2 tog, k18. (39 sts)

Row 25—K18, p3, k18.

Row 26—K18, sl 1—k2 tog—psso, k18. (37 sts)

Repeat Rows 1–26.

VERSION II

Panel of 37 sts.

Row 1 (Wrong side)—Purl.

Row 2—K16, k2 tog, yo, k1, yo, ssk, k16.

Row 3—P15, p2 tog-b, yo, p3, yo, p2 tog, p15.

Row 4—K14, (k2 tog, yo) twice, k1, (yo, ssk) twice, k14.

Row 5—P13, p2 tog-b, yo, p7, yo, p2 tog, p13.

Row 6—K12, k2 tog, yo, k1, k2 tog, yo, k3, yo, ssk, k1, yo, ssk, k12.

Row 7—P11, p2 tog-b, yo, p11, yo, p2 tog, p11.

Row 8—K10, k2 tog, yo, k2, (k2 tog, yo) twice, k1, (yo, ssk) twice, k2, yo, ssk, k10.

Rows 9, 11, and 13—Purl.

Row 10—K9, k2 tog, yo, k2, (k2 tog, yo, k1) twice, yo, ssk, k1, yo, ssk, k2, yo, ssk, k9.

Row 12—K2, yo, ssk, k4, (k2 tog, yo, k2) twice, k2 tog, yo, k1, (yo, ssk, k2) twice, yo, ssk, k4, k2 tog, yo, k2.

Row 14—K3, yo, ssk, (k2, k2 tog, yo) 3 times, k3, (yo, ssk, k2) 3 times, k2 tog, yo, k3.

Row 15—P4, yo, p2 tog, p4, p2 tog-b, yo, p13, yo, p2 tog, p4, p2 tog-b, yo, p4.

Row 16—K5, yo, sl 1—k2 tog—psso, yo, k1, k2 tog, yo, k3, k2 tog, yo, k5, yo, ssk, k3, yo, ssk, k1, yo, k3 tog, yo, k5.

Row 17—P6, yo, p2 tog, p2 tog-b, yo, p17, yo, p2 tog, p2 tog-b, yo, p6.

Row 18—K7, k2 tog, yo, k6, yo, ssk, k3, k2 tog, yo, k6, yo, ssk, k7.

Rows 19, 21, and 23—Purl.

Row 20—K16, yo, ssk, k1, k2 tog, yo, k16.

Row 22—K17, yo, sl 2 knitwise—k1—p2sso, yo, k17.

Row 24—Knit.

Repeat Rows 1–24.

Diagonal Spanish Lace

The diagonal line is typical of a number of Spanish lace patterns (see Madeira Diamond Stitch and Diagonal Madeira Lace) but these patterns differ considerably from one another. They are both beautiful and strikingly novel. An insertion of a diagonal lace stitch up the front of a blouse or dress is very pretty and perhaps even more appealing than an entire garment done in the same pattern.

Multiple of 8 sts plus 4.

Row 1 (Right side)—K2, * yo, ssk, k1, k2 tog, yo, k3; rep from *, end k2.
Row 2—P2, * p5, p2 tog-b, yo, p1; rep from *, end p2.
Row 3—K2, * k2, yo, ssk, k1, k2 tog, yo, k1; rep from *, end k2.
Row 4—P2, * p3, p2 tog-b, yo, p3; rep from *, end p2.
Row 5—K1, * k2 tog, yo, k3, yo, ssk, k1; rep from *, end k3.
Row 6—P2, * p1, p2 tog-b, yo, p5; rep from *, end p2.
Row 7—K2, * k1, k2 tog, yo, k3, yo, ssk; rep from *, end k2.
Row 8—P1, * p2 tog-b, yo, p6; rep from *, end p3.

Repeat Rows 1–8.

Diagonal Spanish Lace

Madeira Diamond Stitch

Here is another beautiful Spanish pattern that features the diagonal line. It has a rather tricky "p3 tog-b" in Rows 4 and 8, which might be more conveniently worked as follows: p2 tog, then sl the st just worked back to left needle; then with the point of right needle sl the next st beyond over this st and off left needle; then sl the same st back to right needle and proceed.

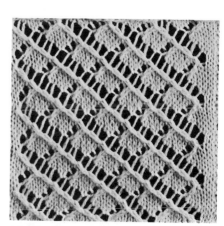

Multiple of 8 sts plus 4.

Row 1 (Right side)—K2, * yo, ssk, k6; rep from *, end k2.
Row 2—P2, * yo, p2 tog, p3, p2 tog-b, yo, p1; rep from *, end p2.
Row 3—K2, * k2, yo, ssk, k1, k2 tog, yo, k1; rep from *, end k2.
Row 4—P2, * p2, yo, p3 tog-b, yo, p3; rep from *, end p2.
Row 5—K2, * k4, yo, ssk, k2; rep from *, end k2.
Row 6—P2, * p1, p2 tog-b, yo, p1, yo, p2 tog, p2; rep from *, end p2.
Row 7—K2, * k1, k2 tog, yo, k3, yo, ssk; rep from *, end k2.
Row 8—P1, p2 tog-b, * yo, p5, yo, p3 tog-b; rep from *, end yo, p5, yo, p2 tog, p2.

Repeat Rows 1–8.

Madeira Diamond Stitch

Bead Stitch

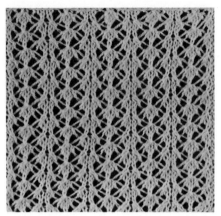

Bead Stitch

Bead Stitch is a basic Shetland lace pattern used as a construction unit in more complicated laces (See Four Sisters Medallion Pattern, Shetland Twins, etc.) Little "beads" formed in this manner are found in Spanish lace patterns as well, demonstrating the Spanish ancestry of Shetland lace. Bead Stitch also makes a pretty allover lace when panels are repeated continuously as shown, on a multiple of 7 stitches; or, one, two, three or more plain knit stitches may be inserted between panels to make a more solid fabric with vertical columns of lace.

Panel of 7 sts.

Row 1 (Right side)—K1, k2 tog, yo, k1, yo, ssk, k1.
Row 2—P2 tog-b, yo, p3, yo, p2 tog.
Row 3—K1, yo, ssk, k1, k2 tog, yo, k1.
Row 4—P2, yo, p3 tog, yo, p2.

Repeat Rows 1–4.

Four Sisters Medallion Pattern

Four Sisters Medallion Pattern

This dainty lace, of Spanish origin, makes a beautiful allover pattern as well as an insertion. It must be well stretched when blocked.

Panel of 15 sts.

Row 1 (Right side)—K5, k2 tog, yo, k1, yo, ssk, k5.
Row 2—P4, p2 tog-b, yo, p3, yo, p2 tog, p4.
Row 3—K3, k2 tog, yo, k5, yo, ssk, k3.
Row 4—P2, p2 tog-b, yo, p1, yo, p2 tog, p1, p2 tog-b, yo, p1, yo, p2 tog, p2.
Row 5—K1, k2 tog, yo, k3, yo, k3 tog, yo, k3, yo, ssk, k1.
Row 6—P2, yo, p5, yo, p1, yo, p5, yo, p2. (Increased to 19 sts)
Row 7—(K3, yo, ssk, k1, k2 tog, yo) twice, k3.
Row 8—P4, p3 tog, yo, p5, yo, p3 tog, p4. (17 sts)
Row 9—K6, yo, ssk, k1, k2 tog, yo, k6.
Row 10—P3, p2 tog-b, p2, yo, p3 tog, yo, p2, p2 tog, p3. (15 sts)

Repeat Rows 1–10.

The Shetland Twins

The "twins" are really two patterns, similar but not identical. Either one may be worked alone if desired, and for this reason they are given separately. Rows 1, 2, 3, 15, 16, 17, and 18 are exactly alike in both patterns; the other rows differ. To work the two patterns in vertical stripes, cast on a multiple of 14 stitches plus 1 and work Row 1 of Pattern A on the first 15 stitches, then work from * of Row 1, Pattern B, on the next 14 stitches, then work from * of Pattern A's first row again, and so on. For each row follow this plan, beginning each succeeding row with the next row of whichever pattern was used last. To alternate the patterns in check fashion as shown, simply exchange their positions after every 18th row.

These patterns are tricky, and some of the "p2 tog-b" directions are awkward to work because one or the other of the two stitches that are to be purled together is a yo. For the method of accomplishing this more easily, see Lace Medallion.

The Shetland Twins

Multiple of 14 sts plus 1.

PATTERN A:

Row 1 (Right side)—K1, * k4, k2 tog, yo, k1, yo, ssk, k5; rep from *.
Row 2—P1, * p3, p2 tog-b, yo, p3, yo, p2 tog, p4; rep from *.
Row 3—K1, * k2, (k2 tog, yo) twice, k1, (yo, ssk) twice, k3; rep from *.
Row 4—P1, * p1, (p2 tog-b, yo) twice, p3, (yo, p2 tog) twice, p2; rep from *.
Row 5—K1, * (k2 tog, yo, k2, yo, ssk, k1) twice; rep from *.
Row 6—P1, * yo, p2 tog, p3, yo, p3 tog, yo, p3, p2 tog-b, yo, p1; rep from *.
Row 7—K1, * (yo, ssk, k2, k2 tog, yo, k1) twice; rep from *.
Row 8—P1, * yo, p2 tog, p1, p2 tog-b, yo, p3, yo, p2 tog, p1, p2 tog-b, yo, p1; rep from *.
Row 9—K1, * yo, ssk, k2, yo, ssk, k1, k2 tog, yo, k2, k2 tog, yo, k1; rep from *.
Rows 10, 11, and 12—Repeat Rows 6, 7, and 8.
Row 13—K1, * (k1, yo, ssk) twice, k1, (k2 tog, yo, k1) twice, k1; rep from *.
Row 14—P1, * p2, yo, p2 tog, p1, yo, p3 tog, yo, p1, p2 tog-b, yo, p3; rep from *.
Row 15—K1, * k3, yo, ssk, k3, k2 tog, yo, k4; rep from *.
Row 16—P1, * p4, yo, p2 tog, p1, p2 tog-b, yo, p5; rep from *.
Row 17—K1, * k5, yo, sl 1—k2 tog—psso, yo, k6; rep from *.
Row 18—Purl.

Repeat Rows 1–18.

PATTERN B:

Row 1 (Right side)—K1, * k4, k2 tog, yo, k1, yo, ssk, k5; rep from *.
Row 2—P1, * p3, p2 tog-b, yo, p3, yo, p2 tog, p4; rep from *.
Row 3—K1, * k2, (k2 tog, yo) twice, k1, (yo, ssk) twice, k3; rep from *.
Row 4—P1, * p1, p2 tog-b, yo, p7, yo, p2 tog, p2; rep from *.

Row 5—K1, * (k2 tog, yo) twice, k1, yo, sl 1—k2 tog—psso, yo, k1, (yo, ssk) twice, k1; rep from *.

Rows 6, 8, 10, and 12—P1, * yo, p2 tog, p9, p2 tog-b, yo, p1; rep from *.

Row 7—K1, * yo, ssk, (k1, yo, sl 1—k2 tog—psso, yo) twice, k1, k2 tog, yo, k1; rep from *.

Row 9—K1, * yo, ssk, k2 tog, yo, k1, yo, sl 1—k2 tog—psso, yo, k1, yo, ssk, k2 tog, yo, k1; rep from *.

Row 11—Repeat Row 7.

Row 13—K1, * k1, yo, ssk, k2, yo, sl 1—k2 tog—psso, yo, k2, k2 tog, yo, k2; rep from *.

Row 14—P1, * p2, yo, p2 tog, p5, p2 tog-b, yo, p3; rep from *.

Row 15—K1, * k3, yo, ssk, k3, k2 tog, yo, k4; rep from *.

Row 16—P1, * p4, yo, p2 tog, p1, p2 tog-b, yo, p5; rep from *.

Row 17—K1, * k5, yo, sl 1—k2 tog—psso, yo, k6; rep from *.

Row 18—Purl.

Repeat Rows 1–18.

Madeira Leaf Stitch Border

Madeira Leaf Stitch Border

This very beautiful old Spanish pattern makes a charming border indeed, but may be carried on more than once to repeat the horizontal leaf motif up through the entire fabric. For a single repeat, simply go through Rows 1–49 once; to continue the pattern upward, omit the first 4 rows and the last 5 rows and proceed with the pattern rows.

Multiple of 10 sts plus 4.

Rows 1, 3, and 5 (Right side)—Knit.

Rows 2, 4, and 6—Purl.

Row 7—K2, * yo, ssk, k8; rep from *, end k2.

Row 8—P9, * p2 tog-b, yo, p8; rep from *, end last rep p3.

Row 9—K2, * (yo, ssk) twice, k6, rep from *, end k2.

Row 10—P7, * p2 tog-b, yo, p8; rep from *, end last rep p5.

Row 11—K2, * (k1, yo, ssk) twice, k4; rep from *, end k2.

Row 12—P5, * p2 tog-b, yo, p8; rep from *, end last rep p7.

Row 13—K2, * (k2, yo, ssk) twice, k2; rep from *, end k2.

Row 14—P3, * p2 tog-b, yo, p8; rep from *, end p1.

Row 15—K2, * (k3, yo, ssk) twice; rep from *, end k2.

Row 16—P6, * p2 tog-b, yo, p8; rep from *, end last rep p6.

Row 17—K3, * k4, yo, ssk, k2, yo, ssk; rep from *, end k1.

Row 18—P4, * p2 tog-b, yo, p8; rep from *.

Row 19—K2, * yo, ssk, k5, yo, ssk, k1; rep from *, end k2.

Row 20—P2, * p2 tog-b, yo, p8; rep from *, end p2.

Row 21—K3, * yo, ssk, k6, yo, ssk; rep from *, end k1.

Row 22—P10, * p2 tog-b, yo, p8; rep from *, end last rep p2.

Row 23—K3, * yo, ssk, k8; rep from *, end k1.

Row 24—Knit.

Row 25—K2, * yo, ssk; rep from *, end k2.
Row 26—Knit.
Row 27—K2, * k2 tog, yo, k8; rep from *, end k2.
Row 28—P1, * yo, p2 tog, p8; rep from *, end last rep p1.
Row 29—K2, * p2 tog, yo, k6, k2 tog, yo; rep from *, end k2. ("P2 tog" in this
   row is *not* a mistake.)
Row 30—P3, * yo, p2 tog, p8; rep from *, end p1.
Row 31—K1, * k2 tog, yo, k5, k2 tog, yo, k1; rep from *, end k3.
Row 32—P5, * yo, p2 tog, p8; rep from *, end last rep p7.
Row 33—K2, * k4, k2 tog, yo, k2, k2 tog, yo; rep from *, end k2.
Row 34—P7, * yo, p2 tog, p8; rep from *, end last rep p5.
Row 35—K1, * (k3, k2 tog, yo) twice; rep from *, end k3.
Row 36—P4, * yo, p2 tog, p8; rep from *.
Row 37—K3, * k2 tog, yo, k2, k2 tog, yo, k4; rep from *, end k1.
Row 38—P6, * yo, p2 tog, p8; rep from *, end last rep p6.
Row 39—K2, * k2 tog, yo, k1, k2 tog, yo, k5; rep from *, end k2.
Row 40—P8, * yo, p2 tog, p8; rep from *, end last rep p4.
Row 41—K1, * (k2 tog, yo) twice, k6; rep from *, end k3.
Row 42—P10, * yo, p2 tog, p8; rep from *, end last rep p2.
Row 43—K1, * k2 tog, yo, k8; rep from *, end k3.
Rows 44, 46, and 48—Purl.
Rows 45, 47, and 49—Knit.

Lace Medallion

Here is an exquisite Italian lace pattern which appears simple
but is actually a bit tricky to work, due to the position of the
yo's which makes them hard to decrease with the stitch along-
side on the next row. The main difficulty will be with the
second "p2 tog-b" in Row 4, and the "p2 tog-b" of Row 6.
These decreases may be more easily accomplished in the following manner: purl the first stitch (that is, the yo of the
previous row) and slip this stitch back to the left needle; then
with the right needle pass the next stitch over it and off the left
needle; then slip the same stitch back to the right needle and
proceed with the following yo.

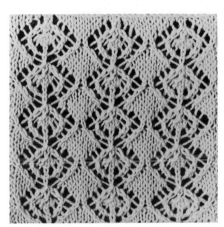

Lace Medallion

Multiple of 11 sts.

Row 1 (Right side)—* K3, k2 tog, yo, k1, yo, ssk, k3; rep from *.
Row 2—* P2, p2 tog-b, yo, p3, yo, p2 tog, p2; rep from *.
Row 3—* K1, (k2 tog, yo) twice, k1, (yo, ssk) twice, k1; rep from *.
Row 4—* (P2 tog-b, yo) twice, p3, (yo, p2 tog) twice; rep from *.
Row 5—* K1, (yo, ssk) twice, k1, (k2 tog, yo) twice, k1; rep from *.
Row 6—* P2, yo, p2 tog, yo, p3 tog, yo, p2 tog-b, yo, p2; rep from *.
Row 7—* K3, yo, ssk, k1, k2 tog, yo, k3; rep from *.
Row 8—* P4, yo, p3 tog, yo, p4; rep from *.

Repeat Rows 1–8.

Diamond Mesh

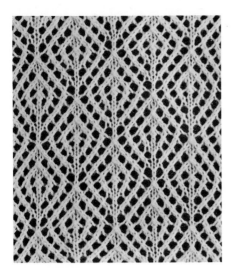

Diamond Mesh

Here is one of the most beautiful of mesh patterns, similar to Openwork Diamonds in form but having the diamonds themselves also made of openwork. Like Arrowhead Lace, to which this mesh is related, it has only two simple pattern rows. One row is repeated three times, the other twice, and then the entire pattern is alternated on the half-drop principle.

Multiple of 12 sts plus 1.

Row 1 (Wrong side) and all other wrong-side rows—Purl.

Rows 2, 6, and 10—K1, * (yo, ssk) twice, yo, sl 1—k2 tog—psso, yo, (k2 tog, yo) twice, k1; repeat from *.

Rows 4 'and 8—K1, * k1, (yo, ssk) twice, k1, (k2 tog, yo) twice, k2; repeat from *.

Rows 12, 16, and 20—K2 tog, yo, * (k2 tog, yo) twice, k1, (yo, ssk) twice, yo, sl 1—k2 tog—psso, yo; repeat from *, end (k2 tog, yo) twice, k1, (yo, ssk) 3 times.

Rows 14 and 18—K1, * (k2 tog, yo) twice, k3, (yo, ssk) twice, k1; repeat from *.

Repeat Rows 1–20.

Lace Chain

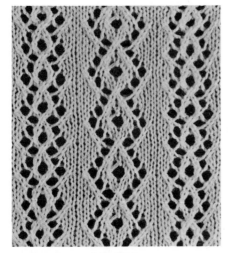

CENTER PANEL: *Lace Chain*
SIDE PANELS: *Little Lace Chain*

Panel of 10 sts.

Row 1 (Wrong side) and all other wrong-side rows—Purl. Note: On Row 7 work (k1, p1) into the double yo of previous row.

Row 2—K2, k2 tog, yo, k2 tog but do not slip from needle, insert right-hand needle between the sts just knitted tog and knit 1st st again; then sl both sts from needle together; yo, ssk, k2.

Row 4—K1, k2 tog, yo, k4, yo, ssk, k1.

Row 6—K2 tog, yo, k1, k2 tog, (yo) twice, ssk, k1, yo, ssk.

Row 8—K2, yo, ssk, k2, k2 tog, yo, k2.

Row 10—K3, yo, ssk, k2 tog, yo, k3.

Repeat Rows 1–10.

VARIATION: *LITTLE LACE CHAIN*

Panel of 8 sts.

Row 1 (Wrong side) and all other wrong-side rows—Purl. Note: On Row 5 work (k1, p1) into the double yo of previous row.

Row 2—K1, k2 tog, yo, twist the next 2 sts as in Row 2 above, yo, ssk, k1.

Row 4—K2 tog, yo, k2 tog, (yo) twice, ssk, yo, ssk.

Row 6—K2, yo, ssk, k2 tog, yo, k2.

Repeat Rows 1–6.

Antique Diamond Pattern

This is one of the oldest known forms of Openwork Diamonds. In the ancient Spanish fashion it uses yo's and decreases on both sides of the fabric. Another point of archaic style is that the basis of the pattern is Garter Stitch. These Antique Diamonds are beautiful in their way; but like all laces of this early type the pattern requires certain special attentions. It should be worked in very fine yarn with an easy tension, and the fabric must be well stretched vertically when it is blocked.

Multiple of 10 sts plus 1.

Row 1 (Right side)—K1, * yo, ssk, k5, k2 tog, yo, k1; repeat from *.
Row 2—P1, * p1, yo, p2 tog, k3, p2 tog-b, yo, p2; repeat from *.
Row 3—K1, * k2, yo, ssk, k1, k2 tog, yo, k3; repeat from *.
Row 4—K1, * k2, p1, yo, p3 tog, yo, p1, k3; repeat from *.
Row 5—K1, * k2, k2 tog, yo, k1, yo, ssk, k3; repeat from *.
Row 6—K1, * k1, p2 tog-b, yo, p3, yo, p2 tog, k2; repeat from *.
Row 7—K1, * k2 tog, yo, k5, yo, ssk, k1; repeat from *.
Row 8—P2 tog, * yo, p1, k5, p1, yo, p3 tog; repeat from *, end last repeat p2 tog instead of p3 tog.

Antique Diamond Pattern

Repeat Rows 1–8.

Smiling Diamonds

This is a combination of two popular lace patterns. It begins as a multiple chevron, and ends as a diamond. The combination is a happy one; each little diamond seems to be wearing a wide grin!

Multiple of 12 sts plus 1.

Row 1 (Wrong side) and all other wrong-side rows—Purl.
Row 2—K1, * yo, ssk, k7, k2 tog, yo, k1; rep from *.
Row 4—K1, * k1, yo, ssk, k5, k2 tog, yo, k2; rep from *.
Row 6—K1, * (yo, ssk) twice, k3, (k2 tog, yo) twice, k1; rep from *.
Row 8—K1, * k1, (yo, ssk) twice, k1, (k2 tog, yo) twice, k2; rep from *.
Row 10—K1, * (yo, ssk) twice, yo, sl 1—k2 tog—psso, yo, (k2 tog, yo) twice, k1; rep from *.
Row 12—K1, * k3, k2 tog, yo, k1, yo, ssk, k4; rep from *.
Row 14—K1, * k2, k2 tog, yo, k3, yo, ssk, k3; rep from *.
Row 16—K1, * k1, (k2 tog, yo) twice, k1, (yo, ssk) twice, k2; rep from *.
Row 18—K1, * (k2 tog, yo) twice, k3, (yo, ssk) twice, k1; rep from *.
Row 20—K2 tog, yo, * (k2 tog, yo) twice, k1, (yo, ssk) twice, yo, sl 1—k2 tog—psso, yo; rep from *, end (k2 tog, yo) twice, k1, (yo, ssk) 3 times.

Smiling Diamonds

Repeat rows 1–20.

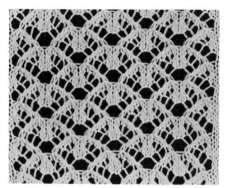

Shower Stitch

Shower Stitch

This is an exquisite old French lace, unsurpassable for its openness and delicacy. Any garment made in this pattern would be a garment to be proud of. The pattern is not difficult, but it does require care in working. There is a "p3 tog-b" in Rows 4 and 8 which might prove a little awkward; it can be easily worked as follows: p2 tog, then sl the resulting st back onto left needle; with right needle pass the next st beyond over this st; then sl the same st to right needle again and proceed.

Multiple of 12 sts plus 4.

Row 1 (Right side)—K2, * k2 tog, yo, k2, k2 tog, (yo) twice, ssk, k2, yo, ssk; rep from *, end k2.

Row 2—P2, * p3, p2 tog-b, yo, (k1, p1) into the 2 yo's of previous row, yo, p2 tog, p3; rep from *, end p2.

Row 3—K2, * k2, k2 tog, yo, k4, yo, ssk, k2; rep from *, end k2.

Row 4—P2, * p3 tog-b, yo, p1, yo, p4, yo, p1, yo, p3 tog; rep from *, end p2.

Row 5—K2, * yo, ssk, k2, yo, ssk, k2 tog, yo, k2, k2 tog, yo; rep from *, end k2. (Note that the yo's at the beginning and the end form a "yo twice").

Row 6—P2, * p1, yo, p2 tog, p6, p2 tog-b, yo, k1; rep from *, end p2. (Note that the "p1" at the beginning and the "k1" at the end form a "k1, p1 into the 2 yo's of previous row", as in Row 2.)

Row 7—K2, * k2, yo, ssk, k4, k2 tog, yo, k2; rep from *, end k2.

Row 8—P2, * p2, yo, p1, yo, p3 tog, p3 tog-b, yo, p1, yo, p2; rep from *, end p2.

Repeat Rows 1–8.

Wave and Leaf Pattern

Wave and Leaf Pattern

This beautiful lace, a traditional Italian pattern, incorporates two lace designs into one. Either may be worked singly. The "wave" design, a miniature Continental-Style Chevron, can be worked by repeating Rows 1–6. The "leaf" pattern is developed by Rows 7–16.

In working the double yo's from the wrong side, care must be taken to keep the "k1, p1" and "p1, k1" in their proper places, otherwise the strands supporting the leaf motifs will not be correctly twisted. Note also the 5-stitch decrease that occurs in Rows 11, 15, 27, and 31.

Multiple of 10 sts plus 5.

Row 1 (Right side)—K2, * yo, ssk, k8; rep from *, end yo, ssk, k1.

Row 2—P2, * p1, yo, p2 tog, p5, p2 tog-b, yo; rep from *, end p3.

Row 3—K2, * k2, yo, ssk, k3, k2 tog, yo, k1; rep from *, end k3.

Row 4—P2, * p3, yo, p2 tog, p1, p2 tog-b, yo, p2; rep from *, end p3.

Row 5—K2, * k4, yo, sl 1—k2 tog—psso, yo, k3; rep from *, end k3.

Row 6—Purl.

Row 7—K2, k2 tog, * (yo) twice, ssk, k3, k2 tog, (yo) twice, sl 1—k2 tog—psso; rep from *, end (yo) twice, ssk, k3, k2 tog, (yo) twice, ssk, k2.

Row 8—P2, * p1, (p1, k1) into 2 yo's, p5, (k1, p1) into 2 yo's; rep from *, end p3.

Row 9—K2, * k2, (yo) twice, sl 1—k2 tog—psso, k1, k3 tog, (yo) twice, k1; rep from *, end k3.

Row 10—P2, * p2, (p1, k1) into 2 yo's, p3, (k1, p1) into 2 yo's, p1; rep from *, end p3.

Row 11—K2, * k3, (yo) twice, sl 2—k3 tog—p2sso, (yo) twice, k2; rep from *, end k3.

Row 12—P2, * p3, (k1, p1) into 2 yo's, p1, (p1, k1) into 2 yo's, p2; rep from *, end p3.

Row 13—K2, * k1, k3 tog, (yo) twice, k3, (yo) twice, sl 1—k2 tog—psso; rep from *, end k3.

Row 14—P2, * p2, (k1, p1) into 2 yo's, p3, (p1, k1) into 2 yo's, p1; rep from *, end p3.

Row 15—K2, k3 tog, * (yo) twice, k5, (yo) twice, sl 2—k3 tog—p2sso; rep from *, end (yo) twice, k5, (yo) twice, sl 1—k2 tog—psso, k2.

Row 16—P2, * p1, (k1, p1) into 2 yo's, p5, (p1, k1) into 2 yo's; rep from *, end p3.

Row 17—K2, * k5, yo, ssk, k3; rep from *, end k3.

Row 18—P2, * p3, p2 tog-b, yo, p1, yo, p2 tog, p2; rep from *, end p3.

Row 19—K2, * k2, k2 tog, yo, k3, yo, ssk, k1; rep from *, end k3.

Row 20—P2, * p1, p2 tog-b, yo, p5, yo, p2 tog; rep from *, end p3.

Row 21—K2, k2 tog, * yo, k7, yo, sl 1—k2 tog—psso; rep from *, end yo, k7, yo, ssk, k2.

Row 22—Purl.

Row 23—K2, * k2, k2 tog, (yo) twice, sl 1—k2 tog—psso, (yo) twice, ssk, k1; rep from *, end k3.

Row 24—Repeat Row 12.

Row 25—K2, * k1, k3 tog, (yo) twice, k3, (yo) twice, sl 1—k2 tog—psso; rep from *, end k3.

Row 26—Repeat Row 14.

Row 27—K2, k3 tog, * (yo) twice, k5, (yo) twice, sl 2—k3 tog—p2sso; rep from *, end (yo) twice, k5, (yo) twice, sl 1—k2 tog—psso, k2.

Row 28—Repeat Row 8.

Row 29—K2, * k2, (yo) twice, sl 1—k2 tog—psso, k1, k3 tog, (yo) twice, k1; rep from *, end k3.

Row 30—Repeat Row 10.

Row 31—K2, * k3, (yo) twice, sl 2—k3 tog—p2sso, (yo) twice, k2; rep from *, end k3.

Row 32—P2, * p3, (p1, k1) into 2 yo's, p1, (k1, p1) into 2 yo's, p2; rep from *, end p3.

Repeat Rows 1–32.

CHAPTER ELEVEN

Cables

It is curious, but true, that many people who have knitted for years have somehow managed to avoid trying their hands at even simple cables. This is a mistake, as some of the most interesting patterns in knitting are formed with the cable needle. The marvelous "fisherman sweaters" that are so popular today are made simply by combining different cable patterns in the same garment, and this is easier to do than you might think if you have never worked with cables. It is only a matter of keeping track of rows (the knitter's pencil-and-paper is one of the most essential parts of a fisherman sweater)! Even an otherwise plain garment is much improved, and acquires much more of the hand-knitted look, with the addition of a few cables. It really pays to become handy with the cable needle, and the technique, while a little awkward at first (like knitting itself, or any other skill) is soon mastered. Once it has been learned, the knitter can choose at will from a multitude of delightful combinations virtually without limit.

The cable needle is used for one simple purpose: to cross a stitch or group of stitches over another stitch or group of stitches. To do this, the nearer or right-hand stitches are held without being worked on the cable needle while other stitches beyond them are being worked. If the stitches slipped on to the cable needle are to cross behind, they are held in back of the work. Then they will be concealed by stitches drawn to the right in front of them. If the stitches slipped on to the cable needle are to cross in front, they are held in front and thus will be drawn to the left, across the other stitches.

Nearly all cable patterns (with a few exceptions, like the all-over patterns of Basket Cable and Aran Honeycomb) are composed of knit stitches on a purl-stitch ground. When worked in a vertical direction, knit stitches tend to stand up away from purl stitches, giving an embossed effect. (In the horizontal direction, the opposite is true: purl stitches stand up in ridges against knit stitches.) Since most cables are used singly, the directions for them are given here in "panels", beginning and ending with the purl stitches on either side. (See Glossary on panels.)

In designing your own cable-stitch garments, or putting cable panels into a garment pattern which calls for plain stockinette, it is well to remember that cables tend to pull the fabric together laterally, so that more stitches are required to make the proper width. If you wish to insert a number of cable patterns into a sweater that is supposed to be done in plain knitting, it is a good idea to make it a size or two larger.

It is a very good habit to use a cable needle a size or two *smaller* than the needles being used for the rest of the work. This insures that the stitches will not be too much stretched while being cabled.

Cables (as well as other patterns) are sometimes worked in twisted stitches for a distinctive and different "corded" effect. This is not given with most of the following directions for various cables but you may try it out on any cable that you like, simply by knitting through the *back* loops of all the knit stitches on the right side that make up the cable, and purling through the *back* loops of the same stitches on the wrong side.

SPECIAL NOTE ON DESIGNING FISHERMAN SWEATERS

Everyone loves a fisherman sweater. How dazzling it is, heavily encrusted with fascinating embossed designs, the wonder and the envy of every inexperienced knitter! She can only admire it and think regretfully, "I could never make anything like that."

Nonsense. She can not only make it, she can even design it herself. Anyone who can use a cable needle can plan and work, not just any fisherman sweater, but an original fisherman sweater, using cable combinations that have never been put together in that particular way before. The result: a really unique garment, one of a kind, like no other sweater in the world. And it's actually very easy to do!

How to begin? All you need to start with is a number: the number of stitches required to reach halfway around the body of the person who will wear the sweater. This number is arrived at by taking the gauge of a cable swatch, or better yet the average of several different cable swatches, and multiplying by inches. For instance, let's say your own personal gauge on cable patterns, using a certain size needle and a certain yarn, is 6 stitches to the inch. Then, let's say you want your sweater to measure 20 inches across each of the front and back sections. 6 x 20 is 120 stitches; there's the number you need to start. An even easier (though rougher) way to get the number is to take it right from a commercial cable-sweater pattern. You simply look up the number of stitches given for a desired size, being sure that the gauge is the same as your own. If you are inexperienced, it is a good idea to continue following the same commercial pattern in regard to shaping the pieces as you go along. This eliminates the need for further measurements to establish when to begin decreases and so on.

All right, you have the number. Now comes the fun part. What patterns to use? There are dozens of traditional Aran patterns, all of them very beautiful, but you need not restrict yourself to these. Any cable or cable-stitch pattern is yours to create with. Leaf through this book and pick out half a dozen that you like. Other patterns not in the cable sections (such as Jacob's Ladder, Twist-Stitch Diamond Pattern, Trinity Stitch, Bobbles, etc.) are also traditionally used for fisherman sweaters but you need not stick to these either. So many hundreds of stunning combinations are possible! The only thing that puts any limit at all to your choice is the matter of vertical gauge. For instance, slip-stitch patterns are usually unsuitable because they will require more rows than cables do for a given length. Of course all patterns that you consider using should be tried out first in test swatches.

Having selected some patterns that you would like to use, next take a piece of paper (graph paper is very good for this purpose) and mark off the panels of your sweater, beginning at the center. Let's say you have chosen a cable pattern of 20 stitches for your central panel. Mark 20 stitches, or 20 squares on the graph paper, for this panel. Next, on either side, you might mark another cable which happens to have a panel of 10 stitches, not forgetting to insert one knit stitch between panels to set them off. Now you have a center panel of 20 stitches, one knit stitch on either side, and two 10-stitch panels. 42 of your 120 stitches are used up. Add two more plain knit stitches on each side and continue building outward from the center in the same way, adding whatever patterns you like, until you have used almost all of the 120 stitches. Suppose you have five patterns all together—the center panel, which we will call A, Pattern B on each side of it, Pattern C next on each side, then two Pattern D's, and on the outside edges, two Pattern E's—each panel set off by single knit stitches between. At the end you have, say, 6 stitches left over on each side edge. These 12 edge stitches can be worked plain, or in any simple knit-purl texture pattern. The patterns most commonly used for this are Seed Stitch, Moss Stitch, and Double Seed Stitch.

Now you have established your patterns. You prepare to cast on for the back of your sweater. It is customary and desirable, when working any garment in cable patterns, to cast on fewer stitches for the ribbing and then increase to the desired number of stitches before beginning the cables themselves. This insures a better fit, as the cables will tighten the fabric above the ribbing. As a general rule you should cast on about 9 ribbing stitches for every 10 garment stitches. So you cast on 110 stitches, work in ribbing for as many inches as desired (twisted or fancy ribbing is preferable for fisherman sweaters), and then increase 10 stitches evenly spaced across the piece. You now have 120 stitches. On the next row set the patterns, following your diagram as you work across. To help out at the start, you can slip markers on the needle in between panels.

The best way to proceed, keeping track of which pattern row is being worked in each panel, is to write the names of the patterns (or A, B, C, D, and E) at the top of your paper and jot the number of each row under each pattern as you go along. Then, even though one pattern may have an 8-row repeat, another a 12-row repeat, and a third a 20-row repeat, you won't get them mixed up. It is very helpful sometimes to *know*, not just guess, that the row you are working on contains Row 9 of Pattern B and Row 13 of Pattern C and Row 3 of Pattern D. So do *not* try this sort of work without pencil and paper. If a mistake should be made, so that you have to unravel a few rows back to correct it, the written row count is an invaluable aid. It will tell you not only how many rows need to be taken out but also where to pick up each pattern when you begin again.

And there you are, launched on your own, unique, original fisherman sweater. The care and planning comes at the start. After the first repeat of the patterns has been worked, it's very easy indeed. Continue working just like a plain sweater, following a commercial pattern or using your own measurements for binding off and shaping above the underarm line. The sleeves are planned, set, and worked in the same way; and on the sleeves you can use those other different cables that you wanted to put in the body and didn't have room for—they need not match the body patterns.

When you are finished, you can be proud indeed. You will have a garment that is not only dazzling in its apparent complexity, but also totally *you*. You will have made your own individual creative contribution to the ancient art of knitting.

Simple Cables

Probably no pattern in knitting is capable of so much variation as the Simple Cable. But the cable action is always the same. It consists of taking half of the stitches composing the cable on a double-pointed needle, holding them in back or in front of the work, knitting the other half of the stitches, then knitting the first group from the double-pointed needle. This creates the cable twist. If the double-pointed needle with the slipped stitches is held in back of the work, the twist will be to the right (back cross); if the double-pointed needle is held in front of the work, the twist will be to the left (front cross). Whenever two Simple Cables are used on either side of a common center, one of them should be crossed in front and the other in back, to give symmetry and balance to the design.

The variations depend upon the number of stitches composing the cable, and the number of rows between cabling rows. Generally speaking, the most shapely cables are created by having the same number of rows to the pattern as there are stitches in the cable (i.e., a six-stitch cable would be crossed every 6th row, etc.) But this is hardly a firm rule. Many knitters prefer the slightly looser cable made with two more rows than there are stitches. And the number of rows may vary in the same pattern (See Eccentric Cable, below). Five possible variations on the Simple Cable are given, but there are dozens more. How you arrange a Simple Cable is largely up to you.

Simple Cables

LEFT TO RIGHT:
1. *Four-Stitch Cable crossed every 4th row.*
2. *Six-Stitch Cable crossed every 6th row.*
3. *Six-Stitch Cable crossed every 8th row.*
4. *Eccentric Cable*
5. *Eight-Stitch Cable crossed every 10th row.*

1. FOUR-STITCH CABLE CROSSED EVERY FOURTH ROW

Panel of 8 sts.

Rows 1 and 3 (Wrong side)—K2, p4, k2.

Row 2—P2, k4, p2.

Row 4—P2, sl next 2 sts to dpn and hold in back (or in front); k2, then k2 from dpn, p2.

Repeat Rows 1–4.

2. SIX-STITCH CABLE CROSSED EVERY SIXTH ROW

Six stitches is the most popular size for cables, though it is by no means necessary to stick to this number.

Panel of 10 sts.

Rows 1 and 3 (Wrong side)—K2, p6, k2.
Row 2—P2, k6, p2.
Row 4—P2, sl next 3 sts to dpn and hold in back (or in front); k3, then k3 from dpn, p2.
Row 5—As 1 and 3.
Row 6—As 2.

Repeat Rows 1–6.

3. SIX-STITCH CABLE CROSSED EVERY EIGHTH ROW

Panel of 10 sts.

Rows 1 and 3 (Wrong side)—K2, p6, k2.
Row 2—P2, k6, p2.
Row 4—P2, sl next 3 sts to dpn and hold in back (or in front); k3, then k3 from dpn, p2.
Rows 5 and 7—As 1 and 3.
Rows 6 and 8—As 2.

Repeat Rows 1–8.

4. ECCENTRIC CABLE

This is only one example of the many ways in which the pattern rows can be varied in the same cable. A long "wrapped-ribbon" effect can be had, for instance, by cabling only once in 20 or 30 rows. Or two cable rows may be placed close together and then three or four times as many rows worked plain in between. Once the principle is understood it can be applied at will.

Panel of 10 sts.

Rows 1 and 3 (Wrong side)—K2, p6, k2.
Row 2—P2, k6, p2.
Row 4—P2, sl next 3 sts to dpn and hold in back (or in front); k3, then k3 from dpn, p2.
Rows 5, 7, 9, 11, 13, 15, and 17—As 1 and 3.
Rows 6 and 8—As 2.
Row 10—As 4.
Rows 12, 14, 16, and 18—As 2.

Repeat Rows 1–18.

5. EIGHT-STITCH CABLE CROSSED EVERY TENTH ROW

This is a bulky, bold cable suitable for heavy sports sweaters and for coats.

Panel of 12 sts.

Rows 1 and 3 (Wrong side)—K2, p8, k2.
Row 2—P2, k8, p2.
Row 4—P2, sl next 4 sts to dpn and hold in back (or in front); k4, then k4 from dpn, p2.
Rows 5, 7, and 9—As 1 and 3.
Rows 6, 8, and 10—As 2.

Repeat Rows 1–10.

Double Cable or Horseshoe Cable

Just as in Simple Cables, many alterations in the appearance of a Double Cable may be made by varying the number of rows between cabling rows and the number of stitches composing the cable. The only limitation is that each cable must be made up of a number of stitches divisible by four, so that even crossings can be made on either side. There are two ways of cabling: (1) a back cross first and a front cross second, which opens the cable outward from the center; and (2) a front cross first and a back cross second, which closes the cable toward the center (Reverse Double Cable).

LEFT: *Double Cable or Horseshoe Cable*
CENTER: *Reverse Double Cable*
RIGHT: *Bulky Double Cable*

Panel of 12 sts.

Rows 1, 3, 5, and 7—(Wrong side)—K2, p8, k2.
Row 2—P2, sl next 2 sts to dpn and hold in back, k2, then k2 from dpn; sl next 2 sts to dpn and hold in front, k2, then k2 from dpn; p2.
Rows 4, 6, and 8—P2, k8, p2.

Repeat Rows 1–8.

REVERSE DOUBLE CABLE

Directions as above, except: read "hold in front" instead of "hold in back", and vice versa, in Row 2.

BULKY DOUBLE CABLE

Panel of 16 sts.

Rows 1, 3, 5, 7, and 9—(Wrong side)—K2, p12, k2.
Row 2—P2, sl next 3 sts to dpn and hold in back, k3, then k3 from dpn; sl next 3 sts to dpn and hold in front, k3, then k3 from dpn; p2.
Rows 4, 6, 8, and 10—P2, k12, p2.

Repeat Rows 1–10.

Wheat Ear Cable

This is a dense cable having the same basic structure as Double Cable, but with the cabling rows closer together and one additional stitch in the center. The same Wheat Ear pattern may be worked on a panel of 13 sts, with a 9-stitch cable (reading "2" for "3" in Row 3.)

Panel of 17 sts.

Row 1 (Right side)—P2, k13, p2.
Row 2—K2, p13, k2.
Row 3—P2, sl next 3 to dpn and hold in back, k3, k3 from dpn, k1, sl next 3 to dpn and hold in front, k3, k3 from dpn, p2.
Row 4—K2, p13, k2.

Repeat Rows 1–4.

VARIATION: *REVERSE WHEAT EAR CABLE*

Work the same as Wheat Ear Cable, except exchange the words "back" and "front" in Row 3. This variation is useful for making a classic Wheat Ear in a garment worked from the top down; or it may be done in reverse fashion from the bottom up if the knitter prefers.

LEFT: *Wheat Ear Cable*
RIGHT: *Reverse Wheat Ear Cable*

Plait Cable

This type of cable is a little more sophisticated than a Simple Cable, but just as easy to work.

Panel of 13 sts.

Row 1 (Right side)—P2, k9, p2.
Row 2—K2, p9, k2.
Row 3—P2, sl next 3 sts to dpn and hold in front, k3, then k3 from dpn; k3, p2.
Rows 4 and 6—As Row 2.
Row 5—As Row 1.
Row 7—P2, k3, sl next 3 sts to dpn and hold in back, k3, then k3 from dpn; p2.
Row 8—As Row 2.

Repeat Rows 1–8.

LEFT: *Plait Cable*
CENTER: *Little Plait Cable*
RIGHT: *Reverse Plait Cable or Branch Cable*

VARIATION

If a *back* cross is worked in Row 3 (i.e., "hold in back" instead of "hold in front") and a *front* cross in Row 7 (i.e., "hold in front" instead of "hold in back"), all other directions remaining the same, the pattern is reversed. This Reverse Plait is sometimes known as Branch Cable.

LITTLE PLAIT CABLE

Panel of 10 sts.

Rows 1 and 3 (Wrong side)—K2, p6, k2.
Row 2—P2, sl next 2 sts to dpn and hold in front, k2, then k2 from dpn; k2, p2.
Row 4—P2, k2, sl next 2 sts to dpn and hold in back, k2, then k2 from dpn; p2.

Repeat Rows 1–4.

Wave Cable or Ribbon Stitch

LEFT TO RIGHT:
1. *Wave Cable or Ribbon Stitch*
2. *Elongated Wave Cable*
3. *Chain Cable or Double Ribbon Stitch*
4. *Elongated Chain Cable*

Instead of being twisted in the usual way, the cabled stitches here are moved back and forth to form an embossed wave. Wave Cable is a popular Aran pattern, often used—along with its relative, the Chain Cable—in fisherman sweaters. When two Wave Cables are worked, one on either side of a common center, then one of the cables should be started with Row 1 and the other with Row 7, so that the "waves" will balance each other.

Panel of 10 sts.

Row 1 (Wrong side) and all other wrong-side rows—K2, p6, k2.
Row 2—P2, sl next 3 sts to dpn and hold in back, k3, then k3 from dpn; p2.
Rows 4 and 6—P2, k6, p2.
Row 8—P2, sl next 3 sts to dpn and hold in front, k3, then k3 from dpn; p2.
Rows 10 and 12—P2, k6, p2.

Repeat Rows 1–12.

VARIATION: ELONGATED WAVE CABLE

There are a number of ways of varying a Wave Cable, both in the number of stitches and the number of rows. This Elongated Wave Cable shows one method of variation.

Panel of 8 sts.

Row 1 (Wrong side) and all other wrong-side rows—K2, p4, k2.
Row 2—P2, sl next 2 sts to dpn and hold in back, k2, then k2 from dpn; p2.
Rows 4, 6, and 8—P2, k4, p2.
Row 10—P2, sl next 2 sts to dpn and hold in front, k2, then k2 from dpn; p2.
Rows 12, 14, and 16—P2, k4, p2.

Repeat Rows 1–16.

Chain Cable or Double Ribbon Stitch

(*See illustration, page 245*)

This famous cable is the basis of the Aran Honeycomb, which is essentially a number of Chain Cables worked side by side, and in contact with each other, across the entire fabric.

Panel of 12 sts.

Row 1 (Wrong side) and all other wrong-side rows—K2, p8, k2.
Row 2—P2, sl next 2 sts to dpn and hold in back, k2, then k2 from dpn; sl next 2 sts to dpn and hold in front, k2, then k2 from dpn; p2.
Row 4—P2, k8, p2.
Row 6—P2, sl next 2 sts to dpn and hold in front, k2, then k2 from dpn; sl next 2 sts to dpn and hold in back, k2, then k2 from dpn; p2.
Row 8—P2, k8, p2.

Repeat Rows 1–8.

VARIATION: *ELONGATED CHAIN CABLE*

In this version the Chain Cable is elongated by only two more rows inserted between cabling rows. Four more could be used also. The Elongated Wave Cable verges on the Medallion Cable, which has a similar form but somewhat larger proportions.

Panel of 12 sts.

Row 1 (Wrong side) and all other wrong-side rows—K2, p8, k2.
Row 2—P2, sl next 2 sts to dpn and hold in back, k2, then k2 from dpn; sl next 2 sts to dpn and hold in front, k2, then k2 from dpn; p2.
Rows 4 and 6—P2, k8, p2.
Row 8—P2, sl next 2 sts to dpn and hold in front, k2, then k2 from dpn; sl next 2 sts to dpn and hold in back, k2, then k2 from dpn; p2.
Rows 10 and 12—P2, k8, p2.

Repeat Rows 1–12.

Medallion Cable

This is similar to the Chain Cable, except that it has one additional stitch in the center and more rows between cable rows. The Medallion Cable lends itself readily to extra ornamentation in the center of the "medallion", for instance with a Bobble formed in the center stitch at each repetition of Row 1.

Panel of 17 sts.

Rows 1 and 3 (Right side)—P2, k13, p2.
Rows 2 and 4—K2, p13, k2.

Row 5—P2, sl next 3 to dpn and hold in front, k3, k3 from dpn, k1, sl next 3 to dpn and hold in back, k3, k3 from dpn, p2.

Rows 6, 8, and 10—K2, p13, k2.

Rows 7, 9, and 11—P2, k13, p2.

Row 12—K2, p13, k2.

Row 13—P2, sl next 3 to dpn and hold in back, k3, k3 from dpn, k1, sl next 3 to dpn and hold in front, k3, k3 from dpn, p2.

Row 14—K2, p13, k2.

Row 15—P2, k13, p2.

Row 16—K2, p13, k2.

Repeat Rows 1–16.

LEFT: *Medallion Cable*
CENTER: *Tyrolean Medallion*
RIGHT: *Round Cable*

Tyrolean Medallion

The large round medallion traditionally is ornamented with bobbles or embroidered flowers, or both.

Panel of 19 sts.

Row 1 (Wrong side)—K2, p15-b, k2.

Row 2—P2, sl next 3 sts to dpn and hold in front, k3-b, then k3-b from dpn; k3-b, sl next 3 sts to dpn and hold in back, k3-b, then k3-b from dpn; p2.

Rows 3 and 5—K2, p15-b, k2.

Rows 4 and 6—P2, k15-b, p2.

Row 7—K2, p15-b, k2.

Row 8—P2, sl next 3 sts to dpn and hold in back, k3-b, then k3-b from dpn; k3-b, sl next 3 sts to dpn and hold in front, k3-b, then k3-b from dpn; p2.

Rows 9–16—Repeat Rows 3 through 6 twice.

Repeat Rows 1–16.

Round Cable

Panel of 12 sts.

Rows 1, 3, and 5 (Wrong side)—K4, p4, k4.

Rows 2 and 4—P4, k4, p4.

Row 6—P2, sl next 2 sts to dpn and hold in back, k2, then p2 from dpn; sl next 2 sts to dpn and hold in front, p2, then k2 from dpn; p2.

Rows 7, 9, and 11—K2, p2, k4, p2, k2.

Rows 8 and 10—P2, k2, p4, k2, p2.

Row 12—P2, sl next 2 sts to dpn and hold in front, p2, then k2 from dpn; sl next 2 sts to dpn and hold in back, k2, then p2 from dpn; p2.

Repeat Rows 1–12.

Gull Stitch

LEFT: *Gull Stitch*
CENTER: *Triple Gull-Stitch Cable*
RIGHT: *Inverted Gull Stitch*

Sometimes known as Wishbone Cable, this is a very beautiful old pattern often seen in Aran sweaters.

Panel of 10 sts.

Row 1 (Wrong side)—K2, p6, k2.
Row 2—P2, k2, sl 2 wyib, k2, p2.
Row 3—K2, p2, sl 2 wyif, p2, k2.
Row 4—P2, sl next 2 sts to dpn and hold in back, k1, then k2 from dpn; sl next st to dpn and hold in front, k2, then k1 from dpn; p2.

Repeat Rows 1–4.

Triple Gull-Stitch Cable

Panel of 10 sts.

Row 1 (Right side)—P2, k6, p2.
Row 2—K2, p6, k2.
Row 3—P2, k6, p2.
Row 4—K2, p2, sl 2 wyif, p2, k2.
Row 5—P2, sl next 2 to dpn and hold in back, k1, k2 from dpn; sl next st to dpn and hold in front, k2, k the st from dpn, p2.
Rows 6–9—Repeat Rows 4 and 5 twice more.
Row 10—K2, p6, k2.
Row 11—P2, k6, p2.
Row 12—K2, p6, k2.

Repeat Rows 1–12.

Inverted Gull Stitch

This cable is not a true Gull Stitch because the stitches are not slipped before being cabled. However, it does resemble a Gull Stitch widened and turned upside down. Note that there is an extra stitch in the center, as in Wheat Ear Cable.

Panel of 13 sts.

Rows 1 and 3 (Wrong side)—K2, p9, k2.
Row 2—P2, sl next st to dpn and hold in front, k3, then k1 from dpn; k1, sl next 3 sts to dpn and hold in back, k1, then k3 from dpn; p2.
Row 4—P2, k9, p2.

Repeat Rows 1–4.

Braid Cables

Braid Cables (not to be confused with Plait Cables) consist of three knit ribs traveling across a purl-stitch ground, and crossing one another alternately in true braid fashion. Braid Cables are novel in appearance and interesting to work. Also, they are capable of much variation. Three types of Braid Cable are given: Close, Barred, and Twisted. Other variations, of course, are possible.

LEFT: *Close Braid Cable*
CENTER: *Barred Braid Cable*
RIGHT: *Twisted Braid Cable*

CLOSE BRAID CABLE

Panel of 13 sts.

NOTE: Front Cross (FC)—sl 2 sts to dpn and hold in front, p1, then k2 from dpn. Back Cross (BC)—sl 1 st to dpn and hold in back, k2, then p1 from dpn.

Row 1 (Wrong side)—K3, p4, k2, p2, k2.
Row 2—P2, FC, BC, FC, P2.
Row 3 and all subsequent wrong-side rows—Knit all knit sts and purl all purl sts.
Row 4—P3, sl next 2 sts to dpn and hold in back, k2, then k2 from dpn; p2, k2, p2.
Row 6—P2, BC, FC, BC, p2.
Row 8—P2, k2, p2, sl next 2 sts to dpn and hold in front, k2, then k2 from dpn; p3.

Repeat Rows 1–8.

BARRED BRAID CABLE

Panel of 16 sts.

NOTE: FC and BC—same as for Close Braid Cable.

Row 1 (Right side)—P2, FC, p2, BC, FC, p3.
Row 2—K3, (yo, p2, pass yo over 2 purled sts, k2) 3 times, k1.
Row 3—P3, FC, BC, p2, FC, p2.
Row 4—K2, yo, p2, pass yo over 2 purled sts, k4, (yo, p2, pass yo over 2 purled sts) twice, k4.
Row 5—P4, sl next 2 sts to dpn and hold in back, k2, then k2 from dpn; p4, k2, p2.
Row 6—As Row 4.
Row 7—P3, BC, FC, p2, BC, p2.
Row 8—As Row 2.
Row 9—P2, BC, p2, FC, BC, p3.
Row 10—K4, (yo, p2, pass yo over 2 purled sts) twice, k4, yo, p2, pass yo over 2 purled sts, k2.
Row 11—P2, k2, p4, sl next 2 sts to dpn and hold in front, k2, then k2 from dpn; p4.
Row 12—As Row 10.

Repeat Rows 1–12.

TWISTED BRAID CABLE

Panel of 11 sts.

NOTE: Front Cross (FC)—sl 1 st to dpn and hold in front, p1, then k1-b from dpn. Back Cross (BC)—sl 1 st to dpn and hold in back, k1-b, then p1 from dpn.

Row 1 (Wrong side)—K3, p2-b, k4, p1-b, k1.
Row 2—P1, FC, p2, BC, FC, p2.
Row 3 and all subsequent wrong-side rows—K all knit sts and p-b all purl sts.
Row 4—P2, FC, BC, p2, FC, p1.
Row 6—P3, sl next st to dpn and hold in back, k1-b, then k1-b from dpn; p4, k1-b, p1.
Row 8—P2, BC, FC, p2, BC, p1.
Row 10—P1, BC, p2, FC, BC, p2.
Row 12—P1, k1-b, p4, sl next st to dpn and hold in front, k1-b, then k1-b from dpn; p3.

Repeat Rows 1–12.

Tree of Life

This is a famous old Aran pattern.

Panel of 15 sts.

Row 1 (Right side)—P2, k1, p4, sl 1 wyib, p4, k1, p2.
Row 2—K2, sl 1 wyif, k4, p1, k4, sl 1 wyif, k2.
Row 3—P2, sl 1 to dpn and hold in front, p1; k1 from dpn (Front Cross or FC); p3, sl 1 wyib, p3; sl 1 to dpn and hold in back, k1; p1 from dpn (Back Cross or BC); p2.
Row 4—K3, sl 1 wyif, k3, p1, k3, sl 1 wyif, k3.
Row 5—P3, FC, p2, sl 1 wyib, p2, BC, p3.
Row 6—K4, sl 1 wyif, k2, p1, k2, sl 1 wyif, k4.
Row 7—P4, FC, p1, sl 1 wyib, p1, BC, p4.
Row 8—K5, sl 1 wyif, k1, p1, k1, sl 1 wyif, k5.
Row 9—P2, k1, p2, FC, sl 1 wyib, BC, p2, k1, p2.
Row 10—K2, sl 1 wyif, k4, p1, k4, sl 1 wyif, k2.

On subsequent repeats omit Rows 1 and 2 and repeat Rows 3–10.

CENTER PANEL: *Tree of Life*
SIDE PANELS: *Twisted Tree*

Twisted Tree

This is a variant on the Tree of Life theme, but in reverse; the Twisted Tree does not droop but rather opens its "branches" upward. Note also the contrast between the large loose slip-stitches of the classic Tree of Life, and the tightly twisted stitches in this pattern.

Panel of 9 sts.

Row 1 (Right side)—P3, k3-b, p3.
Row 2—K3, p3-b, k3.
Row 3—P2, sl next st to dpn and hold in back, k1-b, then p1 from dpn (Back Cross, BC); k1-b, sl next st to dpn and hold in front, p1, then k1-b from dpn (Front Cross, FC); p2.
Row 4—K2, (p1-b, k1) twice, p1-b, k2.
Row 5—P1, BC, p1, k1-b, p1, FC, p1.
Row 6—K1, (p1-b, k2) twice, p1-b, k1.
Row 7—BC, p1, k3-b, p1, FC.
Row 8—P1-b, k2, p3-b, k2, p1-b.

Repeat Rows 1–8.

Staghorn Cable

This is a graceful, easy pattern for any spot where a wide cable is needed. The method of doing it in reverse is handy for a Staghorn effect in any garment that is knitted from the top down. Also, the Reverse Staghorn is a pretty cable in its own right. Staghorn and Reverse Staghorn are attractive when used together in alternate panels.

Panel of 20 sts.

NOTE: Back Cross (BC)—sl 2 sts to dpn and hold in back, k2, then k2 from dpn. Front Cross (FC)—sl 2 sts to dpn and hold in front, k2, then k2 from dpn.

Rows 1, 3, and 5 (Wrong side)—K2, p16, k2.
Row 2—P2, k4, BC, FC, k4, p2.
Row 4—P2, k2, BC, k4, FC, k2, p2.
Row 6—P2, BC, k8, FC, p2.

Repeat Rows 1–6.

LEFT: *Staghorn Cable*
RIGHT: *Reverse Staghorn Cable*

REVERSE STAGHORN CABLE

Panel of 20 sts.

NOTE: BC and FC—as above.

Rows 1, 3, and 5 (Wrong side)—K2, p16, k2.
Row 2—P2, FC, k8, BC, p2.
Row 4—P2, k2, FC, k4, BC, k2, p2.
Row 6—P2, k4, FC, BC, k4, p2.

Repeat Rows 1–6.

Triple-Braided Diamonds

This is a fascinating pattern of large diamonds intricately braided together, ideal for a central panel in a fancy sweater.

CENTER PANEL: *Triple-Braided Diamonds*
SIDE PANELS: *Wave of Honey Cable or Little Chain*

Panel of 30 sts.

NOTES: Front Cross or FC—sl 2 k sts to dpn and hold in front, p1, then k2 from dpn.

Back Cross or BC—sl 1 p st to dpn and hold in back, k2, then p the st from dpn.

Front Double Knit Cross or FDKC—sl 2 k sts to dpn and hold in front, k2, then k2 from dpn.

Back Double Knit Cross or BDKC—sl 2 k sts to dpn and hold in back, k2, then k2 from dpn.

Row 1 (Wrong side)—K7, (p4, k2) twice, p4, k7.
Row 2—P6, (BC, FC) 3 times, p6.
Row 3 and all other wrong-side rows—Knit all knit sts and purl all purl sts.
Row 4—P5, BC, (p2, BDKC) twice, p2, FC, p5.
Row 6—P4, BC, p2, (BC, FC) twice, p2, FC, p4.
Row 8—P3, (BC, p2) twice, FDKC, (p2, FC) twice, p3.
Row 10—(P2, BC) 3 times, (FC, p2) 3 times.
Row 12—Knit all k sts and purl all p sts.
Row 14—(P2, FC) 3 times, (BC, p2) 3 times.
Row 16—P3, (FC, p2) twice, FDKC, (p2, BC) twice, p3.
Row 18—P4, FC, p2, (FC, BC) twice, p2, BC, p4.
Row 20—P5, FC, (p2, BDKC) twice, p2, BC, p5.
Row 22—P6, (FC, BC) 3 times, p6.
Row 24—P7, (FDKC, p2) ·twice, FDKC, p7.

Repeat Rows 1–24.

Wave of Honey Cable or Little Chain

This beautiful little cable is the designing unit of Wave of Honey Stitch (which see). It is very decorative and has many uses. Try, for instance, a continuous row of Wave of Honey Cables, with two purl stitches between, for a fancy ribbing.

Panel of 8 sts.

Rows 1 and 3 (Wrong side)—K2, p4, k2.
Row 2—P2, sl next st to dpn and hold in front, k1, then k1 from dpn; sl next st to dpn and hold in back, k1, then k1 from dpn; p2.
Row 4—P2, sl next st to dpn and hold in back, k1, then k1 from dpn; sl next st to dpn and hold in front, k1, then k1 from dpn; p2.

Repeat Rows 1–4.

Valentine Cable

A hand-knitted gift sweater is surely a labor of love, and all the more evidently so when it carries this handsome heart-shaped pattern. Note that the first 3 rows are preparatory, not to be repeated after the pattern has been started.

CENTER PANEL: *Valentine Cable*
SIDE PANELS: *Ribbed Cable*

Panel of 16 sts.

Rows 1 and 3 (Wrong side)—K6, p4, k6.
Row 2—P6, sl next 2 sts to dpn and hold in front, k2, then k2 from dpn; p6.
Row 4—P5, sl next st to dpn and hold in back, k2, then p1 from dpn (Back Cross, BC); sl next 2 sts to dpn and hold in front, p1, then k2 from dpn (Front Cross, FC); p5.
Row 5—K5, p2, k2, p2, k5.
Row 6—P4, BC, p2, FC, p4.
Row 7—(K4, p2) twice, k4.
Row 8—P3, BC, p4, FC, p3.
Row 9—K3, p2, k6, p2, k3.
Row 10—P2, (BC) twice, (FC) twice, p2.
Row 11—K2, (p2, k1, p2, k2) twice.
Row 12—P1, (BC) twice, p2, (FC) twice, p1.
Row 13—(K1, p2) twice, k4, (p2, k1) twice.
Row 14—P1, k1, sl 1 st to dpn and hold in front, p1, then k1 from dpn (Single FC); FC, p2, BC, sl 1 st to dpn and hold in back, k1, then p1 from dpn (Single BC); k1, p1.
Row 15—(K1, p1) twice, k1, p2, k2, p2, k1, (p1, k1) twice.
Row 16—P1, k1, p1, Single FC. FC, BC, Single BC, p1, k1, p1.
Row 17—K1, p1, k2, p1, k1, p4, k1, p1, k2, p1, k1.
Row 18—P1, Single FC, Single BC, p1, sl next 2 sts to dpn and hold in front, k2, then k2 from dpn; p1, Single FC, Single BC, p1.
Row 19—K2, sl next st to dpn and hold in back, k1, then k1 from dpn; k2, p4, k2, sl next st to dpn and hold in front, k1, then k1 from dpn; k2.

Omit Rows 1 through 3, repeat Rows 4–19.

Ribbed Cable

The Ribbed Cable is very elegant, and is frequently seen in fisherman sweaters. Note that there are two ways of working Row 2, and that in both cases the knit stitches are purled and the purl stitches knitted in the 4-stitch group. When two Ribbed Cables are used on either side of a common center, one should be done by the front-cross method and the other by the back-cross method, to balance the patterns. For a Ribbed Wave Cable, work the front-cross and back-cross methods alternately, every 10th row in the same cable.

Panel of 11 sts.

Row 1 (Wrong side)—K2, (p1-b, k1) 3 times, p1-b, k2.
Row 2—For a front-cross cable work Row 2 as follows: P2, sl next 3 sts to dpn and hold in front, (k1-b, p1) twice on next 4 sts, then from dpn k1-b, p1, k1-b the 3 sts, p2.

For a back-cross cable work Row 2 as follows: P2, sl next 4 sts to dpn and hold in back, k1-b, p1, k1-b on next 3 sts, then from dpn (p1, k1-b) twice, p2.
Rows 3, 5, 7, and 9—As Row 1.
Rows 4, 6, 8, and 10—P2, (k1-b, p1) 3 times, k1-b, p2.

Repeat Rows 1–10.

Superimposed Double Wave

This is a beautiful pattern of four separated waves interpenetrating each other, two on top and two beneath. Very good for fancy sweaters.

Panel of 16 sts.

NOTES: Front Cross or FC—sl 2 k sts to dpn and hold in front, p1, then k2 from dpn. Back Cross or BC—sl 1 p st to dpn and hold in back, k2, then p the st from dpn. Front Double Knit Cross or FDKC—sl 2 k sts to dpn and hold in front, k2, then k2 from dpn.

Row 1 (Right side)—K2, p3, k2, p2, k2, p3, k2.
Row 2—and all other wrong-side rows—Knit all k sts and purl all p sts.
Row 3—FC, p2, FC, BC, p2, BC.
Row 5—P1, FC, p2, FDKC, p2, BC, p1.
Row 7—P2, (FC, BC) twice, p2.
Row 9—P3, FDKC, p2, FDKC, p3.
Row 11—P2, (BC, FC) twice, p2.
Row 13—P1, BC, p2, FDKC, p2, FC, p1.
Row 15—BC, p2, BC, FC, p2, FC.
Row 16—See Row 2.
Rows 17 through 32—work exactly as Rows 1–16 *except* in Rows 5, 9, and 13 substitute *Back* Double Knit Cross for FDKC. This is worked as FDKC but hold the sts in back instead of in front.

Repeat Rows 1–32.

NOTE: If Rows 1–16 *only* are repeated, then the cable will be twisted in the usual cable fashion, instead of being superimposed.

CENTER PANEL: *Superimposed Double Wave*
SIDE PANELS: *Oxox Cable*

Oxox Cable

This curiously named cable is a variation on Chain Cable. Its name describes it: the "chain" cabling action is staggered so that the cable looks like little O's and little X's. It is a good example of how a simple alteration in row order can give very different results.

Panel of 12 sts.

Rows 1 and 3 (Wrong side)—K2, p8, k2.

Row 2—P2, k8, p2.

Row 4—P2, sl next 2 sts to dpn and hold in back, k2, then k2 from dpn; sl next 2 sts to dpn and hold in front, k2, then k2 from dpn; p2.

Rows 5, 6, and 7—Repeat Rows 1, 2, and 3.

Row 8—P2, sl next 2 sts to dpn and hold in front, k2, then k2 from dpn; sl next 2 sts to dpn and hold in back, k2, then k2 from dpn; p2.

Rows 9–12—Repeat Rows 5–8.

Rows 13–16—Repeat Rows 1–4.

Repeat Rows 1–16.

Hourglass Cable

The Hourglass Cable is a beautiful variation on a recurrent theme in Aran patterns. These gracefully curved lines are seen in many other combinations.

Panel of 14 sts.

Row 1 (Wrong side)—K4, p1-b, k1, p2-b, k1, p1-b, k4.

Row 2—P3, sl next st to dpn and hold in back, k1-b, then p1 from dpn (Back Cross, BC); BC again; sl next st to dpn and hold in front, p1, then k1-b from dpn (Front Cross, FC); FC again; p3.

Row 3 and all subsequent wrong-side rows—K all knit sts and p-b all purl sts.

Row 4—P2, BC, sl next st to dpn and hold in back, k1-b, then k1-b from dpn; p2, sl next st to dpn and hold in front, k1-b, then k1-b from dpn; FC, p2.

Row 6—P1, (BC) twice, FC, BC, (FC) twice, p1.

Row 8—(P1, k1-b) twice, p2, k2-b, p2, (k1-b, p1) twice.

Row 10—P1, (FC) twice, BC, FC, (BC) twice, p1.

Row 12—P2, (FC) twice, p2, (BC) twice, p2.

Row 14—P3, (FC) twice, (BC) twice, p3.

Row 16—P4, k1-b, p1, k2-b, p1, k1-b, p4.

Repeat Rows 1–16.

CENTER PANEL: *Hourglass Cable*
SIDE PANELS: *Notched Cable*

Notched Cable

This is a novelty cable suitable for use with other cable patterns. Since the design is small and rather unobtrusive, the Notched Cable is best worked in a heavy yarn on big needles so that it may show up well.

Panel of 11 sts.

Row 1 (Wrong side)—K1, p2, k2, p1, k2, p2, k1.
Row 2—P1, sl next 2 sts to dpn and hold in front, p2, then k2 from dpn; k1, sl next 2 sts to dpn and hold in back, k2, then p2 from dpn; p1.
Rows 3, 5, and 7—K3, p5, k3.
Rows 4 and 6—P3, k5, p3.
Row 8—P1, sl next 2 sts to dpn and hold in back, k2, then p2 from dpn; k1, sl next 2 sts to dpn and hold in front, p2, then k2 from dpn; p1.

Repeat Rows 1–8.

Aran Diamonds with Popcorns

Panel of 19 sts.

CENTER PANEL: *Aran Diamonds with Popcorns*
LEFT SIDE PANEL: *Flying Buttress, right*
RIGHT SIDE PANEL: *Flying Buttress, left*

NOTES: Back Cross (BC)—sl 1 p st to dpn and hold in back, k2, then p the st from dpn. Front Cross (FC)—sl 2 sts to dpn and hold in front, p1, then k2 from dpn.

Row 1 (Wrong side)—P1, k3, k in front, back, front, back, front of next st (5 sts from 1) and sl the worked st off left-hand needle (Popcorn made); k2, p2, k1, p2, k2, popcorn in next st as before, k3, p1.
Row 2—K1, p3, k5 tog-b (completing popcorn); p2, sl next 3 sts to dpn and hold in front, k2, sl the p st from dpn back to left-hand needle and p it, then k2 from dpn; p2, k5 tog-b, p3, k1.
Row 3—P1, k6, p2, k1, p2, k6, p1.
Row 4—K1, p5, BC, p1, FC, p5, k1.
Row 5—P1, k5, p2, k3, p2, k5, p1.
Row 6—K1, p4, BC, p3, FC, p4, k1.
Row 7—P1, k4, p2, k2, popcorn, k2, p2, k4, p1.
Row 8—K1, p3, BC, p2, k5 tog-b, p2, FC, p3, k1.
Row 9—P1, k3, p2, k7, p2, k3, p1.
Row 10—K1, p2, BC, p7, FC, p2, k1.
Row 11—P1, k2, p2, k2, popcorn, k3, popcorn, k2, p2, k2, p1.
Row 12—K1, p1, BC, p2, k5 tog-b, p3, k5 tog-b, p2, FC, p1, k1.
Row 13—P1, k1, p2, k11, p2, k1, p1.
Row 14—K1, p1, k2, p11, k2, p1, k1.
Row 15—P1, k1, p2, k3, popcorn, k3, popcorn, k3, p2, k1, p1.
Row 16—K1, p1, FC, p2, k5 tog-b, p3, k5 tog-b, p2, BC, p1, k1.

Row 17—P1, k2, p2, k9, p2, k2, p1.
Row 18—K1, p2, FC, p7, BC, p2, k1.
Row 19—P1, k3, p2, k3, popcorn, k3, p2, k3, p1.
Row 20—K1, p3, FC, p2, k5 tog-b, p2, BC, p3, k1.
Row 21—P1, k4, p2, k5, p2, k4, p1.
Row 22—K1, p4, FC, p3, BC, p4, k1.
Row 23—P1, k5, p2, k3, p2, k5, p1.
Row 24—K1, p5, FC, p1, BC, p5, k1.

Repeat Rows 1–24.

Panel includes 2 k sts, one on either side.

Flying Buttress

Compared to most cable patterns, the Flying Buttress is almost stark in its simplicity. It consists of a single rib of two knit stitches, traveling diagonally on a purled ground, either (1) to the right, or (2) to the left. The Right version is done with a series of back crosses, the Left with front crosses. When worked on either side of a common center, as shown, these two versions should be used, one on each side. For a Double Flying Buttress, cast on a panel of 20 stitches and work one version on the first 10, the other on the second 10—reversing the order, of course, on the opposite side of the fabric.

(1) FLYING BUTTRESS, RIGHT

(See illustration, page 256)

Panel of 10 sts.

Row 1 (Wrong side)—P2, k6, p2.
Row 2—K2, p5, sl next st to dpn and hold in back, k2, then k1 from dpn.
Row 3—P3, k5, p2.
Row 4—K2, p4, sl next st to dpn and hold in back, k2, then k1 from dpn, k1.
Row 5—P4, k4, p2.
Row 6—K2, p3, sl next st to dpn and hold in back, k2, then *p1* from dpn (Back Cross, BC), k2.
Row 7—P2, k1, p2, k3, p2.
Row 8—K2, p2, BC, p1, k2.
Row 9—(P2, k2) twice, p2.
Row 10—K2, p1, BC, p2, k2.
Row 11—P2, k3, p2, k1, p2.
Row 12—K2, BC, p3, k2.
Row 13—P2, k4, p4.
Row 14—K1, BC, p4, k2.
Row 15—P2, k5, p3.
Row 16—BC, p5, k2.

Repeat Rows 1–16.

(2) FLYING BUTTRESS, LEFT

(*See illustration, page 256*)

Panel of 10 sts.

Row 1 (Wrong side)—P2, k6, p2.

Row 2—Sl 2 sts to dpn and hold in front, k1, then k2 from dpn, p5, k2.

Row 3—P2, k5, p3.

Row 4—K1, sl next 2 sts to dpn and hold in front, k1, then k2 from dpn, p4, k2.

Row 5—P2, k4, p4.

Row 6—K2, sl next 2 sts to dpn and hold in front, *p1,* then k2 from dpn (Front Cross, FC), p3, k2.

Row 7—P2, k3, p2, k1, p2.

Row 8—K2, p1, FC, p2, k2.

Row 9—(P2, k2) twice, p2.

Row 10—K2, p2, FC, p1, k2.

Row 11—P2, k1, p2, k3, p2.

Row 12—K2, p3, FC, k2.

Row 13—P4, k4, p2.

Row 14—K2, p4, FC, k1.

Row 15—P3, k5, p2.

Row 16—K2, p5, FC.

Repeat Rows 1–16.

Figure-Eight Diamond Pattern

CENTER PANEL: *Figure-Eight Diamond Pattern*
SIDE PANELS: *Figure-Eight Cable*

Both this pattern and the Figure-Eight Cable are popular Aran designs, often used together in the same garment.

Panel of 22 sts.

Row 1 (Wrong side)—K9, p4, k9.

Row 2—P9, sl next 2 sts to dpn and hold in back, k2, then k2 from dpn; p9.

Row 3 and all subsequent wrong-side rows—Knit all knit sts and purl all purl sts.

Row 4—P8, sl next st to dpn and hold in back, k2, then p1 from dpn (Back Cross, BC); sl next 2 sts to dpn and hold in front, p1, then k2 from dpn (Front Cross, FC); p8.

Row 6—P7, BC, p2, FC, p7.

Row 8—P6, BC, p4, FC, p6.

Row 10—P5, BC, p1, k4, p1, FC, p5.

Row 12—P4, BC, p1, BC, FC, p1, FC, p4.

Row 14—P3, BC, p1, BC, p2, FC, p1, FC, p3.

Row 16—(P2, BC, p2, FC) twice, p2.

Row 18—P1, (BC, p4, FC) twice, p1.

Row 20—P1, k2, p6, sl next 2 sts to dpn and hold in back, k2, then k2 from dpn; p6, k2, p1.
Row 22—P1, (FC, p4, BC) twice, p1.
Row 24—(P2, FC, p2, BC) twice, p2.
Row 26—P3, FC, p1, FC, p2, BC, p1, BC, p3.
Row 28—P4, FC, p1, FC, BC, p1, BC, p4.
Row 30—P5, FC, p6, BC, p5.
Row 32—P6, FC, p4, BC, p6.
Row 34—P7, FC, p2, BC, p7.
Row 36—P8, FC, BC, p8.

Repeat Rows 1–36.

Figure-Eight Cable

See Figure-Eight Diamond Pattern.

Panel of 12 sts.

Row 1 (Wrong side)—K5, p2, k5.
Row 2—P4, k4, p4.
Wrong-side rows from 3 through 19—Knit all knit sts and purl all purl sts.
Row 4—P3, sl next st to dpn and hold in back, k2, then p1 from dpn (Back Cross, BC); sl next 2 sts to dpn and hold in front, p1, then k2 from dpn (Front Cross, FC); p3.
Row 6—P2, BC, p2, FC, p2.
Row 8—P2, FC, p2, BC, p2.
Row 10—P3, FC, BC, p3.
Row 12—P4, sl next 2 sts to dpn and hold in back, k2, then k2 from dpn; p4.
Rows 14, 16, 18, and 20—Repeat Rows 4, 6, 8, and 10.
Row 21—K4, p4, k4.
Rows 22, 24, and 26—P5, k2, p5.
Rows 23, 25, and 27—K5, p2, k5.
Row 28—P5, k2, p5.

Repeat Rows 1–28.

Double-Braided Cable

The construction of this cable is similar to that of Triple-Braided Diamonds, but a bit simpler, as there are only four crossing ribs instead of six.

Panel of 22 sts.

NOTES: FC (Front Cross): sl 2 sts to dpn and hold in front, p1, then k2 from dpn.

CENTER PANEL: *Double-Braided Cable*
SIDE PANELS: *Scotch Faggoting Cable*

BC (Back Cross): sl 1 st to dpn and hold in back, k2, then p1 from dpn.

FDKC (Front Double Knit Cross): sl 2 sts to dpn and hold in front, k2, then k2 from dpn.

BDKC (Back Double Knit Cross): sl 2 sts to dpn and hold in back, k2, then k2 from dpn.

Rows 1 and 3 (Wrong side)—K2, p2, k3, p2, k4, p2, k3, p2, k2.

Row 2—P2, k2, p3, k2, p4, k2, p3, k2, p2.

Row 4—P2, (FC, p2) twice, (BC, p2) twice.

Row 5 and all subsequent wrong-side rows—Knit all knit sts and purl all purl sts.

Row 6—P3, FC, p2, FC, BC, p2, BC, p3.

Row 8—P4, FC, p2, BDKC, p2, BC, p4.

Row 10—P5, (FC, BC) twice, p5.

Row 12—P6, FDKC, p2, FDKC, p6.

Row 14—P5, (BC, FC) twice, p5.

Row 16—P4, BC, p2, BDKC, p2, FC, p4.

Row 18—P3, BC, p2, BC, FC, p2, FC, p3.

Row 20—P2, (BC, p2) twice, (FC, p2) twice.

Rows 22, 24, and 26—As Row 2.

Repeat Rows 1–26.

Scotch Faggoting Cable

This novel openwork cable is rarely seen, but it is so attractive and so easy to work that the reason for its rarity can only be that it is so little known. A panel is given, but the motif is easily converted into an all-over pattern by working it on a multiple of 6 sts plus 2 (2 purl sts between cables). When repeating across the fabric, it is a good idea to begin every alternate cable with Row 9, so that the crossings will be staggered. If desired, every other cable may be worked with a back cross instead of a front cross.

Panel of 8 sts.

Row 1 (Right side)—P2, k2, yo, k2 tog, p2.

Row 2—K2, p2, yo, p2 tog, k2.

Rows 3 and 5—As Row 1.

Rows 4 and 6—As Row 2.

Row 7—P2, sl 2 to dpn and hold in front, k2, then k2 from dpn, p2.

Row 8—As Row 2.

Rows 9, 11, 13, and 15—As Row 1.

Rows 10, 12, 14, and 16—As Row 2.

Repeat Rows 1–16.

Trellis With Moss Stitch

This is another traditional Aran pattern.

Panel of 28 sts.

Row 1 (Right side)—P5, sl next 2 sts to dpn and hold in front, k2-b, then k2-b the sts from dpn (Front Double Knit Cross or FDKC); p10, FDKC, p5.

Row 2 and all other wrong-side rows—Knit all knit sts and purl all purl sts.

Row 3—P4, sl next st to dpn and hold in back, k2-b, then p st from dpn (Back Cross or BC); sl next 2 sts to dpn and hold in front, k1, then k2-b the sts from dpn (Front Cross or FC); p8, BC, FC, p4.

Row 5—P3, * BC, k1, p1, FC, * p6, rep from * to *, p3.

Row 7—P2, * BC, (k1, p1) twice, FC, * p4, rep from * to *, p2.

Row 9—P1, * BC, (k1, p1) 3 times, FC, * p2, rep from * to *, p1.

Row 11—* BC, (k1, p1) 4 times, FC; rep from *.

Row 13—K2-b, (k1, p1) 5 times, FDKC, (k1, p1) 5 times, k2-b.

Row 15—* Sl 2 sts to dpn and hold in front, PURL 1, then k2-b the sts from dpn (Front Purl Cross or FPC); (k1, p1) 4 times, BC; rep from *.

Row 17—P1, * FPC, (k1, p1) 3 times, BC, * p2, rep from * to *, p1.

Row 19—P2, * FPC, (k1, p1) twice, BC, * p4, rep from * to *, p2.

Row 21—P3, * FPC, k1, p1, BC, * p6, rep from * to *, p3.

Row 23—P4, FPC, BC, p8, FPC, BC, p4.

Row 24—See Row 2.

Repeat Rows 1–24.

A Bobble or other decoration may be worked into the purled diamonds at the center of pattern, or these diamonds may be formed of some other texture stitch if desired.

Coin Cable

This pretty little cable is made with a rather novel cabling technique that forms small round medallions with the side stitches crossed in front. The central portion of the "coins" is slightly indented, instead of lifting forward as most cables do.

CENTER PANEL: *Trellis with Moss Stitch*
SIDE PANELS: *Coin Cable*

Panel of 9 sts.

Row 1 (Wrong side)—K2, p5, k2.

Row 2—P2, sl next 4 sts to dpn and hold in back, k1, then sl the last 3 of the sts from dpn back to left-hand needle; then (before knitting the sts) bring dpn with the last st to *front* between needles, passing to the left of the yarn; then knit the 3 sts from left-hand needle; then knit the last st from dpn; p2.

Rows 3 and 5—Repeat Row 1.

Rows 4 and 6—P2, k5, p2.

Repeat Rows 1–6.

Fancy Bobble Cable

Usually bobbles are made out of one stitch, but in this pattern they are made of two stitches. This way of making bobbles is useful for any pattern that is worked on an even number of stitches, so that there are two instead of a single central stitch; when it is desirable to place a bobble in the center, it can be made from both central stitches.

CENTER PANEL: *Fancy Bobble Cable*
SIDE PANELS: *Fast-Traveling Rib, or Snake Rib*

Panel of 16 sts.

Row 1 (Right side)—P2, k4, p4, k4, p2.
Row 2—K2, p4, k4, p4, k2.
Row 3—P2, sl 2 sts to dpn and hold in front, k2, then k2 from dpn; p4; sl 2 sts to dpn and hold in back, k2, then k2 from dpn; p2.
Row 4—Repeat Row 2.
Row 5—P2, k4, p1, Make Bobble as follows: (k1, p1, k1) into *each* of the next 2 sts, turn and p6; turn and k1, ssk, k2 tog, k1; turn and (p2 tog) twice, turn and k2, completing Bobble; p1, k4, p2.
Rows 6, 8, and 10—Repeat Row 2.
Row 7—Repeat Row 3.
Row 9—Repeat Row 1.
Row 11—(Sl 2 sts to dpn and hold in back, k2, then p2 from dpn; sl next 2 sts to dpn and hold in front, p2, then k2 from dpn) twice.
Rows 12 and 14—P2, k4, p4, k4, p2.
Row 13—K2, p4, k4, p4, k2.
Row 15—(Sl 2 sts to dpn and hold in front, p2, then k2 from dpn; sl next 2 sts to dpn and hold in back, k2, then p2 from dpn) twice.
Row 16—Repeat Row 2.

Repeat Rows 1–16.

Fast-Traveling Rib, or Snake Rib

Most "traveling" cables move across the background one stitch at a time on every other row, the cabling action taking place on right-side rows only. This one is different. It travels "fast" because the rib is moved on every row, both right and wrong sides. Hence, the knit stitches of which the rib is composed are somewhat stretched and sleeked. This smooth, slick appearance of the ribs as they undulate across the panel does rather remind one of a snake waving its way along.

When two panels of this pattern are used on either side of a common center, as shown, one of the panels should start with Row 1 and the other with Row 13. If desired, panels can be made narrower by working over a smaller number of stitches.

Panel of 12 sts.

NOTES: Front Cross (FC): sl 2 sts to dpn and hold in front, p1, then k2 from dpn. Reverse Front Cross (RFC): sl 1 st to dpn and hold in front (i.e., at the *wrong* side, which is facing the knitter), p2, then k1 from dpn. Back Cross (BC): sl 1 st to dpn and hold in back, k2, then p1 from dpn. Reverse Back Cross (RBC): sl 2 sts to dpn and hold in back (i.e., at the *right* side, which is facing away from the knitter), k1, then p2 from dpn.

Row 1 (Wrong side)—K10, p2.
Row 2—FC, p9.
Row 3—K8, RFC, k1.
Row 4—P2, FC, p7.
Row 5—K6, RFC, k3.
Row 6—P4, FC, p5.
Row 7—K4, RFC, k5.
Row 8—P6, FC, p3.
Row 9—K2, RFC, k7.
Row 10—P8, FC, p1.
Row 11—RFC, k9.
Row 12—P10, k2.

Row 13—P2, k10.
Row 14—P9, BC.
Row 15—K1, RBC, k8.
Row 16—P7, BC, p2.
Row 17—K3, RBC, k6.
Row 18—P5, BC, p4.
Row 19—K5, RBC, k4.
Row 20—P3, BC, p6.
Row 21—K7, RBC, k2.
Row 22—P1, BC, p8.
Row 23—K9, RBC.
Row 24—K2, p10.

Repeat Rows 1–24.

Off-Center Trellis

This novel and interesting pattern incorporates moss stitch diamonds in a braided trellis pattern. Excellent for sleeve panels or elsewhere in fancy sweaters.

Panel of 25 sts.

NOTES: Front Purl Cross or FPC—sl 2 k sts to dpn, hold in front, p1, then k2 from dpn.

Back Purl Cross or BPC—sl 1 p st to dpn, hold in back, k2, then p1 from dpn.

Front Knit Cross or FKC—sl 2 k sts to dpn, hold in front, k1, then k2 from dpn.

Front Double Knit Cross or FDKC—sl 2 k sts to dpn, hold in front, k2, then k2 from dpn.

Back Double Knit Cross or BDKC—sl 2 k sts to dpn, hold in back, k2, then k2 from dpn.

CENTER PANEL: *Off-Center Trellis*
SIDE PANELS: *Open Cable*

Row 1 (Wrong side)—P2, k6, p4, (k1, p1) 3 times, p4, k3.
Row 2—P2, BPC, FPC, (k1, p1) twice, BPC, FKC, p4, BPC.
Row 3 and all other wrong-side rows—Knit all knit sts and purl all purl sts.
Row 4—P1, BPC, p2, FPC, k1, p1, BPC, k1, p1, FKC, p2, BPC, p1.
Row 6—BPC, p4, FPC, BPC, (k1, p1) twice, FKC, BPC, p2.
Row 8—K2, P6, BDKC, (k1, p1) 3 times, BDKC, p3.
Row 10—FPC, p4, BPC, FKC, (k1, p1) twice, BPC, FPC, p2.
Row 12—P1, FPC, p2, BPC, k1, p1, FKC, k1, p1, BPC, p2, FPC, p1.
Row 14—P2, FPC, BPC, (k1, p1) twice, FKC, BPC, p4, FPC.
Row 16—P3, FDKC, (k1, p1) 3 times, FDKC, p6, k2.

Repeat Rows 1–16.

Open Cable   *(See illustration, page 263)*

This is a traditional and very handsome form of cable, sometimes made with a Bobble worked in the central stitch on Row 8.

Panel of 11 sts.

Row 1 (Wrong side)—K3, p2, k1, p2, k3.
Row 2—P3, sl next 3 to dpn and hold in back, k2, sl the p st back to left-hand needle and p it, k2 from dpn, p3.
Row 3—As Row 1.
Row 4—P2, sl next p st to dpn and hold in back, k2, p the st from dpn (*Back Cross*); p1, sl next 2 to dpn and hold in front, p1, k2 from dpn (*Front Cross*); p2.
Row 5—K2, p2, k3, p2, k2.
Row 6—P1, *BC*, p3, *FC*, p1.
Row 7—K1, p2, k5, p2, k1.
Row 8—P1, k2, p5, k2, p1.
Row 9—As Row 7.
Row 10—P1, *FC*, p3, *BC*, p1.
Row 11—K2, p2, k3, p2, k2.
Row 12—P2, *FC*, p1, *BC*, p2.

Repeat Rows 1–12.

Aran Diamonds with Moss Stitch

More than any other pattern, this one typifies Aran knitting. It is pure, classic Aran: a fully developed design, symmetrical, clean, and refined by generations down to a deceptive simplicity. Sometimes it is worked on a panel of 15 stitches, with the borders of the diamonds made of two knit stitches instead of one.

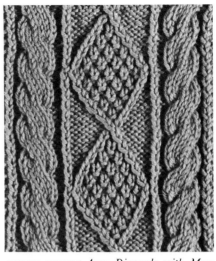

Panel of 13 sts.

Row 1 (Wrong side)—K5, p1, k1, p1, k5.

Row 2—P5, sl next 2 sts to dpn and hold in front, k1-b, then sl the purl st from dpn to left-hand needle and purl it, then k1-b from dpn; p5.

Row 3—Repeat Row 1.

Row 4—P4, sl next st to dpn and hold in back, k1-b, then p1 from dpn (Back Cross, BC); k1; sl next st to dpn and hold in front, p1, then k1-b from dpn (Front Cross, FC); p4.

Row 5 and all subsequent wrong-side rows—Knit all knit sts and purl all purl sts.

Row 6—P3, BC, k1, p1, k1, FC, p3.

Row 8—P2, BC, (k1, p1) twice, k1, FC, p2.

Row 10—P1, BC, (k1, p1) 3 times, k1, FC, p1.

Row 12—BC, (k1, p1) 4 times, k1, FC.

Row 14—FC, (p1, k1) 4 times, p1, BC.

Row 16—P1, FC, (p1, k1) 3 times, p1, BC, p1.

Row 18—P2, FC, (p1, k1) twice, p1, BC, p2.

Row 20—P3, FC, p1, k1, p1, BC, p3.

Row 22—P4, FC, p1, BC, p4.

Repeat Rows 1–22.

CENTER PANEL: *Aran Diamonds with Moss Stitch*
LEFT SIDE PANEL: *Uneven Cable, front cross*
RIGHT SIDE PANEL: *Uneven Cable, back cross*

Uneven Cable

This is an archaic form of Simple Cable, an "ancestral cable" as it were. Long ago all cables were worked on uneven stitches, the larger number of stitches being crossed in front and a smaller number behind. Today, most cables cross half-and-half, which gives a tighter twist to the cable. However, the Uneven Cable is interesting and a little different, for the very reason that it is so seldom used in modern times.

Panel of 10 sts.

Rows 1, 3, and 5 (Wrong side)—K2, p6, k2.

Row 2—P2, k6, p2.

Row 4—For a Back Cross cable (twist to the right) work Row 4 as follows: p2, sl next 2 sts to dpn and hold in back, k4, then k2 from dpn, p2. For a Front Cross cable (twist to the left) work Row 4 as follows: p2, sl next 4 sts to dpn and hold in front, k2, then k4 from dpn, p2.

Row 6—Repeat Row 2.

Repeat Rows 1–6.

Double Zigzag

CENTER PANEL: *Double Zigzag*
LEFT SIDE PANEL: *Crossed Cable, front*
RIGHT SIDE PANEL: *Crossed Cable, back*

This is a basic pattern; the knit zigzag ribs on a background of purl occur in dozens of different shapes and sizes. Sometimes the ribs are made of a single stitch instead of two stitches. Sometimes there are only two zigzagging ribs instead of four; sometimes there are six (three on each side) or eight (four on each side) or more. Sometimes there is a central rib worked vertically straight. Sometimes there are more pattern rows, hence longer zigzags. (See also Fast-Traveling Rib.)

Panel of 20 sts.

NOTES: Back Cross (BC): sl 1 st to dpn and hold in back, k2, then p1 from dpn. Front Cross (FC): sl 2 sts to dpn and hold in front, p1, then k2 from dpn.

Row 1 (Wrong side)—K3, p2, k3, p4, k3, p2, k3.
Row 2—(P2, BC) twice, (FC, p2) twice.
Row 3 and all subsequent wrong-side rows—Knit all knit sts and purl all purl sts.
Row 4—P1, (BC, p2) twice, FC, p2, FC, p1.
Row 6—(BC, p2) twice, (p2, FC) twice.
Row 8—(FC, p2) twice, (p2, BC) twice.
Row 10—P1, (FC, p2) twice, BC, p2, BC, p1.
Row 12—(P2, FC) twice, (BC, p2) twice.

Repeat Rows 1–12.

Crossed Cable

This pretty branch-like cable can be worked with a back cross, as given, or with a front cross by substituting "hold in front" for "hold in back" in Row 1. For two cables symmetrically balanced, cross one in back, the other in front.

Panel of 12 sts.

Row 1 (Right side)—P4, sl 2 to dpn and hold in back, k2, then k2 from dpn, p4.
Row 2—K4, p4, k4.
Row 3—P3, sl 1 to dpn and hold in back, k2, then k1 from dpn (Back Cross or BC); sl next 2 to dpn and hold in front, k1, then k2 from dpn (Front Cross or FC), p3.
Row 4—K3, p6, k3.
Row 5—P2, BC, k2, FC, p2.
Row 6—K2, p8, k2.
Row 7—P1, BC, k4, FC, p1.
Row 8—K1, p10, k1.

Repeat Rows 1–8.

Box Cable

This is an unusual form of Double Cable, incorporating ridges of Garter Stitch to widen the pattern. The panel is alternately extended and tightened from side to side, so that the border stitches will take on a slight wave.

Panel of 16 sts.

Row 1 (Right side)—P2, k2, p2, k4, p2, k2, p2.
Row 2—K2, p2, k2, p4, k2, p2, k2.
Rows 3 and 5—Repeat Row 1.
Rows 4 and 6—Repeat Row 2.
Row 7—P2, sl next 4 sts to dpn and hold in back, k2, then p2 and k2 from dpn; sl next 2 sts to dpn and hold in front, k2, p2, then k2 from dpn; p2.
Rows 8 and 10—Repeat Row 2.
Rows 9 and 11—Repeat Row 1.
Rows 12, 13, 14, 15, and 16—Knit.

Repeat Rows 1–16.

CENTER PANEL: *Box Cable*
SIDE PANELS: *Lovers' Knot*

Lovers' Knot

This is a delightful old French pattern that can be used not only in a cable panel but also as a spot-pattern to decorate a purl fabric. It is related to a Zigzag Rib but has a few unique touches.

Panel of 9 sts.

Row 1 (Wrong side)—(P1, k3) twice, p1.
Row 2—Sl 1 st to dpn and hold in front, p1, then k1 from dpn (Front Cross, FC); p2, k1, p2, sl 1 st to dpn and hold in back, k1, then p1 from dpn (Back Cross, BC).
Rows 3, 5, 7, 9, 11, 13, and 15—Knit all knit sts and purl all purl sts.
Row 4—P1, FC, p1, k1, p1, BC, p1.
Row 6—P2, FC, k1, BC, p2.
Row 8—P2, BC, k1, FC, p2.
Row 10—P1, BC, p1, k1, p1, FC, p1.
Row 12—Repeat Row 4.
Row 14—Repeat Row 6.
Row 16—P3, left running thread between the st just worked and the next st, and purl into the back of this thread (Make One purlwise); sl 1—k2 tog—psso, Make One purlwise, p3.
Rows 17 and 19—Knit.
Rows 18 and 20—Purl.

Repeat Rows 1–20.

Bobble Fans

Panel of 15 sts.

Row 1 (Right side)—Purl.

Row 2—Knit.

Row 3—P7, Make Bobble (MB) as follows: (k1, yo, k1, yo, k1) in next st, turn and p5, turn and k5, turn and p2 tog, p1, p2 tog; turn and sl 1—k2 tog—psso, completing Bobble; p7.

Row 4—K7, p1-b, k7.

Row 5—P4, MB, p2, k1-b, p2, MB, p4.

Row 6—K4, p1-b, k2, p1, k2, p1-b, k4.

Row 7—P2, MB, p1, sl next st to dpn and hold in front, p1, then k1 from dpn (Front Cross, FC); p1, k1-b, p1, sl next st to dpn and hold in back, k1, then p1 from dpn (Back Cross, BC); p1, MB, p2.

Row 8—K2, p1-b, k2, (p1, k1) 3 times, k1, p1-b, k2.

Row 9—P2, FC, p1, FC, k1-b, BC, p1, BC, p2.

Row 10—K3, BC, k1, p3, k1, FC, k3.

Row 11—P4, FC, Make One (M1) purlwise by lifting running thread and purling into the *back* of this thread; sl 1—k2 tog—psso, M1 purlwise, BC, p4.

Row 12—K5, BC, p1, FC, k5.

Row 13—P5, purl into front and back of next st, sl 1—k2 tog—psso, purl into front and back of next st, p5.

Row 14—K7, p1, k7.

Rows 15 and 16—Repeat Rows 1 and 2.

Repeat Rows 1–16.

CENTER PANEL: *Bobble Fans*
SIDE PANELS: *Little Twist Cable*

Little Twist Cable

Panel of 10 sts.

Rows 1 and 3 (Wrong side)—K2, p6, k2.

Row 2—P2, sl next st to dpn and hold in front, k2, then k1 from dpn; sl next 2 sts to dpn and hold in back, k1, then k2 from dpn; p2.

Row 4—P2, k2, k2 tog but do not slip from needle; insert right-hand needle between the sts just knitted tog and knit the 1st st again; then sl both sts from needle together; k2, p2.

Repeat Rows 1–4.

Banana Tree

Panel of 18 sts.

NOTES: Front Cross (FC)—sl 1 st to dpn and hold in front, p1, then k1 from dpn. Front Knit Cross (FKC)—same as FC, but *knit* both sts. Front Purl Cross (FPC)—same as FC, but *purl* both sts.

Back Cross (BC)—sl 1 st to dpn and hold in back, k1, then p1 from dpn. Back Knit Cross (BKC)—same as BC, but *knit* both sts. Back Purl Cross (BPC)—same as BC, but *purl* both sts.

Row 1 (Wrong side)—K2, p3, k3, p4, BPC, k4.
Row 2—P3, BKC, k1, BC, k2, p3, FC, k1, p2.
Row 3—K2, p2, k4, p2, k1, p3, BPC, k2.
Row 4—P2, k3, BC, p1, k1, FKC, p3, FC, p2.
Row 5—K6, FPC, p2, k2, p4, k2.
Row 6—P2, k2, BC, p2, k1, (FKC) twice, p5.
Row 7—K4, FPC, p4, k3, p3, k2.
Row 8—P2, k1, BC, p3, k2, FC, k1, FKC, p3.
Row 9—K2, FPC, p3, k1, p2, k4, p2, k2.
Row 10—P2, BC, p3, BKC, k1, p1, FC, k3, p2.
Row 11—K2, p4, k2, p2, BPC, k6.
Row 12—P5, (BKC) twice, k1, p2, FC, k2, p2.

Repeat Rows 1–12.

Nosegay Pattern

Panel of 16 sts.

NOTES: Front Cross (FC)—sl 1 st to dpn and hold in front, p1, then k1 from dpn. Front Knit Cross (FKC)—same as FC, but *knit* both sts. Back Cross (BC)—sl 1 st to dpn and hold in back, k1, then p1 from dpn. Back Knit Cross (BKC)—same as BC, but *knit* both sts.

Row 1 (Wrong side)—K7, p2, k7.
Row 2—P6, BKC, FKC, p6.
Row 3—K5, FC, p2, BC, k5.
Row 4—P4, BC, BKC, FKC, FC, p4.
Row 5—K3, FC, k1, p4, k1, BC, k3.
Row 6—P2, BC, p1, BC, k2, FC, p1, FC, p2.
Row 7—(K2, p1) twice, k1, p2, k1, (p1, k2) twice.
Row 8—P2, Make Bobble (MB) as follows: (k1, p1) twice into next st, turn and p4, turn and k4, turn and (p2 tog) twice, turn and k2 tog, completing Bobble; p1, BC, p1, k2, p1, FC, p1, MB, p2.
Row 9—K4, p1, k2, p2, k2, p1, k4.
Row 10—P4, MB, p2, k2, p2, MB, p4.

Repeat Rows 1–10.

LEFT: *Banana Tree*
RIGHT: *Nosegay Pattern*

Birdcage Cable

Panel of 22 sts.

NOTES: Front Cross (FC)—sl 1 st to dpn and hold in front, p1, then k1 from dpn. Front Knit Cross (FKC)—same as FC, but *knit* both sts. Back Cross (BC)—sl 1 st to dpn and hold in back, k1, then p1 from dpn. Back Knit Cross (BKC)—same as BC, but *knit* both sts.

Row 1 (Wrong side)—K10, p2, k10.
Row 2—P9, BKC, FKC, p9.
Row 3—K8, FC, p2, BC, k8.
Row 4—P7, BC, BKC, FKC, FC, p7.
Row 5—K6, FC, k1, p4, k1, BC, k6.
Row 6—P5, BC, p1, BC, k2, FC, p1, FC, p5.
Row 7—K4, FC, k2, p1, k1, p2, k1, p1, k2, BC, k4.
Row 8—P3, BC, p2, BC, p1, k2, p1, FC, p2, FC, p3.
Rows 9, 11, 13, 14, 15, 17, and 19—Knit all knit sts and purl all purl sts.
Row 10—(P2, BC) twice, p2, k2, p2, (FC, p2) twice.
Row 12—P1, BC, (p2, BC) twice, (FC, p2) twice, FC, p1.
Row 16—P1, FC, (p2, FC) twice, (BC, p2) twice, BC, p1.
Row 18—(P2, FC) twice, p2, k2, p2, (BC, p2) twice.
Row 20—P3, FC, p2, FC, p1, k2, p1, BC, p2, BC, p3.
Row 21—K4, BC, k2, p1, k1, p2, k1, p1, k2, FC, k4.
Row 22—P5, FC, p1, FC, k2, BC, p1, BC, p5.
Row 23—K6, BC, k1, p4, k1, FC, k6.
Row 24—P7, (FC) twice, (BC) twice, p7.
Row 25—K8, BC, p2, FC, k8.
Row 26—P9, FC, BC, p9.
Row 27—K10, p2, k10.
Row 28—P10, k2, p10.

Repeat Rows 1–28.

CENTER PANEL: *Birdcage Cable*
SIDE PANELS: *Two-Texture Rib*

Two-Texture Rib

This is a traveling rib pattern that alternates half-diamonds of purl and moss stitch. If there are two panels in symmetrical opposition, the pattern should be reversed in one of them.

Panel of 7 sts.

Row 1 (Wrong side)—K5, p2.
Row 2—Sl 2 sts to dpn and hold in front, p1, then k2 from dpn (Front Cross, FC); p4.
Row 3 and all other wrong-side rows—Knit all knit sts and purl all purl sts.

Row 4—K1, FC, p3.

Row 6—P1, k1, FC, p2.

Row 8—K1, p1, k1, FC, p1.

Row 10—(P1, k1) twice, FC.

Row 12—(K1, p1) twice, sl next st to dpn and hold in back, k2, then p1 from dpn (Back Cross, BC).

Row 14—P1, k1, p1, BC, p1.

Row 16—K1, p1, BC, p2.

Row 18—P1, BC, p3.

Row 20—BC, p4.

Repeat Rows 1–20.

CHAPTER TWELVE

Cable-Stitch Patterns

In addition to the many forms of cables, which are arranged in vertical panels, there are other patterns worked with the cable needle which are intended to make an interesting all-over fabric. Just as cables may be repeated, panel by panel, across the fabric, so some of these all-over cable-stitch patterns may be worked in panels of two or three repeats if desired.

When working any cable-stitch pattern across an entire fabric, remember that the cabling action will pull stitches together laterally and narrow the piece. Be sure to cast on enough stitches.

Wave of Honey Stitch

A single-stitch version of the Aran Honeycomb which makes a beautiful three-dimensional lattice pattern when used over a large number of stitches. It is somewhat tedious to work, due to the necessity of using the cable needle for every stitch on every right-side row. But if you are handy with the cable needle, the results of this pattern are well worth the trouble.

Multiple of 4 sts.

Rows 1 and 3 (Wrong side)—Purl.
Row 2—* Sl 1 to dpn and hold in back, k1, k the st from dpn; sl next st to dpn and hold in front, k1, k the st from dpn; rep from * across.
Row 4—* Sl 1 to dpn and hold in front, k1, k the st from dpn; sl next st to dpn and hold in back, k1, k the st from dpn; rep from * across.

Wave of Honey Stitch

Repeat Rows 1–4.

Aran Honeycomb

The Aran Honeycomb is a number of Chain Cables repeated across the fabric, which gives a three-dimensional effect. It is frequently used in fisherman sweaters.

Multiple of 8 sts.

Row 1 (Wrong side) and all other wrong-side rows—Purl.
Row 2—* Sl 2 to dpn and hold in back, k2, k2 from dpn; sl 2 to dpn and hold in front, k2, k2 from dpn; rep from * across.
Row 4—Knit.
Row 6—* Sl 2 to dpn and hold in front, k2, k2 from dpn; sl 2 to dpn and hold in back, k2, k2 from dpn; rep from * across.
Row 8—Knit.

Repeat Rows 1–8.

VARIATION: *ELONGATED ARAN HONEYCOMB*

If desired, the Honeycomb can be elongated by inserting two extra plain rows between cabling rows. This gives the "honey-cells" a rather square shape.

Multiple of 8 sts.

Row 1 (Wrong side) and all other wrong-side rows—Purl.
Row 2—As Row 2, above.
Rows 4 and 6—Knit.
Row 8—As Row 6, above.
Rows 10 and 12—Knit.

Repeat Rows 1–12.

ABOVE: *Aran Honeycomb*
BELOW: *Elongated Aran Honeycomb*

Shadow Cable

This is an allover pattern related to Basket Cable, except that the cabled stitches are staggered and do not cross one another.

Multiple of 8 sts plus 2.

Row 1 (Wrong side) and all other wrong-side rows—Purl.
Row 2—Knit.
Row 4—K1, * sl next 2 sts to dpn and hold in back, k2, k2 from dpn, k4; rep from *, end k1.
Row 6—Knit.
Row 8—K1, * k4, sl next 2 sts to dpn and hold in front, k2, k2 from dpn; rep from *, end k1.

Repeat Rows 1–8.

Shadow Cable

CABLE-STITCH PATTERNS   273

Basket Cable

Basket Cable

This pattern is exceedingly dense in the lateral dimension, as might be expected when 4 stitches are cabled over 4 stitches all the way across the row. Basket Cable is popularly used in panel form for fancy cable sweaters, though in fact the Close-Woven Basket Lattice gives much the same effect with a much neater appearance. When Basket Cable is used as a panel, the 4 edge stitches may be omitted or converted into purl stitches.

Multiple of 8 sts plus 4.

Rows 1, 3, and 5 (Wrong side)—K2, purl to last 2 sts, k2.
Rows 2 and 4—Knit.
Row 6—K2, * sl next 4 sts to dpn and hold in back, k4, then k4 from dpn; rep from *, end k2.
Rows 7, 9, and 11—K2, purl to last 2 sts, k2.
Rows 8 and 10—Knit.
Row 12—K6, * sl next 4 sts to dpn and hold in front, k4, then k4 from dpn; rep from *, end k6.

Repeat Rows 1–12.

Clustered Cable or Cable Check

Clustered Cable or Cable Check

This is a simple German pattern consisting of knit-purl checks, with a single cable cross worked into each knit check.

Multiple of 12 sts plus 6.

Rows 1 and 3 (Right side)—P6, * k6, p6; rep from * across.
Rows 2 and 4—K6, * p6, k6; rep from * across.
Row 5—P6, * sl next 3 to dpn and hold in back, k3, k3 from dpn, p6; rep from *.
Row 6—K6, * p6, k6; rep from * across.
Row 7—P6, * k6, p6; rep from * across.
Row 8—K6, * p6, k6; rep from * across.
Rows 9 and 11—K6, * p6, k6; rep from * across.
Rows 10 and 12—P6, * k6, p6; rep from * across.
Row 13—* Sl 3 to dpn and hold in back, k3, k3 from dpn, p6; rep from *, end sl 3 to dpn and hold in back, k3, k3 from dpn.
Row 14—P6, * k6, p6; rep from * across.
Row 15—K6, * p6, k6; rep from * across.
Row 16—P6, * k6, p6; rep from * across.

Repeat Rows 1–16.

Lace Cable or Germaine Stitch

This pattern is ideal for the knitter who wants to use a dainty openwork but likes to work a few cables into everything. The lace portion of the pattern is recognizable as Little Arrowhead. The same combination comes out equally well with the larger-patterned Arrowhead Lace: simple cables worked in between the lace panels.

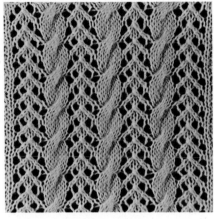

Multiple of 11 sts plus 7.

Row 1 (Wrong side) and all other wrong-side rows—Purl.

Row 2—K1, * yo, ssk, k1, k2 tog, yo, k6; rep from * to last 6 sts, end yo, ssk, k1, k2 tog, yo, k1.

Row 4—K2, * yo, sl 1—k2 tog—psso, yo, k1, sl next 3 sts to dpn and hold in back, k3, then k3 from dpn, k1; rep from * to last 5 sts, end yo, sl 1—k2 tog—psso, yo, k2.

Row 6—Repeat Row 2.

Row 8—K2, * yo, sl 1—k2 tog—psso, yo, k8; rep from * to last 5 sts, end yo, sl 1—k2 tog—psso, yo, k2.

Repeat Rows 1–8.

Lace Cable or Germaine Stitch

Diagonal Wave

This pattern has one feature that is unique among cable patterns—it looks the same on both sides. As given, the waves run upward to the right. It is a simple matter to reverse the diagonals, making the waves run to the left, by slipping 3 knit sts to the cable needle, holding them in front, and purling 3 sts behind.

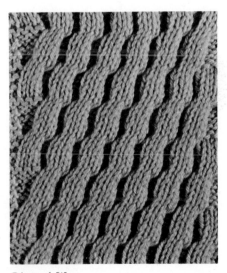

Multiple of 6 sts plus 3.

Rows 1, 3, and 5—(Wrong side)—K3, * p3, k3; rep from *.

Rows 2 and 4—P3, * k3, p3; rep from *.

Row 6—* Sl 3 sts to dpn and hold in back, k3, then p3 from dpn; rep from *, end k3.

Rows 7, 9, and 11—P3, * k3, p3; rep from *.

Rows 8 and 10—K3, * p3, k3; rep from *.

Row 12—P3, * sl next 3 sts to dpn and hold in back, k3, then p3 from dpn; rep from *.

Repeat Rows 1–12.

Diagonal Wave

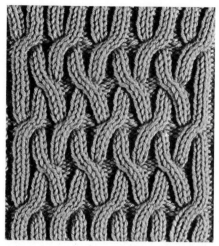

Lattice Cable

Lattice Cable

An allover pattern of knit stitches woven across a purl-stitch ground.

Multiple of 8 sts plus 2.

Rows 1, 3, 5 and 7 (Wrong side)—K2, * p2, k2; rep from *.

Rows 2, 4, and 6—P2, * k2, p2; rep from *.

Row 8—P2, * sl next 4 to dpn and hold in back, k2, sl the 2 p sts from dpn back to left-hand needle and p them; k2 from dpn, p2; rep from *.

Rows 9–15—Repeat Rows 1–7.

Row 16—P2, k2, * p2, sl the next 4 sts to dpn and hold in front, k2, sl the 2 p sts from dpn back to left-hand needle and p them; k2 from dpn; rep from *, end p2, k2, p2.

Repeat Rows 1–16.

Basic Lattice

The cabled lattice is referred to as "basic" because so many other cable-stitch patterns are developed from it. The principle is simply that knit stitches are "traveled" diagonally across a ground of purl stitches, using the cable needle to move them along.

Note that in this pattern the Back Knit Cross and Front Knit Cross may be omitted from Rows 1 and 9, instead working these rows in straight knit and purl stitches as Row 2. In this case the lattice does not cross or "weave", but forms alternating waves which create a pattern known as Hourglass.

Another pleasing variation is made when all knit stitches on the right side are knitted through the back loops, thus being crossed.

Basic Lattice

Multiple of 8 sts.

NOTES: Back Cross (BC)—Sl 1 st to dpn and hold in back, k1, then p the st from dpn.

Front Cross (FC)—sl 1 st to dpn and hold in front, p1, then k the st from dpn.

Back Knit Cross (BKC)—sl 1 st to dpn and hold in back, k1, then k the st from dpn.

Front Knit Cross (FKC)—sl 1 st to dpn and hold in front, k1, then k the st from dpn.

Row 1 (Right side)—P3, BKC, * p6, BKC; rep from *, end p3.

Row 2 and all other wrong-side rows—Knit all knit sts and purl all purl sts.

Row 3—P2, * BC, FC, p4; rep from *, end BC, FC, p2.

Row 5—P1, * BC, p2, FC, p2; rep from *, end BC, p2, FC, p1.

Row 7—* BC, p4, FC; rep from *.
Row 9—K1, * p6, FKC; rep from *, end p6, k1.
Row 11—* FC, p4, BC; rep from *.
Row 13—P1, * FC, p2, BC, p2; rep from *, end FC, p2, BC, p1.
Row 15—P2, * FC, BC, p4; rep from *, end FC, BC, p2.
Row 16—See Row 2.

Repeat Rows 1–16.

Ribbed Lattice With Bobbles

Bobbles made by this method are nubby and stiff, rather than loose and "bobbly". This is a decided advantage if the knitted article is to withstand hard use. Note that Row 1 is a preparation row, omitted from subsequent repeats.

Ribbed Lattice with Bobbles

Multiple of 20 sts plus 2.

NOTES: Back Cross (BC): sl 1 st to dpn and hold in back, k1-b, then p1 from dpn. Front Cross (FC): sl 1 st to dpn and hold in front, p1, then k1-b from dpn.

Row 1 (Right side–preparation)—P6, * (k1-b, p1) twice, k2-b, (p1, k1-b) twice, p10; rep from *, end last repeat p6.
Row 2—K6, * (p1-b, k1) twice, p2-b, (k1, p1-b) twice, k10; rep from *, end last repeat k6.
Row 3—P6, * k1-b, p1, k1-b, on next 4 sts Make Bobble (MB) as follows: (k4, turn, p4, turn) 3 times, then pick up a loop from the first row of bobble and knit it tog with 1st st on left-hand needle; k2, then pick up a loop from 1st row of bobble and knit it tog with next st, completing bobble; k1-b, p1, k1-b, p10; rep from *, end last repeat p6.
Row 4—K6, * (p1-b, k1) twice, p2-b, (k1, p1-b) twice, k10; rep from *, end last repeat k6.
Row 5—P5, * (BC) 3 times, (FC) 3 times, p8; rep from *, end last repeat p5.
Row 6 and all subsequent wrong-side rows: Knit all knit sts and p-b all purl sts.
Row 7—P4, * (BC) 3 times, p2, (FC) 3 times, p6; rep from *, end last repeat p4.
Row 9—P3, * (BC) 3 times, p4, (FC) 3 times, p4; rep from *, end last repeat p3.
Row 11—P2, * (BC) 3 times, p6, (FC) 3 times, p2; rep from *.
Row 13—P1, * (BC) 3 times, p8, (FC) 3 times; rep from *, end p1.
Row 15—P1, MB on next 4 sts, k1-b, * p10, k1-b, p1, k1-b, MB on next 4 sts, k1-b, p1, k1-b; rep from *, end p10, k1-b, MB on next 4 sts, p1.
Row 16 (Wrong side)—K1, * (p1-b, k1) twice, p1-b, k10, (p1-b, k1) twice, p1-b; rep from *, end k1.
Row 17—P1, * (FC) 3 times, p8, (BC) 3 times; rep from *, end p1.
Row 19—P2, * (FC) 3 times, p6, (BC) 3 times, p2; rep from *.
Row 21—P3, * (FC) 3 times, p4, (BC) 3 times, p4; rep from *, end last repeat p3.
Row 23—P4, * (FC) 3 times, p2, (BC) 3 times, p6; rep from *, end last repeat p4.
Row 25—P5, * (FC) 3 times, (BC) 3 times, p8; rep from *, end last repeat p5.

Omitting Row 1, repeat Rows 2–25.

Close-Woven Basket Lattice

Close-Woven Basket Lattice

This pattern gives a dense texture in which the illusion of diagonal basketweaving is extremely realistic.

Multiple of 6 sts plus 2.

Row 1 (Wrong side)—K2, * p4, k2; rep from *.

Row 2—P2, * sl 2 sts to dpn and hold in back, k2, then k2 from dpn; p2; rep from *.

Row 3 and all other wrong-side rows—Knit the knit sts and purl the purl sts.

Row 4—P1, * sl 1 st to dpn and hold in back, k2, then p the st from dpn (Back Cross or BC); sl next 2 sts to dpn and hold in front, p1, then k2 from dpn (Front Cross or FC); rep from *, end p1.

Row 6—P1, k2, p2, * sl next 2 sts to dpn and hold in front, k2, then k2 from dpn; p2; rep from *, end k2, p1.

Row 8—P1, * FC, BC; rep from *, end p1.

Repeat Rows 1–8.

Interlocking Lattice

Interlocking Lattice

In this fascinating pattern the sides of the lattice diamonds are twisted around one another. (See Basic Lattice).

Multiple of 6 sts plus 2.

NOTES: For Back Cross, Front Cross, Back Knit Cross and Front Knit Cross, see Notes to Basic Lattice.

Row 1 (Wrong side)—K1, p1, * k4, p2; rep from *, end k4, p1, k1.

Row 2—P1, * FC, p2, BC; rep from *, end p1.

Row 3 and all other wrong-side rows—Knit all knit sts and purl all purl sts.

Row 4—P2, * FC, BC, p2; rep from *.

Row 6—P3, * BKC, p4; rep from *, end last rep p3.

Row 8—P2, * BC, FC, p2; rep from *.

Row 10—P2, * FC, BC, p2; rep from *.

Row 12—As Row 6.

Row 14—P2, * BC, FC, p2; rep from *.

Row 16—P1, * BC, p2, FC; rep from *, end p1.

Row 18—BC, p4, * FKC, p4; rep from *, end FC.

Row 20—K1, p4, * BC, FC, p2; rep from *, end p2, k1.

Row 22—K1, p4, * FC, BC, p2; rep from *, end p2, k1.

Row 24—FC, p4, * FKC, p4; rep from *, end BC.

Repeat Rows 1–24.

Double Hourglass

This is a very handsome pattern of the lattice type, excellent for sweaters. It can be enriched with bobbles or embroidery— a "lazy-daisy", a "snowflake", or some small cross-stitch motif in the center of each diamond of purl. For further embellishment, the knit stitches can be either Crossed or Twisted.

For a single "Hourglass", see Basic Lattice.

Double Hourglass

Multiple of 14 sts plus 2.

NOTES: Back Cross (BC)—sl 1 st to dpn and hold in back, k1, then p1 from dpn. Front Cross (FC)—sl 1 st to dpn and hold in front, p1, then k1 from dpn.

Row 1 (Wrong side)—K1, * p1, k2, p1, k6, p1, k2, p1; rep from *, end k1.
Row 2—P1, * FC, p1, FC, p4, BC, p1, BC; rep from *, end p1.
Row 3 and all other wrong-side rows—Knit all knit sts and purl all purl sts.
Row 4—P1, * (p1, FC) twice, p2, (BC, p1) twice; rep from *, end p1.
Row 6—P1, * p2, FC, p1, FC, BC, p1, BC, p2; rep from *, end p1.
Row 8—Knit all knit sts and purl all purl sts.
Row 10—P1, * p2, BC, p1, BC, FC, p1, FC, p2; rep from *, end p1.
Row 12—P1, * (p1, BC) twice, p2, (FC, p1) twice; rep from *, end p1.
Row 14—P1, * BC, p1, BC, p4, FC, p1, FC; rep from *, end p1.
Row 16—Knit all knit sts and purl all purl sts.

Repeat Rows 1–16.

Fancy Moss Stitch Lattice

This pattern has an unusual three-stitch cross from the wrong side in Rows 1 and 9, which imparts a slightly spiral pull to the diagonal ribs of the lattice. If desired, the reverse cross can be omitted from Rows 1 and 9, instead working these three stitches simply "p1, k1, p1". The resulting pattern will be a most attractive Moss Stitch Hourglass.

Fancy Moss Stitch Lattice

Multiple of 14 sts plus 13.

NOTES: Front Cross (FC): Sl 2 sts to dpn and hold in front, p1, then k2 from dpn. Back Cross (BC): Sl 1 st to dpn and hold in back, k2, then p1 from dpn. Reverse Front Cross (RFC; worked from wrong side): Sl 2 sts to dpn and hold in front, p1, then sl the knit st from dpn back to left-hand needle and knit it, then p1 from dpn. Reverse Back Cross (RBC; worked from wrong side): Sl 2 sts to dpn and hold in back, p1, then sl the knit st from dpn back to left-hand needle and knit it, then p1 from dpn.

Row 1 (Wrong side)—P2, * (k1, p1) 5 times, RBC, p1; rep from *, end (k1, p1) 4 times, k1, p2.

Row 2—FC, (p1, k1) 3 times, p1, BC, * k1, FC, (p1, k1) 3 times, p1, BC; rep from *.

Rows 3, 5, and 7—Knit all knit sts and purl all purl sts.

Row 4—K1, FC, (p1, k1) twice, p1, BC, k1, * p1, k1, FC, (p1, k1) twice, p1, BC, k1; rep from *.

Row 6—P1, k1, FC, p1, k1, p1, BC, k1, p1, * k1, p1, k1, FC, p1, k1, p1, BC, k1, p1; rep from *.

Row 8—K1, p1, k1, FC, p1, BC, k1, p1, k1, * (p1, k1) twice, FC, p1, BC, k1, p1, k1; rep from *.

Row 9—(P1, k1) twice, * p1, RFC, (p1, k1) 5 times; rep from *, end p1, RFC, p1, (k1, p1) twice.

Row 10—P1, k1, p1, BC, k1, FC, p1, k1, p1, * (k1, p1) twice, BC, k1, FC, p1, k1, p1; rep from *.

Rows 11, 13, and 15—Knit all knit sts and purl all purl sts.

Row 12—K1, p1, BC, k1, p1, k1, FC, p1, k1, * p1, k1, p1, BC, k1, p1, k1, FC, p1, k1; rep from *.

Row 14—P1, BC, (k1, p1) twice, k1, FC, p1, * k1, p1, BC, (k1, p1) twice, k1, FC, p1; rep from *.

Row 16—BC, (k1, p1) 3 times, k1, FC, * p1, BC, (k1, p1) 3 times, k1, FC; rep from *.

Repeat Rows 1–16.

LEFT: *Traveling Cable, left*
RIGHT: *Traveling Cable, right*

Traveling Cable

In this pattern the cables can be moved either to the right or to the left. Either version is pretty as an allover pattern, but if there are two panels of Traveling Cable, one on each side of a common center, then one of each version should be used.

TRAVELING CABLE, LEFT

Multiple of 5 sts plus 1.

Rows 1 and 3 (Right side)—P1, * k4, p1; rep from *.

Rows 2, 4, and 6—K1, * p4, k1; rep from *.

Row 5—P1, * sl next 2 sts to dpn and hold in front, k2, then k2 from dpn (Front Cross, FC), p1; rep from *.

Rows 7 and 9—K1, * p1, k4; rep from *.

Rows 8, 10, and 12—* P4, k1; rep from *, end p1.

Row 11—K1, * p1, FC; rep from *.

Rows 13 and 15—K2, * p1, k4; rep from *, end p1, k3.

Rows 14, 16, and 18—P3, * k1, p4; rep from *, end k1, p2.

Rows 17—K2, * p1, FC; rep from *, end p1, k3.

Rows 19 and 21—K3, * p1, k4; rep from *, end p1, k2.
Rows 20, 22, and 24—P2, * k1, p4; rep from *, end k1, p3.
Row 23—K3, * p1, FC; rep from *, end p1, k2.
Rows 25 and 27—* K4, p1; rep from *, end k1.
Rows 26 and 28—P1, * k1, p4; rep from *.
Row 29—* FC, p1; rep from *, end k1.
Row 30—P1, * k1, p4; rep from *.

Repeat Rows 1–30.

TRAVELING CABLE, RIGHT

Multiple of 5 sts plus 1.

Rows 1 and 3 (Right side)—P1, * k4, p1; rep from *.
Rows 2, 4, and 6—K1, * p4, k1; rep from *.
Row 5—P1, * sl next 2 sts to dpn and hold in back, k2; then
    k2 from dpn (Back Cross, BC), p1; rep from *.
Rows 7 and 9—* K4, p1; rep from *, end k1.
Rows 8, 10, and 12—P1, * k1, p4; rep from *.
Row 11—* BC, p1; rep from *, end k1.
Rows 13 and 15—K3, * p1, k4; rep from *, end p1, k2.
Rows 14, 16, and 18—P2, * k1, p4; rep from *, end k1, p3.
Row 17—K3, * p1, BC; rep from *, end p1, k2.
Rows 19 and 21—K2, * p1, k4; rep from *, end p1, k3.
Rows 20, 22, and 24—P3, * k1, p4; rep from *, end k1, p2.
Row 23—K2, * p1, BC; rep from *, end p1, k3.
Rows 25 and 27—K1, * p1, k4; rep from *.
Rows 26 and 28—* P4, k1; rep from *, end p1.
Row 29—K1, * p1, BC; rep from *.
Row 30—* P4, k1; rep from *, end p1.

Repeat Rows 1–30.

Traveling Rib Pattern

Multiple of 6 sts plus 4.

Rows 1 and 3 (Wrong side)—P1, * k2, p1; rep from *.
Row 2—K1, * p2, k1; rep from *.
Row 4—* Sl 3 sts to dpn and hold in back, k1, then holding
    yarn in front, sl the 2 purl sts from dpn back to left-hand
    needle and purl them; then knit remaining st from dpn
    (Cross 4); p2; rep from *, end Cross 4.
Rows 5, 6, and 7—Repeat Rows 1, 2, and 3.
Row 8—K1, p2, * Cross 4, p2; rep from *, end k1.

Repeat Rows 1–8.

Traveling Rib Pattern

CABLE-STITCH PATTERNS 281

Bell Rib Pattern

This pattern tends to draw together quite strongly when being worked, and in blocking it must be well stretched laterally. The texture is quite pretty. After it is stretched, the little indented "bells" in purl stitches can be seen.

Multiple of 4 sts plus 2.

Rows 1, 3, and 5 (Wrong side)—P2, * k2, p2; rep from *.

Rows 2 and 4—K2, * p2, k2; rep from *.

Row 6—K1, * sl next st to dpn and hold in front, p1, skip 1 st and knit the next st inserting the point of needle into the st and then around the right-hand side of skipped st to catch yarn, then complete the knitting of this st drawing it *over* the skipped st and off needle; yarn to front and knit the st from dpn; then p1 (the skipped st); rep from *, end k1.

Rows 7, 9, and 11—K2, * p2, k2; rep from *.

Rows 8 and 10—P2, * k2, p2; rep from *.

Row 12—K1, skip next st and knit the 2nd st drawing it over skipped st as before; purl the skipped st, * repeat from * of Row 6, end sl 1 to dpn and hold in front, p1, k1 from dpn, k1.

Repeat Rows 1–12.

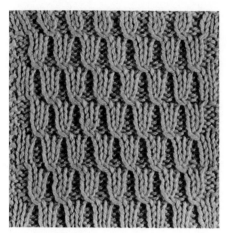

Bell Rib Pattern

Diamond Window Pattern

Most cable patterns are composed of motifs in knit stitches, displayed against a purled background. This pattern is the reverse: the diamond motifs are purled (and therefore indented) while the borders and background are made of knit stitches. If desired, the pattern can be worked the other way, with knit diamonds on a purled ground, simply by reading "knit" for "purl" and vice versa.

This is a very handsome pattern for a sweater, and readily lends itself to further embellishment with touches of embroidery or bobbles or some other accent worked into the center of each diamond.

Multiple of 26 sts.

NOTES: Back Knit Cross (BKC): sl 1 st to dpn and hold in back, k2, then k1 from dpn. Front Knit Cross (FKC): sl 2 sts to dpn and hold in front, k1, then k2 from dpn. Back Purl Cross

Diamond Window Pattern

(BPC): sl 1 st to dpn and hold in back, k2, then p1 from dpn.

Front Purl Cross (FPC): sl 2 sts to dpn and hold in front, p1, then k2 from dpn.

Row 1 (Wrong side)—* K5, p16, k5; rep from *.

Row 2—* P4, BKC, k12, FKC, p4; rep from *.

Row 3 and all subsequent wrong-side rows—Knit all knit sts and purl all purl sts.

Row 4—* P3, BKC, k4, BPC, FPC, k4, FKC, p3; rep from *.

Row 6—* P2, BKC, k4, BPC, p2, FPC, k4, FKC, p2; rep from *.

Row 8—* P1, BKC, k4, BPC, p4, FPC, k4, FKC, p1; rep from *.

Row 10—* BKC, k4, BPC, p6, FPC, k4, FKC; rep from *.

Row 12—* K6, BPC, p8, FPC, k6; rep from *.

Row 14—* K6, FKC, p8, BKC, k6; rep from *.

Row 16—* FPC, k4, FKC, p6, BKC, k4, BPC; rep from *.

Row 18—* P1, FPC, k4, FKC, p4, BKC, k4, BPC, p1; rep from *.

Row 20—* P2, FPC, k4, FKC, p2, BKC, k4, BPC, p2; rep from *.

Row 22—* P3, FPC, k4, FKC, BKC, k4, BPC, p3; rep from *.

Row 24—* P4, FPC, k12, BPC, p4; rep from *.

Repeat Rows 1–24.

Little Bow Twist

This is a charming spot-pattern on a purled fabric.

Multiple of 12 sts plus 7.

Row 1 (Wrong side)—Knit.

Rows 2, 4, 8, and 12—P1, * k1, p3, k1, p7; rep from *, end k1, p3, k1, p1.

Rows 3, 5, 7, 9, 11, and 13—K1, * p1, k3, p1, k7; rep from *, end p1, k3, p1, k1.

Rows 6 and 10—P1, * sl next 4 sts to dpn and hold in back, k1, then sl the 3 purl sts back to left-hand needle and purl them; then knit the last st from dpn; p7; rep from *, end last repeat p1.

Row 14—Purl.

Row 15—Knit.

Rows 16, 18, 22, and 26—P7, * k1, p3, k1, p7; rep from *.

Rows 17, 19, 21, 23, 25, and 27—K7, * p1, k3, p1, k7; rep from *.

Rows 20 and 24—P7, * sl next 4 sts to dpn and hold in back, k1, then sl the 3 purl sts back to left-hand needle and purl them; then knit the last st from dpn; p7, rep from *.

Row 28—Purl.

Repeat Rows 1–28.

Little Bow Twist

Arrow Cable

Arrow Cable

This is a nice pattern for either vertical or horizontal panels.

Multiple of 16 sts plus 4.

NOTES: Front Cross (FC): sl 1 st to dpn and hold in front, p1, then k1 from dpn. Back Cross (BC): sl 1 st to dpn and hold in back, k1, then p1 from dpn. Cable 4: sl 2 sts to dpn and hold in back, k2, then k2 from dpn.

Row 1 (Wrong side)—P4, * p1, k3, p4, k3, p5; rep from *.
Row 2—K4, * FC, p2, k4, p2, BC, k4; rep from *.
Rows 3, 5, and 7—Knit all knit sts and purl all purl sts.
Row 4—Cable 4, * p1, FC, p1, Cable 4, p1, BC, p1, Cable 4; rep from *.
Row 6—K4, * p2, FC, k4, BC, p2, k4; rep from *.
Row 8—Cable 4, * p4, Cable 4; rep from *.

Repeat Rows 1–8.

Acorn Pattern

This is an old English pattern that makes a handsome novelty fabric.

Multiple of 10 sts plus 2.

Acorn Pattern

Row 1 (Right side-preparation row)—K1, p3, k4, * p6, k4; rep from *, end p3, k1.
Row 2—K4, p4, * k6, p4; rep from *, end k4.
Row 3—K1, p1, * sl next 2 sts to dpn and hold in back, k2, then p2 from dpn (Back Cross, BC); insert needle under running thread between st just worked and the next st, and (k1, p1) into this thread; sl next 2 sts to dpn and hold in front, p2, then k2 from dpn (Front Cross, FC); p2; rep from * to last 2 sts, end last repeat p1, k1.
Rows 4 and 6—K2, * p2, k2; rep from *.
Row 5—K1, p1, * k2, p2; rep from *, end k2, p1, k1.
Row 7—K2, * ssk, p6, k2 tog, k2; rep from *.
Row 8—K1, p2, k6, * p4, k6; rep from *, end p2, k1.
Row 9—K1, insert needle under running thread and knit once into this thread, * FC, p2, BC, (k1, p1) into running thread; rep from *, end FC, p2, BC, knit once into running thread, k1.
Rows 10 and 12—K1, p1, * k2, p2; rep from *, end k2, p1, k1.
Row 11—K2, * p2, k2; rep from *.
Row 13—K1, p3, * k2 tog, k2, ssk, p6; rep from *, end k2 tog, k2, ssk, p3, k1.

Omit Row 1, Repeat Rows 2–13.

Cathedral Pattern

This marvelous pattern has a little of everything—lace, cabling, and bobbles. It is classified under Cable Patterns because it does require the use of the cable needle, and the lace part of the pattern is more like a series of accents in an otherwise solid fabric.

The Cathedral is one of those ever-fascinating pictures in yarn. Its realism is astonishing. The beautiful "stained-glass windows" are built up of Vertical Lace Trellis—an indication of how imagination and a general knowledge of simple pattern stitches can be used to make almost any sort of artistic effect.

Cathedral Pattern

Panel of 25 sts.

Row 1 (Right side)—P2, k4, (yo, k2 tog) 7 times, k3, p2.

Row 2—K2, p21, k2.

Row 3—P2, k3, (ssk, yo) 7 times, k4, p2.

Row 4—K2, p21, k2.

Rows 5 through 20—Repeat Rows 1–4 four times more.

Row 21—P2, k4, (yo, ssk) twice, yo, sl 2 knitwise—k1—p2sso, yo, (k2 tog, yo) 3 times, k4, p2.

Row 22—K2, p21, k2.

Row 23—P2, sl next 2 sts to dpn and hold in front, p1, then k2 from dpn (Front Cross or FC); k2, (yo, ssk) twice, yo, sl 2 knitwise—k1—p2sso, yo, (k2 tog, yo) twice, k2, sl next st to dpn and hold in back, k2, then p1 from dpn (Back Cross or BC); p2.

Row 24—K3, p19, k3.

Row 25—P3, FC, k2, yo, ssk, yo, sl 2 knitwise—k1—p2sso, yo, (k2 tog, yo) twice, k2, BC, p3.

Row 26—K4, p17, k4.

Row 27—P4, FC, k2, yo, ssk, yo, sl 2 knitwise—k1—p2sso, yo, k2 tog, yo, k2, BC, p4.

Row 28—K5, p15, k5.

Row 29—P5, FC, k2, yo, sl 2 knitwise—k1—p2sso, yo, k2 tog, yo, k2, BC, p4.

Row 30—K6, p13, k6.

Row 31—P6, FC, k2, yo, sl 2 knitwise—k1—p2sso, yo, k2, BC, p6.

Row 32—K7, p11, k7.

Row 33—P7, FC, k1, k2 tog, yo, k2, BC, p7.

Row 34—K8, p9, k8.

Row 35—P8, FC, k3, BC, p8.

Row 36—K9, p7, k9.

Row 37—P9, FC, k1, BC, p9.

Row 38—K10, p5, k10.

Row 39—P11, k1, make Bobble in center st as follows: (k1, yo, k1, yo, k1) in same st; turn and p5; turn and k5; turn and p1, p3 tog, p1; turn and sl 2 knitwise—k1—p2sso; Bobble completed; k1, p11.

Row 40—K12, p1-b, k12.

Row 41—Purl.

Row 42—Knit.

Repeat Rows 1–42.

Flying Wings Pattern

Flying Wings Pattern

It does not put too heavy a burden on the imagination to see in this pattern a flock of birds in flight. It is an ingenious combination of twist and cable stitches, making a closely woven texture that is attractive either in panels of 3 or 4 repeats or as an allover fabric.

Multiple of 6 sts.

Row 1 (Right side)—Knit.

Row 2—Purl.

Row 3—* Skip 2 sts, knit into 3rd st on left-hand needle and pull through a loop; then knit 1st and 2nd sts and sl all 3 sts from needle together; sl next st to dpn and hold in front, k2, then k1 from dpn; rep from *.

Row 4—P5, * skip 1 st and purl the 2nd st on left-hand needle, then purl the skipped st and sl both sts from needle together; p4; rep from *, end p1.

Repeat Rows 1–4.

Serpentine Cables

Serpentine Cables

When repeated over a large number of stitches, this pattern gives a truly wonderful array of interlinked cables which appear more complicated than they are.

Multiple of 8 sts plus 4. (A minimum of 20 sts is required to show pattern.)

NOTES: Front Cross or FC—sl 2 k sts to dpn, hold in front, p1, then k2 from dpn. Back Cross or BC—sl 1 p st to dpn, hold in back, k2, then p1 from dpn. Front Double Knit Cross or FDKC—sl 2 k sts to dpn, hold in front, k2, then k2 from dpn. Back Double Knit Cross or BDKC—sl 2 k sts to dpn, hold in back, k2, then k2 from dpn.

Row 1 (Wrong side)—K2, p2, * k4, p4; rep from *, end k4, p2, k2.

Row 2—P2, * FC, p2, BC; rep from *, end p2.

Row 3 and all other wrong-side rows—Knit all knit sts and purl all purl sts.

Row 4—P3, * FC, BC, p2; rep from *, end p1.

Row 6—* P4, BDKC; rep from *, end p4.

Row 8—P3, * BC, FC, p2; rep from *, end p1.

Row 10—Knit all knit sts and purl all purl sts.

Row 12—P3, * FC, BC, p2; rep from *, end p1.

Row 14—* P4, BDKC; rep from *, end p4.

Row 16—P3, * BC, FC, p2; rep from *, end p1.

Row 18—P2, * BC, p2, FC; rep from *, end p2.

Row 20—P1, BC, * p4, FDKC; rep from *, end p4, FC, p1.

Row 22—BC, p4, * BC, FC, p2; rep from *, end p2, FC.

Row 24—Knit all knit sts and purl all purl sts.

Row 26—FC, p4, * FC, BC, p2; rep from *, end p2, BC.

Row 28—P1, FC, * p4, FDKC; rep from *, end p4, BC, p1.

Repeat Rows 1–28.

Plaid Lattice

This is a double pattern; a lattice of two-stitch ribs is superimposed upon another lattice of one-stitch ribs. One single panel, 16 sts wide, makes the popular "X-in-a-diamond" cable.

Multiple of 14 sts plus 2.

Row 1 (Wrong side)—K1, * p1, k4, p4, k4, p1; rep from *, end k1.

Row 2—P1, k1-b, * p4, sl 2 sts to dpn and hold in front, k2, then k2 from dpn; p4, sl 1 st to dpn and hold in front, k1-b, then k1-b from dpn; rep from * to last 2 sts, end last repeat k1-b, p1.

Row 3 and all other wrong-side rows—Knit all knit sts and purl all purl sts.

Row 4—P1, * sl 1 st to dpn and hold in front, p1, then k1-b from dpn (Single Front Cross, SFC); p2; sl 1 st to dpn and hold in back, k2, then p1 from dpn (Back Cross, BC); sl 2 sts to dpn and hold in front, p1, then k2 from dpn (Front Cross, FC); p2; sl 1 st to dpn and hold in back, k1-b, then p1 from dpn (Single Back Cross, SBC); rep from *, end p1.

Row 6—P1, * p1, SFC, BC, p2, FC, SBC, p1; rep from *, end p1.

Row 8—Pl, * p2, sl 1 st to dpn and hold in back, k2, then k1-b from dpn (Back Knit Cross, BKC); p4; sl 2 sts to dpn and hold in front, k1-b, then k2 from dpn (Front Knit Cross, FKC); p2; rep from *, end p1.

Row 10—P1, * p1, BC, SFC, p2, SBC, FC, p1; rep from *, end p1.

Row 12—P1, * BC, p2, SFC, SBC, p2, FC; rep from *, end p1.

Row 14—P1, k2, * p4, sl 1 st to dpn and hold in back, k1-b, then k1-b from dpn; p4, sl 2 sts to dpn and hold in back, k2, then k2 from dpn; rep from * to last 3 sts, end last repeat k2, p1.

Row 16—P1, * FC, p2, SBC, SFC, p2, BC; rep from *, end p1.

Row 18—P1, * p1, FC, SBC, p2, SFC, BC, p1; rep from *, end p1.

Row 20—P1, * p2, FKC, p4, BKC, p2; rep from *, end p1.

Row 22—P1, * p1, SBC, FC, p2, BC, SFC, p1; rep from *, end p1.

Row 24—P1, * SBC, p2, FC, BC, p2, SFC; rep from *, end p1.

Repeat Rows 1–24.

Plaid Lattice

Cluster Stitch

Cluster Stitch

In this pattern no stitches are cabled—that is, crossed over each other. But the work does require the use of a cable needle, and so Cluster Stitch is classified as a cable pattern.

Like Bobbles, a series of Clusters can be used as a fancy texture spot-pattern, as shown. Or, Clusters can be worked as a form of Smocking, to tie together various sizes of knit-purl ribs. (See Ribbed Cluster Diamond Pattern.) Larger Clusters can be made by winding the yarn more times; smaller ones by winding fewer times. The winding can be tight or loose, depending on whether the knitter wishes the clustered stitches squeezed together or not.

Multiple of 6 sts plus 5.

Row 1 (Wrong side) and all other wrong-side rows—Purl.
Row 2—Knit.
Row 4—K4, * knit next 3 sts and transfer the 3 sts just knitted onto dpn; then wind yarn 6 times counterclockwise (looking down from top) around these 3 sts under dpn; then return the 3 sts to right-hand needle (Cluster 3); k3; rep from *, end k1.
Row 6—Knit.
Row 8—K1, * Cluster 3, k3; rep from *, end Cluster 3, k1.

Repeat Rows 1–8.

The Anchor

The Anchor

Although this pattern is worked in a panel, it does not continue vertically but is completed, instead, at the end of 42 rows. It may, of course, be started again in the next panel above, or worked horizontally across the fabric by repeating the pattern every 32 stitches. Note that the Front Cross and Back Cross are made on both sides of the fabric to give a shallow slant to the traveling stitches.

Panel of 32 sts.

Row 1 (Right side)—Purl.
Row 2—Knit.
Row 3—P15, k2, p15.

Row 4—K15, p2, k15.

Row 5—P14, sl next st to dpn and hold in back, k1, then k1 from dpn; sl next st to dpn and hold in front, k1, then k1 from dpn; p14.

Row 6—K13, sl next st to dpn and hold in front, *p1,* then k1 from dpn (Front Cross, FC); p2; sl next st to dpn and hold in back, k1, then *p1* from dpn (Back Cross, BC); k13.

Row 7—P12, BC, p1, k2, p1, FC, p12.

Row 8—K11, FC, k2, p2, k2, BC, k11.

Row 9—P10, BC, p3, k2, p3, FC, p10.

Row 10—K9, FC, k4, p2, k4, BC, k9.

Row 11—P8, BC, p5, k2, p5, FC, p8.

Row 12—K7, FC, k6, p2, k6, BC, k7.

Row 13—P6, BC, p7, k2, p7, FC, p6.

Row 14—K5, FC, k8, p2, k8, BC, k5.

Row 15—P4, BC, p9, k2, p9, FC, p4.

Row 16—K1, p1, (k2, p1) twice, k7, p2, k7, (p1, k2) twice, p1, k1.

Row 17—P1, FC, p1, k1, p1, BC, p7, k2, p7, FC, p1, k1, p1, BC, p1.

Row 18—K2, (p1, k1) twice, p1, k8, p2, k8, (p1, k1) twice, p1, k2.

Row 19—P2, FC, k1, BC, p8, k2, p8, FC, k1, BC, p2.

Row 20—K3, p3, k9, p2, k9, p3, k3.

Row 21—P3, Make One (M1) purlwise by lifting running thread between the st just worked and the next st, and purling into the back of this thread; sl 1—k2 tog—psso, M1 purlwise, p9, k2, p9, M1 purlwise, sl 1—k2 tog—psso, M1 purlwise, p3.

Row 22—K4, p1, k10, p2, k10, p1, k4.

Row 23—P10, Make Bobble (MB) as follows: (k1, yo, k1, yo, k1) in next st, turn and p5; turn and k5; turn and p2 tog, p1, p2 tog; turn and sl 1—k2 tog—psso, completing Bobble; p4, k2, p4, MB, p10.

Row 24—K10, p1-b, k4, p2, k4, p1-b, k10.

Row 25—P10, FC, p3, k2, p3, BC, p10.

Row 26—K11, BC, k2, p2, k2, FC, k11.

Row 27—P12, FC, p1, k2, p1, BC, p12.

Row 28—K13, BC, p2, FC, k13.

Row 29—P14, FC, BC, p14.

Row 30—Repeat Row 4.

Row 31—P15, sl next st to dpn and hold in front, k1, then k1 from dpn; p15.

Row 32—K14, FC, BC, k14.

Row 33—P13, BC, p2, FC, p13.

Row 34—K12, FC, k4, BC, k12.

Row 35—P12, k1, p6, k1, p12.

Row 36—K12, p1, k6, p1, k12.

Row 37—P12, FC, p4, BC, p12.

Row 38—K13, BC, k2, FC, k13.

Row 39—P14, FC, BC, p14.

Row 40—K15, skip 1 st and purl the 2nd st, then purl the skipped st and sl both sts from needle together; k15.

Row 41—Purl.

Row 42—Knit.

Cable Chevron

Cable Chevron

This interesting fabric is the result of uniting a series of Double Cables all the way across a row. It looks about the same upside down or right side up—an advantage in some cases when a garment is being worked from the top down, or in an article like a pillow cover or baby blanket that can be turned either way.

Multiple of 12 sts plus 2.

Row 1 (Wrong side) and all other wrong-side rows—Purl.

Row 2—K1, * sl next 3 sts to dpn and hold in back, k3, then k3 from dpn; sl next 3 sts to dpn and hold in front, k3, then k3 from dpn; rep from *, end k1.

Rows, 4, 6, and 8—Knit.

Repeat Rows 1–8.

The Candle Tree

The Candle Tree

On Rows 9–21 of this pattern, cabled crossings are performed on both sides of the fabric to make the graceful spread of the Tree's lower "branches". The upper boughs hold nine Leaf or Candle-Flame motifs, all alike, in a very naturalistic tree-shaped arrangement. The entire panel with its 52 rows is a complete design, roughly square in shape. It may be used only once, as a central ornament in a garment, or it may be placed in blocks at any desired distance from each other. It is an ideal pattern for bedspreads and throws, since it can be made in squares of contrasting colors and the squares then sewn or crocheted together. To repeat the pattern as a vertical panel, work several rows of some other pattern as a horizontal band before beginning the next Candle Tree.

Panel of 35 sts.

NOTES: Front Purl Cross (FPC): sl 1 st to dpn and hold in front, p1, then k1 from dpn. Back Purl Cross (BPC): sl 1 st to dpn and hold in back, k1, then p1 from dpn.

Front Knit Cross (FKC): sl 1 st to dpn and hold in front, k1, then k1 from dpn.

Back Knit Cross (BKC): sl 1 st to dpn and hold in back, k1, then k1 from dpn.

Rows 1, 3, 5, and 7 (Right side)—P16 k3, p16.

Rows 2, 4, 6, and 8—K16, p3, k16.

Row 9—P15, BKC, k1, FKC, p15.

Row 10—K14, FPC, p3, BPC, k14.

Row 11—P13, BPC, p1, k3, p1, FPC, p13.

Row 12—K12, FPC, k2, p3, k2, BPC, k12.

Row 13—P11, BKC, p3, k3, p3, FKC, p11.

Row 14—K10, FPC, p1, k3, p3, k3, p1, BPC, k10.

Row 15—P9, BPC, p1, k1, p3, k3, p3, k1, p1, FPC, p9.

Row 16—K8, FPC, k2, p1, k3, p3, k3, p1, k2, BPC, k8.

Row 17—P7, BKC, p3, yo, k1, yo, p3, k3, p3, yo, k1, yo, p3, FKC, p7.

Row 18—K6, FPC, p1, (k3, p3) 3 times, k3, p1, BPC, k6.

Row 19—P5, BPC, p1, k1, p3, (k1, yo) twice, k1, p3, k3, p3, (k1, yo) twice, k1, p3, k1, p1, FPC, p5.

Row 20—K4, FPC, k2, p1, k3, p5, k3, p3, k3, p5, k3, p1, k2, BPC, k4.

Row 21—P3, BPC, p3, k1, p3, k2, yo, k1, yo, k2, p3, k3, p3, k2, yo, k1, yo, k2, p3, k1, p3, FPC, p3.

Row 22 and all subsequent wrong-side rows: Knit all knit sts and purl all purl and yo sts.

Row 23—P3, yo, k1, yo, p4, k1, p3, ssk, k3, k2 tog, p3, k3, p3, ssk, k3, k2 tog, p3, k1, p4, yo, k1, yo, p3.

Row 25—P3, (k1, yo) twice, k1, p4, k1, p3, ssk, k1, k2 tog, p3, k3, p3, ssk, k1, k2 tog, p3, k1, p4, (k1, yo) twice, k1, p3.

Row 27—P3, k2, yo, k1, yo, k2, p4, yo, k1, yo, p3, sl 1—k2 tog—psso, p2, BPC, k1, FPC, p2, sl 1—k2 tog—psso, p3, yo, k1, yo, p4, k2, yo, k1, yo, k2, p3.

Row 29—P3, ssk, k3, k2 tog, p4, (k1, yo) twice, k1, p5, BPC, p1, k1, p1, FPC, p5, (k1, yo) twice, k1, p4, ssk, k3, k2 tog, p3.

Row 31—P3, ssk, k1, k2 tog, p4, k2, yo, k1, yo, k2, p4, BPC, p2, k1, p2, FPC, p4, k2, yo, k1, yo, k2, p4, ssk, k1, k2 tog, p3.

Row 33—P3, sl 1—k2 tog—psso, p4, ssk, k3, k2 tog, p3, BPC, p3, k1, p3, FPC, p3, ssk, k3, k2 tog, p4, sl 1—k2 tog—psso, p3.

Row 35—P8, ssk, k1, k2 tog, p3, yo, k1, yo, p4, k1, p4, yo, k1, yo, p3, ssk, k1, k2 tog, p8.

Row 37—P8, sl 1—k2 tog—psso, p3, (k1, yo) twice, (k1, p4) twice, (k1, yo) twice, k1, p3, sl 1—k2 tog—psso, p8.

Row 39—P12, k2, yo, k1, yo, k2, p4, yo, k1, yo, p4, k2, yo, k1, yo, k2, p12.

Row 41—P12, ssk, k3, k2 tog, p4, (k1, yo) twice, k1, p4, ssk, k3, k2 tog, p12.

Row 43—P12, ssk, k1, k2 tog, p4, k2, yo, k1, yo, k2, p4, ssk, k1, k2 tog, p12.

Row 45—P12, sl 1—k2 tog—psso, p4, ssk, k3, k2 tog, p4, sl 1—k2 tog—psso, p12.

Row 47—P17, ssk, k1, k2 tog, p17.

Row 49—P17, sl 1—k2 tog—psso, p17.

Row 51—Purl.

Row 52 (Wrong side)—Knit.

Dear Reader:

Do you know any knitting pattern that is not included in this book? I'd like to add your pattern to my collection. Please send your pattern directions to:

Barbara G. Walker
c/o Charles Scribner's Sons
597 Fifth Avenue
New York, N.Y. 10017

Sincerely yours,
Barbara Walker

BIBLIOGRAPHY

Carroll, Alice. *Complete Guide to Modern Knitting and Crocheting.* Wm. H. Wise & Co., Inc., New York, 1949.

Curtis, Carol. *Complete Book of Knitting and Crocheting.* Pocket Books Inc., New York, 1965.

Norbury, James. *The Penguin Knitting Book.* Penguin Books Ltd., Harmondsworth, Middlesex, 1957.

Norbury, James. *Traditional Knitting Patterns.* B. T. Batsford Ltd., London, 1962.

O'Mara, Ruth Hatcher. *Easy Knitting: Children's Sizes 4 to 14.* Pocket Books, Inc., New York, 1965.

Thomas, Mary. *Mary Thomas' Book of Knitting Patterns.* Hodder & Stoughton Ltd., London, 1943.

INDEX

INDEX